My Connecticut Garden

My Connecticut Garden

Personal Experiences of an Amateur Gardener

by
George Valchar

TIMBER PRESS
Portland, Oregon

Mention of a chemical product is for information only. Follow current label directions for legal use and application rates.

ISBN 0-88192-227-7
Printed in Hong Kong

TIMBER PRESS, INC.
9999 S.W. Wilshire, Suite 124
Portland, Oregon 97225

Library of Congress Cataloging-in-Publication Data

Valchar, George.
My Connecticut garden : personal experiences of an amateur gardener / by George Valchar.
p. cm.
Includes bibliographical references and index.
ISBN 0-88192-227-7
1. Plants, Ornamental--Connecticut. 2. Gardens--Connecticut.
3. Valchar, George--Homes and haunts--Connecticut. I. Title.
SB407.V34 1993
635.9'09746--dc20 92-21134
CIP

Contents

Preface

The dedication of a book by an author is inevitably a very personal matter. As I reviewed in my mind the many individuals and sources from whom I derived inspiration, it became evident that they were too numerous to mention. At the same time, to be true to my feelings, I must express my thankful thoughts to at least three people: my wife, my daughter, and an author who will never know how he affected my life with a book he wrote a long time ago.

To my wife, Mary Louise, go my kind and appreciative thoughts not only for her encouragement in the pursuit of my avocation, but for her acceptance of gardening as one of her principal hobbies. Sharing our gardening experiences became the highlight in our lives, especially once our children grew up and left the house and I retired from my job. My sudden and permanent presence in the house could have been an upsetting development had it not been for the activities around the garden that absorbed so much of our time. Together we poured over the seed and plant catalogues during the cold dark days of winter. Sometimes we prepared the beds, the flats, and the planting holes together for the material we ordered, usually in excessive quantities; and together we suffered the disappointments when some of the plants died. It was my wife who brought into my garden a greater awareness of the finer and less obvious plant qualities, such as the fragrance of blossoms and foliage.

My next thoughts of gratitude go to the youngest of my six daughters, Claudia, who gave up weekend upon weekend to type my drafts and revisions without the slightest indication of impatience and blame for any interference with her social life. My attempts to write this volume would have been complicated without her help.

As to the author who impressed me so profoundly many years ago, I came upon his book in a secondhand bookshop. Writing before the Second World War, this English gardener, T. H. G. Stevens, described the trees and shrubs that grew in the relatively balmy environment of his garden at the other end of the Gulf Stream. Since then I have read dozens of books on plants and planting yet none has meant so much in making gardening my hobby as that modest volume. It was the work of an amateur, but his willingness to share his personal successes and failures and his unrestrained love of plants encouraged me to pursue this wonderful activity.

During the decades that followed I was able to garden only sporadically as my family and I moved between houses, countries, and continents. When we finally settled down in Connecticut, I could draw more and more on the advice and experience of the old plantsman. I only wished that he had lived here, in the stern climate of the U.S. Northeast: some of the plants that he was able to grow in his hardiness zone 8 would not have survived in southwestern Connecticut's zone 6.

Hence, I decided to compile a plant roster more suitable to the harsher growing conditions of the Northeast. At first I intended to use this list for my own purposes, but then I thought of my daughters and friends who also gardened in rugged climates. After a few years of becoming acquainted with my garden, I was able to identify and record all (or nearly all) the plants growing in my backyard. The list was longer than I expected; I had no idea so many species and varieties could grow on only 2.4 acres (1 ha).

The thought of expanding that compendium into a book came several years later during one of those never-ending flights from New York to the Far East. With my body suspended for hours at 38,000 ft (11,600 m), lounging in a comfortable seat, feeling relaxed yet bright under the extra oxygen, and pampered by super-attentive flight attendants, my mind functioned at a coolly detached pace that easily inspired an exaggerated self-confidence. And so the idea was born to augment the original list with comments and observations on each plant's hardiness, appearance, and performance.

Throughout my travels, my thoughts kept turning to my garden and to the idea of writing about it. The more exotic and varied the climates and growing conditions in the gardens I encountered, the more compelling was the desire to write. A sheik in the United Arab Emirates showed me a nursery in the desert of Abu Dhabi where thousands of trees flourished under a glaring sun, irrigated by water from a desalting plant on the shores of the Persian Gulf. The cost of water even then was well over a dollar a gallon. In my garden in Buenos Aires grew 10-ft (3-m) tall poinsettias, small bananas, and kumquats. I recall the acres of yellow daisies along the Australian and southern African beaches, and I will never forget the thick air roots 50 ft (15 m) long, hanging from *Monstera deliciosa* (splitleaf philodendron) plants nestled in the crowns of giant trees in the forests of Paraguay. I still have a vivid memory of the 8-ft (2.4-m) long stems of small-blossom orchids reaching out of the murky darkness of a Central American jungle to bathe their flower heads in the brighter light along the narrow road. The years I spent working with plants helped me become attuned to nature everywhere, and this keen awareness of plant life provided a frame of reference, a comforting common denominator among the sometimes bewildering succession of places I lived in and visited.

But nature revealed still another face: the unlimited beauty of plants, the fantastic works of art that human beings have copied, interpreted, stylized, and reflected in their art from time immemorial. Mother Nature continues to produce plants under varied circumstances all over the globe. Given a chance, she fills every square foot of available land with species suited to the latitude, altitude, moisture, and light. The means by which she accomplishes this task is the process of natural selection. A plant will either flourish or perish in a given environment, and only the strongest survive and reproduce. It sometimes amazes me that it took the human race so many generations to notice, identify, and ultimately describe this obvious but uncompromising rule. Charles Darwin, his contemporaries, and his immediate predecessors finally discovered what should have been evident to thinkers and scientists hundreds of years earlier. One can only wonder when this valuable knowledge will be used in our endeavors to better understand and help the human species as well.

Such abstract musings failed to divert my attention from the down-to-earth activities in my garden and the urge to tell about them. Instead, they focused and reinforced my determination to get on with the job of writing. In defining my objectives for this volume I recognized that they would be simple. My book would be the work of a hobbyist to serve as a reference or handbook for other hobbyists. The information it would contain would be competent, but the attitudes it would convey would be those of an enthusiastic devotee convinced that he has encountered something wonderful and that he should pass it on and share it with others.

If you decide to read on, try to leave behind the stresses of the competitive life, the ills of society, the fluctuations of economic cycles, and the complexities of domestic and international politics. Instead, set out on a path lined with the marvelous creations of nature, the living works that will become your friends and family, dependent on you and yet immeasurably rewarding. Thumb through the pages of the plant descriptions and let your attention be captured by a specimen with an interesting name, color, shape, or smell. Then consider how you would plant it, care for it, and make it prosper. It is more than possible that in this process you will find that gardening gives you as much pleasure and satisfaction as it has given me.

A Pastime for All

Is gardening for anyone or for just the select few, those with a "green thumb"? Is it a pastime for men more than for women, or vice versa? Are gardeners born or are they made?

Such questions are sometimes raised in personal discussions or in the gardening sections of newspapers and magazines. While they are mostly irrelevant, they do bring to mind some interesting thoughts. For example, the majority of the great gardens of the world were created by men, and all the famous plant explorers of the past centuries were men, but viewed objectively, these facts are simply a reflection of the position the sexes occupied in the social structure of the times rather than an indication of the natural propensities of men and women. One can hardly imagine women in the 1800s being allowed to organize and undertake the arduous and sometimes fatal journeys into inaccessible areas of western China and Tibet, yet today women are a part of every group that sets out to explore the regions of the globe. In this century some magnificent gardens have been created by women, and, of course, we should not forget Empress Josephine, who 200 years ago, in her garden at Malmaison, brought together the most strikingly beautiful collection of roses ever assembled. As gardeners, both sexes probably excel and fail at an equal rate.

Are successful gardeners and plant lovers blessed with some favored gene that is passed from generation to generation, influencing a person's attitudes and mental processes? Possibly, but I think the answer is more elementary than the question: a "green thumb" is mainly the result of experience. It is the sum of all the unsuccessful attempts to grow the wrong thing in the wrong place at the wrong time, as the legendary, tongue-tripping U.S. baseball player Yogi Berra may have put it.

People who tell themselves that they were made to spend their free time doing other things probably will make poor gardeners, but if they give gardening a reasonable amount of effort and time, about four seasons, then they will be pleasantly surprised at how those minute seeds and tiny plants respond to a little care and attention. And, what can give greater pleasure than bringing into existence a living thing that, without the gardener's intervention, would probably not exist!

PART 1
My Garden

PLATE 1. The brook in early spring lined with the young foliage of *Symplocarpus foetidus* (skunk cabbage).

PLATE 2. The wood in autumn colors.

The Ground

Before proceeding to the plant descriptions, the reader is invited to take an imaginary walk through my garden to become acquainted with it, its background, its origins, and its maintenance.

My garden is located in the southwestern corner of the state of Connecticut, approximately 8 miles (13 km) from Long Island Sound, the great arm of the Atlantic Ocean that moderates to some degree the climate in this part of the state. It is a modest and mostly do-it-yourself garden. For one reason, it is difficult and expensive to find truly knowledgeable and dedicated help. Second, I distrust professional gardeners and gardening companies that dispatch troops of sometimes uncaring helpers who can devastate the fine, selective work I have achieved over the seasons.

I also have a somewhat negative feeling about certain less sensitive gardening architects. I am very impressed by their magnificent stone and wooden structures—their broad, graceful stairways, terraces, and other massive creations, but I have some difficulty accepting the supreme dominance of such construction projects in the garden which, after all, is meant to be primarily a home for plants, with humans as welcome guests. As a result, despite some mechanical interventions, I have managed to keep my garden in a fairly natural state.

My 2.4 acres (about 1 ha) occupy the bottom of a small shallow valley, only a dip on top of a ridge some 460 ft (140 m) above sea level. Through the east side of the roughly square property runs a brooklet which, though dry for a few weeks in most summers, feeds a small pond and keeps it always full (Plate 1). In heavy rains the whole modest watercourse gushes with seemingly uncontrollable fury. The pond has a tiny island on which grow a few plants of *Kalmia latifolia* (mountain laurel), *K. angustifolia* (sheep laurel), young *Betula populifolia* (gray birch), *Rhododendron viscosum* (swamp azalea), and *Lycopodium obscurum* (tree club moss).

In the northwest corner of the lot is a small wood of some 120 trees of various species (Plate 2). *Acer rubrum* (red maple) and *Liriodendron tulipifera* (tulip tree) predominate, but also present are *Nyssa sylvatica* (pepperidge tree), *Betula lenta* (black birch), *B. alleghaniensis* (yellow birch), *Fraxinus americana* (white ash), and *Ulmus rubra* (slippery elm). The low portions of the wood become flooded after heavy rains. To drain the area, the original settlers dug narrow channels to carry the excess water into the pond. The land may even have been used as a cranberry bog. One could imagine the growers damming the brooklet on the east side and flooding the *Vaccinium macrocarpon* (cranberry) vines to harvest the fruit, control insects, or protect the crops from early frost before harvest time. When the fruit was gathered, they would open the dams and the area would revert to its original semidry state. Now, of course, there is no sign of any cranberries, and the bottomland maples (*Acer* spp.) and tulip trees (*Liriodendron* spp.) have aggressively claimed the land.

The remainder of the property is covered by lawns, a small meadow, a 2000-sq-ft (186-sq-m) vegetable garden, a rose garden, a rock garden, and several smaller areas of native and introduced trees and shrubs. Between and through these partly natural islands of vegetation run many paths, from 3- or 4-ft (0.9- or 1.2-m) wide moss-covered walks to broad strips of lawn (Plates 3, 7, 69).

The pond's surface is approximately 4500 sq ft (420 sq m) (Plate 4). It is populated by several species of fish. Every spring their number explodes into large schools of fry only to be effectively brought under control at summer's end by the resident large- and small-mouthed bass as well as by opportunistic raccoons, cats, kingfishers, rails, and an occasional heron. Some years ago, I introduced 12 large triploid carp (white amur) to control the prolific algae. The inspector from the state's Department of Fisheries insisted that a metal mesh be placed at the inflow and outflow points of the pond to assure absolutely that the carp would not invade and populate the local streams and lakes, even though each fish had been made sterile. I installed the barriers but to no avail. The fish are disappearing anyway, mainly courtesy of the skilled fishing raccoons. Occasionally I find a part of a large fish skeleton or a few 0.5-in (1.3-cm) scales where one of the animals had its $25 breakfast. Of the original dozen, only three carp can sometimes be seen warming themselves in the sun in the upper layer of the pond's water. They have grown to 5 or 6 lbs (2 or 3 kg) in the few years I have had them, while keeping the pond's smothering vegetation almost to a manageable level.

The soil in my garden is a sand-and-gravel-based loam. The original moraine was brought from northern New England on the glaciers of the last advances of the Wisconsin glaciation. Besides sand and pebbles of differing sizes, it contained larger stones and even enormous boulders. In the more accessible and fertile areas, generations of farmers collected the rocks, split the boulders, and then stacked them into 3- to 4-ft (0.9- to 1.2-m) high boundary walls. The smaller stones were used to fill

PLATE 3. Grassy paths and areas with native and introduced vegetation: the white *Kalmia latifolia* (mountain laurel), rhododendrons 'Gibraltar' (orange) and 'Klondyke' (yellow), *Osmunda cinnamomea* (cinnamon fern), and the ground cover *Pachysandra terminalis* (spurge).

PLATE 4. The pond and the island under cover of ice and snow.

swamps, make foundations for roads, or just piled into heaps. It is still sometimes said: "Scratch the soil and you'll come up with a rock."

Not all the rocks in my garden were ordinary and uninteresting. Some years ago I came upon a quartz arrowhead, which an archaeologist later identified as a Brewerton Eared-Triangle Point from the Late Archaic Period of 3000 to 2500 B.C. I now feel privileged more than ever to work on land where Native Americans roamed nearly 5000 years ago.

Having collected thousands of stones and pebbles on my property over the decades, and having brought loads of leaf mold from the town leaf-mulch field, I can now say that the planting conditions in my garden are generally acceptable. In fact, the vegetable garden beds are a rich loam that runs through one's fingers like brown gold; not a single rock can be found anywhere, except maybe 18 in (45 cm) below the surface.

While I have tried to depend largely on myself in maintaining the garden, this does not mean that on some occasions I have not used outside help or even employed heavy equipment. Maybe as I become older I will rely even more on the assistance of others. Nonetheless, for now I enjoy not only the spiritual rewards of gardening but the physical ones as well, for gardening keeps me in trimmer shape.

PLATE 5. The blossoms of *Acer rubrum* (red maple), some already maturing into the reddish samaras (fruits).

Climate

My garden is just north of the 41st parallel and west of the 73rd meridian. The warming effect of the Sound is partly offset by the 460-ft (140-m) elevation which places the garden in plant hardiness zone 6b. In most winters, the temperature drops to 0°F (−18°C), and in some years it goes to −10°F (−23°C). Old residents sometimes speak of the terrible winters of our grandparents; for instance, during a severe winter in the early 1930s, the temperature dropped to −25°F (−32°C), and the Sound is said to have frozen solid for a mile (1.6 km) or more from the shore. In 1780, in the depths of our most recent Little Ice Age, New York harbor froze from shore to shore. It is almost certain that during such cold periods some plant species must have perished or receded farther south.

In summer, the temperature reaches 90°F (32°C) in most years, and 95°F (35°C) is not unusual. Deciduous forests cover the area for miles around, but the woods are speckled with residential properties of 2–4 acres (0.8–1.6 ha) each. There are also hundreds of acres of forests that remain undeveloped since they serve as watersheds. The summer humidity can be high, with dew points reaching the discomfort level many times in July and August. In some years, toward the end of summer, mildew on plants can be a problem.

The demanding climate has its compensations. The cold winter temperatures tend to keep certain diseases in check. For example, a new form of powdery mildew has been threatening rhododendron plantings in the more ideal rhododendron climates of the U.S. Northwest, the British Isles, and Australia. Temperatures of 0°F (−18°C) or lower apparently kill the spores of the mildew. The summer heat also has its bright side: it seems to be an important ingredient in the profuse blossoming of evergreen azaleas. In milder regions these plants tend to bloom for a longer period but with only a modest display of flowers at a time. This also applies to native deciduous azaleas which not only tolerate but even seem to relish the annual baking in early summer when they form their flower buds for the next year.

In winter, if New Englanders can live through the unpleasant periods of slush, chilly dampness, or bitter cold, they are rewarded by days when the total calm and restfulness of the wintry countryside, especially when enhanced by snow, far exceed in beauty anything that the tropics or subtropics can offer. Following the winter's thorough cleansing treatment, the urgent and inevitable renewal process forces changes upon all plant life and reflects even in human beings. Soon after the cold season's iron grip has let up in late February, the willow trees (*Salix* spp.) begin to acquire the look of a bright greenish yellow mist, and by late March the maples (*Acer* spp.) begin to blossom into their billows of red haze (Plate 5). On the ground, the plants begin to push through the frozen earth as if it were soft molding clay rather than a concretelike substance. And, after the profusion of summer, not too many places on earth are blessed with the annual magnificence of color that adorns the New England landscape almost to excess each fall (Plate 6).

Yet, the harsh climate does not drastically affect the number and the variety of plants that can be grown here. It sometimes surprises me how similar, in this regard,

PLATE 6. The garden in early fall with yellow and orange foliage of *Betula* (birch) and *Acer* (maple) species and the red foliage of a young *Quercus coccinea* (scarlet oak) in lower left corner.

my garden is to the tens of thousands of gardens around the world. The majority of the human population resides in climates that fall into hardiness zones 5 through 8, a broad band of territory circling the globe. In North America this band stretches from Newfoundland and Nova Scotia south to Georgia and Colorado, encompassing most of the inhabited areas of the Rocky Mountains, and reaching up to the southern coast of Alaska. In Asia it includes the greater part of Japan, the Korean peninsula, northeastern China, and the southeastern coast of Siberia. It covers almost all Europe from central and coastal Scandinavia and Scotland to the southern Alps. In the Southern Hemisphere, the corresponding localities are in the higher elevations of New Zealand, southeastern Australia, southern Africa, and portions of South America.

Many gardeners believe that their climate is among the most trying for maintaining a successful garden; it appears to them that other locations are better in most respects. But, for instance, think about the Connecticut summers, which can be hot, wet, and extremely humid one year, and rainless and arid the next, while winters may vary from sunny, dry, snowless, and bitterly cold to dark, chillingly damp and dank. Like other gardeners, I also believe that my climate is difficult. Any plant that can survive Connecticut's growing conditions should be able to succeed in almost any garden in the four temperate hardiness zones. This would be true especially if a plant that is marginally hardy in a given location were placed in a favorable microclimate. To find an advantageous habitat in a garden, consider the following guidelines:

1. Good air drainage. This means more than just air circulation. It implies the actual flowing of air. For example, on calm, windless, winter nights the heavier cold air flows downward and accumulates in deeper valleys making them considerably colder than the sloping or elevated positions.

2. Wind protection. A strong persistent movement of air desiccates the foliage of evergreens as well as the thin twigs of deciduous plants and dries out exposed soil above the roots. A lee of tall evergreen trees or shrubs provides an excellent shelter.

3. Winter sun. The warming effect of the winter sun can be an important ingredient in creating a balmier microclimate. Nevertheless, to prevent sunscald it is essential that the midday rays be polarized by the bare branches of deciduous trees above the site. A smaller plant may be protected from the sun by the dense branch of a deciduous shrub thrust into the ground on the sunny side. A length of snow fence around a plant will also provide the needed shade without diminishing the warmth in the area.

4. Sufficient moisture. In warm and dry regions, incorporating moisture-retentive organic matter in the soil at planting time, applying heavy mulch, providing high shade during the hottest parts of the day, and sensibly irrigating in rainless periods will considerably improve the chances of heat-sensitive plants.

A perfect climate is, at best, a relative term; more realistically, it does not exist. Fortunately, over millions of years plants have found ways of coping with and adapting to varied and adverse conditions. Their tolerance to cold, heat, and drought is sometimes surprising. Yet, at one time or another, gardeners still try to push their plants' endurance limits beyond the known tolerances; occasionally, though not very often, they succeed.

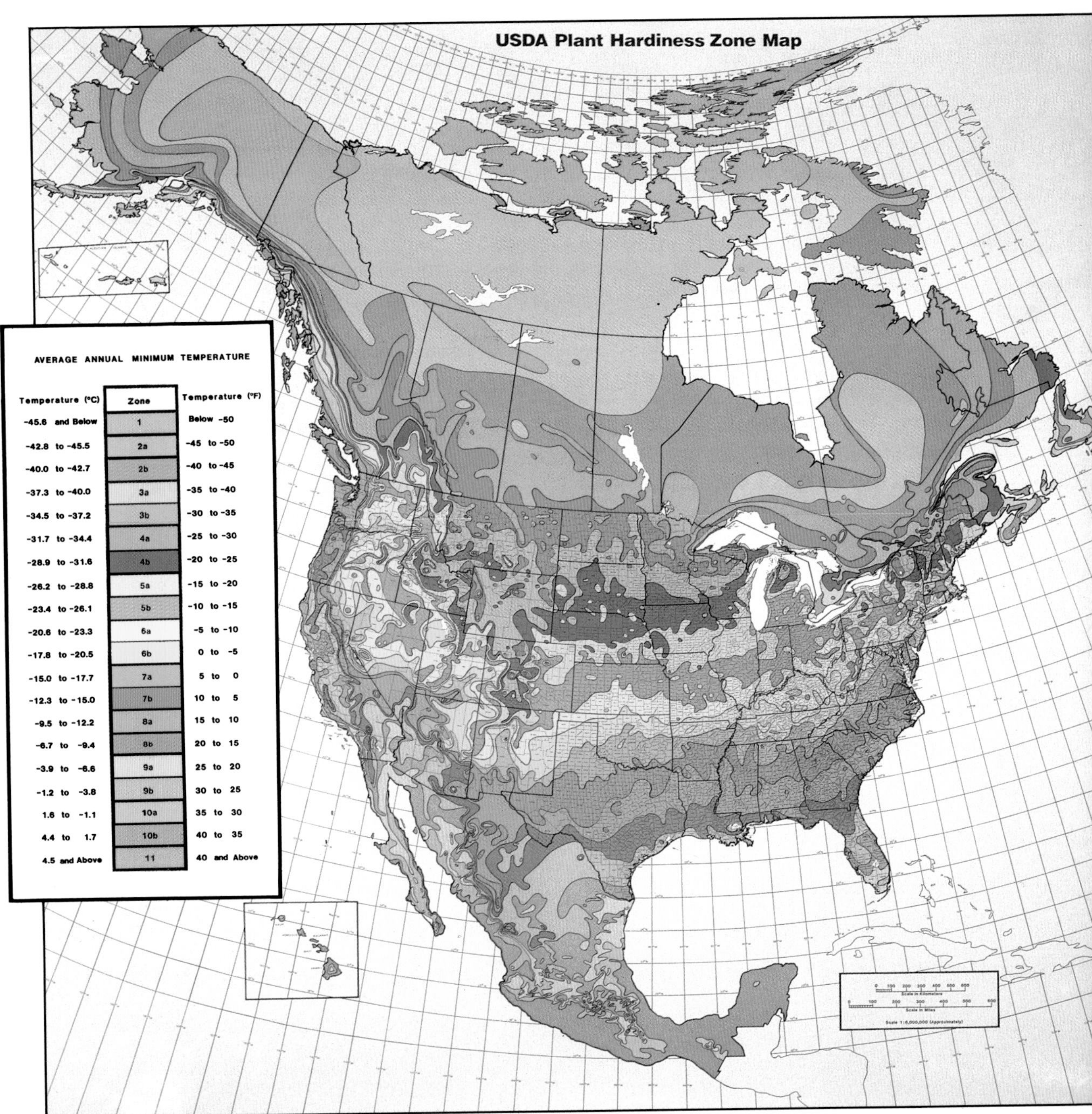
USDA Plant Hardiness Zone Map
AVERAGE ANNUAL MINIMUM TEMPERATURE
Temperature (°C) | Zone | Temperature (°F)
-45.6 and Below | 1 | Below -50
-42.8 to -45.5 | 2a | -45 to -50
-40.0 to -42.7 | 2b | -40 to -45
-37.3 to -40.0 | 3a | -35 to -40
-34.5 to -37.2 | 3b | -30 to -35
-31.7 to -34.4 | 4a | -25 to -30
-28.9 to -31.6 | 4b | -20 to -25
-26.2 to -28.8 | 5a | -15 to -20
-23.4 to -26.1 | 5b | -10 to -15
-20.6 to -23.3 | 6a | -5 to -10
-17.8 to -20.5 | 6b | 0 to -5
-15.0 to -17.7 | 7a | 5 to 0
-12.3 to -15.0 | 7b | 10 to 5
-9.5 to -12.2 | 8a | 15 to 10
-6.7 to -9.4 | 8b | 20 to 15
-3.9 to -6.6 | 9a | 25 to 20
-1.2 to -3.8 | 9b | 30 to 25
1.6 to -1.1 | 10a | 35 to 30
4.4 to 1.7 | 10b | 40 to 35
4.5 and Above | 11 | 40 and Above

HARDINESS ZONE
TEMPERATURE RANGES
°F ZONE °C
below −50 1 below −45
−50 to −40 2 −45 to −40
−40 to −30 3 −40 to −34
−30 to −20 4 −34 to −29
−20 to −10 5 −29 to −23
−10 to 0 6 −23 to −17
0 to 10 7 −17 to −12
10 to 20 8 −12 to −7
20 to 30 9 —7 to −1
30 to 40 10 −1 to 5
NORWAY
SWEDEN
FINLAND
Oslo
Stockholm
Helsinki
USSR
DENMARK
UK
Edinburgh
Dublin
London
Hamburg
NETH
BELG
GERMANY
POLAND
Frankfurt
Prague
CZECHO-SLOVAKIA
Munich
AUSTRIA
SWITZ
Bern
HUNGARY
Budapest
RUMANIA
FRANCE
Paris
Bordeaux
Limoges
Lyon
Marseille
PORTUGAL
SPAIN
Leon
Madrid
Barcelona
Gibralter
ITALY
Rome
YUGO-SLAVIA
Belgrade
BULGARIA
ALBANIA
GREECE
Athens

Native Species and Introduced Plants

When my family and I moved to Connecticut I found a garden that consisted of two or three dozen plants of *Taxus* (yew), *Ilex* (holly), and *Pieris* neatly planted by the builder around the house like a tight necklace. It was the classic "foundation planting," appropriate and perhaps welcome for a smaller urban or suburban lot, but unnecessarily restrictive in our semijungle environment. In the following year or two I transplanted nearly all the plants to a long bed along the street and allowed the house to rise straight out of the green bed of *Pachysandra terminalis* (spurge) that also circled the foundation. Then I proceeded to widen the lawns around the house beyond the 30 or 40 ft (9 or 12 m) allowed by the builder. There had been trees growing against the house and, while I love trees, I also wanted to see the sky and the sun, and allow the breeze to touch the house walls.

As the years went by I continued to expand my sphere of influence deeper into the woods until, finally, I began to perceive the entire property as my garden. The old, overgrown pasture was cleared and became a meadow. The pond was deepened, and paths were cut through the woods to provide access for walking, for wheelbarrows, and, in winter, for cross-country skiing. The horse barn was moved deeper into the woods and made into a tool shed.

While all this was happening, I became keenly aware of the rich native flora and silva that grew everywhere. From the stumps of felled trees I inferred that the vegetation must have begun reclaiming the area over 100 years ago. It was probably in the second half of the 19th century that the inhabitants, whose ancestors originally cleared the land, moved to the more fertile soils of the Midwest. By the time we came, woods again covered nearly every square foot of land. They were full of ferns, *Symplocarpus foetidus* (skunk cabbage), *Arisaema triphyllum* (jack-in-the-pulpit), *Amelanchier* (shadbush), and dozens of other species.

It had occurred to me frequently that I could maintain the property as a garden of purely native plants and exclude all those that were not here before the house was built. After some deliberation, however, I concluded that I was not prepared to accept the status quo; to do so would be to look at the garden as a snapshot of a moment in time, a museum rather than a living, dynamic, and always-changing organism that is nature. Under normal conditions, a struggle goes on constantly between the extant and the new, the strong and the weak, the suitable and the unsuitable. New seeds are blown in by the wind or dispersed in bird droppings. Plant explorers and nurseries introduce a never-ending stream of new plants and, within a few years, distribute them around the globe. Even automobile tires carry seeds which they leave along the road to colonize new territories. Tiny spores are carried by the jet stream, and big coconuts are floated on the oceans from continent to continent.

While patches of virgin prairies and primeval forests do exist and, with considerable effort, are artificially maintained in some locations, I did not feel that I could commit myself to such an endeavor while giving up all the other wonders of the plant world. Therefore, I decided to grow all the varieties of plants that will survive in this climate and under my benign neglect.

There are rhododendron enthusiasts who specialize in growing only species (i.e., plants as they are found in nature); no hybridized specimens are permitted in their gardens. These specialists forgo the exhilaration of seeing large trusses of bloom, in nearly all colors of the rainbow, on thousands of rhododendron hybrids.

Even in the wild, the line between a species and a hybrid is sometimes blurred. For example, the North American plant, *Rhododendron calendulaceum* (flame azalea), as found in nature is perhaps an intermediate between *R. bakeri* (Baker's azalea) and *R. arborescens* (sweet azalea). Furthermore, some hybridization is taking place in nature now, after the individual species have been well defined, although the process was greatly expedited during the decades of the Green Revolution. Hybridizers have increased the yield of corn by many multiples, and thousands of superior flowers, shrubs, and trees have been produced in this process. Hence, to garden without hybrids is to garden in an artificial, somewhat impoverished state to which no gardener should banish himself or herself lightly.

Garden Paths and Benches

Every garden should have a path. Even a small flower border must have some provision to make access easier, to avoid compacting the soil, and to facilitate weeding, transplanting, picking fresh or spent flowers, or just getting a closer look. In a larger garden it is necessary at times to transport soil or peat moss in a cart, a wheelbarrow, or even a tractor. But equally important, paths make it possible to take walks through a garden and enjoy the results of past endeavors as well as to make plans for the future. Walking through a garden at almost any time of the year is one of the sweet rewards for the hard work.

A path can be a few stepping stones, a broad strip of lawn, or anything in between. The first path I built in my garden was a 5-ft (1.5-m) wide track that ran roughly around the perimeter of the property. It was used as a cross-country ski trail and, in snowy winters when the grandchildren come for a visit, we still use it for that purpose. It runs by the pond, along the brook, through an opening in a stone wall, across a corner of the meadow into the woods, and past various rhododendrons (Plate 7). The portion of the path that is in the woods was built on a foundation of

PLATE 7. A wide moss-covered path in April with *Kalmia latifolia* (mountain laurel), *Rhododendron* species, and *Symplocarpus foetidus* (skunk cabbage). Next to the wall on the right, a few remaining yellow blossoms of *Corylopsis pauciflora* (buttercup winter hazel).

large stones. Smaller stones, when used first, disappeared into the swampy ground, and so could be used only as the second layer, which was then covered with the pebbles left over after sifting garden soil. The final layer was a mixture of sand and soil. Now covered with moss, the trail is easy to keep clean of leaves and debris that fall from the trees in the autumn and in wind and ice storms; a few times a year, while trimming my lawns with a hand-held power mower, I run the mower along the length of the path at low RPMs and blow off all loose material.

I have built many other paths since that first one. Each time the wet and marshy sections were filled with stones and covered with sand. Many of the paths lead over old drainage channels and the pond's inlet and outlet; in such locations, narrow culverts were installed or small bridges constructed so that quiet, relaxing walks would not have to be interrupted by undignified leaps (Plate 62).

A few sections of the paths are still only bare ground, but shaded portions are now mostly moss-covered (Plates 7, 73). For moss to cover a path, two or three years are required from the time the surface is raked or otherwise disturbed for the last time. There is plenty of moss in my garden and woods. In Europe, nature lovers used to say that as long as there was moss in an area, the air was not seriously polluted. If true, the air above my garden is uncommonly pure.

The spreading of moss can be speeded up by planting small patches of it in a new path and watering them well. There are also more expeditious ways to reproduce moss. Of the several formulas in existence, the following is worth trying: pour a 12-oz (35-cl) can of beer into a blender container; fill the empty can with fresh moss and add it to the beer; also add a teaspoon (5.5 ml) of sugar. Mix the concoction briefly in the blender, then spread it on damp bare ground, a large stone, or an old log, in shade, and mist it lightly in dry weather. Within two months, moss should cover the area on which the mixture was spread. Milk or buttermilk may be used in place of beer, and water is probably just as effective. Also, mixing the ingredients in a bucket instead of a blender will most likely give the same results.

When I first began experimenting with surfacing materials on my paths, I used sawdust and woodchips, but they both rotted in a couple of years and had to be replenished. Also, the debris and leaves that fell on such paths could not be swept away without losing too much of the surfacing material itself. Therefore, I opted for the sand/soil mixture with the eventual natural cover of moss. There is one disadvantage to this "paving" method, however: a rake cannot be used on the paths as it pulls off the moss.

An ideal width for a path is 4–5 ft (1.2–1.5 m), enough for two people to walk side by side. Nevertheless, a gardener may not be able to set aside that much land everywhere, so 2–3 ft (0.6–0.9 m) have to be adequate in some places (Plate 69). Along the paths there are infinite opportunities for placing fascinating plants such as *Anemone, Aquilegia* (columbine), *Cyclamen, Primula* (primrose), various spring and autumn bulbs, and many other gems from nature's treasury.

All garden paths have that enticing quality of drawing you farther into the distance. They lead around the next bend, a tree, or a shrub, on to a wide open space, or to a long vista with an interesting plant or a bench at its distant end (Plate 18).

I cannot imagine a garden without a place to sit and rest, or just look around and think. The seat itself may be a home-made wooden bench, a store-bought concrete seat, a log from a tree felled long ago, a boulder, or a folding chair—all are equally useful for sitting even if not necessarily equal in their comfort or esthetic value (Plates 26, 33). The gardener or a guest should be able to rest in almost any part of the garden without having to walk very far. No interesting spot or view should go unnoticed without a seat from which to see it. This means, of course, that there will be many places to sit. Some will be inconspicuously hidden in the woods or partly surrounded by shrubs, others will become points of interest in themselves and add an ornamental touch to the landscape (Plates 8, 20). Some will be in shade while others will be in the open, so that though bundled up, one may enjoy the first warm rays of the February sun.

Trellises and arbors are also useful in a garden and can even be beautiful, especially when draped with a flowering vine or a climbing rose; but their number should be kept to a few well-placed applications so as not to overwhelm the garden with a single design feature (Plate 31). As for garden ornaments, I prefer to use them sparingly as well. Most gardeners will agree that in this respect, too, less is more.

PLATE 8. A bench with rhododendrons 'Nova Zembla' (red) and 'Catawbiense Alba' (white) in late May.

The Rose Garden

Moving the old horse barn farther into the woods left a dampish rectangle 20 × 40 ft (6 × 12 m). The north and east ends were enclosed with old boundary walls along which grew a dozen plants of *Rhododendron viscosum* (swamp azalea) and *Vaccinium corymbosum* (highbush blueberry). The south and west ends were left open. The site was well suited for a rose garden provided, however, that the problem of dampness could be resolved. Roses strongly prefer well-drained locations.

The solution lay in raising the ground level above the surrounding grade. After seven or eight truckloads of various materials, including manure and leaf mold, the area seemed drier, but only on the surface. About 1 ft (30 cm) below ground level the soil was still damp, and a somewhat deeper hole quickly attracted 5 in (13 cm) of water at the bottom. Evidently, an underground water-resistant stratum carried rain and melted snow from the nearby and slightly higher corner of the meadow to the pond via my future rosarium.

It occurred to me that the bottom moisture might not be entirely unwelcome in dry summers; the roses could send their roots into this reservoir of dampness and thus better survive the occasional rainless summer. This theory proved generally correct, although water is brought in from the pond in a few exceptionally dry years. Nevertheless, as additional insurance against excessive dampness in normal years, I

PLATE 9. The rose garden in early June.

enclosed the central bed with heavy railroad ties and filled the space to the brim with good soil and leaf mold. The planting level was thus raised by an additional 6 in (15 cm). After the roses were planted, I scattered a heavy layer of pine tree bark on top to give the crowns and roots of the plants some protection from frost in winter and from evaporation in summer. Once this coarse and expensive mulch is in place, it more or less precludes any large-scale disturbance of the surface such as the annual hilling of soil around each bush in late fall, a practice often recommended by suppliers of roses. Nevertheless, I do not follow it; I believe that if a rose bush cannot make it through the winter, even under a generous protection of bark mulch, then it does not belong in my garden.

The elevated rose bed contains up to four dozen bushes, especially in years following mild winters; severe winters cull the hybrids that prove too tender for the climate. The bed measures approximately 8 ft (2.4 m) across and 25 ft (7.6 m) in length. On the outside of the rail ties is a gravel walk that facilitates frequent visits to the rose garden for cutting fresh and spent blossoms, for occasional weeding or spraying, or just for enjoyment (Plate 9). No other planting in my garden provides the same variety of color for nearly 5 months of the year that the rose garden offers. But, it is clearly a labor-intensive enterprise; neglect, even for 3 or 4 weeks during the growing season, can turn this beautiful spot into a bed of diseased fallen leaves and bare stems.

On the south and west sides of the rose garden I placed a 3-ft (1-m) high picket fence with a corner gate. Along the south side I placed thirty plants of white and pink *Anemone* × *hybrida,* far too many, as I belatedly discovered. They keep spreading out of the confines of their bed and must be frequently restrained. On the west I planted three herbaceous peonies (*Paeonia* spp.) that never seem to outgrow the space allocated to them.

The rose garden gives a cultured touch to the surrounding wilder portions of my garden and, despite the price it exacts in labor and care, it is welcome as a source of cut flowers and as a quiet refuge for a short rest and contemplation.

The Vegetable Garden

The vegetable patch in my garden is a 2000-sq-ft (190-sq-m) area over which I have very little authority or responsibility; it is the almost exclusive domain of my wife. My participation is limited to activities such as building and maintaining the fence, constructing raised beds, bringing fresh leaf mold, and attempting, often unsuccessfully, to trap an occasional *Marmota monax* (woodchuck, groundhog) in a Havahart® trap. I did take a greater part in the creation of the vegetable garden when it was being developed in the corner of a worn-out pasture. The thin, sterile soil, consisting mostly of yellowish sand, pebbles, and large stones, was tilled several times and enriched with copious quantities of manure and leaf mold.

After years of experimenting with the configuration and size of the individual planting plots, the elevated-bed pattern was chosen. The beds, which run from north to south, are about 25 ft (8 m) long, 4 ft (1.2 m) wide, 5 in (13 cm) high, and are held together by boards of treated, rot-resistant lumber (Plate 10). At first, there was some concern about the potential toxicity to the vegetables from the long-lasting wood preservative in the boards. Nevertheless, the state agricultural experiment station

PLATE 10. The vegetable garden in mid spring.

advised that tests indicated such effects to be minimal as the preservative was applied under pressure to wood that had been first thoroughly dried. This process allows the chemical to penetrate deeply into each board and remain firmly tied up. Hence, the possibility of leaching is insignificant.

The supply of fresh leaf mold for the garden comes from the town leaf-mulch field. To avoid slippery roads the Department of Public Works vacuums the streets and roads in late autumn, piling the overabundant leaves into heaps 15 ft (4.5 m) high and 300 ft (90 m) long. In spring and summer the leaves are turned over several times with machines. By the following autumn and winter, bacteria consume a large part of the organic matter turning it into a rich substance that makes an ideal soil additive for growing vegetables and other plants. The material is then made available free to local gardeners as well as to the town's parks and nature center. The municipal treasury still comes out ahead in this seemingly altruistic venture because the alternative disposal of leaves in the incinerator would be considerably more costly in terms of fuel and the effects on the environment.

In addition to leaf mold, the vegetable garden receives an annual dressing of compost from our own two-part compost bin into which goes nearly everything that decomposes: weeds, thin leafy branches, and all vegetable household scraps. Meat leftovers are avoided as they would attract raccoons, rats, and other unwanted visitors. While a frequent turning of the compost pile would expedite its decomposition, neither I nor my wife engage very often in this heavy exercise. Consequently, it takes a year or more for the compost to reach a degree of decay when it can be screened and incorporated into soil.

The two parts of the bin permit two piles of compost to mature at alternate intervals; when the material in one side of the bin is used up and a new pile is started in its place, the compost in the other side continues to age. During the decomposition process, the feeding bacteria generate temperatures that destroy the viability of most or all weed seeds. The heat may also neutralize certain pathogens but, to the extent possible, it is best to avoid composting diseased plants and their foliage. The leaves, blossoms, and stems of roses are not recycled; whether healthy or not, they are sent routinely with other garbage to the incinerator.

Compost and leaf mold are most beneficial to plants when they reach a stage of only partial decomposition, with some of the original organic matter remaining undegraded to complete its decay after it is incorporated in the soil. If allowed to mature completely over too many seasons, compost or leaf mold turns into brown soil which will have lost most of its value as a fertilizer, even though it will remain an excellent conditioner.

A vegetable garden is not only a source of the freshest produce, but it is also an esthetically pleasing piece of land that displays the love and labor so generously bestowed upon it. It is a sober, unfrivolous, dignified, and somehow morally justified gardening endeavor that is perhaps a reflection of the great step the human race took 30,000 years ago when it changed from food gathering to food growing.

The Rock Garden, Meadow, and Nursery

During the dredging of the pond two decades ago, the machines brought up a number of large boulders for which I could find no use. In a quick decision I piled them in a heap not far from the pond, hoping to soon make a rock garden. Some of the pond's mucky yet sandy bottom was dumped over the boulders, and the whole disarray was left alone. It became one of those future projects that I always managed to delay by looking the other way. After a few years, it did not even look like an eyesore to me anymore, and I was once taken aback when my youngest daughter mentioned it facetiously. Obviously, she had failed to instruct her brain and eyes not to see it.

But, there was some help from nature. The rains cleaned the rocks and washed the soil between them. On the more stable surfaces, moss began to grow. Finally, one spring some 15 years later, I began noticing the old heap again. Since it was in shade, a typical rock garden was out of the question. Still, there are plants that prefer the screelike conditions (a mixture of pebbles, sand, and soil) with perfect drainage and shade. I brought more moss from the woods to cover the bare spots. Then I scooped out deep pockets between the boulders and in the steeper sides, filling them with rich

PLATE 11. The moss-green and sandstone-gray tones of the rock garden in early fall.

PLATE 12. The entrance to the meadow in early May; *Daphne cneorum* 'Ruby Glow' and *Pieris yakushimanum* in left foreground, and *Cornus florida* (flowering dogwood) in left background. On the right, the corner gate to the rose garden.

leaf mold. In these pockets I planted dwarf specimens of *Rhododendron, Ilex* (holly), *Picea* (spruce), and other shrubs, as well as perennials such as *Hepatica* (liverleaf), *Haberlea rhodopensis, Soldanella,* small bulbs, *Cyclamen,* and anything else that would like the site and was small enough to be in scale. Eventually, the moss had to be pinned to the ground with small sticks inserted vertically through it into the soil, because a flock of overflying robins discovered it and, in an early spring raid, ripped out every inch of moss while looking for worms. After a few years, the old heap became an interesting mound the color of moss-green and sandstone-gray (Plate 11). A few rocks placed as steps make it possible to reach the top and, from there, gain still another perspective on the garden.

The designation meadow for the 11,000-sq-ft (1020-sq-m) former pasture is something of a misnomer. Many years ago I had a vision for this clearing in the woods; I imagined knee-high grass waving in the breeze, dotted with flowers of *Asclepias tuberosa* (butterfly weed), *Campanula* (blue bells), *Chrysanthemum leucanthemum* (daisy), and *Papaver rhoeas* (field poppy). However, when the pasture was cleared, leveled, and seeded, unexpected problems with maintaining a true meadow emerged. Within the first year, hundreds of seedlings from nearby trees and bushes sprouted in the loosened and improved soil. The only means by which I could prevent my clearing from returning to a thicket was either by pulling out the seedlings by hand or by spraying them. Neither method had much appeal, especially when I realized that if mowed with a tractor-mower, my "meadow" could be made neat in half an hour.

So, today only the name remains. The disappointment is only minimal since I still enjoy the meadow's long vistas and the open sky (Plate 12). The meadow also provides an easy access to the side areas; against the eastern wall is a broad bed with strips of *Rubus idaeus* (red raspberry) and *Asparagus officinalis* (asparagus), and on the west side is a shrubbery border with a few flowering trees, including *Styrax japonicus* (styrax), *Cornus florida* (flowering dogwood), *Cladrastis lutea* (yellowwood), and *Sorbus alnifolia* (Korean mountain ash), as well as 24 rhododendrons and tree peonies.

Fifteen years ago, when my vigor was much greater, I double-dug a small triangle of land shaded by a tall maple and protected by a stone boundary wall. Digging out the soil to a depth of 2 ft (60 cm), I heaped it on the side, screened out the rocks, mixed in several wheelbarrows of leaf mold and sand, and returned the good soil back into the hole. Although some maple roots now have penetrated this ideal medium, the place still provides a favored temporary shelter for dozens of small plants. New cuttings (after they are rooted in a glassed porch), layered branches of rhododendrons, plants ordered through catalogues or purchased locally and too small to set out in open sites, or plants I just do not know what to do with at the moment, all go into this tiny nursery. The area is barely 75 sq ft (7 sq m), but it can hold four dozen little plants. They do remarkably well there.

On one side, the nursery is protected by a wall, but otherwise it is surrounded by a snow fence. This keeps out the most damaging potential intruders, namely, the deer. Above the nursery are a few long saplings held horizontally on 4-ft (1.2-m) high cedar posts, and over these rails additional segments of snow fence are unfolded as a flat, slatted roof. The space between the laths is about one and a half times the width of each lath, allowing the amount of light reaching the plants to be reduced by 40 percent; this is sufficient protection from the burn of the afternoon winter sun that beams into that corner of the meadow on clear days.

Light and Water

The question of sun and shade in my garden was one of the more difficult issues to resolve because of my early reluctance to cut any trees. At first I hesitated to cut even the scrawniest saplings, yet later 60-ft (18-m) tall maples had to be removed in certain parts of the garden to obtain sufficient light for smaller plants requiring sun or dappled shade. In my hesitation to thin out unwanted trees, I should have taken a clue from nature and its steady hand in dealing with excessive or overcrowded vegetation: redundant individuals simply perish and fade away.

As my plans for the garden firmed up and my priorities were defined, trees were cut, one by one. With each tree, uncertainty and doubt arose in my mind whether it was really necessary to remove it. Still today as I look back, I cannot think of a single tree that I wish I had not felled. I am also aware, however, that at this stage of the garden's development I must proceed with sensitivity and caution in giving up any more trees. All kinds of alternatives can be explored before the irrevocable final cut; for example, in certain cases it may be possible to avoid felling a tree by trimming its lower limbs and thus letting more light reach the space beneath. In other instances, topping a tree will shorten its shadow and allow more sunshine for the plants on its shady side.

Most plants flower more profusely if they receive more sun. Nonetheless, while heavy blossoming for a week or two is an important reason for growing a plant, it is also desirable that a specimen look attractive during the remaining 50 weeks of the year. As an example, with sufficient moisture some rhododendron varieties bloom exceptionally well in full hot sun, but their foliage may become bleached and unwholesome, clearly a liability for the site they are supposed to beautify throughout the year. It would be better to move the shrubs to a shadier spot where their blossoms may be less abundant but where the plants would feel more at home. Their original site could be used for sun-loving plants such as *Lavandula angustifolia* (lavender) or *Caryopteris* × *clandonensis* (bluebeard), which would become bushy and floriferous there but thin and straggly in shade.

When a new plant is acquired, it is advisable to become familiar with its light preferences. However, even with the best information, the perfect spot is not always chosen. When a specimen begins to show dissatisfaction with a location, it can be moved almost risk-free within one or two years from planting, if the job is done in spring or fall. The success is assured even more if the moving is done in very early spring as soon as the soil can be worked. Even if snow and some frost occur after the move, the specimen will be well established by early summer. If there is not enough rain, adequate irrigation should be provided during the first two or three summers in the new location.

Although the need for watering during a drought can be significantly reduced by mulch, it is not eliminated entirely. Porous soils in elevated and well-drained positions, while desirable in other respects, are especially prone to drying in prolonged periods without rain. To overcome this tendency, I use mulch, but I also incorporate moisture-retentive materials, such as leaf mold and compost, in the soil at time of planting. Nevertheless, in times of extreme drought, the loss of moisture through seepage, evaporation—even when reduced by mulch—and transpiration through foliage may be so complete as to turn the rich brown soil enveloping the roots into dense dust.

Certain types of plants, especially older specimens that have grown in the same location for many years, manage to survive these conditions. Some go dormant and revive with the next abundant rainfall or irrigation. Certain trees, such as ashes (*Fraxinus* spp.), may become partly or totally defoliated, and some shrubs, like rhododendrons, may roll up their leaves to reduce the surface area of evaporation, similar to the defensive posture they assume on very dry, cold, and windy days in winter. Nevertheless, individuals that were planted only one or two years earlier, or plants that are still young, do not have the facility to cope with such severe circumstances. Some may die, and those that survive may perish in the next period of stress, such as a cold winter, or an attack of a disease they could otherwise fight off. Thus, almost every summer I find it necessary to selectively water the plants in my garden that appear to be in need of moisture.

Pruning

Pruning is defined as cutting back or cutting off for the purpose of achieving better shape or more floriferous growth, and for the reduction of unwanted and superfluous parts. Many useful rules have been written on pruning, some of which describe in simplified terms a subject that defies categorization. Every genus, species, and plant has unique pruning requirements that can be discerned only by knowing the specimen well. And yet, ignoring all such rules and concerns, and cutting off whatever a gardener wants to cut in any season, will probably do little harm to the plant if not carried to excess.

I walk through my garden as frequently as I can manage, always carrying in my back pockets two small gardening tools. One is a narrow trowel, handy for little jobs like digging up a weed in the lawn or moving a seedling that volunteered where it cannot remain. The second tool is a pair of hand pruning shears which I use on almost every walk regardless of the season. A thin branch of *Vaccinium corymbosum* (highbush blueberry) reaching across a path should be cut back. A lanky 8-ft (2.4-m) long stem of *Rhododendron viscosum* (swamp azalea), with only a few leaves and two or three flower buds at its tip, ceased to be an asset a long time ago and should be removed. A dead branchlet of an evergreen rhododendron, probably harboring the grub of a stem borer, must be cut off and split open to locate and crush the larva. A few dry stems of *Gentiana andrewsii* (bottled gentian) should be cut at the base, and the seedpods saved. And the yellowed, spent foliage of *Dicentra spectabilis* (bleeding heart) has completed its magnificent spring display of color, form, and texture, and now at the end of summer is ready to be cut and tossed on the compost pile.

After the large-leaved (elepidote) rhododendrons finish blooming in late spring, their spent blossoms are removed. This allows the new vegetative growth and the formation of next year's flower buds to advance without delay and to harden well before winter sets in. This procedure, called deadheading, is practiced widely by rhododendron growers; yet no one performs this task in the wild and the genus continues to flourish. Nonetheless, considering the millions of dustlike seeds rhododendrons produce every year, it is easy to conclude that by not allowing the seed capsules to remain on the bushes to maturity, some of the plants' energy is saved. Deadheading does not appear to affect noticeably the next year's production of blossoms; semiannual bloomers continue to skip a year, and annual bloomers do not seem to need the help. Still, year after year on my early summer walks I instinctively reach up to remove the dry or drying trusses, and sometimes my wife and I undertake a deadheading campaign and spend a couple of hours taking off the redundant clusters. Some of them break off easily with two fingers while others require two hands to make a clean break and to keep the loss of newly sprouted shoots to a minimum. Whether the plants need it or not, I have the feeling that they appreciate this attention, and they certainly look better.

To encourage bushy growth and heavier blossoming, shrubs such as *Spirea japonica* 'Shibori' and *Caryopteris* × *clandonensis* (bluebeard) must be reduced in early spring from last year's height of 2–3 ft (60–90 cm) to a mere 4 in (10 cm). The

PLATE 13. The clouds of blossoms of a tall *Kalmia latifolia* (mountain laurel) in early June against the dark foliage of *Juniperus virginiana* (eastern red cedar).

clematises 'Jackmanii', 'Ville de Lyon', and 'Ernest Markham' are pruned almost to the ground every February, whereas 'Henryi' and 'Lanuginosa Candida' are cut only once in 3 or 4 years.

Roses are pruned twice a year in addition to the frequent cutting of long stems with blossoms through the summer. The first partial pruning is performed in November when the canes are shortened to about 3 ft (90 cm) to prevent their swaying in the strong winds of winter and thus loosening their upper roots and crowns. Then in March or April they are shortened to 8–15 in (20–40 cm). The spring pruning should be done before the vegetative buds swell too much but after the danger of heavier frost has passed to avoid freezing the new shoots promoted by pruning. The spring cut of each cane (always using sharp shears) should be made about 0.5 in (1 cm) above a healthy vegetative bud.

Plants such as the daphnes are almost never pruned because, it is said, they "shrink from the knife." Looking at the thick, fleshy wood of *Daphne* × *burkwoodii* 'Carol Mackie', you can almost feel the plant's pain at being cut into. But even daphnes must be sometimes severely pruned and, according to those who have done it, the shrubs recover remarkably well.

Larger pruning tasks may require a hand saw, a pole saw, or a chain saw. My *Magnolia stellata* (star magnolia) needs major surgery every 2 or 3 years to keep it in bounds; the pruning is done immediately after the blossoms fade so that the new growth has time to produce next year's flower buds. Similar rules apply to *Malus* ('Hopa' crab apple), *Halesia monticola* (mountain silverbell), and other flowering trees that are kept low due to limited space and bushy for greater abundance of blossoms.

Broad-leaved evergreens also need an occasional pruning. Several of my *Kalmia latifolia* (mountain laurel) bushes have grown into small trees (Plate 13). Some of their lower branches, laden with large flower trusses, droop to shoulder height and obstruct the grassy path beneath them. A few rhododendrons let their heavy-foliaged boughs encroach on the narrow path running next to them. This vigorous growth must be headed back, even though pruning broad-leaved evergreens is always a sensitive job that I perform with great reluctance. I avoid it for as long as I can by holding the branches back with thin stakes or by tying the offending parts to the main stem or to a stake driven into the ground away from the roots. Eventually, however, some cutting has to be done.

With *Kalmia latifolia* (mountain laurel) and many *Rhododendron* varieties, it may be well to keep in mind that they do not always sprout near the point where a branch is cut, sometimes leaving a bare stick that eventually dries and has to be removed. Certain species and varieties of rhododendrons, especially some with red flowers, have the genetic trait of losing all dormant buds along their branches one or two years following the unfolding of new terminal foliage; when the leafy tips are pruned off, there may be nothing to replace them. Other types, however, retain a few dormant and viable buds for several years; these almost-imperceptible protuberances, which are awakened when the end foliage is lost, are capable of producing new bushy growth along the bare branch. Some species however old they may be, including the native *R. maximum* (rosebay), can be cut down to a few inches from the ground and in several years develop into rejuvenated, dense bushes.

Branches of large trees may occasionally need to be cut off. For instance, the 1.5-in (4-cm) thick lower limbs of *Juniperus virginiana* (eastern red cedar) have to be removed with a hand saw to enable the nearby *Rhododendron* 'Scintillation' to grow taller and wider. Some slender 60-ft (18-m) high *Acer rubrum* (red maple) trees have developed new growth on their otherwise smooth, silvery trunks; these shoots must be removed with a pole saw to preserve the maples' clean appearance.

The crowns of the tall and top-heavy *Quercus coccinea* (scarlet oak) and *Acer rubrum* (red maple), both growing near the house, must be reduced in their breadth by at least a third to minimize their wind resistance and thus preclude their breaking or uprooting in a hurricane. This task, however, is reserved for the professional tree expert sitting in a basket at the end of a long boom on a heavy crane.

Small and large pruning is unavoidable, but it need not be an enigmatic chore if the plants' growth characteristics and welfare are learned and respected.

Mulch

Several feet below ground level, the temperature of the earth remains relatively constant at somewhat above 50°F (10°C), but the top layer, which is directly affected by the temperature of the air, varies from much below freezing in winter to 70°F (21°C) or higher in summer. Important fluctuations occur even within a 24-hour period. In winter the soil freezes at night and thaws by midday, a process that can dislocate smaller plants by upheaving them and tearing their thin feeder roots. It can also expose sizable portions of entire root systems to the drying effects of the season's sometimes-arid air.

Mulch can make an important difference. The warmth that in winter is conducted from the subsoil upward and normally lost into the atmosphere can be intercepted by a protective covering and partly retained to warm the layer of soil around the roots. In summer the same 50°F (10°C) temperature still radiates from the subsoil, this time cooling the upper layers; in this case mulch interposes itself as a barrier to the heating effects of the hot air above it. Hence, mulch can narrow significantly the temperature extremes of the medium in which the roots exist.

Mulch is beneficial to plants in other respects as well: it reduces evaporation and preserves moisture in dry spells; it prevents soil erosion by rain above the roots; it makes a natural and attractive background for plants; and it controls weeds, most of which require heat, light, and direct contact with soil to germinate. In some parts of a garden, such as lawns, weeds must be controlled by hand, but in shrubbery and perennial borders they can be significantly reduced or totally eliminated by heavy mulch. In some locations similar effects can be achieved with vigorous ground covers such as *Pachysandra terminalis* (spurge) or *Vinca minor* (periwinkle).

Yet, mulch can also be detrimental to plants. In very rainy weather it can keep the soil sodden so that the roots are deprived of oxygen. One extremely wet spring I nearly lost a mature *Rhododendron mucronulatum* (Korean azalea) that was growing in a low, damp location (where it should not have been planted in the first place). The preceding autumn, in my mulching enthusiasm, I had placed 4 in (10 cm) of leaves around the plant. When the heavy spring rains came, the water table rose to a few inches below ground level, and the soil became totally saturated. Suddenly, the plant's leaves acquired dark green blotches, appeared waterlogged, and began to droop. I removed the mulch and within hours the plant began to return to normal. Today, 10 years later, it is flourishing, but I have never again put mulch around it.

In winter, mulch piled close to the stem of a shrub or the trunk of a small tree provides an easy and warm access to the plant for mice and voles, who gnaw on the bark, thus girdling the trunk and killing the plant. I once lost a large *Rhododendron* 'Roseum Elegans' in this manner, so to avoid helping the rodents, I pull the mulch away from each trunk, about 6 in (15 cm) in all directions, especially if the mulch consists of leaves. The winter wind blows some of the leaves back into the empty space, but the layer that accumulates is usually quite thin. Even though a 1-ft (30-cm) wide circle around the trunk is unmulched, most of the beneficial aspects of the cover remain. The outer roots of the plant are still protected, and the entire surrounding area receives the usual benefits that mulch offers (i.e., it remains moist, weed-free, more attractive, warmer in winter, and cooler in summer).

Another possible harmful effect of mulch may come from the retention of excessive dampness during the hot humid weather of mid and late summer. In such conditions it is not unusual to encounter various types of blight, root rot, and other fungal diseases. I have lost several plants of *Rhododendron carolinianum* (Carolina rhododendron) as well as other species and hybrids to these pathogens, especially when the plants were growing in locations with heavier shade and poor air circulation. Some of these diseases are treatable or preventable by fungicide sprays, but others are generally untreatable and terminal. Hence, I do not plant in sensitive locations the varieties that I know are susceptible. It is wise to burn the infected plants or to put them into a garbage bag so they can be burned in the town incinerator.

One example of unsuspected injury from mulch applied at the wrong time is the publicized experience of nursery owners with young plants lined out in the field. In early fall growers would routinely apply mulch around the plants expecting a certain percentage of the plants to perish before spring. Eventually it was discovered that winter losses could be reduced by applying the mulch somewhat later, after several light frosts or even after a thin layer of the soil froze. It appears that during the hardening period young plants need the warmth that rises around them during the night from the bare and still warm earth. After a longer period of chilly weather, the plants complete their winterizing process by draining excess moisture from their cells. At that time the application of mulch begins to yield the expected advantages.

Despite all these hidden and obvious dangers, I could not garden without mulch. If used with discretion and forethought its benefits far outweigh its drawbacks. My favorite mulch is made of pine needles. I put on as much of it as I can find—up to 2 in (5 cm). Pine needles have every advantage a mulch should have. They let the rain go through rather than run off. They allow air to reach the soil and oxygenate it; yet, they still slow down evaporation and keep the soil moist. They last several years, and when they decompose, they leave a mealy, friable, nutritious substance into which the roots reach eagerly. They resist being blown by the wind and still are easy to scatter with a pitchfork or by hand. And they smell beautifully when their resin evaporates into the warm air of summer. Do they have disadvantages? Possibly they may be too acidic for certain plants. I have not found it to be so, but if it were the case the problem would be easy to correct by scattering a handful of limestone around the plant and watering it in. Where do I get all the wonderful needles? The truth is I never have enough, but I rake them up where pines grow in great numbers or I collect the heaps that people accumulate when removing them from their lawns.

My other favorite mulch is made of oak leaves. As the oak leaves dry, they curl up creating pockets which let rain and air reach the roots. Oak leaves can be mixed in a reasonable proportion with other kinds of leaves, including those of maples which, by themselves, tend to lie flat when wet, creating an impenetrable barrier to air and water. I apply 6–8 in (15–20 cm) of oak leaves or the mixture in late fall. By spring, the layer is packed down by rain and snow to 2–3 in (5–8 cm).

The pine bark nuggets that are available at garden supply stores also make an excellent mulch; however, for my purposes, I would need truckloads of them. Also, they look well around the house or on smaller surfaces such as the rose garden, but could look out of place covering vast areas in a natural landscape. Woodchips also make a good mulch, as does sawdust, but there is some concern that while these materials are undergoing decomposition, the bacteria that feed on them deplete the soil of nitrogen, which must then be replaced.

Soil and Fertilizer

The regular use of fertilizer is by no means a universally accepted gardening practice. There are perhaps as many different opinions on this subject as there are gardeners expressing them. During most of my gardening years I have endeavored to grow plants as naturally as I could, allowing for only a few exceptions such as the control of excessive insects and diseases. Accordingly, I have gravitated toward the school of using minimum amounts of fertilizer; years may go by between applications. Instead, I have relied heavily on the two trusted sources of nourishment: leaf mold or compost worked into the soil at planting time, and mulch that slowly decomposes and lets the nutriments leach gradually among the roots.

Nevertheless, there are circumstances when the use of fertilizer becomes almost unavoidable. For instance, I know of no alternative to fertilizer when some specimens of deciduous azaleas grow vigorously but refuse to set flower buds. To wake them from their happy-but-sterile existence, a small helping of superphosphate or a combination of ingredients according to tested recipes becomes the only option. This subject, as well as several formulas, is discussed in detail in the introductory pages to *Rhododendron* found in Part 2 of this volume.

If fertilizers are used, they should be applied at a time when they would not unduly stimulate fresh growth that could freeze in a cold winter. It is generally recommended that no fertilizer be applied after 1 July, as the young shoots that would be thus encouraged to appear would have no time to sufficiently harden; once the plants have gone dormant in early winter, fertilizing is in order.

Most commercially available formulas are a combination of three elements that are shown on the package in percentages of total contents. For example, a product displaying numbers 15–30–15 consists of 15 percent nitrogen (N), 30 percent phosphorus (P), 15 percent potassium (K), and 40 percent inert matter. Nitrogen, a gaseous element that may dissipate into the atmosphere if it is not absorbed by the plants or worked into the soil, is used by plants mainly for the production of foliage. Phosphorus helps to develop hardiness and cell structure and, together with potassium, encourages the development of roots. Both phosphorus and potassium are solid elements that take months to break down before they become available to the plants.

For the correct selection of fertilizer, it is important to know what kind of soil is in a garden. Soil test kits, which are available in garden supply stores and nurseries, are not difficult to use if instructions are followed explicitly. I have used them in past years but have since relied on the more comprehensive and accurate analyses from state or county agricultural offices. Their reviews are available free or for a nominal fee and usually detail not only the elements in which the soil may be deficient, but also the degree of acidity and alkalinity (i.e., its pH value). The pH scale begins with 0.0 and goes to 14.0, with pH 7.0 being the neutral value; soils with pH above 7.0 are alkaline, and those below 7.0 are acidic. Nearly all soils fall between pH 3.5 and pH 9.0; the individual values are usually described in terms similar to those listed below:

pH Value	Description
9.5	Intensely alkaline
9.0	Strongly alkaline
8.5	Definitely alkaline
8.0	Moderately alkaline
7.5	Slightly alkaline
7.0	Neutral
6.5	Very slightly acidic
6.0	Slightly acidic
5.5–5.0	Moderately acidic
4.5	Definitely acidic
4.0	Strongly acidic
3.5	Intensely acidic

The pH values are based on logarithms with 10 as the base. Thus, pH 5.0 is 10 times as acidic as pH 6.0, and pH 4.0 is 10 times as acidic as pH 5.0; hence, pH 4.0 is 100 times more acidic than pH 6.0. The majority of plants grow in soils of pH 6.0 to 7.5; nevertheless, others die in soils with pH higher than 4.5 or 5.0. Some wild flowers, such as *Cypripedium acaule* (pink ladyslipper), require not only definitely acidic soils, but also a symbiotic relationship of their roots with microscopic fungi, the mycorrhizae.

The acidity of soil may be altered with readily available substances such as lime, sulfur, ammonium sulfate, and even a commercial fertilizer. For instance, dissolving about 0.5 cup (12 cl) of commercial superphosphate in 1 gal (4 liters) of water will produce a solution of pH value 3.5. If poured around the roots of a small plant growing in neutral soil, it will change the pH instantly, though temporarily, to well under 5.0. To make the change more permanent, the soil can be dusted a few days later with a tablespoon of powdered sulfur plus an equal amount of ammonium sulfate in an 8-in (20-cm) circle over the outer roots of a plant, avoiding the foliage which could be damaged by the chemicals. On the other hand, an acidic soil may be made neutral or alkaline with the application of a solution of 1 cup (24 cl) of garden limestone in 2 gal (8 liters) of water, and followed with a tablespoon (1.5 ml) of limestone worked into the soil in a circle around the plant.

As in most parts of New England, the natural pH of the soil in my garden is between 4.5 and 6.5, a degree of acidity that grows great specimens of *Kalmia* (mountain laurel), *Rhododendron, Erica* (heath), *Calluna* (heather), *Epigaea repens* (trailing arbutus), and other acid-loving plants.

Diseases and Pests

No garden on earth is free of plant pathogens and pests. Perhaps even the Garden of Eden had a few of each. The fear of plant diseases and the concern about the damage they cause often may be worse than the actual injury. As a rule, their effect is nothing more than an esthetic deterioration or a gradual decline in a plant's health, which could possibly become serious over several years but which can be reversed usually in time to save the specimen. For instance, the various fungal diseases that defoliate plants such as *Rosa* (rose), *Malus* (crab apple), *Syringa* (lilac), or *Kalmia latifolia* (mountain laurel) in one year can be totally cured or avoided the following year or two, probably with only a marginal setback to the plants' health.

The few exceptions to this benign image of plant diseases are deadly pathogens belonging to *Phytophthora,* sometimes called root rot or stem dieback. Among the many plants these pathogens attack are *Syringa* (lilac), *Rosa* (rose), and *Rhododendron,* all of which prefer well-drained locations. Grown on poorly drained sites with inadequate air circulation or stressed by severe drought, these plants may fall prey to this soil-borne affliction.

There are no reliably permanent remedies to totally eliminate these diseases from a garden. Two chemicals, metalaxyl and fosetyl-al, were thoroughly tested in the past 5 years by the Research Foundation of the American Rhododendron Society. Though the results were encouraging, neither chemical offered a complete and permanent eradication, perhaps because the pathogen is always present in the soil and becomes active when conditions are favorable to it. I have not used these chemicals as I have not identified *Phytophthora* as a specific problem in my garden, a task that requires a laboratory test. Over many years I have lost a handful of plants to some kind of root rot but if the situation does not become worse, I do not intend to use the two chemicals. Nevertheless, in every case that a specimen dies of unexplained causes, tools that were used around the plant should be washed thoroughly with diluted bleach before they are used elsewhere and the plant should be burned. Diseases other than *Phytophthora* are usually cured with traditional fungicides, most of which contain natural substances such as sulfur and are readily available in garden supply stores.

In gardens where deer are not a problem, the most harmful pests are likely to be insects. I have found the following species to be the most damaging.

Otiorhynchus sulcatus (black vine weevil, taxus weevil) was imported from Japan many decades ago. It is black and about 0.3 in (1 cm) long. The adults and larvae feed on a variety of plants including *Taxus* (yew), *Rhododendron,* and *Rosa* (rose). At the mature stage, the 0.5-in (13-mm) long insect can be identified easily by its tapering snout, plus the fact that it cannot fly but instead drops to the ground when disturbed. It is seldom seen during the day because it feeds mostly at night. As an adult it damages plants by making small, irregular, sometimes semicircular, notches on or near the margins of leaves. This, however, is only the tip of the iceberg. More serious destruction occurs on the roots where the grubs feed throughout the growing season. In cases of heavy infestation a plant may wilt as if it were in drought. As the larvae eat their way upward, sometimes girdling the main stem, the plant will die.

In prior years the common treatment for black vine weevil involved drenching the soil around the roots with long-lasting chemicals such as chlordane. Since sprays of this type are no longer used, the preferred product is acephate. Because of its short period of effectiveness, acephate must be applied every three weeks from May to October. Even though the highly injurious weevils are present in my garden, I have not yet used any specific insecticides to control them; eventually I may be obliged to seek a remedy, by then, perhaps, one of biologic origin.

Popilia japonica (Japanese beetle) and one or two similar Oriental insects are lethargic but extremely destructive pests. *Popilia japonica* is an oval, shiny brown beetle about 0.3 in (1 cm) long. It occurs in large numbers in midsummer when the adults emerge from the soil, where they spent their immature stage as grubs, and immediately proceed to eat and mate. Injury inflicted by the adults is devastating to blossoms which are sometimes devoured completely. The beetles also injure foliage, eating the tender parts and leaving behind meshlike skeletons of the leaves' veins. Of equal concern are the grubs that feed on the roots of many plants.

Total control of Japanese beetle is impossible because the adult insects fly in from surrounding areas. Nevertheless, there are measures that can keep the population at least partially under control. Shaking the insects gently from the blossoms of roses and other plants into a jar with water or diluted bleach will dispose of hundreds of them within a few days. Traps baited with a sex hormone, which attract the beetles and let them fall into a bag below, sometimes amass pounds of the insects.

Oberea myops (stem borer) is a small beetle that deposits its egg on the current year's growth of rhododendrons, usually in the middle or near the bottom of the new fresh-green shoot. After hatching, the larva eats some of the surface tissue, leaving irregular, light brown areas of injury before burrowing into the center of the stem, where it begins consuming its way through the pith upward toward the new leaves, usually causing the entire young branchlet to wilt and dry. At this point the insect can be controlled completely without insecticide by cutting off the wilted stem just below the areas of injury, then slitting it open and crushing the white larva between the two halves of the stem. If not destroyed, the larva overwinters inside the narrow tunnel, reverses its direction in spring, and eats its way down toward the main stem, drilling tiny holes every few inches through which it expels the sawdustlike material it produces. In the course of the second spring and summer, it will consume the entire central strand of the spongy tissue, causing the death of ever-larger branches. The stem borer grows to 0.5 in (13 mm) or a little more in length by the time it reaches the ground, where it spends the second winter and matures into an adult.

Most young plants thus affected by stem borers will die. I have noticed that the borer occurs also on my *Kalmia latifolia* (mountain laurel) plants, which, however, appear to be more capable of surviving the attack even without the pith. During the winter, birds sometimes peck into the laurel stems and extract the larvae. Applying an insecticide such as carbaryl just as the new growth on rhododendrons begins to firm up would probably prove effective. Nonetheless, I have not used any remedy for the stem borer other than my pruning shears and a sharp pocketknife. On rare occasions an infested branchlet does not wilt and the only way the borer's presence is detected is by the accumulation of sawdust at the mouth of the holes. To locate the larva in such cases, I sometimes have to sacrifice an entire large branch by cutting the wood lower and lower until I reach healthy pith.

Sesia rhododendri (rhododendron borer, clear wing) is a moth with transparent wings that lays its eggs in late May or early June in the crotches of rhododendrons, usually about 12 in (30 cm) above the ground or even at the soil level. By the end of summer, the whitish larvae will have grown to 0.75–1 in (2.0–2.5 cm), sometimes girdling the main trunk and burrowing into it with many small tunnels, leaving sawdustlike remains at the openings. This destructive insect is one of the very few pests that can kill the venerable rhododendron giants that have survived other serious adversities. It can be controlled by spraying the plant's lower trunk with carbaryl several times between early June and early July. I have not experienced any serious infestation of this insect in my garden.

Tetranychus bimaculatus (red spider mite, two-spotted mite) is a minute arachnid that often infests plants growing in hot, sunny locations. It can be controlled with frequent, strong streams of cold water from a hose or with a specific miticide.

Giardomyia rhododendri (midge) is a tiny insect that affects the very young leaves of rhododendrons, leaving them disfigured and curled as they mature. The distorted foliage remains on the plants until it falls off in the second or third year. This nearly invisible insect is difficult to control with insecticide, but if applied in early spring before the new leaves begin to unfold, and again in late July and August when the second flush of new growth occurs in some years, sprays are probably effective. Nevertheless, snapping off infested shoots and disposing of them in a garbage bag has provided an equally effective control in my garden.

All insecticides and fungicides, whether of manufactured or of natural (biologic) origin, are to a certain degree harmful to humans and present a risk also to other mammals, as well as to birds, amphibians, fish, beneficial insects, and arachnids. Most of us view these preparations with a measure of ambivalence. We fear and even hate them, but we suspect that without them our living standards could not be maintained. Almost certainly the world would not have the abundance of food we take for granted. Perhaps it was this kind of public concern that prompted the U.S. Environmental Protection Agency (EPA) to fund an entity called the National Pesticide Telecommunication Network. This organization, which provides both emergency and advisory counsel to anyone who calls, can be reached 24 hours a day, 365 days a year, on a toll-free number: 1-800-858-7378. The staff can answer questions on almost any related subject.

Among the other annoying pests in my garden, slugs are certainly in the top rank. Consuming large quantities of foliage, they cause stunted growth or even death to many plants. They also devour blossoms, preventing formation of seeds. Though I have tried many methods, I have never mastered the control of slugs. Nothing seems to be completely or permanently effective, but neither can I give up entirely and leave the garden to them. Among the ways I have attempted to control slugs are placing shallow plates of beer in infested areas, dusting diatomaceous earth around plants, and inviting a neighbor's pet duck to my garden. These and other measures are partially effective, but many are cumbersome or impractical for a larger garden. At times I have resorted to crushing the slugs with the heel of my boot, then throwing them into the pond to the fish. Last but not least, I have used slug bait in the form of paste or pellets. Since the pellets can possibly be eaten by birds, it is best that they be hidden under stones or in rock cavities. To be effective, a slug bait program must be started in very early spring; late March is not too soon, even though in some years rains and late snows may dissolve the substance, which then must be applied again and again. Using slug bait is my last option, at least until several of the promising biologic controls become available and prove effective and ecologically safe without the likelihood of introducing new and perhaps even more damaging organisms.

Other pests that can sometimes become bothersome are squirrels, chipmunks, and mice. *Cyclamen, Sanguinaria canadensis* (bloodroot), and other vulnerable plants can be protected by a cage made of hardware-cloth (galvanized wire mesh with 0.5 in/13 mm openings). The enclosure is easy to make using heavy leather gloves and a pair of wire-cutting shears. Although it may be of any size, I make a cage to fit a narrow bed 12–24 in (30–60 cm) wide, 3–4 in (7–10 cm) deep, and as long as necessary or desirable. The lid, or top side, is closed permanently only after the enclosure has been placed in a shallow trench, filled with good soil, and planted with tubers 8–10 in (20–25 cm) apart. Once the lid is closed, the entire bed is covered with 1.5–2 in (4–5 cm) of soil, over which I usually scatter a thin mulch of pine or spruce needles or crushed dry leaves.

For some gardeners, deer are welcome visitors, elegant creatures that grace the woods and gardens luckily in increasing numbers. For others, deer are greedy, never-satisfied interlopers that inflict an ever-increasing ecologic and economic injury on woods, farms, and gardens, and a major factor in the spread of Lyme disease. The exclusive wards of the state, deer relentlessly trespass uncontrolled on private lands. If not restrained by costly barriers, they cause damage that far exceeds the combined effects of slugs, rats, mice, mildew, root rot, black spot, and other obstacles to a successful husbandry of agricultural, forestry, and garden plants. Their average food requirement is 4.5 lbs (2 kg) of fresh vegetable matter per day. I shudder at the thought of how many flower buds of azaleas, rhododendrons, and roses, how many rows of string beans and peas, and how many hundredweights of foliage and blossoms from native wild flowers, shrubs, and young trees are needed every month to feed the small herd roaming my neighborhood woods and gardens.

My attitude toward deer has changed very gradually over the years and eventually the innocent pleasure of seeing them in my backyard a few times a year turned into a sense of being mugged several times a week. In the course of this erosion of sympathy, I have tested a number of measures aimed at minimizing the damage while still preserving the opportunity to observe the gorgeous animals prance across my meadow. I have experimented with growing plants that are disagreeable to their taste; though there are still several such varieties in my garden (individually noted in the plant descriptions), the list has grown shorter and shorter the faster the deer population has grown. I have scattered over my plants bags of human hair from local barbershops and bags of dog hair from dog-grooming parlors. I have hung cakes of soap of various trademarks and fragrances on my bushes, covered plants individually with black plastic netting, and spent thousands of dollars on sundry repellents, only to realize that I had too many valued plants to treat them all several times a year.

My ultimate protection is simply a fence. According to the U.S. Department of Agriculture, *Odocoileus virginianus* (white-tailed deer) is capable of surmounting obstacles as high as 9 ft (2.7 m). Thus, to be effective, a fence should be somewhat higher, and it must be uninterrupted around the entire area it is to protect. The deer quickly find even a small opening, a weak spot, or a lesser height, and exploit the weakness within days. They enter the property through a driveway during the day even when cars are standing there with engines still warm.

A dozen years ago I would not have believed that I would ever fence out deer. However, with all natural and unnatural enemies absent in this virtually hunting-free area, the deer population rises 40 percent a year, according to the state's estimate. This means that our current herd will double in slightly over 2 years, and quadruple in 4 or 5 years. If the publicized experience with cattle overgrazing the public range lands is any indication, it is possible to envision this alarming scenario: in several decades, our woods could be totally depleted of native wild flowers, shrubs, and tree seedlings up to 7 ft (2 m) from the ground (the height of the deer's outstretched mouths while standing on their hind legs). As the existing trees live out their cycle in three or four human generations, no seedlings would replace them and our woods, with their summer serenity and striking autumn colors, would turn into sparse grasslands populated by herds of sick and stunted deer.

Color, Fragrance, Texture, and Shape

It would be difficult for me to decide which of these attributes counts most in my garden. Blossom color, of course, comes first to mind, but on most plants that phenomenon lasts only a week or several weeks at best. Happily, other sources of color are present, many of them through all four seasons: the dark green foliage of broad-leaved evergreens and conifers, the bare trunks and branches of deciduous trees that vary from dark brown in rain to shades of gray when dry, the lichens on the stone walls that "bloom" in the humid air of late fall or early spring and glow in subtle green hues when the evening headlights of a car touch them (Plate 53). These and many other gradations of color are always around us.

The one all-or-nothing explosion of color comes in the autumn. When chillier and longer nights begin to follow balmy but shorter days with reduced hours of sunlight, plants accept the change as their signal to slow down the activity within their systems. Reducing their supply of nitrogen, they withdraw sugars and starches from the leaves and store them in the trunks and roots for use in spring. Chlorophyll, the green photosynthetic coloring substance, begins to lose its dominance in the leaves where, until then, it totally obscured the yellow and red colors. With the green gone, these basic colors reveal themselves, with their infinite number of nuances and shades, in an astonishing clarity and intensity (Plate 14).

PLATE 14. The festive foliage of *Acer saccharum* (sugar maple) in early October.

As to fragrance, no garden should be without it. Think of a summer evening walk with the perfume of the blossoms of a tall *Robinia pseudoacacia* (common locust) drifting down to the path. Remember the spicy scent of *Rhododendron viscosum* (swamp azalea) flowers and the delicate bouquet of *Clethra alnifolia* (summersweet, sweet pepperbush). When all the blossoms and smells of summer have gone, crush a leaf of *Myrica pensylvanica* (bayberry) or *Rhododendron* 'Windbeam', step on the fallen foliage of *Pinus strobus* (eastern white pine) or *Juniperus virginiana* (eastern red cedar). A garden would be poor indeed without fragrance.

Shape and texture seem to go together, yet they are distinct. What is a *Picea glauca* var. *albertiana* (Alberta spruce) without its stiff but beautifully trim silhouette (Plate 15)? Yet, even a shapeless drape of *Tsuga canadensis* (eastern hemlock) branches is a thing of beauty with its refined texture (Plate 16). A keen awareness of these and many other inherent characteristics enhances our enjoyment of a garden no matter what time of year.

PLATE 15. A 30-year-old *Picea glauca* var. *albertiana* (Alberta spruce) with a young *Rhododendron* 'Besse Howells' on the left, and rhododendrons 'Atroflo' and 'Vulcan' on the right.

PLATE 16. The supple boughs of *Tsuga canadensis* (eastern hemlock) and the stiffer branches of *Abies balsamea* (balsam fir) far left, weighed down gently by a dusting of snow.

The Design

The following paragraphs contain a few thoughts on how my garden was conceived, and touch on the evolutionary process that led to its present, though perhaps not final, status.

In past centuries, owners of splendid houses the world over employed expert designers and architects to create sweeping landscapes and intimate hideaways. Such large-scale undertakings could not have been accomplished without grand designs and plans expressing the owners' dreams. Nonetheless, my garden did not begin as a representation of a vision on a sheet of draft paper. Rather, it came about by a slow evolution, a gradual process of self-development. If in the beginning there was a master plan, it was the subconscious—and contradictory—desire to leave my property unchanged while at the same time improving it so as to create an environment pleasing to the senses and mind. The garden was to be as natural as possible with only a touch of refinement, a hint of studied nonchalance (Plate 17).

PLATE 17. A shrubbery border in May with the dark-leaved *Acer palmatum* 'Bloodgood' (Japanese maple) above *Rhododendron* 'Delaware Valley White' and *R.* 'Scintillation' (pink buds). Between the two *Juniperus virginiana* (eastern red cedar) trees, a few yellow blossoms of a tall *R. calendulaceum* (flame azalea), and beyond the path, the purple-red flowers of *R. obtusum* 'Amoenum'.

My garden began as an almost impenetrable wilderness of woods and thickets laced with the burning vines of *Rhus radicans* (poison ivy). As it progressed through several stages of openness, a few definitive plans did come to my mind. I even produced sketches of various sections while determining their light and shade intensity, protection from wind, sun, and cold, as well as the amount of space available for the plants I wanted to add. Nevertheless, for the most part, the overall design was confined to a series of unstated, albeit increasingly clarified, principles which may be summarized as follows:

1. The entire property was to be considered a garden, including the wood in the northwest corner that would remain largely untouched except for the construction of several paths to make it accessible, and the planting of additional wild flowers to enhance its natural beauty.
2. The garden would consist of several individual and distinct environments to give it variety and interest. There would be small lawn areas, an open meadow, a dark wood, a pond with sunny banks, a moist area along the brook, a sun-drenched vegetable garden, a shady rock garden, and a bright rose garden. These separate little worlds would be connected by narrow and wide paths, and by patches of lawn.
3. Paths and bridges would be constructed early to create an infrastructure for the development and enjoyment of the more distant sites.
4. Even at the expense of neglecting the beds near the house, the farthest corners would receive the earliest attention and the best plants. This would give the entire lot a feeling of cohesiveness and would reduce the number of forgotten or uncared-for fringe areas that sometimes make a garden appear incomplete and unfulfilled. Work areas would be located near the center of the lot.
5. Interesting and select plants and plantings would be positioned along paths and lawns in such a way that they could be found or encountered unexpectedly and evoke a pleasant surprise. Most of us can remember the sense of youthful adventure and excitement when we explored the woods, and the delight at coming upon a beautiful flower, a shrub, a tree, or a secluded spot. A garden is nothing if it cannot bring back some of that magic.
6. To give the garden a feeling of space, long unobstructed vistas would be created, or preserved where they already existed (Plate 18). New plants would be positioned so that they would not block the views.
7. Throughout the garden, rich native flora would be preserved and intermingled with introduced species and hybrids.

These and similar principles guided my hand over the years. Yet, I am not certain that I would employ them again in a smaller, larger, or equal-sized environment. Much depends on the natural characteristics of the site or the gardener's disposition at the time. There are many ways to create a garden; perhaps in place of open spaces and long vistas, seclusion and intimacy are desirable; and instead of variety, perhaps calming uniformity, the "unified theme" of a one-color garden, is preferred.

Many practical and useful volumes have been written on garden design, from outlines for perennial borders to plans for entire gardens; some are accompanied by specific instructions on how it has to be done. Yet, almost nothing in gardening must be done only one way. Nature offers an infinite latitude of choices. Gardeners can turn in almost any direction and still reach their goals. It is perhaps this freedom of thought, imagination, and action that makes gardening the creative, spiritually relaxing, and enormously satisfying pursuit we enjoy.

PLATE 18. A view along the pond channel and the retaining wall.

PART 2
Plant Descriptions

Introduction

For purposes of this book, I divided the plants in my garden into three categories: trees, shrubs, and nonwoody plants (herbs). The question may be asked, when is a plant a tree and not a shrub, and when is it neither? The distinction is sometimes vague; that is, some trees at maturity may be lower or smaller than certain young shrubs, and some so-called nonwoody plants may have woodier stems than a few subshrubs. Although in most instances the separation between the three groups is clear, there are a few borderline cases in which I relied on custom or simply made a practical decision.

Within each of the three groups, plants are listed by their botanical name in strict alphabetical order, and common names are listed below the corresponding botanical names. (Ferns, too, are listed alphabetically by botanical name, but their shared characteristics are discussed in a separate entry under the common name "Ferns," since a number of genera are involved.) Where several species belong to the same genus, a brief description of the genus precedes the individual species descriptions. The genus's scientific name is given, followed by the family name in parenthesis, and then the genus's common name, if any.

Why are botanical names used instead of the seemingly easier common names that often appear more descriptive, more colorful, and more interesting? Surprising as it may seem, the majority of plants on this planet have no common name. Moreover, the scientific names are accurate and, above all, are uniformly recognized everywhere in the world. Common names, however, are not entirely obsolete. They are used in casual conversation or in situations where even generic names are sufficient to convey a thought. Nevertheless, in many circumstances the use of a scientific name is the only way to avoid a misunderstanding or confusion. I would be reluctant to buy a plant from a nursery or order one from a catalogue under a common name as I could not be certain that the seller knew exactly what I wanted or that I knew exactly what plant was being sold.

An example of the confusion that can result when common names alone are used is the case of the gray birch. Its botanical name, *Betula populifolia,* is recognized by botanists, foresters, nursery professionals, and gardeners all over the world. Yet the common name gray birch will be correctly applied only in certain locations, mainly in the northeastern United States. A few miles away the same tree may be known by one of its other names, such as poplar birch, old field birch, poverty birch, fire birch, or white birch. However, in some locations the name white birch will identify a different species, *B. papyrifera,* which may also be known as paper white birch, paper birch, canoe birch, or silver birch. Yet the name silver birch is sometimes used to identify *B. alleghaniensis,* which is also called yellow birch and, to complete the circle, gray birch.

Botanical or scientific names always have two parts (i.e., they are binomials). Under this system developed by the eighteenth-century Swedish botanist Carolus Linnaeus (born Karl von Linné), the first of the two parts identifies the genus, a class of plants marked by common characteristics. (In turn, genera are grouped into families of plants, the names of which may be recognized by endings such as *-aceae, -osae,* or *-atae.* The family name is often given in parenthesis after the plant's botanical name.) The genus is designated by a Latin or latinized singular noun with the initial letter capitalized (e.g., *Betula*). The second part (the epithet) identifies the species itself (e.g., *populifolia*). Incidentally, the word *species* is used in horticulture for both the singular and the plural forms. It is now recommended that the species designation (the epithet) always begin with a lowercase letter (although the older practice of capitalizing the first letter of epithets derived from names of persons or places is still used by some writers). The epithet often describes the plant's visual qualities (*populifolia* = poplar leaved; *papyrifera* = papery, with paperlike bark), a place of origin (*alleghaniensis* = Alleghenian), the name of a person in whose honor it was designated (*Rhododendron bakeri* = Baker's azalea), or some other identifying feature or fact.

A description of a plant in an article, a book, or a catalogue sometimes includes additional names, such as the name of a subspecies (abbreviated as "ssp."). A subspecies meets the specifications of a species generally, but differs from the type of species in some way, perhaps reflecting the unique growing conditions in a separate geographic area. Other plants are sold under a varietal name (usually abbreviated as "var."). A variety in this sense is a subdivision of a species. For example, a Chinese birch with pinkish brown peeling bark, *Betula albo-sinensis* var. *septentrionalis,* will be offered simply but incompletely as *Betula septentrionalis.* The word *variety* is sometimes used also generically to indicate any indefinite species or hybrid.

The gardening world is filled with wonderful hybrids. The name of a hybrid is sometimes preceded by an ×, as in *Daphne* × *burkwoodii.* The × is read as "the hybrid." Sometimes the parentage of a hybrid is given after its name, customarily in parentheses. Thus, the full name may appear as *Daphne* × *burkwoodii* (*Daphne caucasica* × *Daphne cneorum*).

The names of species and genera are given in italics (e.g., *Rhododendron austrinum*), while hybrid names are not italicized but enclosed in single quotation marks (e.g., *Rhododendron* 'Canary Islands'). Family names and common names are given in roman type.

Each description in this volume includes the maximum height the plant is likely to attain in its lifetime. In the case of rhododendrons, however, it is customary to indicate how tall the plant will be in 10 years, although the ultimate height may be much greater. Following the height is the plant's hardiness zone, reflecting the temperature data shown on the U.S. Department of Agriculture Hardiness Zone Map issued in January 1990. This is the most recent, wide-reaching, and accurate of the many hardiness zone maps that have been compiled for North America in the past hundred years. Several years ago a hardiness zone map was developed also for Europe, but no zone maps are yet available for other parts of the globe.

The description paragraph itself contains information on the plant's place of origin or native range, and its foliage and blossoms. Most descriptions also give the average blossoming period which, however, may vary according to altitude, latitude, and even longitude (e.g., the plant will probably bloom earlier in Oregon than in Connecticut even though both planting sites may be on the seacoast and on the same latitude). Though variable, the flowering time can still be of help in learning the plant's blossoming characteristics.

The *Rhododendron* descriptions include quality ratings based on a scale of 1 to 5, with the lowest number indicating the poorest quality, and the highest indicating superior quality. These ratings do not exist for any other genus nor are they available for all varieties of rhododendrons. Nonetheless, where they exist, they are included in the description paragraph. A rating may appear, for example, as 3/5. The first digit refers to the quality of the flower, and the second to the quality of the plant and its foliage. Ratings are assigned by growers or by the American Rhododendron Society (ARS), which tests registered hybrids in the gardens of its members in various locations. The assigned ratings reflect the average of the growers' experience. The quality of many plants has not been assessed as yet and thus no ratings are given for them.

Some North American nursery growers of rhododendrons use a third quality rating to suggest the plant's performance. I find the third rating to be too subjective and have not used it. Experience seems to indicate that many of the "good" plants do well on the West Coast but are often disappointing in Connecticut no matter what their hardiness ratings indicate. The difference is probably due to various factors one of which, no doubt, is that a given lowest temperature the plant can tolerate, say, 0°F (−18°C), may persist for weeks in gardens on the East Coast, but will last only several nights on the West Coast. Thus, in Connecticut the soil freezes solid around plant roots, depriving the foliage of moisture, but on the West Coast, even if the foliage and branches are affected by a severe cold snap, the root system generally remains functional. It follows then that the plants react differently in the two climates.

Gardeners need to remember that ratings are not infallible. Some rhododendrons of a given rating may prosper in one location but fail in another. The ARS is currently developing a new method to recognize this fact and reflect selectively the quality of the tested material in various areas of the United States. Still, such as they are, the rhododendron quality ratings, as well as their hardiness ratings, are items of information not available in such a concise form for any other group of plants. I find it particularly vexing that the enormous rose-growing industry has never provided similar data for its plants.

Trees

ABIES (PINACEAE) Fir

The genus *Abies* consists of about 40 species of evergreen conifers native to the colder regions of the Northern Hemisphere. These species do not thrive in areas with hot summers and polluted air. Their growth habit is narrowly conical with a central trunk and whorled branches clad with dark green linear foliage.

Abies (fir) is sometimes confused with *Picea* (spruce), but the two genera are readily distinguished by their needles, branchlets, and cones. *Abies* has flat needles, dark green on top, with two whitish bands beneath; branchlets are smooth even where the needles grew before falling off; and female cones are erect, standing like Christmas tree candles toward the ends of the branches. As the seeds in the center of the cone ripen, the individual scales fall off leaving a dry, persistent central stalk. On the other hand, the needles of *Picea* are four-angled or compressed; where needles have fallen off, raised bases remain making branchlets rough to the touch; and the female cones are pendulous and fall off entirely when ripe.

Two species of *Abies* are represented in my garden, both tall-growing plants. To extend their period of usefulness in my limited space, the trees must be periodically topped. Eventually they will have to be felled, but in the meantime I will have enjoyed them for many years.

Abies balsamea — 75 ft (23 m); Zone 3

Balsam Fir

This North American species grows from Labrador to Alberta and south to Virginia. When young, *Abies balsamea* is useful even in a smaller garden. The tree keeps its needled foliage for several years, but as it matures, its lower branches sometimes become dry and the plant loses much of its ornamental aspect. When it outgrows its space in the garden, it can be cut down and used as a Christmas tree; it is well suited for this purpose since indoors it keeps its fragrant foliage for many days.

Abies fraseri — 75 ft (23 m); Zone 5

Fraser Fir; Southern Balsam Fir; She Balsam

Similar though somewhat less hardy than *Abies balsamea, A. fraseri* is native to the higher elevations of the southern Appalachians. It was named for Scottish botanist John Fraser who explored the region in the late 1700s. Southern mountaineers call the tree she balsam because of the plump bulges, filled with resin, that are found on its trunk. The readily apparent aspect by which it differs from *A. balsamea* is its cones, which are somewhat smaller and have bracts that project beyond the cone scales and bend downward at their tips.

ACER (ACERACEAE) Maple

There are over 200 species in the genus *Acer*, mostly deciduous trees growing in the northern temperate zone. Their leaves are usually palmately lobed or sometimes compound. Some maples, such as the Oriental varieties, are decorative dwarfs that are useful in rock gardens, while other maples are the giants of the forests of the Northeast. Four species of *Acer* grow in my garden.

Acer griseum 20–40 ft (6–12 m); Zone 6

Paperbark Maple

The leaves of this deciduous Chinese tree consist of three leaflets that are light green above and silvery beneath. They turn an attractive red and orange in the autumn if grown in the sun. The tree's greatest attribute is the cinnamon-brown exfoliating bark. My young specimen grows in shade, so the fall color of the foliage is less brilliant than it would be if the tree grew in a sunny location. Nevertheless, the attractive peeling reddish bark is already in evidence.

Acer palmatum 20–50 ft (6–15 m); Zone 5

Japanese Maple

There are many varieties of this deciduous species, and most are beautiful because of their growth habit, twisted limbs, or the many-lobed leaves that come in numerous shapes and colors. One of the two specimens in my garden, *Acer palmatum* 'Bloodgood', has dark red leaves in most summers, but if the weather is very hot, dry, and sunny, the bright red pigment is partly masked by green (Plate 17). This could be due to the greater abundance of chlorophyll produced under such conditions, or it could be a reflection of the rather rich soil in which the tree is located which may encourage more vigorous and lush green growth. I planted the tree in a place where the rising sun would shine through the bright scarlet leaves on autumn mornings. Unfortunately, the site is somewhat limited and the plant has begun to outgrow its allotted space. Rather than cut it down, I prune it every 2 or 3 years to a height I can reach with my pruning shears in an outstretched hand while standing on the ground, about 7 ft (2 m). There is no indication that the plant is suffering or is being harmed in any way by the pruning.

Acer rubrum 120 ft (36 m); Zone 3

Red Maple; Swamp Maple; Scarlet Maple; White Maple; Water Maple; Soft Maple

This deciduous North American tree with 3- to 5-lobed leaves ranges from Nova Scotia to Manitoba and south to Florida and eastern Texas. It is a vigorous, even aggressive species, but with enough space it is the glory of the eastern forest. Its roots are close to the surface reaching greedily into every available patch of fertile or moist soil; yet, they are not as aggressive as the roots of *Acer platanoides* (Norway maple) which often produce barren ground so that nothing else will grow under the tree. When planted along streets, *A. platanoides* lifts sidewalks and curbs; I believe it should not be planted since so many superior cultivars of *A. rubrum* are now available.

In very early spring, East Coast forests begin to acquire a red haze that contrasts most attractively with the clear blue sky. This is the flowering time of *Acer rubrum* (red maple), whose blossoms appear before the leaves. Since the blossoms are pollinated by the wind, they have no petals to attract insects but occur in enormous quantities. Their color is usually red or yellowish (Plate 5). In autumn the maple species again bring out the brilliant reds, oranges, and yellows in their foliage (Plate 6).

Acer saccharum 130 ft (40 m); Zone 3

Sugar Maple; Rock Maple; Hard Maple

This large maple is one of the more common trees in the eastern part of North America. Its deciduous leaves are 3- to 5-lobed, 3–5 in (8–13 cm) long and equally wide, dark green above and paler beneath. In autumn, the leaves turn golden-yellow, sometimes suffused with vivid orange-red (Plate 14). The greenish to creamy yellow flowers, which open before the leaves, occur in small clusters without petals. In spring, the sap of *Acer saccharum* is tapped by New Englanders in large volumes and boiled to produce maple syrup.

Amelanchier laevis (Rosaceae) 25 ft (8 m); Zone 4

Shadbush; Shadblow; Shad; Sarviceberry; Serviceberry; Juneberry; Sugarplum

The 25 species in the genus *Amelanchier* are widely distributed over most of North America, with a few species native to Eurasia. *Amelanchier laevis* is a North American species with alternate oval leaves 2.5 in (6.4 cm) long, dark green above and whitened beneath. The plant grows either as a large shrub or a small tree. Its native habitat reaches from Newfoundland to Minnesota and south to Kansas, Alabama, and Georgia. The word *shad* in some of the common names is a reminder of days long ago. The early settlers noticed that with the first appearance of the trees' white flowers, Native Americans in the surrounding countryside migrated to the New England rivers that were beginning to abound with the year's first run of shad. The blossoms of *Amelanchier* species last only a few days, but they come at a time and in a quantity that makes the tree a beloved addition to a landscape. The berries, small red or purple pomes, ripen in June and are very tasty. In autumn the leaves turn bright yellow.

BETULA (BETULACEAE) Birch

The 50 or 60 species in the genus *Betula* are native to the Northern Hemisphere, some growing in the frigid soils of the Arctic. Bark color varies from gleaming white on some species to orange-red, reddish, and nearly black on others. The trees are graceful, often with pendant branches, and deciduous, alternate, ovate, toothed leaves that have pointed tips and are 2–4 in (5–10 cm) long. The usual life span of these species is relatively short. Six species of *Betula* grow in my garden.

Betula albo-sinensis* var. *septentrionalis 100 ft (30 m); Zone 5

This birch from western China has a beautiful brownish orange flaking bark, a feature that is particularly noticeable and attractive in winter. The leaves are ovate, 2.5 in (6.4 cm) long, darker above and paler beneath.

Betula alleghaniensis 90 ft (27 m); Zone 4

Yellow Birch; Silver Birch; Gray Birch

The range of this North American birch reaches from Newfoundland to Manitoba and south to the mountains of Georgia. Its leaves are ovate and 2–4 in (5–10 cm) long, and its wood is the most useful of all native birches because it is hard, close-grained, and strong. As with many species in the genus *Betula*, the bark of *B. alleghaniensis* is its most noteworthy feature: it is yellowish or silvery gray on younger trees, and reddish brown on older specimens, peeling in small, thin filmlike curls (Plate 19). The trees in my garden are forest-grown and thus are tall and slender, branching at 45 ft (14 m).

PLATE 19. The beigy silver flaking bark of *Betula alleghaniensis* (yellow birch), with branches and buds of *Rhododendron* 'Maximum Roseum' in mid June.

Betula lenta 75 ft (23 m); Zone 3

Black Birch; Cherry Birch; Sweet Birch; Mahogany Birch; Mountain Mahogany

The habitat of this North American tree ranges from Maine to Ohio, and farther south along the Appalachians. The leaves are ovate with pointed tips, and 2–4 in (5–10 cm) long. The nearly black bark does not peel but remains smooth, almost cherrylike, during the tree's early years. Only on old trunks does the bark fissure into thick plates closer to the ground. Several *Betula lenta* specimens in my garden have been infected with the trunk canker *Nectria galligena*, a pathogen that eventually kills the trees and for which I know of no remedy.

Betula papyrifera 100 ft (30 m); Zone 2

Paper Birch; White Birch; Paper White Birch; Canoe Birch; Silver Birch

The range of this North American tree begins in the Arctic as far north as any trees will grow, reaching south to Washington State and the northern Rocky Mountains, and east to Pennsylvania. The ovate leaves are 2–3 in (5–8 cm) long. The wood and bark had many uses for Native Americans, especially in construction of canoes. The species is one of the most desirable ornamental trees; few sights in a garden are more arresting than a well-grown, stately *Betula papyrifera* with its startlingly beautiful chalky white or, on some trees, creamy white flaking bark.

Betula pendula 60 ft (18 m); Zone 2

European White Birch; White Birch

Native to Europe and Asia Minor, this birch has been planted as an ornamental throughout the United States, Canada, and other countries in the temperate zone. It is a graceful tree with white bark that flakes somewhat less than the bark of *Betula papyrifera*. On old trees, the bark closer to the ground becomes deeply furrowed, exposing the black inner bark. The ovate leaves are 2–3 in (5–8 cm) long. Though beautiful when healthy, the species is unfortunately susceptible to attacks by *Agrilus anxius* (bronze birch borer) which seriously disfigures even mature specimens. The tree planted some dozen years ago in a shady location in my garden is flourishing undamaged by the insect. However, its trunk must be wrapped with wire mesh to protect it from the bucks that often scrape the bark of saplings with their antlers.

Betula populifolia 30 ft (9 m); Zone 4

Gray Birch; Poplar Birch; Old Field Birch; Poverty Birch; Fire Birch; White Birch

The natural habitat of this birch reaches from Nova Scotia west to Lake Ontario and south to Delaware. It is something of a weed tree, aggressively invading burned-out forest land and any available open space, but living only 25 to 35 years. The leaves are triangular-ovate and 2–3 in (5–8 cm) long, and the bark is chalky white. The tree's stature is usually somewhat irregular, consisting of spindly trunks bending in all directions while reaching toward light. The weight of ice and snow in winter distorts the shape of *Betula populifolia* trees in my garden, so many have been cut down. Although I allow a few seedlings to grow, I usually cut them down before they reach their less attractive stage and the end of their short lifespan.

CARYA (JUGLANDACEAE) Hickory

Most of the 20 to 25 species in the genus *Carya* are native to eastern and central North America, and Central America, with a few species growing in east Asia. The tall, slow-growing deciduous trees have alternate, pinnately compound leaves with five or more leaflets. The foliage is fragrant when crushed. The trees produce nuts, which on some species are inedible but on others are edible and very agreeable to taste. Among the latter is *Carya illinoinensis* (pecan), which grows to 150 ft (46 m) and bears the delicious pecan nuts. I have not grown this species, but two other *Carya* species grow in my garden.

Carya cordiformis 90 ft (27 m); Zone 5

Bitternut Hickory; Swamp Hickory; Pignut

This tree ranges from southern Maine to Minnesota and south to Texas and Florida. Its deciduous compound leaves are up to 10 in (25 cm) long with 7 to 11 leaflets. The bark is light gray, firm, and tight. The nuts are nearly round, about 1 in (2.5 cm) in diameter, with reddish brown shells and of an intensely bitter taste. The few *Carya cordiformis* trees in my garden are tall, with branches high up on their trunks. In the open, they would be fuller near the ground and not as tall.

Carya ovata 120 ft (36 m); Zone 5

Shagbark Hickory; Shellbark Hickory; Scaly Bark Hickory; Upland Hickory

The natural habitat of this deciduous tree is similar to that of *Carya cordiformis*. The most evident distinguishing marks between the two species are the bark, which on *C. ovata* exfoliates in long shaggy strips, and the nuts, which have sweet kernels.

PLATE 20. A path leading into the wood in early May. On the right, the blossoms of *Cercis canadensis* (redbud) above the unfolding croziers of *Osmunda cinnamomea* (cinnamon fern). On the left, *Dicentra spectabilis* (bleeding heart), and in the center near the bench, white blossoms of the creeper *Arabis caucasica* (wall rock cress).

Cercis canadensis (Leguminosae) 40 ft (12 m); Zone 5

Redbud; Judas Tree

The seven species in the genus *Cercis* are native to North America, southern Europe, and Asia. *Cercis canadensis* is the most hardy, growing naturally throughout the northeastern parts of the United States and southern Canada. As with other species of plants with the specific epithet *canadensis,* the redbud is by no means only a Canadian plant. Prior to the American Revolution, botanists awarded the adjective *americanus* or *americana* infrequently, giving preference to other geographic names such as *virginiana, carolinianum, catawbiense,* or *canadensis.*

Cercis canadensis is a small deciduous tree or shrub whose bare branches are covered in spring with bright lavender, rose-pink or, rarely, white pea-shaped flowers (Plate 20). The leaves are alternate, broadly ovate, up to 4 in (10 cm) wide. The two specimens in my garden grow in rich soil that could be too acidic for them. Though they grow and flower well, scattering some lime or wood ashes over their roots may be beneficial.

***Chamaecyparis nootkatensis* 'Pendula'** (Cupressaceae) 100 ft (30 m); Zone 5

Weeping Nootka Cypress; Alaska Cedar

This conifer with acute evergreen leaves is one of seven or eight species that comprise the genus *Chamaecyparis;* all are native to North America and Asia.

Chamaecyparis nootkatensis comes from the parts of Alaska that have relatively warm winters and cool, moist summers, areas that, incredibly, fall into zones 5 to 7. Hopefully, the tree can tolerate some of our dry winters and steamy summers. The small specimen in my garden was planted in a warm corner of the meadow where it is sheltered from winter wind. I look forward to seeing it grow and spread its long graceful branches with their pendant streamers of dark green foliage.

Chionanthus virginicus (Oleaceae) — 30 ft (9 m); Zone 5

Fringe Tree; Old Man's Beard; Flowering Ash

This deciduous tree belongs to a small genus that counts only three or four species among its members: two in North America and one or two in east Asia. *Chionanthus virginicus* grows from Pennsylvania south to Florida, but is fully hardy in southern New England. One of the last plants to leaf out, this species produces its foliage very late in spring. Its leaves are 4–8 in (10–20 cm) long and oval or obovate. The fringe tree is one of North America's handsomest flowering trees. In June it becomes mantled with drooping clusters of fragrant flowers that have creamy white, wispy petals several inches (up to 10 cm) long and only 0.1 in (3 mm) wide. My little plant is only about 2 ft (60 cm) tall, and it will be several more years before it blooms. Some years ago I caused the demise of a 6-ft (1.8-m) tall flowering specimen by overlooking a plastic nameband that girdled its trunk at ground level where it had been hidden by leaves and forest litter.

Cladrastis lutea (Leguminosae) — 50 ft (15 m); Zone 5

Yellowwood; Virgilia

The genus *Cladrastis* contains four deciduous, hardy species native to eastern Asia and eastern North America. *Cladrastis lutea* is one of the rarer North American trees, occurring locally from Arkansas to Illinois, and east to Georgia and North Carolina. It is hardy in Connecticut. The odd-pinnate leaves, with up to 11 leaflets, are 12 in (30 cm) long. In June, racemes of pleasantly fragrant white wisterialike blossoms decorate the tree. After a very slow start, the 10-ft (3-m) sapling in my garden finally spread its branches and began blooming.

CORNUS (CORNACEAE) Dogwood; Cornel

Some 45 species comprise the genus *Cornus*. They range throughout North America and Eurasia with a few coming from South America and Africa. They are usually small trees or shrubs, many with attractive flowers or bracts and ovate leaves. Six *Cornus* varieties grow in my garden.

Cornus alba 'Elegantissima Variegata' — 10 ft (3 m); Zone 3

This is a handsome cultivar of a hardy species, *Cornus alba*, that is native to Siberia, northern China, and Korea. It is a low-growing deciduous tree or shrub that can be kept even lower by pruning the new shoots to the nearest fork; this encourages formation of additional branches and thus produces more of the elegant, light green, ovate to elliptic foliage with silver margins; the leaves are up to 5 in (13 cm) long. The small specimen in my garden is located in a woodsy area where it receives sun for only a few hours a day; it stands out effectively in this slightly darkened environment.

Cornus alternifolia 25 ft (7 m); Zone 5

Alternate-leaved Dogwood; Blue Dogwood; Pagoda Dogwood; Green Osier

This is a small deciduous understory tree of the hardwood forests of eastern North America. Its structure, especially when young, is interesting in that the slender branches spread almost horizontally in regular tiers. The leaves are oval to ovate, 3–5 in (8–13 cm) long, usually alternate or clustered at the tips of the branchlets. The flowers are white cymes 2.5 in (6.4 cm) wide, maturing into small dark blue fruits that attract squirrels and birds. My garden contained many of these trees, and more are seeding themselves every year. These seedlings must be pulled out; a few *Cornus alternifolia* plants in most gardens are sufficient if they are not to become weedy.

Cornus florida 40 ft (12 m); Zone 5

Flowering Dogwood

Native from Maine to Michigan and south to Texas and Florida, this beautiful North American flowering tree has deciduous leaves that are 3–5 in (8–13 cm) long, up to 3 in (8 cm) wide, oval to ovate, entire, with slightly wavy margins. The wood is hard and durable and withstands a substantial amount of heat. According to one source (Everett 1981, 873), the wood used to be made into daggers to skewer and barbecue meat, hence it was called daggerwood. Through corruption, it became dagwood and, eventually, dogwood.

The tiny blossoms are grouped into miniature pincushions less than 1 in (2.5 cm) across, backed by four large petallike bracts, which can vary in color from white or cream to light pink, dark pink, and red (Plate 12). A tree in full bloom can look like a giant ice-cream cone, and in summer the small red fruits add more interest. In autumn, dark red foliage completes the season of color.

Several years ago a series of adverse conditions in northeastern United States began killing flowering dogwoods: successive winters may have been too frigid and summers too humid, and the natural cycles of several diseases, especially the dogwood anthracnose, culminated in the same stretch of time. The species is not especially long lived, so many of the trees that were dying were perhaps reaching the end of their life span. This unhappy combination of factors put the plantings of *Cornus florida* under severe stress. We can only hope that the species will eventually recover its former glory.

Cornus kousa 20 ft (6 m); Zone 5

Kousa Dogwood; Kousa

This dogwood comes from Korea and Japan. Its deciduous leaves are oval to ovate, 3–5 in (8–13 cm) long, up to 3 in (8 cm) wide, and entire. In general appearance this species is similar to the North American species, *Cornus florida,* except that its white bracts are pointed and its flowering time is several weeks later. In my garden, *C. kousa* usually peaks at the end of June or the beginning of July. Instead of the small red berries of *C. florida,* this species has raspberrylike fruits 0.75 in (2 cm) in diameter, which are loved by squirrels and birds, and are very agreeable to people as well (Plate 21).

***Cornus kousa* 'Summer Stars'** 20 ft (6 m); Zone 5

This slightly later blooming version of *Cornus kousa* keeps its bracts much longer so that in most years they are still on the tree when the red fruits ripen. This feature adds interest, but does not make this cultivar any more spectacular than the species. The deciduous leaves of the cultivar are the same size as the leaves of the species.

Trees of the species and the cultivar grow in my garden in partial shade. Though

PLATE 21. The edible and tasty fruit of *Cornus kousa* (Kousa dogwood) in mid September.

both bloom well now, it took several years for them to begin producing blossoms. They seem to need more time after planting to settle down and bloom than do some other *Cornus* trees.

Cornus mas 20 ft (6 m); Zone 5

Cornelian Cherry; Sorbet

The native range of this tree is central and southern Europe and western Asia. The flowers have neither petals nor attractive bracts; rather, they are tiny clusters of yellow stamens that cover the bare branches profusely in very early spring. The total effect from afar is an illusion of a thin, greenish yellow haze. The fruits are dark red, 0.75 in (2 cm) long, and edible.

The plant in my garden is flourishing but mostly just vegetatively. It has not put on the show one is used to seeing in Europe. The very acidic soil in the area where it is growing, which tested pH 4.2, could be the problem, so adding limestone gradually around the plant's roots will probably remedy the condition.

Davidia involucrata (Nyssaceae) 50 ft (15 m); Zone 6

Dove Tree; Handkerchief Tree

The discovery of this deciduous tree, the only member in the genus *Davidia*, created a sensation around the turn of the century. A native to once inaccessible parts of western and southern China, *D. involucrata* was introduced at the Arnold Arboretum, Harvard University, Cambridge, Massachusetts, by the famous plant hunter Ernest Henry Wilson (Chinese Wilson), who went to great difficulties to obtain a specimen in 1904. His pride was crushed, however, when it was revealed that the tree had already been presented a year or so earlier in France. It was named after the French missionary Père Jean-Paul Armand David, who discovered it in 1869 and introduced it in 1903.

The flowers of *Davidia involucrata* have no petals. Instead, similar to *Cornus florida,* their inconspicuous stamens are subtended by two paper-thin, creamy white bracts, the upper small, but the lower up to 7 in (18 cm) long and hanging down like a small handkerchief. The leaves are alternate, simple, ovate, toothed, and up to 6 in (15 cm) long and equally wide.

The trees are still not common in cultivation. Those that are grown do not always bloom, and those that bloom took 20 years to do so. My spindly specimen is now 12 ft (4 m) tall and beginning to branch. I will probably not see it in bloom in my lifetime; but, if given reasonable care in its younger years, it should provide enjoyment for future generations.

Fagus grandifolia (Fagaceae) 100 ft (30 m); Zone 4
American Beech

There are some ten species in the genus *Fagus,* mostly large trees native to the temperate zones of the Northern Hemisphere. *Fagus grandifolia* is a North American species ranging from southern Canada to Florida and Texas. The light gray bark is smooth and appealing, but it is often disfigured by insensitive initial-carvers. The leaves are shiny, dark green above and paler beneath, ovate with sharp tips, and 3–5 in (8–13 cm) long.

The tree is beautiful, but its large size at maturity makes it difficult to accommodate in many gardens. In addition, its surface roots prevent planting of most other species under it. For this reason I have not introduced it in my garden. Still, new seedlings appear every few years, probably dispersed by squirrels who relish the triangular light brown nuts. I pull out most of the young plants, but leave a few to brighten the darkened woods in the bleak days of autumn and winter. The leaves of young beeches, especially those growing in shade, remain on the branches until they become bleached by rain and snow. The little trees then shine in the darkened environment like dim lanterns, the beigy white foliage catching even the smallest amount of light. I keep the height of these trees to about 7 ft (2 m) so that I can easily reach up and cut the leader branch; I also prune the sides to keep the trees more compact. When the saplings become too massive, I cut them down and use their trunks as durable stakes.

Franklinia alatamaha (Theaceae) 25 ft (7.6 m); Zone 6
Franklinia

This relatively rare North American deciduous tree, the only species in the genus *Franklinia,* no longer exists in the wild. It was discovered in 1765 by botanist John Bartram on the banks of the Altamaha River in Georgia (the extra *a* in the botanical epithet may be an attempt to latinize the native name, or perhaps it was just an oversight when the tree was classified). Bartram was traveling with his son, William, who returned to the grove 8 years later and collected seeds which were then grown in Philadelphia. John Bartram named the plant after his friend, Benjamin Franklin. *Franklinia alatamaha* was never again seen in its native habitat, and it is believed that all the trees growing today originated in Bartram's garden.

The leaves are 6 in (15 cm) long, obovate, and glossy above, turning brilliant scarlet in the autumn. The flowers are 3 in (8 cm) wide, with golden yellow stamens and five large white petals opening from August until frost (Plate 22). In some years, during the 6- to 8-week flowering period, many dozens of blossoms are produced on

PLATE 22. An ivory blossom of *Franklinia alatamaha* just before unfolding fully in early September.

my 12-ft (4-m) tall tree. Now some 15 years old, it is the largest of the Franklinias in my garden. Having been severely damaged by a branch dropped on it by a tree surgeon who was cutting a nearby tulip tree, it has now recovered but its original tree-form was lost and instead the plant has acquired the shape of a large shrub some 10-ft (3-m) wide. The species prefers well-drained but moist acidic soil and, although it grows best in full sun, it will flower acceptably in light shade.

Fraxinus americana (Oleaceae) 120 ft (36 m); Zone 4

White Ash

This large, deciduous North American tree is a member of the genus *Fraxinus*, which contains about 65 species. *Fraxinus americana* ranges from Newfoundland to Minnesota and south to Texas and Florida. Its leaves are compound, consisting usually of 7 leaflets. The flowers are inconspicuous, but the samaras (one-seeded winged fruits) are very evident in late summer and autumn when they fly all over the countryside (in the manner of maple seeds) starting little ashes wherever they land. From this standpoint, the tree is somewhat weedy, but its tall and slender stature commands respect. The wood is hard, heavy, elastic, and strong; it is excellent for fine wood products from furniture to farm and athletic equipment.

Halesia monticola (Styracaceae) 100 ft (30 m); Zone 5

Mountain Silverbell; Silver-bell; Silver-bell Tree; Snowdrop Tree

About five species of deciduous trees or shrubs belong to the genus *Halesia*, all native to North America and eastern China.

Halesia monticola is the largest of the five species. Of a lower height, to 40 ft (12 m), is *H. carolina*, sometimes called *H. tetraptera*, which has smaller flowers and fruits. It is also hardy in the north, and is readily available, though I have not grown it yet. A

PLATE 23. A heavily pruned *Halesia monticola* (mountain silverbell) ready to open its white bells in mid May. On the right, the fading yellow blossoms of *Rhododendron* 'Golden Oriole'.

third North American species, *H. diptera*, is native from Florida to Texas, and is hardy only to zone 8. As its epithet indicates, its fruits are two-winged. The last North American member of the genus is *H. parviflora* (little silverbell), with flowers only 0.5 in (13 mm) long and fruits commensurately smaller. It is native to the southern coastal plain, and is probably not hardy in southern New England.

Halesia monticola ranges over the higher elevations of North Carolina, Georgia, and Tennessee. Its light green leaves are elliptic to obovate, and 7 in (18 cm) long. When in bloom, this species truly deserves to be called one of the most beautiful flowering trees. In May it is covered with thousands of 1-in (2.5-cm) long snow-white bells hanging from its slender branches. The blossoms mature into 2-in (5-cm) long, light brown, pendant, four-winged pods that remain on the plant through most of the winter, adding to the tree's attractiveness.

When I ordered my specimen many years ago, the catalogue did not indicate which species of *Halesia* it was offering nor did it suggest the plant's ultimate height. I planted what turned out to be *H. monticola* in a somewhat restricted space and now am faced with a dilemma: I must either cut the tree down or prune it severely. Since I cannot bear doing the former, almost every year, immediately after flowering, I cut the prior year's growth and bring the tree down to a practical 7-ft (2-m) height. As a result of this pruning, my specimen has acquired a low, oval, and symmetrical crown, which at flowering time is densely covered with beautiful white bells (Plate 23). The tree takes the severe pruning without adverse effects and continues to be healthy, vigorous, and floriferous. A few years ago, I struck some of the pruned-off branches in moist soil in a shady spot. Now I have two new Halesias that began to bloom only 4 or 5 years after rooting. Since they are planted in locations where their mature large size will not become a handicap, they will never require pruning.

HAMAMELIS (HAMAMELIDACEAE) Witch Hazel

The genus *Hamamelis* contains about six species of small trees or shrubs native to North America and eastern Asia. The deciduous leaves have toothed margins, and the clusters of flowers with narrow petals open either in late fall or very early spring. In recent years, dozens of new varieties have been introduced with blossom color varying from light yellow to orange and dark red. The plants prefer moist soils, and grow well even in heavier shade. Two varieties of witch hazel grow in my garden.

Hamamelis virginiana 20 ft (6 m); Zone 5
Common Witch Hazel

This North American species ranges from Quebec to Florida and Texas. Its obovate leaves are 6 in (15 cm) long, and its bright yellow flowers, which consist of 20–40 ribbonlike petals 1 in (2.5 cm) long and only 0.06 in (1 mm) wide, appear on the branches from October into November, just as the yellow leaves begin to fall. The subtle blooms, opening so late in the season, are a welcome sight, providing a crown full of translucent golden flowers against the blue autumn sky.

My garden has many *Hamamelis virginiana* seedlings that occasionally need to be weeded out. As I walk through the garden at any time of the year, I pull out the extra plants, cut them up with my pruning shears, and throw the pieces back to the ground to join the other forest litter. If I miss a few plants one day or one year, I can always get them another time.

***Hamamelis* × *intermedia* 'Arnold Promise'** 20 ft (6 m); Zone 5

This hybrid, which was discovered at Harvard University's Arnold Arboretum, is somewhat similar to *Hamamelis virginiana*, except that its blossoms are larger and it blooms in February and March. The yellow flowers sometimes open when the garden is still covered with snow, a sure sign that spring is just around the corner (Plate 24).

PLATE 24. The harbingers of spring, tiny yellow ribbons of *Hammamelis* × *intermedia* 'Arnold Promise' (witch hazel) in late winter.

ILEX (AQUIFOLIACEAE) Holly

The genus *Ilex* counts some 400 species among its members. Many are evergreen, but some are deciduous, growing in temperate as well as in tropical areas of Asia and North and South America. Among them is a large tree, the tender *I. paraguariensis,* grown in the warm regions of South America for its leaves from which *maté* tea is brewed. Others are small plants with tiny foliage and will be described with the shrubs. Two hollies that grow in my garden and can be regarded as trees are described here.

Ilex opaca 50 ft (15 m); Zone 6

American Holly

This North American holly ranges from southern Massachusetts to Florida and Texas. Its 3-in (8-cm) long, evergreen, leathery leaves with margin spines are somewhat lighter in color and less shiny (hence the epithet *opaca*) than those of the often planted *Ilex aquifolium* (European holly), but the plant has the important advantage of greater hardiness. The flowers are inconspicuous, but the bright red berries decorate the tree from late summer to late winter and early spring. Because the fruits are astringent, they are unappealing to birds until they have been exposed to frost and lost some of their bitterness by late spring. Staminate (male) and pistillate (female) flowers occur on separate trees. At least one male must be planted for one or more female trees to produce berries. Since *I. opaca* can reach a significant height, I keep topping my trees at about 7 ft (2 m). The species tolerates pruning well and is sometimes used for hedges.

Ilex verticillata 15 ft (4.6 m); Zone 4

Winterberry; Black Alder

This North American holly is deciduous, but the bright green leaves (arranged in whorls or verticils) often remain on the branches well into autumn, creating a Christmaslike background for the large quantities of red berries that are just then becoming ripe (Plate 25). With heavier frost, the leaves turn black (hence the origin of one of the common names), curl up, and fall, leaving the leafless branches laden with brilliant scarlet fruit that remains on the tree until birds dispose of it or until it falls in late winter. Some of my *Ilex verticillata* plants are shrubs, but several are small trees. As with other hollies, a male must be in close proximity if the females are to bear fruit. The sexes are impossible to distinguish until the plants are with berries or in flower. Even their tiny 0.25-in (6-mm) wide creamy white blooms are identical, except for the very center: in the middle of the female blossom is a minute ball the size of a pinhead, whereas on the male flower the center appears empty. The plants seed themselves freely and their population must be controlled if they are not to become weedy.

Juniperus virginiana (Cupressaceae) 75 ft (23 m); Zone 3

Eastern Red Cedar; Cedar Savin; Red Juniper

Despite some of its common names, this North American tree is a true juniper and not a cedar (Plate 17). Its range reaches from Nova Scotia to the Dakotas and south to Texas and Florida. It has two kinds of evergreen foliage: mature trees have scalelike foliage while younger trees and the more vigorous branches of older plants have prickly awllike foliage. The wood, which is durable outdoors, is mostly yellowish, but the heartwood is bright rose-red, which gives the tree some of its common names. The foliage is fragrant and pleasant to walk on when it falls onto the

PLATE 25. Christmas colors in mid October, the fruit and foliage of *Ilex verticillata* (winterberry).

paths, and the wood, too, has an agreeable smell, but apparently not to moths for it is used to mothproof closets and chests. *Juniperus virginiana* grows almost anywhere, and my garden is no exception. A few of the dozen or more trees are 40 ft (12 m) high. They produce many seedlings which I carefully transplant around the periphery of my property to serve, eventually, as a screen and a windbreak.

Laburnum* × *watereri (Leguminosae) 15 ft (4.6 m); Zone 5
Golden Chain Tree

The genus *Laburnum* comprises four species of which two European species, *Laburnum alpinum* and *L. anagyroides*, were crossed to create *L.* × *watereri*. The leaves are compound and deciduous, and the flowers are in the form of 1-ft (30-cm) long racemes of bright yellow pea-shaped blossoms hanging from the branches (Plate 26). The tree does not succeed in very warm climates, and even in Connecticut it performs best in light afternoon shade. My specimen has been blooming well in such a location. I add fireplace ashes and even small quantities of lime around the tree. Because its parents come from the mostly calcareous alpine regions of Europe, the hybrid most likely also prefers a limy soil. The tree is sometimes sold as *Laburnum* × *vossii*, but the name has no botanical standing and is probably a designation for a cultivar of *Laburnum* × *watereri*.

***Larix decidua* 'Pendula'** (Pinaceae) 150 ft (46 m); Zone 3
European Larch

The genus *Larix* contains about 10 species, all deciduous conifers native to the colder areas of the Northern Hemisphere and hardy from zone 5 to as far north as zone 2. Several are North American plants, including *L. laricina* with the evocative common names of tamarack and hackmatack. *Larix decidua*, which comes from northern and central Europe, has short needle-shaped leaves clustered on short spurs. It can grow into an attractive tree with a pyramidal shape. Its vivid green, soft leaves turn bright yellow before they fall in autumn. In nature, the tree attains its maximum height, but in gardens it generally remains around 50 ft (15 m). The recently planted specimen of *L. decidua* 'Pendula' in my garden is already beginning to display its pendant growth habit. I placed it in the north corner of the meadow where it can keep company with other deciduous conifers, *Metasequoia glyptostroboides,* and *Taxodium distichum.*

Liriodendron tulipifera (Magnoliaceae) 200 ft (61 m); Zone 4

Tulip Tree; Tulip Magnolia; Tulip Poplar; Yellow Poplar; Whitewood

The genus *Liriodendron* has only two species, one from China and the other from North America. *Liriodendron tulipifera* is a deciduous tree that ranges from Massachusetts to Michigan and south to Louisiana and Florida. Its leaves are 5 in (13 cm) long, and its greenish yellow flowers are of the shape and almost the size of tulip blossoms. However, in my garden we can see them only after they, or the twigs on which they grow, are broken by the wind and drop to the ground from the lofty heights of the trees' crowns. This is a most noble giant of the eastern forests where no tree grows taller and more majestic than the mighty tulip tree. I do not even object to having to weed dozens of its seedlings that sprout every year all over my wood.

PLATE 26. A seat made of a felled *Liriodendron tulipifera* (tulip tree) in the shade of a 40-year-old *Rhododendron periclymenoides* (pinxter), and a *Laburnum* × *watereri* (golden chain tree), in mid May.

MAGNOLIA (MAGNOLIACEAE)

There are about 85 species in the genus *Magnolia* that are native to southeastern and eastern Asia and the eastern portions of North and Central America. The genus was named for a French professor of botany at Montpellier, Pierre Magnol. Some of the species are evergreen while others are deciduous, but the majority are highly ornamental trees and shrubs with leathery leaves and large attractive flowers with powerful fragrance. The trees require rich and moist but well-drained sites with acidic soil in sun. Nearly a dozen magnolias grow in my garden belonging to four, possibly five, species and varieties. All are deciduous in Connecticut's climate.

***Magnolia* 'Betty'** 15 ft (4.6 m); Zone 5

This plant is the product of a hybridizing program carried out in the 1950s at the U.S. National Arboretum, Washington, DC. The hybrid is probably a progeny of two species, *Magnolia quinquepeta* and *M. stellata* 'Rosea'. Its leaves are 7 in (18 cm) long, and its rich rose-purple flowers, which open in May, are over 8 in (20 cm) in diameter.

***Magnolia* 'Elizabeth'** 30 ft (9 m); Zone 6

This hybrid was produced and patented by the Brooklyn Botanic Garden in New York and named after its director, Elizabeth Van Brun. It is the first truly hardy yellow magnolia. It has fragrant, clear yellow tulip-shaped flowers.

Magnolia stellata 25 ft (7.6 m); Zone 5

Star Magnolia

This beautiful plant from central Japan is one of the earliest trees to open its flowers. In April it is covered with 3-in (8-cm) wide, fragrant, creamy white blossoms, each with 12–18 fleshy straplike petals that, loosely interpreted, look like ragged stars (Plate 27). My specimen grows in a moist, partly shaded bed of *Pachysandra terminalis* (spurge). It sets flower buds in large quantities that open into handsome flowers every year, except for the occasional spring (once in 5 or 6 years) when a late frost destroys some or even most of the blossoms. Even so, the plant is well worth growing.

As with several other trees in my garden, I did not allow adequate room for this very vigorous specimen that would outgrow its allotted space in 4 or 5 years if I did not prune it severely at least once every 3 years. I use a hand saw to cut the thick central trunks, and pruning shears to shape the tree. Although I sometimes remove as many as three-fourths of the branches, the subsequent year the tree fills out again into a dense rounded shape. Pruning must be done immediately after blossoming or next year's flowers will be lost. *Magnolia* species can take a great deal of pruning with no ill effects. I once saw a Far Eastern gardener trim the magnolias in his tiny garden in an almost topiary fashion.

Several years ago I ordered six additional plants of *Magnolia stellata* and planted them in a border at the north end of the meadow where I thought they would have adequate space to spread out, but they began growing as if they intended to go up to 75 ft (23 m). In fact, that is just what they had in mind. With the first blossoms that opened several years after planting, it became evident that the trees were not the normal, relatively dainty *M. stellata*. I concluded that they were either *M. loebneri* 'Merrill', or a variety of *M. kobus* that can grow to 50 or even 75 ft (15–23 m) in height. The blossoms are similar but larger than those of *M. stellata*, the straps of the petals are wider, and there are fewer petals in each flower. In a few years I will have to cut most of the trees down. For now, however, a good yearly pruning keeps them in line.

PLATE 27. *Magnolia stellata* in late April, 2 years after severe pruning.

Magnolia virginiana 20 ft (6 m); Zone 5

Sweetbay Magnolia; Laurel Magnolia; Swamp Magnolia

This is one of the more desirable North American trees. Its range reaches from Massachusetts to Florida and Texas. In its southern habitat the tree may grow 60 ft (18 m) tall. Its leaves are narrow, up to 5 in (13 cm) long, and evergreen in the South, but deciduous in the North. The flowers, which occur in late June and July, are 2–3 in (5–8 cm) in diameter, white, and deliciously lemon-scented. My specimen, which at our latitude will always remain shrubby, is planted in a damp, woodsy location that should suit it well. Like all magnolias, it requires acidic soil, but contrary to most, it can stand but does not insist on swampy ground.

***Malus* 'Hopa'** (Rosaceae) 15 ft (4.6 m); Zone 4

'Hopa' Crab Apple

There are only about 25 species in the genus *Malus* (apple) but hundreds of cultivars, hybrids, and varieties. The genus is sometimes considered a subgenus of *Pyrus* (pear). *Malus* species, which are native to the Northern Hemisphere from North America to Europe and northern Asia, are deciduous and usually very floriferous trees and shrubs.

Despite the great beauty and ready availability of many ornamental crab apples, *Malus* 'Hopa' is the only member of the genus in my garden. Unfortunately, it is not one of the more carefree. It has two drawbacks. First, it is the alternate-bearing type (i.e., it blooms one year and rests the next). Second, and more serious, it is not resistant to cedar-apple rust, serving with *Juniperus virginiana* (eastern red cedar) as an alternate host for the disease. The rust, which appears on the leaves of apple trees as a sooty, almost black deposit, causes the leaves to drop prematurely, denuding the trees sometimes in mid summer. Before the leaves drop, however, the spores of the rust are dispersed back onto the junipers where they cause the second stage to develop: a 3-in (8-cm) wide lump of orange viscous substance that matures into a dry mass and disperses its spores to the apple leaves. To break the cycle, I spray the 'Hopa' crab with sulfur-based fungicide during spring and summer.

Plenty of Oriental crab apples are more attractive than 'Hopa', bloom every year, and are resistant to cedar-apple rust. It is these species and varieties that should be planted. I have to admit, however, that when the 'Hopa' crab is in full bloom, I have no desire to cut it down. It brightens the garden in late April and early May, and the pink carpet of spent fallen petals further extends the tree's days of modest resplendence.

Metasequoia glyptostroboides (Taxodiaceae) 100 ft (30 m) or more; Zone 5

Dawn Redwood

The only member of the genus *Metasequoia,* this species was thought to be long extinct when its ancient fossils were discovered in 1941. Nevertheless, in 1948, living plants were brought to the attention of botanists in the Sichuan Province of southwestern China. The species is allied to the two North American sequoias, but is considerably hardier and deciduous. In spring it is covered with soft, fresh green, needled foliage that changes to a pinkish beige color in the autum before falling. When I planted this tree about 5 years ago, it was a small twig in a gallon container. Today, it is a 15-ft (4.6-m) tree and growing vigorously. It is planted in a location where its size will not have to be restrained in any way.

Nyssa sylvatica (Nyssaceae) 100 ft (30 m); Zone 4

Pepperidge; Sour Gum; Black Gum; Upland Tupelo

The genus *Nyssa* consists of six or seven species native to North America and eastern Asia. The range of *N. sylvatica,* a North American deciduous species, reaches from Ontario to Michigan, and south to Texas and Florida. The flowers are inconspicuous but the tree produces large quantities of dark blue fruits, about 0.3 in (1 cm) long, which attract birds, squirrels, and chipmunks, and which germinate readily. The shiny, dark green leaves of the pepperidge acquire brilliant red hues in the fall. Although the tree has a deep root system, it suckers prolifically, creating many young plants above its roots which must be periodically removed.

Oxydendrum arboreum (Ericaceae) 80 ft (24 m); Zone 5

Sourwood; Sorrel Tree; Titi

This is the only species in the genus *Oxydendrum.* Though native from southwestern Pennsylvania to southern Indiana, and south to Florida and western Louisiana, this deciduous tree is hardy well north of its natural habitat. The flowers, favored by bees, resemble lily-of-the-valley blossoms and are borne at the tips of branches in drooping panicles up to 10 in (25 cm) long. The white blooms hang downward on their short slender pedicels, but they inexplicably turn upward when they mature into dry brown capsules. The leaves are oblong and lance-shaped, 8 in (20 cm) long, pointed, shiny, and dark green; in the autumn, they change to bright scarlet especially if the tree grows in a dry location and full sun. However, in such sites the growth can be very slow. I planted my *Oxydendrum arboreum* in a partly shaded, moist spot in a bed of *Pachysandra terminalis* (spurge). In 10 years it has reached over 20 ft (6 m) in height.

PICEA (PINACEAE) Spruce

There are some 45 species in the genus *Picea,* all evergreen conifers of narrowly conical growth native to the colder regions of the Northern Hemisphere. The leaves are linear, four-angled or compressed, and the female cones are pendulous. *Picea* trees are similar to *Abies* trees (see *Abies* for a discussion of the differences between the two genera).

Picea abies 150 ft (46 m); Zone 3

Norway Spruce

This European evergreen, which was introduced to North America by early settlers as an ornamental, is one of the most frequently planted conifers. In addition to normal-sized trees, many interesting and odd-looking cultivars of *Picea abies* are available in the nurseries. Some are miniatures, while others have foliage of unusual colors or an interesting growth habit. Many are of interest to rock gardeners and collectors. In my garden, these cultivars are represented by *P. abies* 'Repens', a flat-growing and spreading dwarf planted on a small steep slope of the rock garden.

Picea glauca 100 ft (30 m); Zone 3

White Spruce; Canada Spruce; Cat Spruce; Skunk Spruce

This evergreen North American conifer ranges from Labrador to Alaska, and south to Michigan and New York. The four-angled, bluish green needled leaves, which are 0.75 in (2 cm) long and 0.06 in (2 mm) wide, have a pungent smell when bruised. Pendant cones are 2 in (5 cm) long.

The species offers a large number of unusual forms. Of these, *Picea glauca* var. *albertiana* (Alberta spruce) is probably the best known. It is a very dense, usually symmetrical plant, often of a strict conical shape. It grows very slowly. I rooted a tiny cutting some 30 years ago, which is now barely 3 ft (1 m) in height and about equally wide (Plate 15). This variety is best planted in some shade or with a northern exposure. In a hot, sunny and dry position it is invariably attacked by *Tetranychus bimaculatus* (red spider mite), which will eventually destroy it. These nearly invisible creatures can be controlled by diligent spraying with streams of cold water from a hose during the growing season, or by using specific miticides. Such measures are not needed in my garden because the plant grows in shade.

Other forms of *Picea glauca* growing in my rock garden include the extremely dwarf cultivar *P. glauca* 'Alberta Globe', now 3 in (8 cm) high and expected to reach the height of 12 in (30 cm) in 10 years, and *P. glauca* 'Echiniformis', a blue-green, cushionlike dwarf said to be the smallest of the *P. glauca* cultivars.

Pinus resinosa (Pinaceae) 90 ft (27 m); Zone 3

Red Pine; Norway Pine

Despite one of its common names, this is a purely North American evergreen conifer ranging from Nova Scotia to Manitoba, and south to Pennsylvania and Connecticut. The bright reddish brown bark and the tufts of 5-in (13-cm) long needles make the tree a good ornamental. The single specimen in my garden is only 10 ft (3 m) tall and may never reach maturity. A large stand of this species once grew about 0.5 mile (800 m) away, but *Metsucoccus resinosai* (red pine scale) totally destroyed every one of the 60-ft (18-m) trees, whose white trunks, with the bark fallen off, are lying over each other as if some nasty giant had trampled this once handsome grove.

Pinus strobus (Pinaceae) 120 ft (37 m); Zone 3

White Pine; Eastern White Pine

This is one of North America's outstanding evergreen conifers. It is native from Newfoundland to Manitoba, south to Iowa, east to the Atlantic seacoast and, along the Appalachians, to northern Georgia. The soft, bluish green needles grow five to a bundle and remain on the branches for 3 years. When young, the tree looks fluffy and festive, but as it matures it acquires the dramatic silhouette frequently outlined against the sky and visible from afar as one travels along eastern roads. These striking irregular shapes are the result of the heavy brittle branches having been broken off by snow and wind. The trees appear to be pruning themselves in this manner, possibly so that the diminished crowns would present less resistance to strong winds, thus protecting the trees from death by uprooting.

Pinus strobus is susceptible to a fungus, *Cronartium ribicola* (white pine blister rust), which has an alternate host in certain species and varieties of the genus *Ribes* (currant, gooseberry). These plants should not be grown closer than 500 yds (460 m), especially in climates with long, hot, humid summers. *Pinus strobus* seeds itself readily in my garden. After nurturing the pretty seedlings for a year or two, I plant them along the north side of my property to form a windbreak for the gardener who will husband these acres in the distant future.

PRUNUS (ROSACEAE)

Over 400 species of trees and shrubs belong to the genus *Prunus,* including many fruit-bearing and ornamental plants such as plums, apricots, peaches, and cherries. These species are deciduous, have alternate leaves, and produce white and pink flowers with five petals and sepals. Four *Prunus* varieties, including one native species, grow in my garden.

***Prunus* 'Okame'** 20 ft (6 m); Zone 5

'Okame' Cherry

This beautiful flowering cherry is a hybrid of two Oriental species: *Prunus incisa* from northern Japan and *P. campanulata* from Taiwan. The cross was made before the Second World War by the English hybridizer Collingwood Ingram. The dark pink flower buds open into lighter pink blooms in May.

Prunus serotina 80 ft (24 m); Zone 4

Black Cherry; Wild Black Cherry; Wild Cherry; Rum Cherry; Cabinet Cherry

The range of this North American cherry reaches from Nova Scotia to Minnesota, and south to Texas and Florida. The white, pleasantly fragrant flowers are arranged in pendant racemes up to 6 in (15 cm) long. The small fruit is red to purple-black and has a bitter-sweet taste; it used to be the source of fruit-wine and jelly. This is a true timber tree that was once common in northeastern forests but has been heavily cut for furniture and interior work. Its wood is hard, close-grained, and strong. In my garden birds keep the tree's population high, so the numerous seedlings must be frequently weeded and kept under control.

***Prunus serrulata* 'Kwanzan'** 18 ft (5.5 m); Zone 6

Japanese Flowering Cherry; Oriental Cherry; Kwanzan or Kanzan Cherry

This is probably the hardiest and certainly the most widely planted of the double-flowering cherries from the Far East. The 2.5-in (6.4-cm) wide rose-pink flowers have up to 30 petals. They nearly cover the branches at blossom time, a familiar sight in North American towns and in Washington, DC, along the Potomac River.

I planted five of these trees in my garden but had to wait several years for their blossoms as they needed more sun, which they finally received when I cut an out-of-place maple. My trees will also benefit from superphosphate, and lime (since the soil in which they grow is acidic).

***Prunus serrulata* 'Shogetsu'** 15 ft (4.6 m); Zone 6

This is another of the many varieties (some 120 named in Japan) of *Prunus serrulata*. These trees have been grown in China and Japan for centuries, and a number of good varieties are now grown in North America. *Prunus serrulata* 'Shogetsu', also known as 'Shimidsu', is considered to be among the most beautiful, though it happens to be one of the few that lack fragrance. The 2-in (5-cm) blossoms have up to 30 very light pink petals and cover the tree completely before the leaves appear. Since the flowers remain on the branches only about 2 weeks, I planted my tree in a central location where I can enjoy it fully while the blossoms last.

QUERCUS (FAGACEAE) Oak

The genus *Quercus* comprises about 450 species of deciduous and evergreen trees native to the Northern as well as the Southern Hemisphere in higher elevations. The leaves are alternate, usually lobed; the flowers are slender catkins; and the fruits are acorns of various shapes and sizes.

Most oaks are among the few trees that have a deep root system, so smaller shrubs or shade-loving perennials can be planted relatively close to their trunks. They seed themselves prolifically, thanks to the squirrels who bury the acorns for future use and then forget where they put them. I have to pull out many of the seedlings or cut down the saplings, but always with some hesitation. After all, they are oaks.

Quercus alba 100 ft (30 m); Zone 4

White Oak

This deciduous oak ranges from Maine to Minnesota, and south to eastern Texas and northern Florida. It is one of the largest North American hardwood trees. The leaves have round lobes, and are of the classic form used in the oak-leaf cluster of military decorations. In autumn, the leaves change to beigy brown, remaining on the branches of younger trees through most of the winter. *Quercus alba* is not a tree for small gardens nor is it of any outstanding beauty until it reaches the great age and size for which it is known.

Quercus coccinea 80 ft (24 m); Zone 4

Scarlet Oak

The range of this deciduous North American tree reaches from Maine to Minnesota, and south to Oklahoma and Georgia. The tree is relatively fast growing. One of the saplings in my garden added 4 ft (1.2 m) to its height in one summer! At maturity it would have totally obliterated sunlight in the vegetable garden, so it had to be cut down. The leaves of *Quercus coccinea* are lustrous on top and turn brilliant scarlet in most autumns (Plate 6). Because of its deep taproot, the tree is difficult to transplant. Although I moved a few of the larger seedlings, they took many years to recover from the shock. The largest of the scarlet oaks in my garden towers 70 ft (21 m) over the back lawn. Some autumns its burgundy-red crown creates an impressive sight against the sky.

Robinia pseudoacacia (Leguminosae) 80 ft (24 m); Zone 3
Common Locust; Black Locust; White Locust; Yellow Locust; False Acacia

There are some 20 species in the genus *Robinia,* all native to North America. The original range of this deciduous tree once was limited to the southern Appalachians up to Pennsylvania and certain parts of the Ozark Mountains. Now, however, it is naturalized over the entire eastern United States. Because its wood is durable even when in contact with soil, it is used for fence posts and similar outdoor applications. The leaves are compound, consisting of up to nine leaflets, and the branches have short thorns along their length and at leaf axils. Flowers are drooping clusters of white pea-shaped blooms with a sweet smell that is unmatched in our woods. There are only two *R. pseudoacacia* trees in my garden, both forest grown, with their thin unbranched trunks reaching 50 ft (15 m) into the canopy. When in bloom, their perfume lingers along the paths on many May evenings.

SALIX (SALICACEAE) Willow; Osier

The genus *Salix* consists of some 300 species of trees and shrubs native to most parts of the globe except Australia. Some grow as far north as the Arctic, and all prefer moist soils. Their blossoms, which are in the form of dense catkins, appear usually before the foliage. Two willows grow in my garden.

Salix caprea 25 ft (7.6 m); Zone 5
Goat Willow; Pussy Willow; Florists Willow; Sallow

Native to the European continent, this species has pink catkins that appear before the leaves. If there is enough room, the tree can be a useful and decorative addition in a garden, as well as a source of catkin boughs for bouquets and vases.

Salix* × *sepulcralis 50 ft (15 m); Zone 5
Weeping Willow

This hybrid is a cross between *Salix alba* (white willow) of Europe and *S. babylonica* (weeping willow) of the Near East and possibly China. *Salix* × *sepulcralis* is less weeping than the often-planted *S. babylonica* but more vigorous and hardy. The 15-ft (4.6-m) sapling in my garden was severely damaged by deer who scraped the bark off one side of the trunk. It is now protected by wire mesh.

Sassafras albidum (Lauraceae) 60 ft (18 m); Zone 4
Sassafras

There are three species in the genus *Sassafras;* two are native to eastern Asia, and one, *Sassafras albidum,* is native to North America. The latter reaches from Massachusetts to Michigan, and south to Texas and Florida. A deciduous tree, it has been of interest more for the practical products it used to provide than for the esthetic contribution it makes in a garden: oil distilled in early spring from the bark of its roots was used for sassafras tea; very young leaves and the pith of small branches produced a powder used as a thickening agent for soups; and a substance refined from the tree's bark was used in industry and commerce as attar for soap, a flavoring agent in medicine, and an additive to flavor candy. However, sassafras is now banned from foods and beverages sold in the United States because of the presence of a cancer-inducing ingredient.

In the garden, only one feature of *Sassafras albidum* has a redeeming value: its leaves, when crushed, have a wonderful fragrance. Otherwise the plant is invasive and impossible to keep in bounds, even if allowed more than generous room. It spreads by long underground runners that colonize wide territories. I have tried to eradicate it in my garden and, after years of control, success appears possible.

SORBUS (ROSACEAE) Mountain Ash

The genus *Sorbus* counts about 85 species among its members; all are deciduous trees and shrubs native to the Northern Hemisphere. The leaves may be simple or pinnate, and flowers occur in corymbs that mature into clusters of small pomes.

Sorbus alnifolia 60 ft (18 m); Zone 4

Korean Mountain Ash

This Far East native is probably the most effective of the mountain ashes due to its four-season attractiveness: silver gray bark in winter; clusters of white flowers in spring; bright green, simple, ovate leaves in summer; and clusters of red berries and orange-to-scarlet foliage in the fall. It has an important advantage over some other mountain ashes: it is resistant to borers. However, the specimen in my garden could not resist the deer which scraped its bark and nearly killed it, so the tree is now protected with wire mesh.

Sorbus aucuparia 45 ft (14 m); Zone 2

European Mountain Ash; Rowan; Quickbeam

Native to Europe and Asia Minor, this mountain ash has racemes of white flowers in spring and clusters of bright red fruits in the fall, but the foliage has no autumn color. Frequently, this beautiful and desirable tree is attacked by a borer that enters the trunk near the ground level. Although I sprayed my sapling and filled the borer's holes with wax, I found this enemy difficult to defeat. Eventually my tree became weaker and died. I am not tempted to grow *Sorbus aucuparia* again.

STEWARTIA (THEACEAE)

There are six or seven generally recognized species in the genus *Stewartia*. Two are native to eastern United States and the others are native to Asia. Of the two North American species, *S. malacondendron* is hardy to zone 7 and some specimens grow as far north as the southern coast of Long Island. Stewartias have alternate, simple leaves and showy white flowers. They prefer rich, acidic, moist but well-drained peaty soils.

The name of the genus honors John Stuart, the third Earl of Bute, who grew a plant of a North American species in his English garden. When the plant was named in 1746, probably by Linnaeus, Stuart's name was misspelled, but since that was the first time the genus was afforded an identification, the incorrect spelling stands. Three varieties of Stewartia grow in my garden.

Stewartia ovata* f. *grandiflora 15 ft (4.6 m); Zone 6
Mountain Stewartia; Mountain Camellia

One of two North American species, *Stewartia ovata* is native to small isolated areas from Kentucky to Georgia but hardy to southern New England. It is a very ornamental species in its own right and is even more beautiful in the form *S. ovata* f. *grandiflora,* the best of all Stewartias—Asian or North American.

The specimen in my garden is now 8 ft (2.4 m) high and has been blooming since it was only 2 ft (0.6 m) in height. It differs from the typical species by its larger flowers, 4 in (10 cm) wide versus 2.5 in (6.4 cm), and by the glowing purple stamens of its blossoms rather than the orange stamens on *Stewartia ovata*. Both versions lack the colorful exfoliating bark common in other Stewartias.

Stewartia pseudocamellia 50 ft (15 m); Zone 5
Japanese Stewartia

This Japanese tree is the most widely cultivated *Stewartia* species. It has 2.5-in (6.4-cm) wide blossoms with broad white petals and a cluster of orange-yellow stamens (Plate 28). On older trees, the peeling bark with exposed areas in several colors is among the most beautiful of all trees with exfoliating bark. The species blooms from late June to late July, a time of summer when few woody plants are in flower. My plant is 20 ft (6 m) tall and, although individual flowers stay on the branches only a day, there are usually so many buds on a tree of this size that it is heavily covered with fresh blooms for over a month. After 1–2 years of profuse blossoming, the tree tends to skip a year, producing only a small number of blooms.

***Stewartia pseudocamellia* 'Korean Splendor'** 50 ft (15 m); Zone 5

Originally, this Korean plant was classified as a distinct species, but it has since been re-classified as a cultivar of *Stewartia pseudocamellia*. The seeds were brought in the early 1900s to Harvard University's Arnold Arboretum by E. H. Wilson, then a collector for the institution. The seeds were grown to maturity, and plants from these seedlings are now available in trade. The flowers of the cultivar are more saucer-shaped than those of the species, and they stay on the branches somewhat longer. In autumn, the foliage turns bright yellow or reddish orange while plants of Japanese origin turn burgundy-red.

Styrax japonicus (Styracaceae) 30 ft (9 m); Zone 5
Storax; Japanese Snowbell

The genus *Styrax* comprises about 100 species of shrubs and small trees. Some species grow in tropical regions, while others are hardy to zone 5. Five or more are native to North America and the others are mostly Asian.

Styrax japonicus comes from China and Japan. The alternate, elliptic leaves, up to 3 in (8 cm) long, grow on the upper sides of the branches, leaving the lower sides exposed and allowing thousands of white bell-shaped flowers in late May and June to hang below the foliage. The tree is beautiful, especially when seen from below. The fragrant blossoms hang on long pedicels in racemes of 3–6 bells each. In autumn they mature into 0.6-in (15-mm) wide satiny green spheres that hang in profusion on 2-in

PLATE 28. The blossoms of *Stewartia pseudocamellia* in mid July.

(5-cm) pedicels and add considerable appeal in the late season. As these pods drop into the moist rich soil beneath, the seeds germinate in large numbers. I have been able to give away many seedlings, but many more must be taken out if a thicket is not to develop under my styraxes. Since the species has a long taproot, the young plants must be transplanted when still small. The tree grows best in rich, moist but well-drained soil, with shade provided for part of the day.

Taxodium distichum (Taxodiaceae) 150 ft (46 m); Zone 5

Bald Cypress; Swamp Cypress; Southern Cypress; Tidewater Red Cypress

The genus *Taxodium* contains two conifer species: one from the higher elevations of Mexico, and the other native to wet locations from Delaware to southern Indiana, and south to Texas and Florida. There is evidence, however, that *T. distichum* once grew much farther north. It is a handsome tree that will grow on dry land, as well as in a swamp, or directly out of water. In the latter situation it develops the peculiar aerating projections referred to as "knees," which are large, irregular woody extensions growing up from the roots. Its soft, light green deciduous needled foliage changes to bright yellow before it falls in the autumn. Since the tree grows so tall and is said to live 1000 years or more, I planted my *T. distichum* in the far north corner of the garden where it can keep company with the deciduous *Larix* and *Metasequoia* species and prosper until the end of the third millennium A.D.

Thuja occidentalis (Cupressaceae) 60 ft (18 m); Zone 3
American Arborvitae; Northern White Cedar; Swamp Cypress

The five species of evergreen conifers in the genus *Thuja* are native to North America and eastern Asia. On older branches the leaves are scalelike, but on younger branchlets they are needlelike and flattened in a horizontal plane.

The range of *Thuja occidentalis* extends from Labrador and Manitoba south to New York and, in the mountains, as far south as Tennessee. An important forest tree, this species also makes a versatile garden plant with a number of varieties and cultivars. It can tolerate marshy ground and a fair amount of shade.

Tilia americana (Tiliaceae) 130 ft (40 m); Zone 3
American Basswood; American Linden; Whitewood; Linn; Lime; Beetree

Some 30 species comprise the genus *Tilia*. These large deciduous trees with broadly ovate leaves are native to the Northern Hemisphere. *Tilia americana* ranges from New Brunswick to Manitoba, south to Kansas and east to the Atlantic coast. Its wood is white, light but tough, and is used in many commercial applications. The tree is also valued as a large flowering specimen: in June it is covered with fragrant blossoms that are sometimes dried and used for making a delicious aromatic tea.

There is yet another dimension that *Tilia americana* brings to a garden: the soothing hum of honeybees in its giant crown at blossom time. It was that image that motivated me to plant a 12-ft (4-m) sapling in my garden. Nevertheless, one October morning several years later I found the trunk stripped of its bark. Deer had found it easy to tear off the soft smooth bark, and the following spring my beetree was only a dry skeleton.

Tsuga canadensis (Pinaceae) 80 ft (24 m); Zone 3
Eastern Hemlock

There are some 10 species in the genus *Tsuga*, mostly tall evergreen conifers of east Asia and North America. *Tsuga canadensis* ranges from southeastern Canada to Minnesota, and along the Appalachians south to Alabama and Georgia. The leaves are dark green, needlelike, and 0.75 in (2 cm) long. The most attractive feature of this species is the texture of its foliage, which has a supple softness found on no other North American evergreen conifer (Plate 16). The species grows in shade or sun, in dry or wet soils.

Young plants must be protected from deer which destroy the trees by scraping the bark with their foreheads and antlers, and by eating the foliage to bare sticks. The species has yet another deadly enemy, *Adelges tsugae* (hemlock woolly adelgid), a tiny insect that was carried to the New England hemlock stands in the 1980s on several hurricanes, and brought by birds and mammals from southeastern forests. The insect was introduced from Japan, where it is a harmless inhabitant of several hemlock species, but in North America it has already devastated hemlock groves in two or three southern states. The pest has no natural enemy on this continent and could threaten the existence of *Tsuga canadensis* as a widespread native species.

Ulmus rubra (Ulmaceae) 60 ft (18 m); Zone 4

Slippery Elm; Red Elm; Gray Elm; Moose Elm

The genus *Ulmus* has 18 species of trees native to North America, Europe, and Asia. The range of *U. rubra* reaches from Maine to the Dakotas, and south to eastern Texas and Florida, growing mostly in the bottomlands. The leaves are 7 in (18 cm) long, dark green, and heavily ribbed. This species has not yet been seriously affected by *Ceratocystis ulmi* (Dutch elm disease), which has destroyed nearly all specimens of the beautiful *Ulmus americana* (American elm) in North America. The wood of *U. rubra* is hard and durable and the inner bark, currently used medicinally for coughs, was used also by Native Americans as food. The bark is rather viscid, giving the tree one of its common names. The plant seeds itself, but not objectionably.

Shrubs

Abeliophyllum distichum (Oleaceae) 5 ft (1.5 m); Zone 5

Korean Forsythia; White Forsythia

This deciduous shrub, the only species in the genus *Abeliophyllum,* is native to central Korea. It blooms in early spring, usually before *Forsythia* species to which it is allied. Its outstanding feature is the earliness of its small white blossoms which remain on the shrub for up to three weeks, if the weather is not too hot or too frigid. Arranged in short racemes on long slender branches, the blossoms have a slight but distinct springlike fragrance reminiscent of wild primroses. Some years the shrub reblooms in September and continues to bloom modestly until frost. Once in 6 or 7 years, spring flowers are killed by late frosts but the plant itself is unharmed.

As with many flowering shrubs, *Abeliophyllum distichum* recedes into the landscape largely unnoticed after blossoming. Still, if there is room in the garden for a bush of small proportions, which can be kept even smaller by pruning immediately after flowering, then it is worth growing. The two specimens in my garden become welcome touches of white in early spring, a time of year when the monochromatic landscape needs an uplift. The bushes grow on the south side of a 3-ft (90-cm) high boundary wall where they are protected from the north winds and warmed by 5–6 hours of direct sun.

Andromeda polifolia (Ericaceae) 1 ft (0.3 m); Zone 2

Bog Rosemary

There are two species in the genus *Andromeda.* One, *A. glaucophylla,* up to 2.5 ft (80 cm) tall, is native to the colder parts of North America; I do not grow it in my garden. The second, *A. polifolia,* is a low-growing species with a creeping rootstock, 1.5-in (4-cm) long evergreen leaves, and small, pitcher-shaped, pinkish flowers in terminal umbels, five to six per cluster, appearing in May. It is native to wet, peaty, acidic soils in sunny locations throughout the northern parts of Eurasia and North America. In my garden it grows near the pond in soil that almost never dries out; neverthless, it tolerates drier positions if kept reasonably moist.

ARONIA (ROSACEAE) Chokeberry

There are only a few species in the genus *Aronia,* all North American deciduous shrubs with pointed, alternate, elliptic, 1–3 in (2.5–8 cm) long leaves with sharply toothed margins. The flowers are 0.4 in (1 cm) wide, with five white or light pink petals. The fruit, a 0.25-in (6-mm) wide, berrylike pome, has a taste that is a few degrees beyond astringent! I would not recommend it to anyone. Even the birds leave this fruit alone in winter. The genus is sometimes considered a subgenus of *Pyrus* (pear). Two species of *Aronia* grow in my garden.

Aronia arbutifolia 9 ft (2.7 m); Zone 4

Red Chokeberry

The range of this straggly shrub reaches from Nova Scotia to Michigan, and south to Texas and Florida. The rather attractive white flowers are arranged in flat-topped clusters, and the abundant 0.25-in (6-mm) wide red fruits, together with red autumn foliage, are the shrub's additional assets. I purchased a plant of this species not so much for its inherent value as to achieve variety in my garden, which used to be overrun by its close relative, *Aronia melanocarpa* (black chokeberry). I felt both species should be present as they very often grow together in the wild.

Aronia melanocarpa 9 ft (2.7 m); Zone 4

Black Chokeberry

The range and characteristics of this shrub are almost identical with those of *Aronia arbutifolia,* except that its berries are black. This is one of the plants that I have been trying to eradicate in all parts of my garden, save a small area where I keep a few specimens, plus one plant of *A. arbutifolia*. It is not easy to keep the two species under control because they spread vigorously by pencil-thick underground runners many feet long. Where they end, new plants emerge and continue their colonizing effort farther afield. I have not yet won this battle; a few new shoots continue to appear where I thought they had been cleared.

Azalea. See ***Rhododendron.***

***Buddleia alternifolia* 'Fascination'** (Loganiaceae) 10 ft (3 m); Zone 5

Fountain Butterfly Bush

The genus *Buddleia* consists of more than 100 species of deciduous and evergreen shrubs and small trees native mostly to the warm regions of Central America, Africa, and Asia. The leaves of these species are usually opposite. *Buddeleia alternifolia* is a rare exception: its leaves are alternate and, coming from northwestern China, the species is hardy. Normally, it has purple flowers but 'Fascination' has yellow blossoms appearing in 3–4 in (7–10 cm) long clusters from mid and late summer until frost. The flowers are strongly favored by butterflies and bumblebees.

***Buxus sempervirens* 'Vardar Valley'** (Buxaceae) 2 ft (0.6 m); Zone 4

Boxwood; Box

The genus *Buxus* contains about 30 species of mostly tender, evergreen shrubs and small trees native mainly to the Mediterranean region, east Asia, and a few locations in the Caribbean. *Buxus sempervirens* 'Vardar Valley' was discovered in 1935 along the Vardar River in Macedonia, formerly part of southern Yugoslavia, and introduced by the Arnold Arboretum of Harvard University, Cambridge, Massachusetts. This attractive and hardy boxwood has 1-in (2.5-cm) long, bright green leaves and, as is true for other boxwoods, rather insignificant flowers. In time it spreads to 2–3 ft (60–90 cm). My little plant occupies the top of a steep slope in the rock garden.

***Callicarpa bodinieri* var. *giraldii* 'Profusion'** (Verbernaceae) 10 ft (3 m); Zone 5

Beautyberry

Native to central and western China, this deciduous shrub is an exotic addition to my garden. Its long name is an example of one of the few anomalies in botanical nomenclature, which normally is frugal with words. The genus *Callicarpa* has over 130 species of which *C. bodinieri* is one. Its variety, *giraldii,* is a further refinement of the species, and the trade name 'Profusion' indicates a heavy-bearing individual that must

PLATE 29. A branch with outstandingly brilliant berries of *Callicarpa bodinieri* var. *giraldii* 'Profusion' (beautyberry) in mid October.

be propagated vegetatively (by cuttings, layers, or tissue culture) so that each new clone is identical to the mother plant. Propagation by seed would not assure perfect uniformity, hence the name 'Profusion' could not be used for seedlings.

It is recommended that at least three plants of this variety be grouped together for better pollination and heavier fruiting. The specimens in my garden grow close together in a sunny, protected position. They bloom in July with small purple flowers that are generally not very noticeable. It is the multitude of shiny jewellike, amethyst berries in early fall that is the cause célèbre (Plate 29). They are so unusual and perfect that they look almost artificial. The birds are not discouraged by their odd color, however, and finish them off early. In colder winters, the plants may freeze to the ground but will sprout, bloom, and bear fruit satisfactorily in 1–2 years. Heavy pruning is acceptable, and even recommended, to encourage the development of more fruit-bearing branches.

Calluna vulgaris (Ericaceae) 2 ft (0.6 m); Zone 4
Heather; Ling

This is the only species in the genus *Calluna*. Nevertheless, there are many varieties, all low evergreen shrubs native to Europe and Asia Minor, but widely distributed in other parts of the world by travelers and emigrants. Once extensively used as packing material for goods and furniture, the plants were sometimes discarded at destination and, where the conditions were agreeable, seeded themselves and became naturalized. The coastal regions of the northeastern United States and eastern Canada were particularly suitable to the species as they offered less fertile, acidic, sandy soils of pH 4.5 to 6.0. This species, and the related genus *Erica* (heath), are sentimental favorites with many gardeners who associate them with their ancestral home countries.

Most of the *Calluna vulgaris* plants growing in my garden were easily reproduced from an old specimen. I took cuttings in late August, struck them in a moist medium, and kept them cool and moist through the winter. Most of these cuttings rooted, even though they were less than 1 in (2.5 cm) long.

The flowers of this species are rose-purple, but there are cultivars varying from white through shades of pink and red. Foliage can also vary in color, as can the size and growth habit of the plants. Pruning is a matter of some disagreement but, if done in April, it will do the most good, or the least harm, to the new blossoms.

Several interesting cultivars grow in my garden, of which 'J. H. Hamilton' from England is one of the more distinctive. Its tiny flowers possess perhaps the purest pink among the callunas, having none of the rose-purple hue typical for the genus. The diminutive blooms are double, with tens of almost microscopic petals. The plant grows only about 4 in (10 cm) high but in time spreads to 2 ft (60 cm). 'Sedlonov', named after the location in Czechoslovakia where it was discovered, has no blossoms at all. Instead, it is a uniquely attractive foliage plant of bright green color resembling a dense conifer and growing only 5–6 in (13–15 cm) in each direction. 'Dainty Bess Minor' is only 3 in (8 cm) high with small mauve flowers. 'White Lawn' is a flat dwarf with white blossoms. All four cultivars fit perfectly into little nooks in my rock garden, hugging a boulder or draping over a small steep slope.

***Campsis* × *tagliabuana* 'Madame Galen'** (Bignoniaceae) Vine to 30 ft (9 m); Zone 4
Trumpet Creeper; Trumpet Flower; Crown Plant; Cow Itch

Two species comprise the genus *Campsis*. One is Chinese, *C. grandiflora*, and the other is North American, *C. radicans*. Both are deciduous creeping vines that fasten themselves to brick or wood with rootlike supports. They have red or orange flowers of a distinct trumpet shape and compound leaves up to 15 in (38 cm) long which may irritate the skin of some people. The North American species is native from Connecticut to Illinois and south to Texas and Florida.

The specimen in my garden is a hybrid of the two species. It has sparsely produced rich apricot-colored trumpets up to 3 in (8 cm) wide, growing in groups of five to ten, and opening over a long period from late July or early August until the first frost (Plate 30). Growing in partial sun at the base of a tall thin maple on which it climbs to about 30 ft (9 m), the plant produces flowers high on its stem. From a second story window only 40 ft (12 m) away, it is possible to watch hummingbirds disappear into the trumpets in their quest for nectar. The holdfasts by which the vine clings cause no damage to the tree because they do not penetrate the bark. In strong winds, the upper portion of the vine sometimes becomes detached. I simply cut it off just above the point where it is still attached and new shoots creep up the tree rather quickly. The roots of the vine sometimes develop new plants several feet from the parent. They should be removed so as not to diminish the energy of the main plant and create an unwanted thicket around it.

Caryopteris* × *clandonensis (Verbenaceae) 3 ft (1 m); Zone 5
Bluebeard

There are about six species in the genus *Caryopteris*, a group of deciduous shrubs and subshrubs native to east Asia. *Caryopteris* × *clandonensis* is a hybrid of *C. incana* (zone 7) and *C. mongholica* (zone 3). Its grayish green leaves are 4 in (10 cm) long, and its small, light dusty blue flowers are arranged in terminal cymes several inches across. The plant grows best in well-drained soil, preferably in full sun at Connecticut's latitude. To encourage formation of many stems and branches and thus a

PLATE 30. Still only sparsely clad with its orange bells in mid July, *Campsis* × *tagliabuana* 'Madame Galen' (trumpet creeper) on a slender *Acer rubrum* (red maple).

greater abundance of flowers, the old stalks should be cut down to 4 in (10 cm) in early spring. Light mulch applied in late autumn can be beneficial in cold winters, but should be removed in spring to allow the ground to dry and warm up for an earlier production of blooms and to discourage root rot.

Chaenomeles japonica (Rosaceae) 6 ft (1.8 m); Zone 5
Flowering Quince

There are only three species in the genus *Chaenomeles* but tens of hybrids and hundreds of cultivars whose nomenclature is confused. It is difficult to identify individual plants unless their parentage has been diligently recorded. The genus is of Asian origin. Its name has been changed by botanists several times and, just prior to the current name, the designation *Cydonia* was used.

Chaenomeles plants are grown mostly for their 1.5–2 in (4–5 cm) wide flowers that vary in color from white to shades of pink, orange, and deep red. The fruit, up to 2.5 in (6.4 cm) long, ripens green or yellow and is pleasantly fragrant. In the old days the fruit was often placed, together with a few apples, in suit closets to impart a pleasant smell to the clothes. I still remember the old gentlemen sitting in the pew in front of me whose heavy Sunday woollens emitted the somehow very appropriate fragrance of quince. Theirs was probably the fruit of the common quince, *Cydonia oblonga*, a 20-ft (6-m) tall tree, but the fruit of *Chaenomeles* is similar.

The two plants in my garden that be can identified are the orange-blossomed *Chaenomeles japonica* 'Orange King' and *C. japonica* 'Hollandia' with red flowers and bright yellow stamens. The third plant, still unidentified, has pink flowers. The blossoms of all three plants, appearing with the leaves, are early and attractive. The shiny leaves add considerable appeal if they can be kept from falling off by midsummer.

Many plants have been infected with *Quadraspidiotus perniciosus* (San Jose scale). Systemic insecticide sprinkled or poured around the bushes in early April, as well as an application of dormant or summer oil sprays, may control the problem.

CLEMATIS (RANUNCULACEAE)

The genus *Clematis* is native to many geographic locations in the Northern Hemisphere. It contains over 200 species, most of them woody climbing vines but some non-climbing bush forms and perennial herbs. The familiar, colorful large-flowered vines climbing up old porches and house corners are mostly hybrids of a few species. Their flowers have no petals and by themselves would hardly evoke a comment. Rather, their little bunches of stamens are subtended by large and often spectacular sepals. Some of these flower configurations are up to 10 in (25 cm) in diameter, in colors from pure white to all shades of pink, purple, blue, and vivid red.

Despite the often-mentioned beginner's failure with clematises, the plants are easy to grow and, once established, easy to care for. They are said to strongly prefer limy soils, but I grow five specimens in soils that are naturally acidic and still the plants do well and bloom prolifically. Three grow next to concrete foundations, which may leach some lime, and occasionally I put wood ashes (reported to contain up to 40 percent lime) around the other two, but they did well even before I began that practice. All are situated in relatively well-drained sunny positions in rich organic soil, and their roots are shaded by *Pachysandra terminalis* (spurge) or a small hedge of *Lavandula angustifolia* (lavender) growing at their feet. In the first two years after planting, they required watering because of the dry summers, but once established they seldom need attention. Three are pruned almost to the ground every February, and the other two are shaped only when they become straggly; once in five or six years, they are also cut completely with the others.

I have never lost a clematis plant, but there is reputedly a period of risk soon after planting. A young specimen sometimes dies unexpectedly even a year after it was set out in the garden. If strong wind or careless people did not damage it, then the supposedly dreaded clematis wilt may have caused its demise. Relatively little is known about the disease; it is thought to be caused by *Coniothyrium clematidis,* which may possibly respond to some fungicides. Nevertheless, severe pruning at planting time will probably prevent the disease entirely. Since clematises are such fast-growing plants, often gaining 6 in (15 cm) a day, perhaps they so exhaust themselves when very young that their weakened system is exposed to any pathogen that happens to come by, and which would not affect sturdier, well-established plants. To avoid this condition, it is best to cut new plants about 0.5 in (13 mm) above the pair of the lowest buds, those closest to the roots. When the two buds, or sometimes just one of them, lengthen into shoots 8–10 in (20–25 cm) long and develop a second set of buds, the new central stem should be cut again about 0.5 in (13 mm) above them. If caught in time, nipping the central lead shoot with fingers will accomplish it. Next February or, at the latest early March, and again the following spring, the vines should be cut down to their first or second set of buds. The resulting plants will be certainly sturdier and bushier, and the procedure may even save them from the wilt. All this took much longer to read than it will take to do.

When planting a new clematis, choose a site with full sun and good drainage. Moisture should be available either from a hose or below ground and, if it can be managed, the roots should be shaded with small plants or at least porous mulch. When they first arrive from the nursery, clematises are such limp little twigs it is hard to believe that in a few years it will be necessary to prune off armfuls of vines.

The matter of pruning is another misunderstood mystery in growing clematises. Much has been written about this subject, but there are just two vague rules I observe. All clematis varieties have one period when they bloom more profusely than the remainder of the season. If a plant has its first explosion of color by mid June, it is probably blooming on last year's wood; hence, it should not be pruned in February. If, on the other hand, major blossoming occurs at the end of June or in early July, then the flowers probably are appearing on the current year's growth. In this case, the more it was pruned in February, the more of the blossom-bearing shoots it will have produced. Should the pruning be missed one year, all that will happen is that the flowering portions of the vine will be a little higher or farther from the roots, a situation that can be remedied easily with severe pruning next spring.

The suppliers of young clematises omit the identification of each plant's pruning preferences. Yet, hybridizers and growers know the origins and the parentage of their products and are able to indicate under which pruning practice they are likely to perform best. Lists of the plants in each group are available. It would be helpful if growers would include this information on each plant's name label.

Clematis 'Ernest Markham' — Vine to 10 ft (3 m); Zone 5

This hybrid was named after one of the most important clematis hybridizers in the early part of this century. Ernest Markham, together with William Robinson of Gravetye Manor in Sussex, England, grew and introduced many varieties. Since then, a great number of hybrids have been developed in Europe, Asia, and North America and are available from nurseries and mail-order houses. *Clematis* 'Ernest Markham', introduced in 1926, has red sepals up to 6 in (15 cm) wide. The plant in my garden is located in an open, sunny area where it climbs on a trellis over the entrance to the vegetable garden (Plate 31). I prune it severely in February because it is the later-flowering type. Starting in late June, it blooms intermittently until frost. It is said that the plant sometimes flowers on old wood, but my specimen has not done so.

Clematis 'Henryi' — Vine to 10 ft (3 m); Zone 5

This clematis produces large white flowers over 8 in (20 cm) in diameter that begin to open in mid June on last year's wood. My plant grows at the southwestern corner of the house on a redwood trellis that can be lifted off its supports even when the plant is in full growth. This arrangement comes in handy when the house is being painted. I seldom prune *Clematis* 'Henryi', but have cut it almost to the ground two or three times in the 12 years since it was planted, because it outgrew its bounds. Its best and most numerous flowers appear during the first flowering period in June, and it produces many more blooms before it gives up in October. Having its head under the eaves of the house, the flower buds often escape damage by early frosts. The plant goes also by the name *C.* 'Bangholme Belle'. It was introduced in the mid 1800s by the nursery of Isaac Anderson-Henry, Edinburgh, Scotland.

***Clematis* 'Jackmanii'** Vine to 12 ft (3.7 m); Zone 4

Upon its introduction in 1862, this classic purple hybrid began the clematis mania. Vigorous, tough, and floriferous, it is covered with blooms by late June or early July and continues to flower sporadically until September. I prune my specimen in February to about 1 ft (30 cm) high, a point at which its woody stems, now 1 in (2.5 cm) thick, almost touch the lowest rung of a removable redwood trellis. From there, new shoots reach the trellis easily and cover it completely with new flower-bearing vines by mid June. The roots of this plant, as well as those of the *Clematis* 'Henryi' just around the corner, are shaded by a thick growth of *Pachysandra terminalis* (spurge). The hybrid was produced in 1858 by the nursery of George Jackman and Son, Woking, England.

***Clematis* 'Lanuginosa Candida'** Vine to 15 ft (4.7 m); Zone 4

Although its name sounds like that of the species *Clematis lanuginosa,* this plant is a hybrid or a superior cultivar. Its gorgeous white flowers, especially the first ones of the season that appear on old wood, are almost 10 in (25 cm) in diameter (Plate 31). In my garden, this plant grows on the opposite side of a trellis that also bears the red *C.* 'Ernest Markham', so the two plants grow into each other overhead. Every 2 or 3 years I cut *C.* 'Lanuginosa Candida' to the ground, but some years I prune only half of its vines and leave the rest. Pruning this way expands the plant's blooming period back to early summer when it blossoms on the old vines, while still assuring the October blooms, which appear mostly on current year's wood. This is the most vigorous variety in my garden. Every spring it sends up dozens of new 12-ft (4-m) long stems and, at pruning time, bundles of vines are removed.

PLATE 31. Clematises 'Ernest Markham' and 'Lanuginosa Candida' embellishing the gate to the vegetable garden in early July.

***Clematis* 'Ville de Lyon'** Vine to 9 ft (2.7 m); Zone 5

This hybrid, together with *Clematis* 'Ernest Markham' and C. 'Jackmanii', is pruned heavily in February. Why all the emphasis on February? I have observed my plants for several years and noticed that their buds began to swell by mid March. This vigorous new growth would be cut off if the plants were not pruned by the end of February. Some gardeners prefer autumn pruning, but this practice does not appear to offer any advantages. In some years the plants remain active late into the season, and cutting them too soon may deprive them of the last opportunity to harden and to gather strength for the winter. On the other hand, in warmer autumns, fall pruning may encourage a new pre-winter growth of buds and shoots that would be damaged or destroyed by winter frosts. *Clematis* 'Ville de Lyon' is rather late blossoming; its flowers are red, not excessively large but with an iridescence that contrasts well with the light green foliage.

Clethra alnifolia (Clethraceae) 10 ft (3 m); Zone 3

Sweet Pepperbush; Summersweet

There are about 30 species in the genus *Clethra,* native to east Asia, eastern North America, and two or three locations near the equator. *Clethra alnifolia* is a North American deciduous shrub ranging mostly in coastal areas from Maine to Florida and eastern Texas. In a garden, it must be held firmly in line as it spreads vigorously by underground stems. In my garden it used to form impenetrable thickets with *Aronia melanocarpa,* so both had to be severely restrained. I have reserved a wet area at the edge of the wood where this plant has always grown and where it continues to flourish. Almost everywhere else I keep pulling it out, though admittedly with a sense of regret. *Clethra alnifolia* is a handsome shrub with rich green, firm leaves, and cinnamon-colored slender stems. Its greatest asset, however, is the fragrance of the white flower spikes produced in profusion in July and August. Large sections of my garden are perfumed by this plant, and it is at that time I wish I did not have to keep it under such strict control.

Corylopsis pauciflora (Hamamelidaceae) 6 ft (1.8 m); Zone 6

Buttercup Winter Hazel

The genus *Corylopsis* comprises about 10 species of deciduous shrubs or small trees native to east Asia and the Himalayas. *Corylopsis pauciflora* comes from Japan. It produces light greenish yellow flowers that open in early spring and hang from thin branches like small Christmas ornaments (Plate 7). The flowers have a faint fragrance of primroses. Although the plant is hardy, the flower buds do not always make it through the late frosts. Once in 6 or 7 years they freeze, a penalty well worth paying for the other years of beauty. Whether in bloom or out, the species fits best in a woodsy environment.

Cytisus* × *praecox (Leguminosae) 6 ft (1.8 m); Zone 6

Warminster Broom

There are about 50 species in the genus *Cytisus,* mostly shrubs native to the Mediterranean region and Canary Islands. *Cytisus* × *praecox* is a hybrid of two south European species, *C. multiflorus* and *C. purgans*. In spring, its long, supple green branches, covered with small leaves and pale yellow, pealike flowers, cascade toward the ground like a small sulfur-colored waterfall. A well-grown plant makes a spectacular picture in any landscape, but is particularly effective on sloping ground. I grew two specimens for many years and they flourished and even seeded themselves. Then, one year they were all gone—the mature plants as well as the seedlings. The species is not generally long lived, so the death of the plants was not totally unexpected. Still, one looks for a more direct cause. My soil is acidic, which the shrubs prefer, and their location was sunny, which they like. Perhaps the one requisite I did not provide was perfect drainage, a condition hard to come by in the flat bottomland. I will try them again soon and will do my best to meet their needs more effectively.

DAPHNE (THYMELAEACEAE)

There are over 50 species in the genus *Daphne*, all native to Europe and Asia. Some are evergreen and others are deciduous. Many are intensely fragrant while some have no smell at all. A few are hardy as far north as zone 4. They are said to be temperamental and difficult to grow. I am reminded of the story of an expert gardener who tried to grow daphnes in every suitable spot in his garden, but failed. When the last plant was dying, he pulled it up in frustration and tossed it on the compost pile. Next spring the pile was covered with fragrant pink flowers. The plant had found its home.

Despite their bad reputation, I find daphnes easy to grow. Of the dozen or so that I have grown, just one died and that only because of inexcusable neglect in watering it the first year. The others are still growing, blooming, and flourishing. Another myth that is sometimes repeated is that daphnes insist on limy soil. Some of my plants grow in soils of pH 5.5, where they do splendidly. Nevertheless, one condition that eventually kills every daphne is drought. I water all my plants in dry summers, but those that do best grow in locations that are naturally damp and well drained; most of these sites are slightly elevated or sloping. Daphnes also appear to appreciate some shade. Yet, four or five of my plants grow in full sun. They have access to some deep moisture, of course, and I probably put a bucket of water on them more often than I realize, since they are conveniently close to the pond. Currently, seven varieties grow in my garden.

Daphne arbuscula 6 in (15 cm); Zone 6

This beautiful species comes from central Europe. Its very narrow leaves, about 1 in (2.5 cm) long and 0.1 in (3 mm) wide, are shiny and evergreen. The rose-pink tubular flowers appear in large clusters in early to mid spring. The plant prefers rich, moisture-retentive soil in a location that is not sunbaked. There it will live for many years and grow slowly into a low mound up to 12 in (30 cm) wide. It is a lovely little shrub that fits well into the condensed environment of my shady rock garden.

***Daphne* × *burkwoodii* 'Carol Mackie'** 5 ft (1.5 m); Zone 4

This daphne is an incredible gift from Mother Nature, a genetic mutation that was found around 1970 in the New Jersey garden of Carol Mackie. It is a further refinement of an already superior hybrid, *Daphne* × *burkwoodii*, which was raised by Albert Burkwood of Surrey, England, from two species, *Daphne caucasica* and *D. cneorum*.

If one has ever hesitated to admit that plants have personalities, *D.* × *burkwoodii* 'Carol Mackie' will dispel such doubts. Its major trait is its eagerness to please. It is a vigorous yet gentle and well-mannered plant that in May covers each of its many branches with dozens of 0.5 in (13 mm) wide, creamy white flowers that have a touch of pink and are strongly and deliciously perfumed. The plant is well-shaped, rounded, and tough. On top of all this, its small oval leaves are edged in bright gold. The beautiful foliage is not evergreen in my garden, but it remains on the bush into the winter (Plate 32). In milder climates it is fully evergreen. If cared for reasonably well, it will grow to a substantial height; thus space should be allotted accordingly.

PLATE 32. The gold-edged foliage of *Daphne* × *burkwoodii* 'Carol Mackie' in October.

PLATE 33. On the left, a planting of the fragrant *Daphne cneorum,* and the large ill-scented (when bruised) foliage of *Symplocarpus foetidus* (skunk cabbage) in late May. On the right, the red-and-yellow bells of *Aquilegia canadensis* (columbine) with the last blue cluster remaining from the blossoms of *Mertensia virginica* (Virginia bluebells).

Daphne caucasica 6 ft (1.8 m); Zone 7

As its name indicates, the home of this species is the Caucasus, and west to the mountains of eastern Europe. The plant's beautiful light green foliage is deciduous, and its white flowers are strongly fragrant. The species blooms in May and June, and often reblooms, or continues to bloom at a somewhat reduced rate, in August and September. It is rated for zone 7, but it has survived two winters in my garden in good condition albeit with a heavy mulch of oak leaves. It grows in a partly shaded location at the edge of a woodsy area near a narrow path where its delicious fragrance can be readily enjoyed once it begins blooming.

Daphne cneorum 6 in (15 cm); Zone 4

Garland Flower; Rose Daphne

This beautiful evergreen species comes from central and southern Europe. After several years, it forms a flat, round plant 2 ft (60 cm) in diameter. In May it is covered with hundreds of small, rose-purple, fragrant flowers. Its 1-in (2.5-cm) long narrow leaves are fully evergreen. As is true for all daphnes, it must be kept moist. There are four versions of this attractive species in my garden: several plants of a light purple form (Plate 33); one plant of a deeper red form called *Daphne cneorum* 'Ruby Glow' (Plate 12); one plant of the red-budded *D. cneorum* 'Eximia'; and one plant of the small, white-flowered *D. cneorum* var. *pygmaea* 'Alba'. All are hardy and very fragrant.

Daphne mezereum 3 Ft (0.9 m); Zone 4

February Daphne; Mezereon

This is another beautiful species from central and northern Europe, the Caucasus, and beyond to the Altai Mountains in south-central Siberia. It is an erect, prim deciduous shrub that has become naturalized in England as well as in parts of New England. In late February to early April, its stiff, upright branches become densely clothed with rose-purple, very fragrant flowers that remain on the plant for several weeks, especially if the weather remains cool. The two plants in my garden grow in a sunny position and must be kept moist in dry periods. They have been here for several years, but the species has the reputation of dying unexpectedly. If that occurs, I will surely replace them as I shall always want *Daphne mezereum* in my garden.

***Daphne odora* 'Aureomarginata'** 4 ft (1.2 m); Zone 7

Winter Daphne

This beautiful shrub comes from China. It has 2-in (5-cm) long evergreen leaves that are uniformly green on the species but distinctively edged in gold on the cultivar 'Aureomarginata' (sometimes called 'Marginata'). Its white to light purple flowers have the most powerful and pleasing fragrance of all daphnes. The plant blooms in January, but is not hardy in Connecticut's climate and in winter must be kept in a big pot in a glassed, mostly unheated porch.

Daphne retusa 2 ft (0.6 m); Zone 7

This species from western China is a restrained and beautiful evergreen shrub with dark, leathery, 1-in (2.5-cm) long leaves that are shiny on top. It grows slowly to a rounded, well-shaped bush which in May is adorned with deliciously scented rose-purple flowers maturing into large red berries. It is too tender for Connecticut's climate and in winter requires the shelter of an enclosed porch.

Deutzia gracilis (Saxifragaceae) 5 ft (1.5 m); Zone 5

Slender Deutzia

The genus *Deutzia,* which contains about 40 species and many more hybrids and cultivars, is native to Asia and the mountains of Central America. *Deutzia gracilis* is from Japan. In May it is covered with clusters of snow-white flowers on slender arching branches. Some years the flowers are damaged by late frost but those years are not too frequent. The plant in my garden was started many years ago from a small cutting I broke off from a large bush in a friend's garden. It rooted readily and became a substantial shrub in only a few years.

Empetrum eamesii* ssp. *hermaphroditum (Empetraceae) 1 ft (0.3 m); Zone 2

Rockberry

The genus *Empetrum* consists of three species of low, procumbent evergreen shrublets native to the polar regions of North America and Eurasia, and one species coming from the cold areas of southern Chile. My little plant, 3 in (8 cm) tall and forming a thin mat 1 ft (30 cm) wide, is native from eastern Long Island and New England to the northern regions of Siberia and Europe. The slender branchlets are covered with 0.4-in (1-cm) long awl-shaped leaves and small flowers that are usually purple. The fruit of this subspecies is a juicy black or purple-black berry, while the species has pink or red fruits. The plant grows in sandy or rocky locations with moist peaty soil. With our hot, steamy summers, a northern exposure and some summer shade are needed to give this plant the sufficiently cool environment it requires.

ENKIANTHUS (ERICACEAE)

There are about 10 species in the genus *Enkianthus,* a group of deciduous shrubs from eastern Asia and the Himalayas. Their leaves are alternate, obovate, up to 3 in (8 cm) long, and brightly colored in the autumn. The flowers are in the form of 0.5-in (13-mm) long bells varying in color from pure white to red. These ericaceous plants require acidic, woodsy soil and adequate moisture. Two species of *Enkianthus* grow in my garden.

Enkianthus campanulatus 12 ft (3.7 m) or taller; Zone 4

Redvein Enkianthus

This large species comes from Japan. The plant's structure is one of its distinct assets: the branches grow in tiers and the leaves in whorls. In May, small flowers dangling in profusion from thin branches are reminiscent of lily-of-the-valley blooms, except they are creamy yellow with red tips. A plant in flower is a beautiful sight, an effect that is almost surpassed by the gold and red hues of the autumn foliage.

Enkianthus perulatus 6 ft (1.8 m); Zone 5

White Enkianthus

This species is similar to the preceding one, but it is more compact, its pendulous flowers are pure white, and its autumn color is even more vivid. It requires the same growing conditions as its relative.

Epigaea repens (Ericaceae) 3 in (8 cm); Zone 2

Trailing Arbutus; Mayflower; Ground Laurel

There are two species in the genus *Epigaea*: *E. asiatica* is from Japan and is hardy to zone 6, but I do not grow it in my garden; *E. repens* is native to North America and ranges from Labrador to Florida. Its oval leaves are evergreen and 1–3 in (2.5–7.5 cm) long, and its pinkish white, very fragrant flowers are in terminal clusters. The little plant does not command much attention, except by those gardeners who are eager to grow it and cannot. It is not particularly difficult to grow if its conditions are met: shade, good drainage, and soil with an acidity rating of pH 4.0 to 5.0. To make such soil, if it is not available, take a bucket of well-composed litter from under old pine trees and add some leaf mold or organic matter from the woods and some sand. If the pH of the mixture is not 5.0 or lower, mix in iron sulfate until the reaction is sufficiently acidic. After that, an occasional tablespoon or two (1.5 to 3 ml) of iron sulfate dusted over the plant's roots should be all it needs.

Epigaea repens was once collected in large quantities for Christmas and Easter decorations, so large stands of it have been completely destroyed. It is now possible to propagate it by tissue culture without using any wild plants. Every opportunity should be taken to plant this species in our gardens and then possibly reintroduce it to the areas where it once grew but has been absent for decades.

Erica carnea (Ericaceae) 1 ft (0.3 m); Zone 6

Spring Heath; Snow Heather

The genus *Erica* includes about 500 species of low evergreen shrubs and small trees native to southern Africa and Europe. The majority are tender plants, but a few are hardy to zone 6. *Erica carnea* is a European species with small needlelike leaves whorled around thin, 12-in (30-cm) high stems. In spring, these stalks are topped by terminal racemes of 0.25-in (6-mm) long flowers, usually red but also lighter colors and white. To keep the plants compact, they should be sheared; this encourages thicker growth and more flower-bearing stems. Even without pruning, however, *E. carnea* is an attractive low-growing shrub well suited to small plantings. My garden contains several *Erica* plants, mostly of uncertain origin since they began as cuttings from a garden of a friend who did not keep records. Occasionally, a severe winter may damage *Erica* plants, but they generally recover quickly.

EUONYMUS (CELASTRACEAE) Spindle Tree

The genus *Euonymus* comprises about 170 species native to five continents. These plants are deciduous or evergreen trees and shrubs, or vinelike plants that creep up walls and large trees. A few are decorative bushes with attractive variegated foliage. Two species of *Euonymus* grow in my garden.

Euonymus alata 8 ft (2.4 m); Zone 3

Winged Spindle Tree; Winged Euonymus; Burning Bush

This deciduous shrub is native to eastern Asia. The leaves are elliptic, 2 in (5 cm) long, and sharply toothed on the edges. The plant grows easily and has naturalized in many parts of the world. One of its lesser but still worthy attractions is the bright-colored fruit that becomes evident when its brown shell cracks open; but the plant's main attribute is the red autumn foliage. Less obvious but interesting is the bark, which develops thin ridges along the twigs and branches. These raised strips are well described as wings, hence some of the plant's common names.

The specimens of *Euonymus alata* in my garden grow in partial shade and their fall color is correspondingly less brilliant. The leaves acquire a very light, almost translucent purplish pink hue that creates its own gentle effect in the autumn woods. All the plants in my wood are self-sown, apparently with the help of birds who are attracted by the scarlet-orange aril fruits.

Euonymus atropurpurea 15 ft (4.6 m); Zone 4
Wahoo

This North American deciduous *Euonymus* species ranges from Ontario to Montana, south to Oklahoma and east to Georgia. It has no spectacular features, but the bright scarlet aril fruits become an attraction of sorts after the purplish pink capsules containing them burst upon ripening. I brought three plants of the species to my garden from an open lot before it was bulldozed, but I am not certain that I want to keep them, especially if they continue seeding themselves excessively.

Forsythia* × *intermedia (Oleaceae) 10 ft (3 m); Zone 5
Golden bells

There are about six species in the genus *Forsythia,* all native to southeastern Europe and eastern Asia. Most of the thousands of bushes seen around the world every spring are hybrids, and probably the majority are *Forsythia* × *intermedia* in one or another of its many versions. They are dependable, vigorous growers that require occasional thinning, pruning, or even cutting to the ground. They always come back to brighten the early days of spring.

Fothergilla gardenii (Hamamelidaceae) 5 ft (1.5 m); Zone 5
Witch Alder; Dwarf Fothergilla

Fothergilla is a North American genus of four species, all native to six or seven southeastern states. *Fothergilla gardenii* is a well-behaved shrub that stays where you put it and does not seem to outgrow its space. Many years ago I planted a small specimen in a restricted area near the house; only now is it beginning to spread modestly. In May, it is covered with fascinating honey-scented white flowers that look like 2-in (5-cm) long bottlebrushes (Plate 34). These flowers remain fresh for many days, especially if the weather stays cool. In the fall, the foliage becomes a painter's palette of bright reds, oranges, and yellows. Some leaves have all three colors at the same time plus a few spots of the departing green color.

PLATE 34. The creamy white bottlebrush flowers of *Fothergilla gardenii* (witch alder) in late May.

Fuchsia magellanica (Onagraceae) 4 ft (1.2 m); Zone 6

Hardy Fuchsia; Magellan Fuchsia

This is one of approximately 100 species in the genus *Fuchsia.* A native to southern Chile and Argentina, *F. magellanica* is one of the very few South American plants that has any chance of surviving New England winters. It is classified as a shrub because in warmer climates it grows to 12 ft (3.7 m), and its stems and branches become woody. In my garden, the plant dies to the ground almost every year. If it does not die back entirely, it should be cut close to the soil level so that in spring it will send up more new flowering stalks. If planted in moist soil in a well-drained, warm microclimate in partial shade, and if mulched with 8 in (20 cm) of leaves in winter, it will survive and bloom.

It is said that more garden plants die from deep planting than from any other cause. This does not apply to *Fuschia magellanica.* When first set out in the garden, it should be planted 3–4 in (8–10 cm) deeper than it grew in the pot. Whatever other reasons may demand this practice, it will certainly help protect the roots from frost.

The exotic flowers of this species are in the form of ornamental pendants. At the top of each blossom is a long, narrow tube that further down splits into four sepals. Below the sepals hangs the corolla, which is almost always of a color that contrasts sharply with the color of the sepals. On the plant in my garden, the corolla consists of nearly 20 creamy white wavy petals hanging below the four upward-curving bright rose-red sepals. The blossom, almost unreal in its complexity, is 2.5 in (6.4 cm) in diameter and nearly 3 in (8 cm) long.

When in full bloom, *Fuchsia magellanica* is a very graceful plant. It begins blooming in late June and continues until it is cut down by frost, sometimes into early October. Mulch is applied after the first frost, and any remaining foliage is pruned to the ground the following April.

Gaultheria procumbens (Ericaceae) 4 in (10 cm); Zone 4

Wintergreen; Spicy Wintergreen; Checkerberry; Teaberry; Mountain Tea; Ivry-leaves

The 100 species that comprise the genus *Gaultheria* are distributed around the globe. Some are trees or shrubs, while others are prostrate creepers only a few inches high. The leaves of several species are the source of aromatic oils. *Gaultheria procumbens* is native to the northeastern part of North America, ranging from Newfoundland to Minnesota and along the mountains south to Alabama. From its slender woody stems creeping on or below the surface of the soil rise short stalks with evergreen aromatic leaves and 0.25-in (6-mm) long bell-shaped white flowers that mature into red berries with the taste of wintergreen. The species grows in varied habitats but prefers acidic soils between pH 4.0 and 6.0.

***Hibiscus syriacus* 'Diana'** (Malvaceae) 8 ft (2.4 m); Zone 5

Althea; Shrub Althea; Rose-of-Sharon

Among the 250 species in the genus *Hibiscus,* a few are hardy to zone 5 but many are tropical plants that in my climate can be grown only indoors. *Hibiscus syriacus* 'Diana' is one of many hybrids developed at the U.S. National Arboretum in Washington, DC. In the first two or three years after planting, this hardy hybrid tends to be somewhat tender and may freeze to the ground, so a mulch protection may well be applied in its early life. The plant has simple, palmately veined, 4-in (10-cm) wide leaves and large, pure white flowers, often 6.5 in (16 cm) in diameter, and most of which produce no seeds. The blooms begin emerging from their round ball-shaped buds in late summer and continue till frost. I keep my plant to about 3 ft (1 m) tall by pruning it in late fall, after the last of the great white blossoms has folded and fallen to the ground.

HYDRANGEA (SAXIFRAGACEAE)

There are about 23 species in the genus *Hydrangea*. They are deciduous and evergreen bushes and climbing, stiff vinelike plants native to North and South America and eastern Asia. Their leaves are opposite, often toothed on the edges. The flowers vary from white to pink and clear blue. The plants prefer moist locations in sun but perform well in partial shade. Three varieties of *Hydrangea* grow in my garden.

Hydrangea arborescens 'Annabelle' — 3 ft (1 m); Zone 5
Wild Hydrangea; Hills-of-Snow Hydrangea

Hydrangea arborescens is a North American deciduous shrub that ranges from New York to Missouri and Oklahoma, and south to Florida. Several selected cultivars are available, all with great globular blossoms. Among them, *H. arborescens* 'Annabelle' is one of the best, with possibly the largest blooms of all. It spreads slowly by underground stolons and may have to be occasionally lifted and replanted. It blooms in July and for that reason alone it is welcome. It brightens a darker corner in my garden under *Juniperus virginiana* trees, where it contrasts attractively with the rich green foliage of *Pachysandra terminalis* (spurge).

Hydrangea macrophylla — 5 ft (1.5 m); Zones 6–7
French Hydrangea; Hortensia

This Japanese and Korean species has been hybridized in many countries. A large number of hybrids, varieties, and colors are grown worldwide, and their number is further increased by the plant's tendency to produce pink flowers in alkaline soil and blue flowers in acidic soil.

There are five specimens of this plant in my garden. The largest and oldest has beautiful sky-blue flowers which, however, I see only once in 4 or 5 years because their buds freeze in most winters. The plant was here when we came, and one of these years I will do my wife's bidding and take it out. The next oldest is a pink specimen that has not bloomed since I brought it from a nursery on the south shore of Long Island, probably in zone 7. Next are three small plants that I purchased from a mail-order house located in a colder climate: *Hydrangea macrophylla* 'Nikko Blue', *H. macrophylla* 'Forever Pink', and *H. macrophylla* 'Red'. One of them had a small bloom the year it was planted, but the other two have not blossomed. The northern source of the plants obviously does not guarantee that they were not grown by a southern supplier. I will give them 2 more years to show their colors, and if they do not perform, they will have to make room for hardier souls.

Hydrangea quercifolia 'Snow Queen' — 7 ft (2 m); Zone 5
Oakleaf Hydrangea

This is an excellent North American species ranging mainly in the coastal plains and the piedmont areas of Georgia, and as far west as Louisiana. It is fully hardy in Connecticut. Now that it has become established in my garden, the plant has been beaming with vigor and beauty. Its great oak-leaf-shaped foliage presents a bold background for the large upright panicles of white flowers produced in considerable numbers. In autumn, the leaves turn dark red and the flowers mature to a beige color, remaining on the branches well into fall. When winter claims this finery, the thick tan-colored canes with their papery exfoliating bark carry the plant's appeal into the dormant season. The bush needs plenty of space, as much as 30 sq ft (3 sq m).

ILEX (AQUIFOLIACEAE) Holly

The genus *Ilex* contains evergreen and deciduous shrubs and trees native to North and South America and Asia. The leaves are alternate, often leathery. Two holly trees that grow in my garden are described in the previous section, "Trees," and three holly shrubs are described below.

Ilex crenata 15 ft (4.6 m); Zone 6

Japanese Holly; Box-leaved Holly

Ilex crenata is the typical Japanese holly of foundation plantings. Its native habitat includes the coastal regions of Japan and the Kurile Islands. The evergreen leaves are up to 1.5 in (4 cm) long and 0.4 in (1 cm) wide. The shrub is frequently clipped into small dense cushions or globes, but if left unpruned, it will grow into a large bush or a small tree. The flowers are insignificant, and the black berries on female plants, about 0.4 in (1 cm) in diameter, contribute little interest when they ripen in late summer and autumn.

I allowed my *Ilex crenata* plants to grow unpruned for several years; they are now over 7 ft (2 m) high and as wide, and I am prepared to prune them severely, perhaps as much as 50 percent of their branches, as their generally unkempt appearance adds little value to the landscape. The species has dozens of named cultivars, some of which are more desirable as garden subjects than the type.

***Ilex crenata* 'Convexa'** 8 ft (2.4 m); Zone 6

This is one of the better cultivars of *Ilex crenata*. The unclipped plants in my garden are now 7 ft (2 m) tall and of equal width. Though not pruned, they are denser and more attractive than the species, and their dark green, shiny, convex leaves clothe the branches more heavily. Contrary to common belief that deer do not eat plants of the genus *Ilex*, the 'Convexa' specimens get plenty of pruning from the animals. This cultivar seems to be less hardy than the species, and in severe winters (once every six or seven years), its foliage is either damaged or even falls off completely. The plants themselves are not seriously affected and recover well in spring.

***Ilex crenata* 'Convexa Dwarf Pagoda'** 10 in (25 cm); Zone 6

This little plant is the product of Elwin Orton of Rutgers University in New Jersey. I purchased it for my rock garden because the catalogue description stressed that its height and width in 10 years would be less than 1 ft (30 cm), a perfect size for the site. In 2 years the plant grew in each direction only by the width of one or two of its tiny 0.25-in (6-mm) wide leaves, yet it appears healthy and even vigorous. A second cultivar located next to it is *Ilex crenata* 'Piccolo', which is perhaps even smaller and slower growing.

Juniperus communis (Cupressaceae) 35 ft (11 m); Zone 3

Common Juniper

This species is a member of the same genus as the treelike *Juniperus virginiana*. Its leaves are linear, 0.75 in (2 cm) long, and very prickly. Though the plant grows taller occasionally, it commonly occurs as a shrub 4–6 ft (1–2 m) high. It is native to Eurasia and North America, and under varied growing conditions it acquires many shapes and forms. The flowers are of no consequence, but the blue-black 0.25-in (6-mm) wide fruits are the raw material from which gin used to be made until the introduction of artificial essences and flavors. The berries taste like gin and vice versa.

KALMIA (ERICACEAE)

The genus *Kalmia,* named after the 18th-century botanist Peter Kalm, consists of seven species of shrubs, all evergreen except one, and all native to North America. Five are from the eastern United States, one from the western Rocky Mountains, and one from Cuba. Since they are ericaceous plants they require acidic, peaty, well-drained soils. While individual species differ in size, growth habit, and foliage, one factor they all have in common is their unique flower form. The cup-shaped corolla has a rim undulating into five slightly raised tips, which look like the remains of five petals that grew together over time. Inside the corolla are 10 springy filaments, each the thickness of a heavy thread, rising from the middle and bending under tension toward the sides where their pollen-bearing tips are held in 10 small pouches clearly seen protruding through the outer walls of the corolla. From the center of the filaments ascends the style topped with a stigma that must be pollinated if the flower is to develop into a seed capsule.

When the flower is disturbed, some or all 10 filaments are released from their pouches, springing back toward the center with considerable force and throwing the tiny sticky masses of pollen in the direction of the flower's center where the stigma happens to be. Early observations of this mechanism led to the erroneous conclusion that kalmias were self-pollinating. It has been determined, however, that this system developed so that the pollen would be cast toward the abdomen of an insect alighting on the flower. The insect then carries the pollen to another blossom where it pollinates the stigma.

I grow only two of the seven species in my garden, *Kalmia angustifolia* and *K. latifolia.*

Kalmia angustifolia — 3 ft (0.9 m); Zone 2

Sheep Laurel; Dwarf Laurel; Pig Laurel; Lambkill; Wicky

This evergreen plant is native to eastern United States and eastern Canada. Its 2-in (5-cm) long gray-green leaves cover its branches fully in mild winters and at least partially in severe winters. Its growth is creeping and rather straggly, but the little bushes can be kept neater with some shearing. The flowers, which open late in the season (usually around 15 June), are like miniature *Kalmia latifolia* blossoms, but their color is a radiant pink-purple (Plate 35). I found the plant growing prolifically in my garden when I moved here, and it is still plentiful. As one of its common names suggests, it is poisonous to cattle, but deer nibble on it apparently unharmed.

PLATE 35. The bright blossoms of *Kalmia angustifolia* (sheep laurel) in mid June.

Kalmia latifolia 15 ft (4.6 m); Zone 5

Mountain Laurel; Calico Bush; Spoonwood; Ivybush; Ivy

The native range of this species reaches from Maine and eastern Canada to western Florida, and northwest to Kentucky. It is the largest, most variable, and certainly the most beautiful of the seven *Kalmia* species. In my garden, it was and still is heavily represented (Plates 3, 41). Some specimens are over 15 ft (4.6 m) tall and, if they are not in their off-year, are literally smothered in late May and early June with trusses of beautiful flowers hanging from the top branches like miniature clouds (Plate 13). I transplanted a few and lost one or two that languished for many years in excessively wet locations before they finally succumbed, but otherwise all the plants that were here are still growing, plus several dozen newly sprouted seedlings that I have kept, after giving many others to friends.

A few specimens of the shrub bloom profusely every year but most blossom prolifically only once in two or three years. This tendency is only partly overcome by deadheading (removing spent flowers immediately after they fade). During a year of heavy bloom the plant's energy is directed toward the production of a great amount of seed. In that year there are almost no new leaves and no new flower buds for next spring. The following year the plant usually produces only new foliage and perhaps a few flower buds. Two years elapse before new flowers in acceptable quantities are produced, and it takes three or more years for some plants to accumulate strength for the remarkable eruption of gorgeous blooms that occurs from time to time.

From its discovery in the 1700s by European settlers until the 1960s, *Kalmia latifolia* was given only muted attention from botanists, nursery professionals, and gardeners. When the plant was mentioned, it was virtually always the common white or nearly white form. The shrub had its admirers, however, and became the state flower of Connecticut and Pennsylvania.

Several darker pink and red-budded variants were discovered in the wild and in gardens, and later a few specimens bearing flowers with dark brownish or reddish bands (the 'Fuscata' cultivars) were found. Because the species was difficult to propagate, these forms received only limited distribution. It was taken for granted that the plant possessed uncommonly immutable properties: it occurred principally with white or light pink flowers and there was little point in hybridizing it, which was difficult anyway. The natural beauty of the common form also diffused the urgency to improve it by hybridization or by seeking out new cultivars.

Nevertheless, unknown to most of us, many different forms occurred in nature, and hybridization did prove possible. A few *Kalmia* connoisseurs along the East Coast discovered these cultivars and spread word of their existence, but it took the enthusiasm, knowledge, and perseverance of one individual to finally bring together the scattered bits of information and to use them effectively: Richard A. Jaynes, then horticulturist and plant breeder at the Connecticut Agricultural Experiment Station (CAES) in New Haven, Connecticut. In 1975 Dr. Jaynes published his first work on the subject, *The Laurel Book,* and in 1988 he introduced its updated version, *Kalmia, The Laurel Book II.* In his Broken Arrow Nursery, Hamden, Connecticut, he began gathering and breeding new cultivars, many with patterns and colors never before available or thought possible. In 1987 Jaynes was designated by the Council of the International Society of Horticultural Science as the International Registration Authority for *Kalmia.*

Our eyes have become so accustomed to seeing the usual, though beautiful, blossoms of the common version of *Kalmia latifolia* that we have difficulty imagining the new cultivars without seeing them in real life or at least in a color photograph. Some have dark-red buds that open into white flowers; others have pink buds and pink flowers with white centers; many have narrow or broad bands of red or cinnamon inside their corollas, while others have corollas ringed with maroon dots. A few have corollas that actually divide into separate petals, and the flowers of some are the size of a silver dollar. The foliage and the stature of the plants also vary, several being true miniatures. Listed below are the cultivars I have thus far assembled in my garden. Many more are available and still more, undoubtedly, will be forthcoming.

***Kalmia latifolia* 'A'** 3 ft (0.9 m); Zone 5

This unnamed miniature plant came from R. A. Jaynes. The white buds open into a normal-sized corolla with a broad brown band. The leaves are 1 in (2.5 cm) long, dark green, and narrow. The growth is low, dense, and attractive, although the plant is a shy bloomer.

***Kalmia latifolia* 'Alpine Pink'** 7 ft (2.1 m); Zone 5

On this beautiful cultivar the rich pink buds open to soft, clear pink flowers with nearly white centers. The 3.5-in (9-cm) long leaves are thick, light green, glossy, broad, and heavy. The growth habit is attractive, and the size is normal for the species. By the first week of June, red buds speckle the bush like small, 10-pointed stars, and by mid June radiant pink flowers completely cover the foliage. The plant was selected by J. Eichelser, Olympia, Washington.

***Kalmia latifolia* 'B'** 6 ft (1.8 m); Zone 5

This unnamed red-budded and red-flowered selection also came from R. A. Jaynes. The dark green leaves are 3.5 in (9 cm) long, and the buds as well as the open corolla are bright orange-red, a rare color for a kalmia. The plant blooms heavily every second year, the abundant trusses weighing down the slender branches. The very decorative bud stage begins in early June with the buds covering the green foliage entirely. The bush is in full bloom by mid to late June.

***Kalmia latifolia* 'Bullseye'** 7 ft (2.1 m); Zone 5

This plant has a corolla with a broad purple-cinnamon band covering most of the inside wall. The center and the narrow margin of the corolla are white (Plate 36). The new leaves are often reddish brown, and the growth is vigorous. This plant originated from a cross of a red-budded plant with pollen of a broad-banded specimen at Bristol Nurseries, Bristol, Connecticut, and was introduced by Knight Hollow Nursery, Madison, Wisconsin.

PLATE 36. The unusual pattern in the flowers of *Kalmia latifolia* 'Bullseye' (mountain laurel) in early June.

***Kalmia latifolia* 'Carol'** 4 ft (1.2 m); Zone 5

The intensely red unopened buds on this cultivar contrast well with the nearly white corolla of open blossoms. The intensity of color can diminish somewhat in extremely hot and sunny locations. The foliage is 3.5 in (9 cm) long, broad, thick, and glossy, and the growth habit is compact. The plant originated in 1969 from a controlled CAES cross.

***Kalmia latifolia* 'Freckles'** 7 ft (2.1 m); Zone 5

The flower buds on this bush are light pink, and the inside of the white corolla has a circle of 10 purplish cinnamon dots, each the size of a large pinhead. The foliage and the growth habit of the plant are typical for the species. The cultivar is from a second-generation controlled cross by R. A. Jaynes.

***Kalmia latifolia* 'Hearts Desire'** 4 ft (1.2 m); Zone 5

The flower bud on this cultivar is red and, when open, the corolla is almost entirely cinnamon-red except for the small tips on its outer edge and a tiny circle in the center, which are both white. This combination gives the large and abundant trusses the illusion of rich deep red touched with silver. The 3.5-in (9-cm) long foliage is dark green, and the growth habit is dense and broader than tall. The plant is a selection from a controlled cross by R. A. Jaynes.

***Kalmia latifolia* 'Kaleidoscope'** 7 ft (2.1 m); Zone 5

The bud on this shrub is red, and the open corolla is almost fully cinnamon-red except for the white tips. The plant's blossoms are similar to those of *Kalmia latifolia* 'Hearts Desire', but the white areas are somewhat larger, and the trusses are looser. The 3.5-in (9-cm) long foliage is dark green, and the growth habit is normal for the species. The plant was selected by R. A. Jaynes from a cross of *K. latifolia* 'Sarah' and a sibling of *K. latifolia* 'Bullseye'.

***Kalmia latifolia* 'Minuet'** 2 ft (0.6 m); Zone 5

The bud on this dwarf cultivar is light pink. Inside the open corolla is a wide, bright, cinnamon-red band, and the outer edges and the center of the corolla are white. The flower is large for the size of the plant. The leaves are about 2 in (5 cm) long, glossy, dark green and narrow. The plant, the first miniature *Kalmia latifolia* with a banded flower to be named, is the result of a cross between a miniature plant and a normal-sized banded plant. It was selected by R. A. Jaynes.

***Kalmia latifolia* 'Olympic Fire'** 5 ft (1.5 m); Zone 5

A large red bud on this plant opens into a pink corolla, and the normal-sized foliage, about 3.5 in (9 cm) long, is heavy. Cuttings are easy to root. The plant, a seedling of *Kalmia latifolia* 'Ostbo Red', was selected and originally propagated by J. Eichelser, Olympia, Washington.

***Kalmia latifolia* 'Olympic Wedding'** 6 ft (1.8 m); Zone 5

Light pink buds on this plant open into a whitish corolla with a broken maroon band, and the 3.5-in (9-cm) long leaves are dark green, broad, and flat. The cultivar is a 1984 selection from a cross of *Kalmia latifolia* 'Ostbo Red' and *K. latifolia* 'Fresca' by J. Eichelser, Olympia, Washington.

***Kalmia latifolia* 'Ostbo Red'** 7 ft (2.1 m); Zone 5

The buds of this old cultivar are iridescent red, especially in a fully sunny location, and the corolla opens light pink. The brilliant color of the buds is the standard by which other red-budded cultivars are judged. The foliage of the bush is normal for the species. It was selected in the 1940s on the West Coast from material supplied by the well-known rhododendron grower C. O. Dexter of Sandwich, Massachusetts. It was the first red-budded selection to be named.

***Kalmia latifolia* 'Raspberry Glow'** 7 ft (2.1 m); Zone 5

Deep burgundy-red buds on this shrub open into very dark red flowers (Plate 37). The color holds well in partial shade. The dark green foliage is of normal size, and the growth habit is excellent. The plant is from a 1974 controlled cross, and was selected, propagated, and commercially introduced by a Connecticut nursery in 1985.

PLATE 37. The strong colors of *Kalmia latifolia* 'Raspberry Glow' in mid June.

***Kalmia latifolia* 'Richard Jaynes'** 6 ft (1.8 m); Zone 5

This plant was selected and named in honor of Richard A. Jaynes in 1977 by the nurseryman and hybridizer Edmund V. Mezitt, Weston Nurseries, Hopkinton, Massachusetts. The buds are red to dark raspberry, and the opened corolla has a silvery white cast over pink. At the time of its selection, the plant was considered by Mezitt to be a major breakthrough in his breeding endeavors because the outside red color of the bud penetrated relatively undiminished into the inside of the corolla. He considered it to be a significant step toward a true-red *Kalmia latifolia*. The bush is a heavy annual bloomer, reaching its optimal flowering time in mid June. The leaves are glossy and somewhat wavy.

***Kalmia latifolia* 'Sarah'** 5 ft (1.5 m); Zone 5

Buds on this gorgeous cultivar are red and the corolla, when fully open, is pink-red. This is possibly the truest red *Kalmia latifolia* that has been created thus far. The leaves and growth habit are excellent. The plant, a selection of CAES, was introduced by a Wisconsin nursery in 1983.

***Kalmia latifolia* 'Snowdrift'** 5 ft (1.5 m); Zone 5

This white-flowered selection was a seedling from seeds collected in an isolated stand of white flowering plants. The 3-in (8-cm) long leaves are dark green and broad, and the growth habit is compact, thickly branched, and densely foliaged. It was selected by R. A. Jaynes.

***Kalmia latifolia* 'Yankee Doodle'** 6 ft (1.8 m); Zone 5

The buds on this plant are red, and the open corolla is white with a narrow, interrupted maroon band. The 3.5-in (9-cm) long foliage is yellow-green. The cultivar was selected in 1975 and introduced by a Connecticut nursery in 1985.

Lavandula angustifolia (Labiatae) 3 ft (0.9 m); Zone 5

Lavender; True Lavender

Approximately 20 species comprise the genus *Lavandula,* all native to a region encompassing the Mediterranean shores from the Atlantic Ocean to the Middle East, east to India, and south along the Red Sea to Ethiopia. The south European *L. angustifolia* is one of the two species whose flowers yield the perfumery oil of lavender. This species is widely cultivated for ornamental reasons, but its fragrance alone makes it a must in every sunny garden. The purple blossoms exude a pleasant smell, and when they disappear, and throughout the year, the silvery 1-in (2.5-cm) long linear leaves give out the beautiful perfume when crushed or bruised.

The long row of *Lavandula angustifolia* planted along the fence of my wife's vegetable garden is clipped in late summer to a height and width of about 1.5 ft (50 cm). The little hedge is an airy sight in late spring when the new long flower spikes become covered with abundant small blooms. The planting consists mostly of the light purple cultivar *L. angustifolia* 'Munstead' plus a few plants of *L. angustifolia* 'Hidcote', which has pretty but uncharacteristically dark purple blooms. The species needs not only full sun, but also perfect drainage, conditions which I am not fully able to provide. Tall trees on the east and west sides allow only about five or six hours of direct sun, and the site is in a flat meadow that tends to remain moist after rain. Because of these circumstances, and due to an occasional harsh winter, I lose a few plants almost every year, but they are easy and inexpensive to replace. Since the soil is acidic, I scatter fireplace ashes or a few handfuls of ground limestone over the bed in winter.

LEUCOTHOE (ERICACEAE) Fetterbush

There are about 50 species of deciduous or evergreen shrubs in the genus *Leucothoe,* all native to eastern Asia, western Africa, and South as well as North America. The leaves are alternate, elliptic, and pointed at the base and the tip. The bell-shaped flowers are white or pink and 0.4 in (1 cm) long. The plants prefer acidic, moist, peaty, and sandy soils. Two varieties of *Leucothoe* grow in my garden.

Leucothoe axillaris 6 ft (1.8 m); Zone 7

Coastal Leucothoe

The native range of this North American evergreen species includes the coastal plain from Virginia to Florida, and west to Mississippi. The plant is not reliably hardy in Connecticut. I have grown it for several years, and while it manages to survive some winters unharmed, most years it suffers damage that varies from minor to significant. Eventually, it may have to be discarded, however, thus far it has always recovered by mid spring. The new shiny brownish foliage and the small bell-shaped, white, and fragrant flowers that look like lily-of-the-valley blossoms seem to come on schedule. It also has the advantage that deer are not fond of it. The plant requires moist, acidic soil in a partly shaded protected location, but it also obviously prefers the climate of zone 7.

***Leucothoe fontanesiana* 'Folia Multicolor'** 6 ft (1.8 m); Zone 4

Girard's Rainbow Drooping Leucothoe; Doghobble; Switch Ivy

Although *Leucothoe fontanesiana* is similar to *L. axillaris* and their native haunts cover about the same geographic area, the former is much hardier, possibly because it comes from the mountainous parts of the range. The cultivar 'Folia Multicolor' (rainbow leucothoe) is a chance seedling of the species from Girard Nurseries, Geneva, Ohio. The stems and the 4-in (10-cm) long leaves occur in several colors at the same time—in varying shades of light green, yellow, white, and red—though the hues are not particularly strong. The plant is vigorous, hardy, and attractive, especially when its long, arching branches are covered with the fragrant flowers in late May. I have never protected this shrub, which has grown eagerly and blossomed prolifically. It looks best in a woodsy environment. The present name of the species, *L. fontanesiana,* is of a relatively recent origin. Previously, it was called *L. catesbaei,* and prior to that, *Andromeda catesbaei*.

Lindera benzoin (Lauraceae) 15 ft (4.6 m); Zone 4

Common Spicebush; Benjamin Bush; Wild-allspice

The genus *Lindera* is a group of about 100 species of aromatic trees and shrubs native mostly to the tropical regions of south and eastern Asia. Two species are native to the eastern part of North America, but only *L. benzoin* is hardy. Its native range reaches from Maine to Iowa and south to Texas and Florida. It is a deciduous shrub growing in acidic soils on damp, wooded sites. It blooms in late April in my wood where it brightens the early spring days with small but abundant, yellow, aromatic unisexual flowers appearing before the leaves unfold. In late summer, bright red berries, 0.5 in (13 mm) long, decorate the branches and contrast attractively with the lush green foliage that changes to bright yellow in early autumn. The species is dioecious, and only the individuals with pistillate flowers bear fruit. All parts of the shrub are spicy-fragrant. The leaves have been used for brewing tea, and the dried and powdered berries were used as a substitute for allspice. The plant seeds itself generously. I allow as many of its seedlings to develop as space permits.

Myrica pensylvanica (Myricaceae) 6 ft (1.8 m); Zone 4

Bayberry; Candleberry; Swamp Candleberry

Most of the 50 species in the genus *Myrica* grow only in warmer climates. *Myrica pensylvanica,* however, ranges from Newfoundland to North Carolina, and northwest to the southern shores of the Great Lakes. It is an aromatic, deciduous to semi-deciduous unisexual shrub that grows in poor and dry sandy soils or even sand dunes; in my garden it grows in damp places as well. Most of the plants that have grown naturally are somewhat leggy, but the species can be shaped into an attractive shrub if pruned when young. The fragrant, leathery, alternate leaves are 2–4 in (5–10 cm) long, and the plentiful grayish blue berries, 0.25 in (6 mm) in diameter, remain on the branches until late fall (Plate 38). Because of their fragrance, the leaves were once used as a substitute for bay leaves in cooking, and the berries are used in making aromatic bayberry candles.

PLATE 38. The aromatic foliage and fruit of *Myrica pensylvanica* (bayberry) in mid September.

Paeonia suffruticosa. See under **"Nonwoody Plants."**

Paxistima canbyi (Celastraceae) 12 in (30 cm); Zone 5

Mountain Lover; Canby Paxistima; Cliff Green

The genus *Paxistima* (sometimes incorrectly called *Pachistima* or *Pachystima*) has only two species: *P. myrsinites* is native to the western Rocky Mountains, while *P. canbyi* ranges from central Pennsylvania and Ohio to Kentucky and West Virginia, and is hardy to southern New England. *Paxistima canbyi* is a low, mat forming evergreen shrublet with upright, four-sided branches, growing on rocky slopes in its native habitat. Its flowers and fruit are not too noteworthy, but the plant as a whole is very useful and attractive for small spaces such as rock gardens. The leaves are dark green, 1 in (2.5 cm) long and only 0.1 in (3 mm) wide, with minute teeth on the edges; in the autumn they acquire a bronze tint. The plant needs an acidic, well-drained soil.

***Philadelphus* × *lemoinei* 'Belle Etoile'** (Saxifragaceae) 6 ft (1.8 m); Zone 5

Mockorange

The genus *Philadelphus* has 65 species, mostly native to North America, east Asia, and Europe. There are many hybrids and some, though not all, are fragrant. The famous and prolific hybridizer of the 19th century, Pierre Louis Victor Lemoine of Nancy, France, produced many of the excellent plants grown today. *Philadelphus* × *lemoinei* 'Belle Etoile', a hybrid of *P. coronarius* and *P. microphyllus*, is among the best. It blooms in June to July; the delightfully scented white flowers have four cupped petals and an attractive pink-purple eye inside the base of the flower. The ovate leaves, 2 in (5 cm) long, are slightly hairy on the underside. The bush is not a tall grower, but if pruning is necessary, it should be done immediately after flowering, as the blooms appear on last year's wood. It prefers a sunny, well-drained position but will grow in partial shade where it will produce fewer flowers.

PIERIS (ERICACEA)

There are about eight species of evergreen shrubs and trees in the genus *Pieris*. Two are from North America, *P. floribunda* and *P. phillyreifolia*, and the others are Asian. Botanists of the late 18th and early 19th centuries named this genus *Andromeda*, but the use of that term as a botanical name for the genus was abandoned long ago and is used less and less even as a common name. Instead, the name *Pieris* is increasingly used even in the trade to avoid confusion with the true *Andromeda* (bog rosemary).

Pieris japonica 9 ft (2.7 m); Zone 5

Japanese Pieris; Lily-of-the-valley Bush

Pieris japonica is grown throughout the temperate zone of the world. Its dark evergreen leaves are 3 in (8 cm) long, and its pendant lily-of-the-valley-shaped flowers are very attractive. As an ericaceous plant, this species requires acidic, peaty, and moist but well-drained soil. It is easy to grow and propagate. Though it will succeed and bloom well in a sunny position, it is best grown in partial shade where it can more easily escape the disfiguring effects of *Aleurothrixus interrogatonis* (pieris white fly). The insect multiplies rapidly on bushes grown in hot, dry, sunny locations where it can turn the normally beautiful, shiny green leaves into dry-looking, nearly white foliage by sucking the sap, and with it, the green chlorophyll. In addition, the honeydew secreted by the insects falls onto the leaves below, causing a growth of sooty mold that inhibits the production of carbohydrates in the plant. In my garden grow several unidentified cultivars of *P. japonica*. Some have coppery new foliage, while the new leaves on others are greenish bronze; one plant, *P. japonica* 'Red Mill', has beautiful scarlet new foliage.

Pieris taiwanensis 6 ft (1.8 m); Zone 7

Chinese Pieris; Formosa Pieris

The original home of this species is Taiwan, as well as the southern parts of mainland China, and Myanmar (formerly Burma). The species strongly resembles *Pieris japonica*; its new leaves have a bronzy hue, and the long racemes of white flowers are similar to those of the Japanese species. The plant is rated hardy to zone 7, but it has grown in my nursery for at least 4 years without any winter damage. I am anxious to see how it does in a more open position where it will have to be moved soon because it is beginning to outgrow its sheltered home.

Pieris yakushimanum 2 ft (0.6 m); Zone 6

This is the smallest and most endearing *Pieris* in my garden. It comes from the high, fog-shrouded slopes of Yakushima Island in southern Japan. Of dwarf growth, it has reached 12 in (30 cm) in height in 5 years (Plate 12). The leaves are about 2.5 in (6.4 cm) long, and the flowers, which are large for a plant of its size, are somewhat sensitive to frost, suffering some damage in severe winters.

Potentilla fruticosa (Rosaceae) 4 ft (1.2 m); Zone 2

Shrubby Cinquefoil; Bush Cinquefoil; Golden Hardhack; Widdy

There may be as many as 500 species in the genus *Potentilla*. Most are weedy herbs, but several are shrubs worthy of the best gardens. *Potentilla fruticosa* is native in North America from coast to coast, as well as in the Eurasian continent from the British Isles to the Far East. Its range reaches from the circumpolar regions to the temperate zones. The species grows in many types of soil and under varied conditions, but it should always have sun or only very light shade. The small foliage is gray-green, deciduous, with an abundance of small leaves frequently consisting of five leaflets, from which the species derives some of its common names. The flowers have five petals and are up to 1.5 in (4 cm) in diameter; their color may be white, yellow, orange, rose, or red. The plants begin to bloom in June and continue intermittently through the summer until frost. There are two cultivars in my garden: *P. fruticosa* 'Abbotswood' with pure white petals and yellow stamens and *P. fruticosa* 'Red Ace' with flowers of intense red which, however, may bleach into yellowish red if the location and the weather are too sunny and hot.

There is another species of *Potentilla* in my garden, *P. nepalensis* 'Miss Willmott'. This is an open, herbaceous plant with 1-in (2.5-cm) wide, carmine-rose flowers, and rich green, strawberrylike leaves. The stems reach up to 1.5 ft (50 cm) with the flowers at their tips. The plant comes from the Himalayas and is hardy to zone 5.

RHODODENDRON (ERICACEAE)

The genus *Rhododendron,* which includes azaleas and rhododendrons, counts about 1000 species among its members. Some species grow in arctic regions, while others are native to tropical forests; some are evergreen, others are deciduous; and some are 1-in (2.5-cm) high dwarfs, while others are 45-ft (14-m) trees covered with trusses of bright-colored blooms. A few species are native to Europe, two dozen or more come from North America, and the remainder are from southeastern and eastern Asia.

Members of the genus *Rhododendron* are probably the most frequently planted ornamental shrubs. No other genus in recent history has inspired greater enthusiasm and loyalty. In the past century, plant explorers braved trips to unknown and dangerous areas to bring out more and more new species. Botanists and gardeners still conduct excursions to the same regions, but now their purpose is to observe the plants in their native habitats, and perhaps by a stroke of good luck to discover one more new species that the multitudes of plant hunters before somehow missed. In recent decades, interest has been focused on *Vireya* rhododendrons from Malaysia and the tropical isles of Indonesia. In colder climates, these species can be grown only indoors.

From the early 1800s till now, many thousands of hardy and tender *Rhododendron* hybrids have been produced by crossing various species with each other, then species with hybrids and, inevitably, hybrids with hybrids. The pedigree of some modern crosses may include a dozen or more known and identified ancestors. It is not difficult to see why the genus inspired such strong fidelity and dedication among its followers. There probably is no other group of plants that is more beautiful and decorative, whether in bloom or out, that will survive such varied growing conditions, and that is so easy to grow and so relatively trouble free.

Some 200 years ago, growers and hybridizers in the Low Countries were the leading force in the culture of the genus, especially the deciduous azaleas. They were succeeded by British hybridizers in the second half of the 19th century. Now, the U.S. rhododendron community is also taking a strong initiative, and active groups of growers and hybridizers have emerged in Germany, Canada, the Low Countries, Czechoslovakia, some Scandinavian countries, Australia, New Zealand, and Japan. The American Rhododendron Society (ARS) has members from all these countries, as well as the United States.

I, too, have easily succumbed to the temptation to grow rhododendrons in my garden. The group of five or six evergreen varieties planted on my lot by the builder has increased to over 300 specimens. About two dozen are clones (from layers) of the original plants; the others (in some cases several of the same variety) have been introduced over the years, despite periodic promises to myself that I would refrain from additional acquisitions. Further, when I came to Connecticut, there were also two or three dozen native deciduous azaleas on the land, all belonging to *Rhododendron viscosum* (swamp azalea) and *R. periclymenoides* (pinxter azalea). I have preserved nearly all these plants, but soon will have to begin thinning them out as they are demanding more and more space. Transplanting native deciduous azaleas can be risky, but no matter how tall they are, if they are cut down to the ground and moved in March, they will probably survive. With adequate moisture, they send up new shoots from the root ball and bloom in a few years.

Currently, over 200 species and varieties of the genus *Rhododendron* grow in my garden. Of these, about 150 are evergreen and the remainder are deciduous. All are described here. The descriptions include a quality rating (see "Introduction" for an explanation of the ratings) and, where known, the plant's parentage. Incidentally, many plants in my garden have low quality ratings, but I would not part with them because they are the old ironclads that recover their composure quickly after a devastating winter or a rainless summer. Their flower buds almost never freeze, and their flowers, albeit only of the ordinary purple/pink, white, or red colors, unfailingly arrive on schedule while some of the highly rated hybrids struggle to come back from the dead. The parentage of hybrids is shown in parentheses after the name of the hybrid. In some instances this information is not available. This is the case, for example, with the many magnificent hybrids introduced in the late 1920s by the prolific U.S. hobbyist-hybridizer C. O. Dexter. By 1930, Dexter was growing 10,000 seedlings annually at his estate on Cape Cod, Massachusetts, from which he selected only a handful of the best plants. However, he kept no records. If a plant was excellent, he proceeded to introduce it to the world. He brought to life a great amount of beauty, but he also left a void that can never be filled.

In the early days of modern botany, when plants now comprising the genus *Rhododendron* were being classified, Linnaeus and certain taxonomists (classifiers) placed them in two completely separate groups: rhododendrons and azaleas. In practice, this division still persists among gardeners and nursery growers, reflecting the readily noticeable visual aspects of the two groups, but there are no constant botanical differences between them; they are merely two parts of a genus. In this volume all descriptions state whether a plant is a rhododendron or an azalea, and, if a rhododendron, whether its leaves are lepidote (scaly) or elepidote (scaleless), a distinction that can be usually ascertained only with a magnifying glass. For practical purposes, however, lepidote leaves are usually quite small, while elepidote leaves are generally longer, broader, and more lush.

Azaleas may be deciduous or evergreen. The leaves of deciduous azaleas fall off completely every autumn, leaving only clean vegetative and terminal flower buds; on the other hand, when the term *evergreen* is used for azaleas, it is employed with some license. It does not mean that a plant's foliage is as evergreen as the foliage of an evergreen rhododendron. Evergreen azaleas have dimorphic leaves (i.e., leaves occurring in two forms). The first set of leaves appears in spring, usually in late May or early June, and falls off by late autumn in cold climates or by late winter in warmer areas. The second set of leaves appears in late June to August. Compared to the spring leaves, the summer leaves are smaller and a darker green. They persist on the branches until replaced by new summer leaves the following year. Thus, although the so-called evergreen azaleas look half-bare or almost-bare in winter, they still have at least a few narrow leaves at the tips of their branches and an altogether different look than the fully deciduous azaleas, which do not have even a semblance of a leaf around their buds after November. Also, before the leaves of deciduous azaleas drop off, they often change color to yellow or red, similar to other deciduous shrubs, but when evergreen azalea leaves change color in cold weather, it will be toward the bronze-red or purple-brown hues.

Despite the variety of conditions in which the genus will flourish, all members of the *Rhododendron* genus have several strict requirements in common. Since they are ericaceous plants, they must have acidic soils (pH between 4.5 and 6.5) that are sandy/peaty and moist but well drained; they are best grown on cool, partly shaded sites. These conditions ensure that their relatively shallow masses of roots never dry out, and that their beautiful foliage does not bake in the summer's heat or suffer winter-burn in the frigid season's sun. In North America, these growing requirements are for the most part easily met on the East and the West coasts. Nevertheless, with better understanding of their preferences, more sensitive selection of appropriate species and hybrids for a given climate, and the extra effort that many gardeners are more than willing to give, rhododendrons can now be grown almost everywhere in the United States and many parts of Canada. New cold-hardy hybrids are being produced in Minnesota, and dozens of heat-tolerant native species and hybrids are being selected and crossed in the Deep South. The problem created by clayey and/or limy soil is easily remedied by the use of raised beds: heap a foot or two of the correct acidic mixture (one-third each) of sand, peat, and loam on top of the native earth, keep it damp, and mulch it well. Mulch keeps the roots moist and cool in summer and warmer in winter, plus it gives the plants some organic matter to feed on. In very dry weather rhododendrons require watering, especially those that have been planted within the past 2 or 3 years.

Fertilizing rhododenrons and azaleas is normally not required and often even discouraged by some growers. Nevertheless, there are exceptions. For example, some deciduous azaleas that fail to produce abundant flowers can be induced to bloom by a dressing of sulfate of potash, applied to the root perimeter at a rate of 1 oz (30 g) per 1 sq yd (1 sq m) in mid to late June. Another formula, which is sometimes recommended, is 4 oz (110 g) of superphosphate for every 2 ft (60 cm) of plant spread, applied in autumn after the plants become dormant. Donald Wyman presents a third formula in *Shrubs and Vines for American Gardens* (1969, 357):

> The late C. O. Dexter of Sandwich, Massachusetts, experimented with many fertilizers for rhododendrons and azaleas until he finally found one that seemed to force his plants into remarkable productiveness. This was made of 10 lbs (4.5 kg) of nitrate of potash and 20 lbs (9 kg) of superphosphate. He applied this at reasonable rates in early spring to all his azaleas and rhododendron specimens, with remarkable success. Nitrogenous fertilizers leaving an acid reaction in the soil will promote vegetative growth, but the above-recommended formula might well be tried for forcing plants into profuse bloom.

Although I have used fertilizers on rhododendrons and azaleas only sparingly, I have tested all three of the above suggestions and am leaning toward the Dexter formula; nevertheless, I add 10 lbs (4.5 kg) of gypsum to provide calcium for my soils of pH 4.2–5.5 without making them limy.

***Rhododendron* 'Alexander'** (*R. nakaharae* × *R.* 'Kin no-sai') 10 in (25 cm); Zone 5

In time this prostrate azalea spreads to a 24-in (60-cm) mat. Its leaves are 1.5 in (4 cm) long, and its flowers, which open in late June to early July, are 2 in (5 cm) in diameter and salmon-red with a purple-red blotch. It is one of many ground-hugging evergreen azaleas from the garden of Polly Hill, North Tisbury, Martha's Vineyard Island, Massachusetts. Most of Hill's hybrids have *Rhododendron nakaharae* as one parent, a tender species from Taiwan that seldom grows more than 5 in (13 cm) high. The hybrids are hardier than the species.

***Rhododendron* 'Allure'** (*R. simsii* × *R. mucronatum*) 5 ft (1.5 m); Zone 6

This evergreen azalea, blooming in mid May, was introduced in the late 1940s by the U.S. Department of Agriculture, Glenn Dale, Maryland. The leaves are 1.5 in (4 cm) long, and the pale rose-pink flowers are up to 2.5 in (6.4 cm) wide. Of the great number of plants that Glenn Dale produced, only some are hardy in my garden. *Rhododendron* 'Allure' goes through most, though not all; Connecticut winters in good condition.

***Rhododendron* 'Aloha'** (*R.* 'Vulcan' × *R. yakushimanum*) 3 ft (0.9 m); Zone 5

This is an elepidote rhododendron of slow, compact growth with 3.5-in (9-cm) long narrow, strap-shaped leaves that are shiny above and indumented with a thick felt beneath. The leaves remain on the branches for 3 years. The growth habit is dense and rounded. Bright red buds open in early May to 3-in (8-cm) wide deep pink funnel-shaped flowers with five wavy-edged lobes. The flower buds withstand temperatures of only −10°F (−23°C), but the plant is hardy to −15°F (−26°C). The cross was made in 1973 by Carl Phetteplace, Leasburg, Oregon.

***Rhododendron* 'Always Admired'** (*R.* 'Scintillation' × *R. haematodes*)
4 ft (1.2 m); Zone 5

This elepidote rhododendron has attractive 3.5-in (9-cm) long light green leaves. The pink flowers, 2 in (5 cm) wide, are darker toward the edges and have a yellowish blotch, thus creating an overall effect of peach color. They open in mid May. The plant in my garden is in a well-drained woodsy location with partial high shade that protects it from the summer as well as the winter sun. It is rated 4/4.

***Rhododendron* 'Anah Kruschke'** (*R.* 'Purple Splendor' × *R. ponticum*)
5 ft (1.5 m); Zone 5

This elepidote rhododendron has 6-in (15-cm) long dark green, pointed leaves with a noticeably depressed midrib. The foliage is rather dense for a plant of its height. The plant is sometimes listed merely as a *Rhododendron ponticum* seedling. Opening in late May, the flowers vary slightly from plant to plant. The bush in my garden has rich, deep reddish purple blooms up to 3 in (8 cm) wide, arranged in large, abundant round trusses of up to 12 blossoms each. Rated 3/4, this is one of a limited number of hybrids originating on the West Coast that do well in my garden, although a Long Island gardener once mentioned that this plant, too, was a disappointment for him. It was developed by F. Kruschke, Clackamas, Oregon, and introduced by A. Wright, Sr., and A. Wright, Jr., in 1973.

***Rhododendron* 'Anita Gehnrich'** (*R.* 'The Honourable Jean Marie de Montague' × *R. yakushimanum*) 4 ft (1.2 m); Zone 6

This elepidote rhododendron has 5-in (13-cm) long elliptic leaves thinly covered with light green film beneath, and held for 3 years. Unfolding in early June, the flowers are 3.5 in (9 cm) wide and funnel-shaped, with red buds opening deep pink and fading to purplish pink with a red blotch. The hybrid is the product of Bud Gehnrich, Long Island, New York. It is rated 3/4.

***Rhododendron* 'Anna Baldsiefen'** (*R.* 'Pioneer' self-pollinated) 3 ft (0.9 m); Zone 6

This lepidote rhododendron has 1-in (2.5-cm) long oval leaves and small 1-in (2.5-cm) wide flowers of clear purplish pink with darker margins, growing in terminal trusses of up to 17 blossoms each, and opening in mid April. A plant of dense growth, this rhododendron flowers prolifically in most years, though the flower buds are somewhat tender and may be damaged in very cold winters. Developed by Warren Baldsiefen, Bellvale, New York, it is rated 3/3.

***Rhododendron* 'Anna Kehr'** (*R.* 'Triomphe' × *R.* 'Rosebud') 4 ft (1.2 m); Zone 6

This evergreen azalea has 2-in (5-cm) long leaves and 2.5-in (6.4-cm) wide double, pink flowers that cover the branches in late May. It was produced by the well-known azalea hybridizer, August E. Kehr, Hendersonville, North Carolina. The plant, a compact but vigorous grower, performs well in my garden and appears to be hardier than what is sometimes indicated.

Rhododendron arborescens 5–20 ft (1.5–6 m); Zone 6

Smooth Azalea; Sweet Azalea; Tree Azalea

This North American deciduous azalea ranges from Pennsylvania to Kentucky and south to Alabama and Georgia. The 2.5-in (6.4-cm) long leaves are light green, and the very fragrant flowers are white or sometimes pink and 1.5 in (4 cm) wide, with a long corolla tube that is sticky on the outside. The blossoms open in July and August. The species is rated 3/3.

***Rhododendron* 'Arctic Pearl'** (selected seedling of *R. dauricum* var. *album*) 4 ft (1.2 m); Zone 5

This is a lepidote rhododendron with attractive, dark green 1.5-in (4-cm) long leaves and 2-in (5-cm) wide pure white flowers appearing in profusion in April in trusses of up to five blossoms each. The plant, a selection of a species from Dauria in eastern Siberia, was named in 1971 by Warren Baldsiefen, Rochelle Park, New Jersey. It requires a well-drained site and has a rating of 4/3.

Rhododendron atlanticum 4 ft (1.2 m); Zone 5

Coast Azalea; Dwarf Azalea

This North American deciduous azalea ranges along the coastal plains from Pennsylvania to Georgia and west to Alabama. Its bluish green leaves are 2 in (5 cm) long, and its 1.5-in (4-cm) wide tubular flowers are white to light purplish or light yellow, sticky, and very fragrant. They occur in mid May in trusses of 4–10. Some plants are stoloniferous but generally spread at a slow pace. The species is rated 3/3.

***Rhododendron* 'Atroflo'** (*R.* 'Atrosanguineum' × *R. floccigerum*) 5 ft (1.5 m); Zone 6

This is an elepidote rhododendron with 6-in (15-cm) long leathery leaves heavily indumented beneath with a silver felt. The 2.5-in (6.4-cm) wide flowers are very bright rose-red and open in late May (Plate 15). Several versions of this hybrid exist in the trade (representing a grex). The plant in my garden may contain a few genes of *Rhododendron smirnowii*, as evidenced by its very heavy indumentum and the rather narrow leaves. It is a beautiful, if somewhat tender, specimen that, I believe, could earn a higher quality rating than the 3/3 it carries. It is a 1940 introduction of Joseph B. Gable, Stewartstown, Pennsylvania.

Rhododendron austrinum 5 ft (1.5 m); Zone 6

Florida Flame Azalea

This North American deciduous azalea ranges from Georgia and Florida to Alabama, but is almost hardy in Connecticut, especially if planted in a protected site. The leaves are 2 in (5 cm) long, and the tubular, 1-in (2.5-cm) wide fragrant flowers are usually yellow or orange and arranged in trusses of up to 15. They open in mid May. In my garden, the flower buds are killed by frost in about two out of three or four winters. The species is rated 3/3.

Rhododendron bakeri 4 ft (1.2 m); Zone 5

Cumberland Azalea; Baker's Azalea

This North American deciduous azalea is native to the Cumberland Plateau from Kentucky south across Tennessee to Georgia and Alabama. The 2-in (5-cm) long leaves are light green, and the 2-in (5-cm) wide tubular flowers are usually red or orange but may be salmon, apricot, or yellow. Their intense color, contrasting attractively with the bright green foliage, makes up for their lack of fragrance (Plate 39). The plant was first identified and described by its discoverers (Lemmon and McKay) in 1937, and named for Professor Woolford F. Baker of Emory University, Atlanta, Georgia. It is one of the native deciduous azaleas that do not seem to mind a hot summer exposure and never fail to bloom prolifically, although an occasional soaking in dry summers and cool mulch throughout the year enhance flower production considerably. The plants in my garden begin to open their flowers in the last week of June and bloom into July. The species is rated 3/3.

PLATE 39. Among the brightest hues of the early summer garden, the orange-red blossoms of *Rhododendron bakeri* (Baker's azalea).

***Rhododendron* 'Bellringer'** (parentage unknown but probably *R. litiense* × *R. fortunei*) 5 ft (1.5 m); Zone 5

This elepidote rhododendron with 4-in (10-cm) long leaves and ruffled, 2.5-in (6.4-cm) wide creamy white flowers was produced from original C. O. Dexter hybrids by A. Consolini, Sandwich, Massachusetts. The flower buds are hardy only to −5°F (−21°C), but the plant itself withstands temperatures of up to −15°F (−26°C).

***Rhododendron* 'Besse Howells'** (*R.* 'Boule de Neige' × *R. catawbiense* red seedling) 3 ft (0.9 m); Zone 4

This elepidote rhododendron has 4-in (10-cm) long leaves and 2.5-in (6.4-cm) wide frilled, bright red flowers in abundant round trusses, opening in late May (Plate 15). A 1964 hybrid of A. M. Shammarello, South Euclid, Ohio, it is rated 3/4.

***Rhododendron* 'Betty Hume'** (parentage unknown, probably *R. fortunei* hybrid) 6 ft (1.8 m); Zone 5

This elepidote rhododendron has lush green 7-in (18-cm) long leaves and 4-in (11-cm) wide pink, ruffled, fragrant flowers in trusses of up to 10 blossoms, opening in late May. The plant is one of the original C. O. Dexter hybrids introduced by Baldsiefen and Effinger in 1962. It is bud hardy to only −5°F (−21°C) and carries a rating of 4/3.

***Rhododendron* 'Blaauw's Pink'** (*R.* 'Kurume' hybrid) 4 ft (1.2 m); Zone 6

This evergreen azalea has 2-in (5-cm) long light green leaves and 2-in (5-cm) wide hose-in-hose salmon-pink flowers with lighter shadings, opening in late May. It is an old, reliable hybrid introduced by J. Blaauw Nursery, Boskoop, Holland. The fact that it is planted frequently does not diminish its considerable value. It is rated 3/3.

***Rhododendron* 'Blue Ensign'** (probably *R. ponticum* hybrid) 4 ft (1.2 m); Zone 5

This elepidote rhododendron has 6-in (15-cm) long dark green leaves and 3-in (8-cm) wide purplish blue flowers with a bold dark-purple blotch. The blossoms stand out dramatically in the landscape. This hybrid was introduced in 1934 by the W. C. Slocock Nursery, Woking, England, and is rated 4/3.

***Rhododendron* 'Blue Peter'** (probably *R. ponticum* hybrid) 4 ft (1.2 m); Zone 6

This elepidote rhododendron has 6-in (15-cm) long dark green leaves and 3-in (8-cm) wide purplish blue flowers similar to *Rhododendron* 'Blue Ensign'. The only differences between the two shrubs are their hardiness and their growth habit, which is more straggly on *R.* 'Blue Peter'. The plant was introduced in 1933 by John Waterer, Bagshot, England. It is rated 4/2.

***Rhododendron* 'Boule de Neige'** (*R. caucasicum* × *R. catawbiense* hybrid) 4 ft (1.2 m); Zone 4

This is an elepidote rhododendron with 4-in (10-cm) long dark green leaves and 2.5-in (6.4-cm) wide pure white blossoms arranged in loose trusses and opening in mid May. The plant is able to withstand very sunny locations; however, in that position it suffers frequently because of *Stephanitis rhododendri* (lace wing fly). My plant does exceedingly well in rather dense but high shade. It was introduced by Mr. Oudieu in France in 1878 and is rated 4/4.

Rhododendron brachycarpum* ssp. *fauriei* f. *nematoi 3 ft (0.9 m); Zone 6

This elepidote rhododendron has 5-in (13-cm) long oval, light green leaves, shiny above as well as beneath, and 1-in (2.5-cm) wide white to yellowish broadly funnel-shaped flowers, in trusses of 12–15, which open from late July to early August. The plant comes from Korea, northern Japan, and the Kurile Islands. The subspecies was named for a French missionary in China, Rev. L. R. Faurie. My plant, though 5 years old and propagated by layering, is only 1.5 ft (50 cm) high and growing very slowly. As is common for the species, it is not only of slow growth, but is also somewhat reluctant to bloom. It is rated 3/3.

***Rhododendron* 'Brown Eyes'** (probably *R. fortunei* hybrid) 5 ft (1.5 m); Zone 4

This is an elepidote rhododendron with large glossy leaves and 3.5-in (9-cm) wide clear pink flowers with a reddish brown blotch, opening in mid May. When young, its growth is somewhat leggy, but the plant fills out with age. This floriferous variety is another original hybrid of C. O. Dexter. It was introduced by Paul Bosley, Mentor, Ohio, in 1958. It is bud hardy to −15°F (−26°C), plant hardy to −20°F (−29°C), and is rated 3/3.

Rhododendron bureavii 4 ft (1.2 m); Zone 6

This elepidote rhododendron comes from the high elevations of the subtropical mountains in Yunnan Province, China. The dark green leaves and young branches are covered with rust-colored or gray indumentum. The 1-in (2.5-cm) wide flowers are white to rose with crimson spots and open in May. *Rhododendron bureavii* is one of the Taliense series of plants that are famous for their superior foliage. It requires perfect drainage and shade, a position I have given it, but the plant still has not shown any particular vigor in the 4 years it has grown here. The species is rated 3/5.

***Rhododendron* 'Burma'** (*R.* 'Mars' × *R.* 'Fanfare') 5 ft (1.5 m); Zone 4

This elepidote rhododendron has dark green 4.5-in (11-cm) long leaves with wavy margins and 3-in (8-cm) wide dark red flowers that open in mid May. It was produced by David G. Leach, North Madison, Ohio, in 1958 and registered in 1984. It bears the rating of 4/4.

Rhododendron calendulaceum 5 ft (1.5 m); Zone 4

Flame Azalea

This North American deciduous azalea ranges from Pennsylvania and Ohio south to Alabama and Georgia. The 3.5-in (9-cm) long leaves are bright green, and the 2-in (5-cm) wide tubular flowers are yellow to orange or scarlet, opening with leaves or later, generally in late May to early June (Plate 17).

The tallest of the *Rhododendron calendulaceum* plants in my garden is now 9 ft (2.7 m) high and still growing. This individual is obviously even more vigorous than what is normal for the species, which is triploid. The normally given 10-year height of 5 ft (1.5 m) clearly does not apply to it. The bush is beautiful in spring when in flower, but a well-grown plant, with its brilliant light green foliage, is no less an asset even out of bloom. In autumn, the bright yellow leaves further add to its appeal. It is rated 4/3.

Rhododendron calophytum 6 ft (1.8 m); Zone 5

This elepidote rhododendron is native to an elevation of 8000 ft (2400 m) in the warm Sichuan Province of central China. It is probably hardy in Connecticut; thus far my young plant has survived several winters, albeit with the protection of a burlap enclosure and heavy oak-leaf mulch. Everything on the shrub is large. The prominently veined, bright green leaves grow as much as 16 in (40 cm) long, and at maturity the plant can reach a height of 20 ft (6 m) in cultivation and up to 50 ft (15 m) in the wild. The fragrant flowers, opening in mid April, are 3 in (8 cm) wide, with five to seven lobes, in trusses of 20 and even 30 blooms. The color is usually white with a bright red blotch. The species is rated 4/4.

Rhododendron campylogynum* var. *myrtilloides 1 ft (0.3 m); Zone 6

This is a lepidote rhododendron, but the scales usually fall off as the leaves mature. It is native to altitudes of up to 15,000 ft (4600 m) in Tibet (Xizang), Myanmar (formerly Burma), and the Yunnan Province of China. The tiny leaves are from 0.3–1 in (6–25 mm) long, shiny, dark green on top, and paler green beneath. There are several varieties of the species differing in height from 2 in (5 cm) to 4 ft (1.2 m), the largest relative variation in size in any species. Variety *myrtilloides* is one of the smaller versions, producing twin, bell-shaped, white to pink flowers 0.5 in (13 mm) wide, which open in mid May. I planted my little specimen on a shaded southern slope of the rock garden where thus far it has survived several winters in good condition. It carries the rating of 3/4.

Rhododendron canadense 2 ft (0.6 m); Zone 4

Rhodora

This North American deciduous azalea ranges from Labrador and Quebec to New York and Pennsylvania, growing in cold bogs and moist barrens. The 2-in (5-cm) long leaves are bluish green, and the 1-in (2.5-cm) wide flowers, which appear before the leaves, are rose-purple and two-lipped with a short tube, in clusters of up to six blossoms. They open in mid April. The little shrubs create an airy effect when in full bloom. Some of the plants in my garden are in the full shade of deciduous trees while others are in full sun. All are prospering but need constant moisture. The species is closely related to *Rhododendron vaseyi*; it is rated 4/3.

***Rhododendron* 'Canary Islands'** [({[*R. catawbiense* 'Album' × (*R. discolor* × *R.* 'Fabia')] × *R.* 'Mary Belle'} × *R.* 'Catalgla') × *R.* 'Peking'] 5 ft (1.5 m); Zone 5

This complex elepidote hybrid rhododendron is the creation of David G. Leach, North Madison, Ohio. It is the yellowest of the hardy yellows. The coveted color is not exceedingly rare among more tender plants, but it is very difficult to achieve in the hardy elepidote hybrids. A true strong yellow has been eluding northern hybridizers for decades, and the challenge endures. The leaves on this shrub are 4 in (10 cm) long, and the flowers are 2 in (5 cm) wide, yellowish cream, in trusses of 10, opening in mid May. The plant is rated 3/3.

Rhododendron carolinianum 4 ft (1.2 m); Zone 4

Carolina Rhododendron; Piedmont Rhododendron; Small Rhododendron

This North American lepidote rhododendron ranges from North Carolina and eastern Tennessee to Georgia and Alabama. The leaves are 1–3.5 in (2.5–9 cm) long, glossy green above and heavily covered with scales beneath. The flowers are 1.5 in (4 cm) wide, funnel-shaped, usually purple, in trusses of six or seven. They open in mid to late May.

In addition to several specimens of color typical for the species, I grow a number of plants with flowers that are nearly, but not entirely, white; they were obtained as *Rhododendron carolinianum* 'Album'. While attractive, they are not the true *R.*

carolinianum var. *album,* which is almost a separate species and has pure white blossoms, somewhat larger than the species itself, that bloom a week later. All three versions do well in my garden, but need good drainage and good air circulation. Several specimens that were planted in very moist areas died of root rot. The species bears the rating of 3/3.

***Rhododendron* 'Catawbiense Alba'** (parentage unknown) 6 ft (1.8 m); Zone 4

This is an elepidote rhododendron with 5.5-in (14-cm) long firm, lush-green pointed leaves and attractive 2-in (5-cm) wide ivory white blossoms with five petals and a yellow-green blotch, opening in mid May (Plates 8, 71). The plant is wonderfully vigorous and hardy, and almost never suffers winter damage. It is rated 3/3. I planted a considerable number of plants of this cultivar along the boundary lines of my garden where they provide excellent screen. Despite the similarity in names, this plant is a hybrid and not the rare and beautiful white form of the species, *Rhododendron catawbiense* var. *album,* which I do not grow as yet.

***Rhododendron* 'Catawbiense Boursault'** (*R. catawbiense* × unknown) 5 ft (1.5 m); Zone 4

This is an elepidote rhododendron of significant hardiness. Its leaves are rounded, up to 5 in (13 cm) long, and the 2.5-in (6.4-cm) wide flowers, opening in late May, are blue-purple with a light-green blotch, in rounded trusses of 10 blossoms. It is not certain whether this is a hybrid or a selection of the species, *Rhododendron catawbiense,* by Boursault. It carries a rating of 3/3.

***Rhododendron* 'Cecile'** (Exbury hybrid) 7 ft (2.1 m); Zone 4

This deciduous azalea, hybridized at the Exbury Estate, Southampton, England, was introduced in 1947 by Edmund de Rothschild, son of Exbury's founder. The plant is tall and vigorous. The 4-in (10-cm) long leaves are bright green, and the 3.5-in (9-cm) wide blooms begin as dark pink buds that eventually open into very large salmon-pink flowers with a yellow flare (Plate 41). The total effect of the shrub is very beautiful as it reaches full bloom in late May.

This hybrid is one of many thousands of deciduous azaleas that have been introduced in Europe, North America, and other parts of the world over the past two centuries. Among the first wild plants that were sent by the early plant explorers from North America to Europe were *Rhododendron arborescens, R. calendulaceum, R. periclymenoides,* and *R. viscosum.* Hybridizers in the Low Countries added the East European species *R. luteum* to this mixture, which became known as the Ghent azaleas. With the addition of the Chinese and the Japanese deciduous azaleas (now both considered part of a single species *R. molle*), the new blend became the Mollis azaleas. By the end of the 19th century, the well-known hybridizer Anthony Waterer of Knap Hill Nursery, Woking, England, imported many of these shrubs from Belgium and crossed them with each other and with the North American species *R. occidentale.* The new generation became known as the Knap Hill azaleas.

When Baron Lionel de Rothschild completed construction of his gardens at Exbury Estate, the Knap Hills were the foundation of a hybridizing program of unprecedented proportions. De Rothschild produced hundreds of thousands of seedlings from which he selected and introduced only the few that he considered to be the very best. Several decades later, he presented some of these plants to King George of England and from them arose the Windsor hybrids. These were followed by the Ilam hybrids (from de Rothschild's gift to Edgar Stead of New Zealand). Subsequently came the hybrids developed by Lionel de Rothschild's son, Edmund (sometimes referred to as the Solent hybrids), and they, in turn, were followed by many new North American hybrids that are just now reaching the market. Two hundred years ago the handsome North American plants left their homeland to have their genes enriched with foreign species. Now they are returning even more beautiful than when they left.

***Rhododendron* 'Centennial Celebration'** (*R.* 'Purple Lace' × *R. yakushimanum*) 4 ft (1.2 m); Zone 5

This elepidote rhododendron has 3.5-in (9-cm) long leathery leaves and light purple, frilled flowers with a greenish blotch, opening in mid to late May. The plant name commemorates the centennial of Washington State. The little hybrid in my nursery is still too small and too protected to be able to determine whether it will live up to its 4/4 rating in my climate. The cross was made by F. Peste and registered by B. Briggs, Olympia, Washington.

***Rhododendron* 'Chesapeake'** (*R. pubescens* × *R. keiskei*) 3 ft (0.9 m); Zone 4

This lepidote rhododendron with 1.5-in (4-cm) long grayish, lightly pubescent leaves has light apricot flowers fading to white that open in late April. It is an upright, thinly branched bush that does not demand much square footage, but which is interesting and attractive even after its annual display of blooms fades away. It was introduced in 1950 by Guy G. Nearing, Ramsey, New Jersey, and is rated 3/2.

***Rhododendron* 'Chetco'** (*R.* 'Hugh Wormald' × *R.* 'Marion Merrimen') 5 ft (1.5 m); Zone 4

This deciduous azalea from the Exbury Estate has 3.5-in (9-cm) long bright green foliage and large clear yellow flowers with an orange blotch. The plant blooms in late May.

***Rhododendron* 'Chionoides'** (*R. ponticum* hybrid) 4 ft (1.2 m); Zone 6

This is an elepidote rhododendron of compact growth, with 4-in (10-cm) long leaves and 2.5-in (6.4-cm) wide white flowers with yellow centers, which open in late May. My plant grows in a sunny position where it budded well until the deer ate it to bare sticks. With protection, it is recovering and should bloom soon. An old hybrid (exhibited before 1886) produced by John Waterer, Bagshot, England, it is rated 3/4.

***Rhododendron* 'Christmas Cheer'** (*R. caucasicum* × unknown) 4 ft (1.2 m); Zone 6

This elepidote rhododendron has 5-in (13-cm) long leaves and 2-in (5-cm) wide light pink flowers opening in the early part of the blooming season. It was raised by Thomas Methven & Son, Edinburgh, Scotland, and is rated 3/4. Normally, this hybrid grows into a low, compact shrub, but due to an oversight, I allowed my plant to grow into a thin, straggly bush. It began to lose its good form several years ago when each of its upright branches produced only one new terminal vegetative bud, which then lengthened into a single shoot. This process was repeated in subsequent springs, resulting in long, thin stems growing in the manner of bamboo. This straggly appearance could have been avoided when the plant was young by removing the single lead bud on each branch, which would have encouraged the development of several side buds; these, in turn, would have grown into side shoots. In place of each long, whiplike stem, there would have been several branches the first year, each of which would have had several branches in the following year.

David G. Leach, in his authoritative work titled *Rhododendrons of the World* (1961, 88), writes that the lead bud produces a hormone that discourages the development of side buds and favors its own eager progress. When, however, the single lead bud is pinched or snapped off in late winter, the production of the hormone diminishes, side buds begin to appear, and from them side branches develop. The pinching is not necessary if, in place of the lead vegetative bud, there is a big, plump flower bud which does not discourage the development of side branches. Hence, when a rhododendron plant is still small, the lead vegetative buds should be removed in late winter from all branches. If this is done 2 or 3 years in a row, it will produce a bushy plant with many branches each of which will have the potential of developing a flower. The plant will be denser and more floriferous. There are rhododendron growers who do not believe in such "mutilation" of young plants. I think, however, that if they could see my *Rhododendron* 'Christmas Cheer' they would change their mind.

***Rhododendron* 'Conewago Improved'** (*R. carolinianum* × *R. mucronulatum*)
5 ft (1.5 m); Zone 4

This lepidote rhododendron has 2-in (5-cm) long leaves that are shiny on top, and small light lilac flowers covering the thin, twiggy branches in early to mid April. Because of its early blossoming, the plant is very welcome in my garden where it flourishes in full high shade with light coming only from the north. The hybrid was introduced in 1958 by Joseph B. Gable, Stewartstown, Pennsylvania. I think that it is underrated with a rating of 2/3.

***Rhododendron* 'Coral Velvet'** (*R. yakushimanum* × unknown) 3 ft (0.9 m); Zone 5

This elepidote rhododendron has heavily indumented 3-in (8-cm) long narrow leaves and salmon-pink flowers that open in early May, a few at a time over a period of 2 or 3 weeks. Originally thought to be a form of the species *Rhododendron yakushimanum,* it is now considered an open-pollinated cross. It is rated 3/3.

***Rhododendron* 'County of York'** (*R. catawbiense* var. *album* × *R.* 'Loderi King George') 6 ft (1.8 m); Zone 5

Also known as *Rhododendron* 'Catalode', this elepidote rhododendron with broad, exotic-looking 10-in (25-cm) long light green leaves bears 4-in (10-cm) wide white flowers with green throat, in trusses of 13. It blooms in early to mid May. A 1936 introduction of Joseph B. Gable, Stewartstown, Pennsylvania, it is rated 3/3.

***Rhododendron* 'Czech Beauty'** (*R.* 'Goldsworth Yellow' × unknown)
6 ft (1.8m); Zone 6

This elepidote rhododendron has dark green, shiny foliage held for 3 years and 3.5-in (9-cm) wide pale yellow flowers with orange spotting, up to 11 per truss, appearing in late May (Plate 40). A vigorous and fast-growing bush, it is the product of the Long Island, New York, hybridizer Louis A. Hindla, who registered it in 1979. In the process of developing this plant, Hindla created two other similar hybrids, which have remained unregistered and unnamed; they are identified as *Rhododendron* 'Hindla's Cream No. 1' and *R.* 'Hindla's Cream No. 4'. The latter is a particularly lovely plant. Though its flowers are only about 2.5 in (6.4 cm) in diameter, their color appears deeper, and the flower buds are possibly hardier than those of *R.* 'Czech Beauty', which are damaged at about −5°F (−21°C). Some winters, the beautiful foliage on all three plants suffers from winter-burn in my garden.

PLATE 40. The creamy yellow open blooms, and the reddish unopened buds of *Rhododendron* 'Czech beauty' in late May.

Rhododendron dauricum 4 ft (1.2 m); Zone 4

This lepidote rhododendron comes from Dauria on the northeastern coast of Siberia. The 1.5-in (4-cm) long shiny evergreen leaves have scales above and beneath; the bright lavender-pink flowers, 1 in (2.5 cm) in diameter, form small, round, dense trusses of up to 18 blossoms that open in some years as early as late March. Rated 4/3, the plant is a close relative of *Rhododendron mucronulatum* which, however, is usually deciduous.

***Rhododendron* 'David Gable'** (*R.* 'Atrosanguineum' × *R. fortunei*) 5 ft (1.5 m); Zone 5

This elepidote rhododendron has attractive 6-in (15-cm) long bright green leaves and 3.5-in (9-cm) wide pink flowers with red throat in large trusses. It blooms in mid May. The plant was produced by Joseph B. Gable, Stewartstown, Pennsylvania, who registered it in 1962. It is known also by its synonym, 'Gable's Pink No. 1', and bears a rating of 4/4.

***Rhododendron* 'Delaware Valley White'** 3 ft (0.9 m); Zone 5

This evergreen azalea originated several decades ago at the Delaware Valley Nurseries. It has become the standard for white azaleas, with its 2–3 in (5–8 cm) wide pure white blossoms set against fresh green foliage. It grows more compact in the sun, but is more lush in partial shade. The blossoms open in early May (Plate 17).

***Rhododendron* 'Dexter's Champagne'** (parentage unknown) 4 ft (1.2 m); Zone 5

This elepidote rhododendron from C. O. Dexter, Sandwich, Massachusetts, has 4.5-in (11-cm) long light green leaves and beigy white flowers, 3 in (8 cm) wide, opening in early May. The plant is not a very vigorous grower, and the foliage tends to bleach in the summer as well as the winter sun. A protected, partly shaded location is best for it. The shrub is bud hardy to −10°F (−23°C).

***Rhododendron* 'Dora Amateis'** (*R. carolinianum* × *R. ciliatum*) 3 ft (0.9 m); Zone 5

This lepidote rhododendron has 3.5-in (9-cm) long, shiny, pointed leaves that acquire a touch of bronze in cold weather. The profusely borne white fragrant flowers, opening in late April to early May, are lightly spotted with green. They are 2 in (5 cm) across and grow in clusters of five. The plant is a hybrid of Edmond Amateis, Brewster, New York, registered in 1958, and is rated 4/4.

***Rhododendron* 'Elisabeth Hobbie'** (*R.* 'Essex Scarlet' × *R. forestii* var. *repens*) 1.5 ft (0.5 m); Zone 6

This lepidote rhododendron has 2.5-in (6.4-cm) long oval leaves that in spring begin coppery brown and gradually change to green. The 2-in (5-cm) wide bell-shaped, brilliant scarlet flowers grow in loose trusses, opening in late April to early May. Despite the often indicated −5°F (−21°C) hardiness, the plants in my garden survive our winters in relatively good condition, even though a few flower buds are lost in most years. This lovely hybrid is the product of the German hybridizer Dietrich Hobbie, who introduced it in 1945. It carries a rating of 4/4.

***Rhododendron* 'Ellie'** (*R.* 'Cunningham's White' × *R. catawbiense* red seedling) 5 ft (1.5 m); Zone 6

This elepidote rhododendron has 4-in (10-cm) long leaves and 2.5-in (6.4-cm) wide bright red flowers with deeper pink blotch, in conical trusses. It blooms in late April to early May. The plant was introduced in 1958 by A. M. Shammarello, South Euclid, Ohio, and is rated 2/2.

***Rhododendron* 'Fairy Bells'** (*R.* 'Yozakura' × *R.* 'Kagaribi') 3 ft (0.9 m); Zone 6

This evergreen azalea with dark-green 1-in (2.5-cm) long leaves has 2.5-in (6.4-cm) wide, pendulous, salmon-pink flowers with red margins. It blooms in mid May. The plant was produced by the U.S. Department of Agriculture (USDA), in Glenn Dale, Maryland.

Rhododendron flammeum 3 ft (0.9 m); Zone 5
Oconee Azalea

This North American deciduous azalea is native to the piedmont regions of Georgia and South Carolina. The leaves are light green and up to 3 in (8 cm) long, and the funnel-shaped 2-in (5-cm) wide flowers are orange to scarlet, opening in late June to early July. The species is rated 3/3.

***Rhododendron* 'Flava'** (*R. yakushimanum* × *R. wardii*) 3 ft (0.9 m); Zone 5

This elepidote rhododendron has 4-in (10-cm) long bright shiny foliage and light-yellow flowers 3 in (8 cm) in diameter, with a red blotch. The blossoms open in early June. The plant was raised by Dietrich Hobbie in Germany and, similar to his other hybrids, it is of low, compact growth suitable for smaller areas and gardens.

Rhododendron fortunei 6 ft (1.8 m); Zone 5

This elepidote rhododendron has 6–8 in (15–20 cm) long leaves and flat, wide open fragrant flowers up to 4 in (10 cm) wide, crinkled around the edges, light pink fading to a very light and delicate purple. It blooms in late May. On other forms, the flowers of *Rhododendron fortunei* are smaller and stronger pink. The species was discovered in China by the famous Scottish plant explorer Robert Fortune, who introduced it in 1856. It has been used extensively by C. O. Dexter as a parent for his hybrids and by hybridizers all over the world. Its attractive foliage is resistant to insects. Two distinct forms grow in my garden. The more beautiful form came from Bill Dodd's Nursery in Semmes, Alabama (now, regrettably, closed). Its light bluish green leaves are beautifully shaped, and the delicate flowers are of a loveliness seldom seen on a species rhododendron of such hardiness. The other two plants came from a northeastern nursery. Their leaves are apple-green, and the flowers are smaller and darker pink. The species carries the rating of 4/4.

***Rhododendron* 'Francesca'** (*R.* 'Britannia' × *R.* 'Dexter No. 202')
8 ft (2.4 m); Zone 6

This elepidote rhododendron has an open growth habit and large leaves. The buds are dark red and, in late May, open into bright carmine-red 3.5-in (9-cm) wide flowers. The plant in my garden grows in a shady spot at the edge of a woodsy area where it receives adequate shade in summer. However, in autumn, when the tall trees above it lose their leaves and the sun's zenith lowers in the winter sky, the noon rays reach the plant unobstructed and bleach its leaves almost to the color of a lemon. The bush recovers in summer, but it is evident that it needs more winter shade. It was introduced by A. Consolini, Sandwich, Massachusetts, in 1972 and is rated 4/3.

***Rhododendron* 'Freckles'** (*R.* 'Jacksonii Pink' × *R. catawbiense* hybrid)
6 ft (1.8 m); Zone 6

This elepidote rhododendron has 5-in (13-cm) long dark green leaves and large trusses of bright pink flowers, each 2.5 in (6.4 cm) wide, with six crinkled lobes, heavily and attractively spotted with maroon dots. It blooms in late May to early June. The shrub is vigorous and floriferous. It is a 1953 hybrid of Joseph B. Gable, Stewartstown, Pennsylvania; it was described and registered in 1991 by the Gable Study Group, Vienna, Virginia. It is available only occasionally in a few East Coast nurseries. There is another unregistered plant by the same name, which is even less known and which was raised by W. E. Whitney, Brinnon, Washington.

Rhododendron furbishi 5 ft (1.5 m); Zone 5

This North American deciduous azalea with 2.5-in (6.4-cm) long light green leaves has 2-in (5-cm) wide tubular flowers, mostly in shades of orange, orange-red, and pink, with a yellow blotch. It blooms in mid June. The plant was found in a single colony in northern Georgia and once was thought to be a separate species. Now it is considered a natural hybrid between *Rhododendron arborescens* and *R. bakeri* or a late blooming *R. calendulaceum*. It is rated 3/3.

***Rhododendron* 'Gertrude Saxe'** (*R. carolinianum* × *R. mucronulatum* 'Paul's Hot Pink') 5 ft (1.5 m); Zone 4

This lepidote rhododendron with 2-in (5-cm) long smooth, shiny leaves has 2-in (5-cm) wide clear pink flowers opening in late May. It is a product of Richard Murcott, East Norwich, Long Island, New York.

PLATE 41. An island of vegetation in late May, with white trusses of *Kalmia latifolia* (mountain laurel), red blossoms of *Rhododendron* 'Nova Zembla' in the background, and deciduous azaleas *R.* 'Gibraltar' (orange), *R.* 'Klondyke' (yellow), and *R.* 'Cecile' (pink).

***Rhododendron* 'Gibraltar'** (Exbury hybrid) 5 ft (1.5 m); Zone 4

This deciduous azalea with 2.5-in (6.4-cm) long light green leaves has brilliant orange blossoms that contrast attractively with the foliage (Plate 41). It blooms in late May. The plant is relatively compact for a deciduous azalea.

***Rhododendron* 'Gi-Gi'** (parentage unknown) 4 ft (1.2 m); Zone 5

This elepidote rhododendron has 4.5-in (11-cm) long leaves and 3-in (8-cm) wide rose-red flowers with deep red spots, up to 18 blooms in each 6-in (15-cm) wide truss. This is another C. O. Dexter hybrid with unknown parentage. The plant is floriferous and of a somewhat spreading habit, becoming wider than tall. It blooms in late May to early June and is bud hardy to −5°F (−21°C). It was introduced in 1973 and is rated 4/3.

***Rhododendron* 'Gillie'** (Robin Hill hybrid) 3 ft (0.9 m); Zone 6

This azalea with 1.5-in (4-cm) long leaves has 2-in (5-cm) wide profusely produced blossoms of dark apricot to light orange, a color seldom seen with such intensity on an evergreen azalea. It blooms in late May. The plant is the product of Robert D. Gartrell and his largely amateur Robin Hill Nursery, Wyckoff, New Jersey.

***Rhododendron* 'Gina Hohman'** (*R.* 'Kurume' hybrid) 4 ft (1.2 m); Zone 6

This evergreen azalea has 1-in (2.5-cm) long leaves that turn bright red in late fall, and 1.5-in (4-cm) wide hose-in-hose, orange to apricot flowers, hanging singly like bells from the thin branches. It blooms in late April. The plant was hybridized by Henry J. Hohman, Kingsville Nurseries, Kingsville, Maryland.

***Rhododendron* 'Ginny Gee'** (*R. keiskei* prostrate form × *R. racemosum*)
2 ft (0.6 m); Zone 7

This lepidote rhododendron has 1-in (2.5-cm) long leaves and small pinkish white flowers that open in late April. It is a plant of tight dwarf growth, with considerable heat tolerance. The 0°F (−18°C) hardiness rating quoted in some catalogues appears to be somewhat understated; in my garden it has survived several winters with lower temperatures in good condition. It was introduced by Warren Berg, Kent, Washington, in 1979 and is rated 5/5.

***Rhododendron* 'Girard Arista'** (*R.* 'Girard 117 KD' × *R.* 'Strawberry Rose')
5 ft (1.5 m); Zone 5

This deciduous azalea has 3-in (8-cm) long leaves and 3-in (8-cm) wide fragrant, deep to light pink flowers with an orange blotch, opening in late May. The trusses are up to 6 in (15 cm) wide. This and the following six azaleas were produced at Girard Nurseries, Geneva, Ohio.

***Rhododendron* 'Girard Mount Saint Helens'** (*R.* 'Cecile' × *R.* 'G 181')
6 ft (1.8 m); Zone 5

This deciduous azalea with 3.5-in (9-cm) long bright green leaves has deep orange-red 3-in (8-cm) wide flowers in trusses of up to 15, opening in late May. It is a strong, upright grower introduced in 1970.

***Rhododendron* 'Girard Pink Delight'** [*R.* 'Homebush' × (*R.* 'G 117 KD' × *R.* 'Cecile')]
6 ft (1.8 m); Zone 5

This deciduous azalea with 3-in (8-cm) long leaves has 3.5-in (9-cm) wide pink fragrant hose-in-hose flowers, up to 24 per truss, which open in late May.

***Rhododendron* 'Girard Red Pom Pom'** (*R.* 'Crimson Tide' × *R.* 'Select Red 116 GD')
5 ft (1.5 m); Zone 5

This deciduous azalea has red, fragrant, double, long-lasting flowers in trusses 4.5 in (11 cm) wide, opening in late May. The plant is a compact grower.

***Rhododendron* 'Girard Wedding Bouquet'** [*R.* 'Homebush' × (*R.* 'White Swan' × *R.* 'Persil')]
5 ft (1.5 m); Zone 5

This deciduous azalea has apple-blossom pink, fragrant hose-in-hose frilled blossoms in trusses of 25. It blooms in late May.

***Rhododendron* 'Girard White Clouds'** (*R.* 'White Swan' × *R.* 'Persil')
5 ft (1.5 m); Zone 5

This deciduous azalea has white flowers that open in early to mid May.

***Rhododendron* 'Girard Yellow Pom Pom'** {*R.* 'White Swan' × [*R.* 'Klondyke' × (*R.* 'Homebush' × *R.* '1129')]}
5 ft (1.5 m); Zone 5

This deciduous azalea of complex parentage has light green leaves and bright lemon-yellow, fragrant, long-lasting flowers in perfectly round trusses 5 in (13 cm) wide. The plant is of compact growth.

***Rhododendron* 'Golden Oriole'** (Knap Hill hybrid) 6 ft (1.8 m); Zone 5

This deciduous azalea produces 3.5-in (9-cm) wide golden-yellow flowers with an orange blotch, opening in late April (Plate 23). It was hybridized by Knap Hill Nursery, Woking, England.

Rhododendron 'Great Eastern' (parentage unknown) 5 ft (1.5 m); Zone 5

This elepidote rhododendron is another beautiful product of C. O. Dexter's hybridizing work. It is almost certain that the plant's mysterious background includes *Rhododendron fortunei*, as suggested by the large leaves with pink petioles. The fragrant pink flowers, 3.5 in (9 cm) in diameter, have six slightly crinkled pink lobes, darker toward the edges, and a harmonizing yellow blotch in the throat which gives them a golden-pink glow; they open in late May. The plant is often rated bud hardy to −5°F (−21°C), but the two specimens in my garden have flowered well after almost every one of the dozen winters they have grown here.

Rhododendron 'Gumpo Pink' (of Japanese origin) 1 ft (0.3 cm); Zone 7

This low-growing evergreen azalea spreads in time to a low mat 3–5 ft (0.9–1.5 m) wide. The 2.5-in (6.4-cm) wide flowers are soft pink, somewhat darker toward the margins, and open from mid June to August. The plant makes an attractive ground cover for a sunny, protected spot. The origin of the gumpo azaleas is hidden behind generations of Far Eastern azalea culture. They are sometimes called the Satsuki clones, after the Japanese Satsuki Society; the famous plant hunter E. H. Wilson considered them as selected clones of *Rhododendron simsii* var. *eriocarpum*. My plant is in a protected position, but some years it suffers damage to its foliage because it is exposed to too much midday winter sun. Since it flowers so late, the buds usually escape serious harm.

Rhododendron 'Guy Yerkes' (*R. kaempferi* × *R.* 'Snow') 3 ft (0.9 m); Zone 6

This is an evergreen azalea of average height and a somewhat spreading habit, with 2-in (5-cm) wide hose-in-hose salmon-pink flowers that have dark pink spots in the throat; they open in late April. The shrub is a product of the Ornamental Plants Section of the Plant Industry Station, U.S. Department of Agriculture, Beltsville, Maryland. It was named for Guy E. Yerkes, who initiated an extensive hybridizing program at the station.

Rhododendron 'Henry R. Yates' (*R. wardii* ssp. *wardii* [Litiense group] × unknown) 4 ft (1.2 m); Zone 6

This elepidote rhododendron has 4-in (10-cm) long dark green leaves and 2.5-in (6.4-cm) wide ivory white flowers with a bold flare, up to 11 per truss, which open in late April. The low, spreading plant was introduced by Joseph B. Gable, Stewartstown, Pennsylvania, in 1971.

Rhododendron 'Herbert' (*R. poukhanense* × *R.* 'Hex') 4 ft (1.2 m); Zone 6

This evergreen azalea of broad habit grows up to 5 ft (1.5 m) wide; in early May it bears 1.5-in (4-cm) wide purple hose-in-hose flowers with a dark purple blotch and frilled margins. My plant grows at the edge of the wood where it presents a striking sight against the darkened background. It is a hybrid of Joseph B. Gable, Stewartstown, Pennsylvania.

Rhododendron 'Hershey Red' (*R.* 'Kurume' hybrid) 3 ft (0.9 m); Zone 6

This evergreen azalea of low growth produces very bright, rose-red hose-in-hose flowers that stand out attractively in the green landscape.

Rhododendron 'Hino-Crimson' (*R. obtusum* 'Amoenum' × *R.* 'Hinode Giri') 3 ft (0.9 m); Zone 6

This evergreen azalea is covered with 1.5-in (4-cm) wide bright red flowers in late April or early May. The 2-in (5-cm) long leaves turn reddish bronze in cold weather.

***Rhododendron* 'Hinode Giri'** (*R.* 'Kurume' hybrid) 2.5 ft (0.8 m); Zone 6

This evergreen azalea of low, spreading growth has 2-in (5-cm) long leaves and many single, 1.5-in (4-cm) wide crimson-red flowers that clothe the plant completely in late April. It is one of the most frequently planted red azaleas in the world. Although there is evidence that it was known in North America in the late 1800s, it was among the original "Wilson Fifty" azaleas brought in 1919 from Japan to Harvard University's Arnold Arboretum by E. H. Wilson, who was then the arboretum's president. The other 49 varieties are seldom available in the trade, but a complete collection of these Kurumes is still maintained at the Royal Horticultural Society's Garden at Wisley, England. Another complete set has been maintained in the garden of Thomas Wheeldon, Richmond, Virginia.

Rhododendron hippophaeoides 3 ft (0.9 m); Zone 4

This lepidote rhododendron comes from high elevations in the subtropical Yunnan Province of China. The plant is of thin, twiggy growth and is clad with gray-green 1-in (2.5-cm) long leaves. The blue-purple flowers (the shade of blue varies from plant to plant), only 0.5 in (13 mm) wide, unfold in late April into diminutive 1.5-in (4-cm) wide trusses of four to eight blooms. It is said to be one of very few rhododendrons that tolerate wet ground. One of my little plants grows near the pond where the soil is waterlogged most of the year. It has survived several winters in that location. The other specimen grows in a drier situation. The species is rated 4/2.

***Rhododendron* 'Hockessin'** (*R. pubescens* × *R. keiskei*) 3 ft (0.9 m); Zone 4

This lepidote rhododendron has 2-in (5-cm) long gray-green leaves and 1-in (2.5-cm) wide apricot flowers fading to white. It blooms in mid April. It is a hybrid of Guy Nearing, Ramsey, New Jersey, and is almost identical to his *Rhododendron* 'Chesapeake', except that it is somewhat larger. The plant bears the rating of 3/2.

***Rhododendron* 'Homebush'** (Knap Hill hybrid) 5 ft (1.5 m); Zone 5

This deciduous azalea has 4-in (10-cm) long light green leaves; in late May it produces vibrant carmine-red, semi-double, 2.5-in (6.4-cm) wide flowers in perfectly round trusses 5 in (13 cm) in diameter, with up to 16 blossoms per truss. It was introduced in 1925 by Knap Hill Nursery, Woking, England.

***Rhododendron* 'Hong Kong'** (*R.* 'Catalgla' × *R.* 'Crest') 5 ft (1.5 m); Zone 5

This elepidote rhododendron with 6-in (15-cm) long glossy leaves and light yellow flowers in late May was the yellowest elepidote hybrid of David G. Leach, North Madison, Ohio, until the introduction of his *Rhododendron* 'Canary Islands'. *Rhododendron* 'Hong Kong' is rated 4/4.

***Rhododendron* 'Hudson Bay'** (*R. carolinianum* var. *album* × *R. dauricum* var. *album*) 4 ft (1.2 m); Zone 5

This lepidote rhododendron has 1.5-in (4-cm) long firm, leathery leaves held for 2 years. In early April, it produces 1.5-in (4-cm) wide clear white flowers with wavy lobes in small but abundant clusters. It was raised by David G. Leach, North Madison, Ohio, in 1968 and introduced in 1974.

***Rhododendron* 'Ice Cube'** (*R.* 'Catalgla' × *R.* 'Belle Heller') 5 ft (1.5 m); Zone 5

This elepidote rhododendron with 6-in (15-cm) long olive-green leaves has 2.5-in (6.4-cm) wide funnel-shaped ivory white flowers with a lemon-yellow blotch. It blooms in late May. It was introduced by A. M. Shammarello, South Euclid, Ohio, in 1973, and is rated 4/3.

***Rhododendron* 'Ignatius Sargent'** (*R. catawbiense* hybrid) 5 ft (1.5 m); Zone 4

This elepidote rhododendron with 6-in (15-cm) long leaves has large, slightly fragrant deep rose flowers in late May. It was introduced in the late 19th century by Anthony Waterer, Knap Hill Nursery, Woking, England.

***Rhododendron* 'Ilam Red Letter'** (parentage unknown) 5 ft (1.5 m); Zone 5

This plant is a member of a grex of deciduous azaleas with large orange-red and red flowers, similar to the Knap Hills and the Exburys. It blooms in early May. The hybrid was developed by Edgar Stead of New Zealand from plants received from Lionel de Rothschild of the Exbury Estate, Southampton, England. The Ilam strain was produced during the 1930s and 1940s. Ten years later it began appearing in North American gardens, yet even today it remains relatively unknown.

***Rhododendron* 'Illusion'** (*R. indicum* × *R.* 'Momozono') 4 ft (1.2 m); Zone 6

This evergreen azalea has dark, glossy 2-in (5-cm) long leaves and 2.5-in (6.4-cm) wide rose-pink flowers with a darker blotch, in groups of two to three blooms, opening in early to mid April. It is normally a dense bush of average height and spread, but I trained my plant into a small tree, now about 6 ft (1.8 m) high, with a thin crown and a slender, slightly twisted trunk. The hybrid was produced by the U.S. Department of Agriculture, Glenn Dale, Maryland.

Rhododendron impeditum 1 ft (0.3 m); Zone 5

This lepidote rhododendron has 0.5-in (13-mm) long blue-green leaves with scales above and below and 1-in (2.5-cm) wide lavender-pink to purplish blue flowers opening in late April. In the wild, the plant carpets open slopes and pastures up to 15,000 ft (4500 m) in its native Yunnan Province, China. My two specimens are planted on a shady slope of the rock garden where they will probably never bloom so prolifically nor grow so dense as they would with a sunny or at least a more open exposure. The species is rated 4/4.

***Rhododendron indicum* 'Balsaminiflora'** 2 ft (0.6 m); Zone 6

This evergreen azalea has 1.5-in (4-cm) long leaves and beautifully shaped 2-in (5-cm) wide double flowers of vivid orange-pink, resembling miniature roses, and containing as many as 40 petals (Plate 42). The flowers open in mid May to mid June and have no pistils or stamens. The plant is a clone of *Rhododendron indicum,* which was known in Holland as early as 1680 when it was brought from the Far East via Java and India, probably by the sailors of the Dutch East India Company. It is rated 5/5.

PLATE 42. The ancient and beautiful Far East cultivar, *Rhododendron indicum* 'Balsaminiflora', in early June.

Rhododendron 'Janet Blair' (parentage unknown) 6 ft (1.8 m); Zone 5

This elepidote rhododendron with 5.5-in (14-cm) long rich green leaves produces beautiful 3-in (8-cm) wide frilled, fragrant pinkish mauve flowers with a golden-brown dorsal blotch, in trusses of nine, opening in early May (Plate 44). It is bud hardy to −15°F (−26°C) and is rated 4/4. Another plant from C. O. Dexter's hybridizing program, it was previously known by its synonym, *Rhododendron* 'John Wister'. It was introduced by David G. Leach, North Madison, Ohio, in 1962.

Rhododendron japonicum 3 ft (0.9 m); Zone 5

Until recently, this elepidote rhododendron was called *Rhododendron metternichii*. It has 3-in (8-cm) long dark green, leathery leaves that are smooth and shiny above and covered with light beige plastered indumentum beneath. The 1.5-in (4-cm) wide funnel-shaped, light rose flowers open in mid May in trusses of up to 15. The species is native to many of the islands of Japan. The three plants in my garden are the Oki-Islands form, from a group of islands in the eastern part of the Sea of Japan. The species is rated 4/4.

Rhododendron keiskei 1–5 ft (0.3–1.5 m); Zone 6

This lepidote rhododendron has thin, light green leaves up to 3 in (8 cm) long and yellow, broadly bell-shaped flowers, 2 in (5 cm) in diameter, up to six in a loose cluster (Plate 43). The species is native to the central islands of Japan. Three distinct forms of *Rhododendron keiskei* grow in my garden, differing only in size and hardiness. The tallest is now over 3 ft (90 cm) in height; its flowers are damaged occasionally by late frosts or can be injured when exposed to direct winter sun. Next is a form that does not exceed 1.5–2 ft (50–60 cm) in height and is probably hardy to −10°F

PLATE 43. The loose lemon-yellow trusses of *Rhododendron keiskei*, the only yellow Rhododendron species at least marginally hardy in southern New England.

(−23°C). The third and smallest will probably always remain lower than 10 in (25 cm); it is denser and also hardier than the other forms. *Rhododendron keiskei* is the only yellow-flowered evergreen species that will survive and perform reasonably well in my climate. All three forms bloom in late April to early May. The species is rated 4/3.

Rhododendron keleticum 1 ft (0.3 m); Zone 5

This lepidote rhododendron has tiny aromatic leaves, 0.5 in (13 mm) long, shiny above, silvery and densely scaly below. The flowers, which open in early June, are bright purple, over 1 in (2.5 cm) wide, and seem large for the minute shrub. *Rhododendron keleticum* comes from Tibet (Xizang), Yunnan, and the upper parts of Myanmar (previously Burma), growing in open sites with scree soil conditions. One of the two plants in my rock garden is over 1 ft (30 cm), and the other less than 5 in (13 cm) tall. Both are thinner than the dense, matted form David G. Leach describes in his *Rhododendrons of the World* (1961, 182). They are, nevertheless, well suited for their small environment. The species is rated 4/4.

***Rhododendron* 'Kettledrum'** (*R. catawbiense* × unknown) 5 ft (1.5 m); Zone 4

This elepidote rhododendron has 5-in (13-cm) long leaves and 2.5-in (6.4-cm) wide purplish crimson flowers that open in late May. The plant is an old hybrid seldom seen today in gardens and catalogues. As one of the hardiest elepidotes available, it is used occasionally by hybridizers to pass its hardiness on to its offspring. In the memory of old growers, this rhododendron stands out as one of the few that survived the very harsh northeastern winters of the 1930s unscathed. It was introduced by Anthony Waterer, Knap Hill Nursery, Woking, England, in 1877.

Rhododendron kiusianum 2 ft (0.6 m); Zone 6

This evergreen azalea from Japan has 1-in (2.5-cm) long leaves and 1.5-in (4-cm) wide flowers that vary from pure white on some forms to rose and shades of crimson on others. It blooms from early to late May. The plant grows slowly, always remaining a dwarf. One of the two plants in my rock garden is light rose, and the other is white. Since they grow in full shade, they tend to be of thin growth, but they still bloom relatively well. The species is rated 5/5.

***Rhododendron* 'Klondyke'** (Exbury hybrid) 6 ft (1.8 m); Zone 5

This deciduous azalea has bright orange-yellow flowers with a darker blotch (Plate 41). The plant blooms in late May and is a product of the Exbury Estate, Southampton, England.

***Rhododendron* 'Knap Hill Red'** (Knap Hill hybrid) 6 ft (1.8 m); Zone 5

This deciduous azalea has deep red, very vivid, long-lasting flowers. The bush towers over surrounding shrubbery and its bright blooms are visible from a distance. My 12-year-old shrub is now at least 8 ft (2.4 m) tall and still growing. It is an introduction of Knap Hill Nursery, Woking, England.

***Rhododendron* 'La Bar's White'** (*R. catawbiense* white clone or natural hybrid) 5 ft (1.5 m); Zone 5

This elepidote rhododendron, with 5-in (13-cm) long leaves, has white flowers with a yellowish blotch in the throat. It blooms in late May. The plant was found in the wild and moved to the former La Bar's Rhododendron Nursery, Stroudsburg, Pennsylvania. It is one of several white *Rhododendron catawbiense* varieties that are used extensively in hybridizing. It is rated 3/3.

***Rhododendron* 'Ladifor'** (*R.* 'Lady Clementine Mitford' × *R. fortunei*)
5 ft (1.5 m); Zone 5

This elepidote rhododendron has 6-in (15-cm) long rich green leaves and 2.5-in (6.4-cm) wide light pink flowers that open in mid May. It is a vigorous hybrid of Joseph B. Gable, Stewartstown, Pennsylvania, who introduced it before 1958.

***Rhododendron* 'Lady Grey-Egerton'** (*R. catawbiense* × unknown)
5 ft (1.5 m); Zone 5

This elepidote rhododendron has 6-in (15-cm) long lush green leaves and silvery, pale lilac flowers growing in tight conical trusses. It blooms in late May. Produced before 1888, this hybrid of Anthony Waterer, Knap Hill Nursery, Woking, England, is rated 2/2.

***Rhododendron* 'Lady Robin'** (Robin Hill hybrid) 10 in (25 cm); Zone 6

This evergreen azalea has 1.5-in (4-cm) long dark green leaves and attractive flowers that sometimes are ivory-white flushed or striped with pink and red but at other times are pink streaked with white. Opening in late May, all the flowers are exquisite, ruffled at the edges, and very large for a shrublet only a few inches high (Plate 61). There are sometimes as many as a dozen of the beautiful blooms on one short branch, each flat blossom measuring 4 in (10 cm) in diameter. The plant is hardy and eventually covers an area 2–3 ft (60–90 cm) wide. It is another beautiful creation of Robert D. Gartrell's Robin Hill Nursery, Wyckoff, New Jersey. Using the Satsuki azalea hybrids as parents, Gartrell once observed that 'Lady Robin' plants might be somewhat genetically unstable, which may account for the variable color patterns in their blossoms.

***Rhododendron* 'Laetevirens'.** See *R.* 'Wilsonii'.

***Rhododendron* 'Lee's Dark Purple'** (*R. catawbiense* hybrid) 6 ft (1.8 m); Zone 5

This elepidote rhododendron has 4-in (10-cm) long dark green leaves and rich purple flowers that open in late May. The plant was introduced in England in the mid 1800s. It is rated 2/3.

***Rhododendron* 'Llenroc'** (*R. carolinianum* var. *album* × *R. mucronulatum* 'Cornell Pink')
3 ft (0.9 m); Zone 5

This lepidote rhododendron, whose name is *Cornell* spelled backwards, has 2-in (5-cm) long leaves and bright light pink flowers that open in early April. It was introduced by Edmund V. Mezitt, Weston Nurseries, Hopkinton, Massachusetts, and is rated 4/3.

***Rhododendron* 'Lodestar'** (*R. catawbiense* var. *album* × *R.* 'Belle Heller')
5 ft (1.5 m); Zone 5

This elepidote rhododendron with 5-in (13-cm) long leaves has 3-in (8-cm) wide flowers, usually white to pale lavender, with darker, greenish yellow dorsal blotch, up to 15 per truss. The bush blooms in late May and grows wider than tall. It was introduced by David G. Leach, North Madison, Ohio, in 1965, and is rated 3/3.

Rhododendron luteum 4 ft (1.2 m); Zone 5

This deciduous azalea is native to eastern Europe from the Baltic Sea in the north to the Caucasus Mountains in the south. The leaves are 5 in (13 cm) long, and the flowers, opening from early May to mid June, are up to 2 in (5 cm) wide, bright yellow, and very fragrant, and grow as many as 12 per truss. The species is rarely successful on the East Coast, possibly because of the hot and humid summers. It is subject to stem borer to a greater extent than other species. The small plant in my garden has survived several winters and summers in a shady position with good air circulation and a heavy winter mulch. The species is too beautiful not to try to accommodate it, even if the attempt should ultimately fail. It is rated 3/3.

Rhododendron makinoi 3 ft (0.9 m); Zone 6

This elepidote rhododendron is native to Japan. Its most outstanding feature is its foliage, which gives the plant an interesting and exotic appearance. The leaves are 7 in (18 cm) long and less than 1 in (2.5 cm) wide, with margins rolled downward. The entire leaf curves gently down the entire central vein. A well-grown bushy plant can make an attractive contribution to a landscape. The foliage is shiny above and heavily indumented beneath with a thick grayish felt. The new shoots, which appear very late in the growing season, sometimes in late July or August, are completely covered with indumentum. The flowers, which come in late May and early June, are blush-white to clear-pink, in trusses of as many as 20. *Rhododendron makinoi* was recently reclassified. No longer a separate species, it is now considered a subspecies of *R. yakushimanum*. The plant will thus be described as *R. yakushimanum* ssp. *makinoi*. It is rated 3/3.

***Rhododendron* 'Mars'** (*R. griffithianum* × unknown) 4 ft (1.2 m); Zone 6

This elepidote rhododendron has light green leaves up to 6 in (15 cm) long and 3-in (8-cm) wide true-red flowers. The blossoms, which open in late May, are bell-shaped, with white stamens that contrast well with the red petals. The plant prefers some noon and afternoon shade. The hybrid was probably produced in the 19th century by Anthony Waterer, Knap Hill Nursery, Woking, England, but it could also be a 1928 introduction by an unknown English hybridizer.

***Rhododendron* 'Mary Belle'** (*R.* 'Atrier' × *R.* 'Dechaem') 5 ft (1.5 m); Zone 5

This elepidote rhododendron has 5.5-in (14-cm) long light-green leaves and 4-in (10-cm) wide flowers in colors varying from bright salmon-pink to buff-yellow and apricot. It blooms in late May. It is floriferous and hardy but, in an occasional winter, a portion of the buds freeze. Nevertheless, there are usually enough of them undamaged to put on a good display. This beautiful plant was introduced in 1964 by Joseph B. Gable, Stewartstown, Pennsylvania. It is rated 4/4.

***Rhododendron* 'Mary Fleming'** (*R. racemosum* × *R. keiskei*) 3 ft (0.9 m); Zone 4

This lepidote rhododendron has attractive 1.5-in (4-cm) long leaves that turn bronze in cold weather and small, abundant flowers, usually white or beigy yellow, with streaks of salmon. The bush blooms in late April. It was introduced by Guy G. Nearing, Ramsey, New Jersey, in 1972 and is rated 4/3.

***Rhododendron* 'Mary Kittle'** (unknown dwarf white × *R.* 'Mrs. P. Ouden')
3 ft (0.9 m); Zone 6

This elepidote rhododendron has 5-in (13-cm) long leaves and plentiful pink flowers that open in mid May. The plant is compact and rounded. It was introduced by Edmund V. Mezitt, Hopkinton, Massachusetts, in 1963.

***Rhododendron* 'Maxhaem Salmon'** (*R. maximum* × *R. haematodes*)
5 ft (1.5 m); Zone 5

This elepidote rhododendron has 5-in (13-cm) long leaves and 2-in (5-cm) wide five-lobed, light salmon-pink flowers that are darker at the margins and have a small golden blotch. The plant blooms in late May. It is a 1935 hybrid of Joseph B. Gable, Stewartstown, Pennsylvania, and was described and registered in 1991 by the Gable Study Group, Vienna, Virginia. The plant is rated 3/3.

Rhododendron maximum 5 ft (1.5 m); Zone 4
Rosebay; Great Laurel

This North American elepidote rhododendron is native from southwestern Maine to Ontario, south to Ohio and New York, and along the Appalachians to Georgia and Alabama. The glossy, dark green, leathery leaves can be as long as 10 in (25 cm), and the modest whitish flowers, which form small trusses of up to 20 blooms, open in the last days of June and continue until mid to late July. In nature, especially in the southern part of its range, the shrub may grow more than 30 ft (9 m) high, but in cultivation and in northern locations it reaches only half that height in many years. One of the *Rhododendron maximum* plants in my garden began a dozen years ago as a tiny seedling in a swampy part of the wood where the dustlike seed must have been blown by the wind or dropped off the feathers of a bird. I moved the little plant to a drier location, and today it is 8 ft (2.4 m) in each direction. The species is rated 3/3.

***Rhododendron* 'Maximum Roseum'** (*R. ponticum* × *R. maximum*)
6 ft (1.8 m); Zone 5

This elepidote rhododendron has 6-in (15-cm) long dark green narrow leaves. The 2.5-in (6.4-cm) wide lilac flowers with darker margins are beautifully complemented by 10 deep purple stamens and a blotch of pure gold; they begin to open in mid to late June. The plant eventually grows quite tall and wide; it provides a rather attractive screen in my rhododendron planting along the street (Plate 19). Known also by its synonym *Rhododendron* 'Ponticum Roseum', its origins are unknown, but it is propagated and distributed by the Orlando S. Pride Nursery, Butler, Pennsylvania.

***Rhododendron* 'Melford Lemon'** 5 ft (1.5 m); Zone 5

This deciduous azalea has 3-in (8-cm) long light green leaves and bright yellow flowers with an apricot blotch. The blossoms open in late May.

Rhododendron metternichii. See ***Rhododendron japonicum.***

***Rhododendron* 'Midsummer'** (*R. maximum* × unknown) 6 ft (1.8 m); Zone 5

This elepidote rhododendron with 5-in (13-cm) long leaves has 2.5-in (6.4-cm) wide bright rose-pink flowers, darker at the edges, with a pronounced golden-yellow blotch and clear purple stamens. The blossoms are doubly welcome since they do not open until mid to late June when most other rhododendrons have completed their flowering. This tall grower was produced by John Waterer, Bagshot, England.

Rhododendron minus 4 ft (1.2 m); Zone 5
Piedmont Rhododendron; Small Rhododendron

This North American lepidote rhododendron is native to the piedmont and the lower mountain elevations from North Carolina and Tennessee to Georgia and Alabama. It was mistakenly named by early botanists to imply small stature, yet it is the largest of all North American rhododendrons, occasionally reaching well over 30 ft (9 m) in its native habitat. In cultivation, it attains 10 ft (3 m) in height if grown in favorable locations. The leaves are 2–4 in (5–10 cm) long, elliptic, pointed at both ends, leathery, with small brownish scales beneath. The flowers are white to deep rose, bell-shaped, and 1.5 in (4 cm) wide. Three to seven blooms are produced from each bud, and they open from early May to mid June. There is a considerable variation in size among the forms of *Rhododendron minus,* which may explain the early naming error. One of the plants in my garden is a tall-growing bush with light green leaves, while the others are dwarfs with dark green foliage that have grown to less than 12 in (30 cm) since they arrived 7 years ago from Bill Dodd's Nursery, Semmes, Alabama. Both types grow well in considerable shade. The species is rated 2/2.

Rhododendron molle 4 ft (1.2 m); Zone 5

This deciduous azalea is native to China and Japan. Until recently, the plants of Japanese origin were classified as a separate species called *Rhododendron japonicum* (a name that has now been assigned to the former *R. metternichii*). The Chinese plants, also previously considered a separate species, were called *R. mollis*. The two forms are almost identical except that the Japanese plants tend to be hardier. *Rhododendron molle* has 4-in (10-cm) long leaves that unfold only after the blossoms have been open for some time. The funnel-formed 3-in (8-cm) wide flowers, in colors varying from yellow to orange and brick-red, open in early May.

The plant in my garden grew and bloomed for 2 or 3 years until one spring it failed to produce blossoms as well as new growth. This occurred after a winter in which I had applied the "Dexter formula" fertilizer to my deciduous azaleas. It appears, but there is no real evidence, that the plant's decline may have been due to the fertilization, which is thought to be sometimes harmful to rhododendron species but may be harmless and at times beneficial to rhododendron hybrids. The plant's demise may have been also caused by a difficult winter. Further, it is possible that the plant was not the "Japanese azalea" it was purported to be by the nursery and, instead, was the more tender Chinese strain. Nevertheless, I have since refrained from applying fertilizer to species rhododendrons. The plant is rated 3/3.

***Rhododendron* 'Mrs. Charles E. Pearson'** (*R.* 'Coombe Royal' × *R.* 'Catawbiense Grandiflorum') 6 ft (1.8 m); Zone 6

This elepidote rhododendron has large foliage and light pink flowers with a purple-brown blotch. It blooms in mid May. There are several rhododendrons in my garden with a hardiness rating of −5°F (−21°C) which, though occasionally damaged, manage to survive many of Connecticut's winters generally in good condition. *Rhododendron* 'Mrs. Charles E. Pearson' is not one of them. I planted this hybrid about 16 years ago; it flowered the first 2 years and never again. Its flower buds as well as many of its vegetative buds usually freeze. The plant should be discarded, but I keep hoping that some friend from the shores of Long Island Sound will take it and give it a climate that is just a touch warmer. The plant is the product of the M. Koster & Zonen Nursery, Boskoop, Holland. It is rated 4/4.

***Rhododendron* 'Mrs. Furnival'** (*R. griffithianum* hybrid × *R. caucasicum* hybrid) 4 ft (1.2 m); Zone 5

This elepidote rhododendron has 4.5-in (11-cm) long dark green leaves and 3-in (8-cm) wide soft pink funnel-shaped flowers with a vivid red blotch, in tightly packed trusses, opening in mid May (Plate 44). A well-grown plant of *Rhododendron* 'Mrs. Furnival' can be a spectacular sight. Even though in my garden it is damaged in an

PLATES 44 . *Rhododendron* 'Mrs. Furnival' in late June, with its magnificent dark blotches. To the left, the pinkish blooms of *R.* 'Janet Blair .

PLATE 45. *Rhododendron* 'Mrs. Tom H. Lowinsky' in early July, together with *R.* 'Mrs. Furnival', perhaps the most decorative additions to a garden.

occasional winter, I consider it a very desirable plant. It was introduced in 1920 by Anthony Waterer, Knap Hill Nursery, Woking, England, and is rated 5/3.

***Rhododendron* 'Mrs. Tom H. Lowinsky'** (probably a combination of *R. catawbiense, R. maximum,* and *R. ponticum*) 5 ft (1.5 m); Zone 5

This elepidote rhododendron with 4.5-in (11-cm) long dark green leaves has 3-in (8-cm) wide white funnel-shaped flowers with a dramatic dark orange-brown blotch, in trusses of 14 (Plate 45). This old, very attractive English hybrid is possibly somewhat less hardy than the −15°F (−26°C) rating indicated by some sources. In my garden it is injured in one of five or six winters, but it is more than worth growing; it blooms late, opening its blossoms toward the end of June. It was produced by Messrs. Lowinsky and Waterer, Knap Hill Nursery, Woking, England, in 1919 and carries the rating 4/3. There is another hybrid with a similar name (*Rhododendron* 'Mrs. T. H. Lowinsky') that has a different parentage and is probably not readily available.

Rhododendron mucronulatum 5 ft (1.5 m); Zone 5

Though sometimes called the Korean azalea, this is a deciduous lepidote rhododendron with thin 3.5-in (9-cm) long leaves scaly on both surfaces, and widely funnel-shaped 1.5-in (4-cm) wide flowers in a color that varies from bright mauve on most bushes to clear pink on the rarer forms. The plant is native to the northeastern part of the Asian landmass and the northern islands of Japan. Its flowers open very early, sometimes too early in warmer climates, exposing themselves to late winter frosts. In my garden, they wait until early April when the chances of extremely low temperatures have somewhat diminished. However, even then there are years when the early buds get nipped; still, there are usually enough of the tardy buds that some blooms appear every year. I planted three distinct forms of *Rhododendron mucronulatum*: the oldest and tallest is the common mauve-colored version; then there are a few plants with pink flowers; and the latest acquisition is a Korean dwarf, which hugs a large stone on the small northern slope of the rock garden, a site that becomes cold and windswept on frigid winter days and nights. The species is rated 3/3.

***Rhododendron* 'Myrtifolium'** (*R. minus* × *R. hirsutum*) 3 ft (0.9 m); Zone 5

This lepidote rhododendron has attractive 2-in (5-cm) long, dark green leaves that turn bronze in winter. The flower is a narrow tube that spreads into a 1-in (2.5-cm) wide corolla of pretty lilac-pink, opening in my garden the second week of June. This old hybrid was exhibited as early as 1917. It is rated 3/5. There is also a species with the name *Rhododendron myrtifolium* that is native to the Balkan mountains but which I do not grow.

***Rhododendron* 'Nancy of Robinhill'** (*R.* 'Vervaeneana' × *R.* 'Lady Louise')
1 ft (0.3 m); Zone 6

This evergreen azalea has 1-in (2.5-cm) long leaves and 2-in (5-cm) wide clear pink flowers with a darker rose-colored blotch. It blooms in late May. Robert D. Gartrell, Wyckoff, New Jersey, considered this hybrid to be his finest. In informal comments titled *Notes to the New Hybridizer—My Experiences in Developing the Robin Hill Azaleas* (1977, 3), he wrote with enthusiasm about the parentage and background of the plant:

> The cross was made with 'Vervaeneana' (a tender Ghent hybrid much used as a 'florist' azalea) as the seed parent, and 'Lady Louise' ('Louise Gable' × 'Tama Giku') as the pollen plant. All seed came from a single capsule. Twenty seedlings were grown on. 'Nancy' appeared as a surprise—none of the other seedlings of this cross had any similarity to 'Nancy'. 'Nancy' had the virtue of being equal to the tender Ghent in appearance, but most important, it is hardy to at least −10 degrees—the genes for hardiness coming from 'Lady Louise'.

Though the name of his private nursery (Robin Hill) was properly spelled as two words, Gartrell was obliged to make one word of it when naming this plant to comply with the botanical nomenclature rule limiting the names of newly registered hybrids to three words.

***Rhododendron* 'Nile'** (*R. catawbiense* var. *album* × *R. wardii*) 6 ft (1.8 m); Zone 5

This elepidote rhododendron has large, shiny green leaves and pale yellow flowers with a bright red spot in the throat of the calyx. It blooms in mid May. It was hybridized by David G. Leach, North Madison, Ohio, and introduced in 1973. It carries a rating of 3/3.

***Rhododendron* 'Normandy'** (*R.* 'Newburyport Beauty' × *R.* 'Newburyport Belle') 3 ft (0.9 m); Zone 5

This elepidote rhododendron has dark green leaves and bright pink flowers that are darker at the margins. It blooms in late May. The growth habit is broad and rounded. A hybrid of David G. Leach, North Madison, Ohio, it was introduced in 1968, and is rated 4/4.

***Rhododendron* 'Nova Zembla'** (*R.* 'Parson's Grandiflorum' × hardy red hybrid) 5 ft (1.5 m); Zone 4

This elepidote rhododendron has dark green leaves with somewhat wavy margins and 2.5-in (6.4-cm) wide vivid red flowers that open in early May (Plates 8, 41, 71). It was named after a Russian island in the Arctic Sea, presumably a reference to the hybrid's considerable hardiness. The plant is of a somewhat spreading habit and should be shaped when young by removing the lead vegetative buds on all branches; otherwise it will grow into a thin, sprawling shrub that must be often supported by stakes. This is one of my "back-up" rhododendrons. I have scattered nearly a dozen *Rhododendron* 'Nova Zembla' plants throughout my garden to form the backbone of new plantings should we be stricken with a ruinously cold winter. This cultivar was introduced by M. Koster & Zonen Nursery, Boskoop, Holland, in 1902, and is rated 3/3.

***Rhododendron obtusum* 'Amoenum'** 4 ft (1.2 m); Zone 6

This evergreen azalea has small dark green leaves changing to an attractive reddish brown shade in the autumn. The 1.5-in (4-cm) wide hose-in-hose flowers are rich magenta and open in early May (Plate 17). This is a vigorous cultivar; some of the plants in my garden have reached a height of 10 ft (3 m) in 15 years. Yet, they can be easily clipped to a tight hedge, which at blooming time becomes a solid cushion of hot purple-red. Once popular, this color has gone out of favor in recent decades, but, fortunately, nature pays no heed to fashion; the bushes look very lovely when they are clad in that exotic hue. The plant is rated 4/3.

***Rhododendron* 'Olga Mezitt'** (*R. minus* var. *minus* × *R. minus* var. *minus*)
3 ft (0.9 m); Zone 4

This lepidote rhododendron has 2-in (5-cm) long shiny leaves that turn dark bronze in winter. The 1.5-in (4-cm) wide bright pink flowers, in small tight trusses of up to 12 blossoms, open in late April. The plant is attractive and compact, well suited for a garden or site of limited dimensions. It was registered by Edmund V. Mezitt, Weston Nurseries, Hopkington, Massachusetts, in 1983, and is rated 4/3.

Rhododendron ovatum 3 ft (0.9 m); Zone 7

This elepidote rhododendron is something of an oddity in the genus: the leaves have no scales, but they have the general appearance and small size of lepidote leaves; and the flowers do not have the 10 or more stamens common among the elepidotes, but instead have only 5 stamens, as do azaleas. The plant comes from China and is rated for temperatures of 5°F (−15°C). Nevertheless, I have grown two small specimens in my nursery for more than 5 years and they are still in good condition. They are, however, in the lee of a stone wall that shelters them from sun and wind in winter and summer. Neither plant has flowered as yet; I will move one of them outside the nursery in a year or two to test its hardiness in the open. The flowers of *Rhododendron ovatum* are white to pink, 1 in (2.5 cm) in diameter, opening in late May. The new foliage is colorful when it first unfolds, ranging from bronze to reddish-brown. In the wild, the plant is said to reach 15 ft (4.6 m) in height, but in cultivation 6 ft (1.8 m) is presumed to be its limit. The species is rated 3/3.

***Rhododendron* 'Palestrina'.** See ***R.* 'Wilhelmina Vuyk'.**

***Rhododendron* 'Parker's Pink'** (parentage unknown) 5 ft (1.5 m); Zone 5

This elepidote rhododendron has 6.5-in (16-cm) long leaves of attractive form and color and 3.5-in (9-cm) wide fragrant flowers of dark pink fading to white at the margins, heavily spotted with red, up to 12 per truss, opening in early May. The bush is floriferous and grows broader than tall. It was introduced in 1973 by P. Vossberg, Westbury, New York, but it is a C. O. Dexter-related hybrid raised by Parker, who used also the synonym, 'Parker's No. 1', for the plant. It is rated 2/3.

***Rhododendron* 'Party Pink'** (*R.* 'Mrs. Furnival' × *R. catawbiense* var. *album*)
5 ft (1.5 m); Zone 5

This elepidote rhododendron with 4.5-in (11-cm) long leaves bears 3-in (8-cm) wide lavender pink flowers with bronze spotting fading to a lighter shade toward the center. The flowers, which open in late May, grow in 6-in (15-cm) wide trusses with up to 18 blossoms each. The hybrid was introduced by David G. Leach, North Madison, Ohio, in 1973, and is rated 4/4.

***Rhododendron* 'Pat Erb'** 1 ft (0.3 m); Zone 6

This evergreen azalea has small leaves and 2-in (5-cm) wide double flowers that open in early June. The blossoms, which are clear soft pink, must have reminded the hybridizer, Robert D. Gartrell, Wyckoff, New Jersey, of his good friend when he named this plant. All Gartrell's Robin Hill azaleas in my garden are unusual in different ways, and all are beautiful, although the flower buds on this hybrid are somewhat tender and are damaged in severe winters.

***Rhododendron* 'Percy Wiseman'** (*R. yakushimanum* × *R.* 'Fabia Tangerine' selfed)
3 ft (0.9 m); Zone 6

This elepidote rhododendron has firm 4-in (10-cm) long leaves and peach-yellow flowers that fade to cream. It blooms in early May. The plant is a hybrid of John Waterer, Bagshot, England, who introduced it in 1971. It is rated 4/4.

Rhododendron periclymenoides 5 ft (1.5 m); Zone 5
Pinxter; Pinxterbloom; Pink or Purple Azalea; Purple Honeysuckle

This North American deciduous azalea is native from Massachusetts and New York to Illinois and south to Georgia. The leaves are 3.5 in (9 cm) long, and the flowers are tubular, 1.5 in (4 cm) wide, in shades of white to light pink or light purple (Plate 26). The name *Pinxter* is from the Dutch word *Pinkster,* which means Whitsuntide, a time on the calendar when the earliest Connecticut immigrants (who came from Holland) saw the plant in bloom. The species was well represented on the property when my family and I came, and I have kept all the plants that were here, moving a few to new locations. Transplanting native azaleas may at times be risky, but the effort is usually successful if carried out as early in spring as the soil is workable (March is best), and if the plant is cut to the ground. There is no reason for saving a stem or two, or even a part of a stem, as it will eventually dry anyway; at best, the thin trunk of a shortened stem sends out a few meager shoots that are quickly overshadowed by the new growth from the base. After transplanting, the root mass should be kept moist and mulched. A few vigorous fresh green shoots will come up the same spring, and additional growth will appear the following spring. As a rule, the plant will blossom in 4 or 5 years from moving. Until about 20 years ago, the species was known as *Rhododendron nudiflorum*. It is rated 3/3.

***Rhododendron* 'Pink Cameo'** (red *R. catawbiense* hybrid × *R.* 'Boule de Neige')
5 ft (1.5 m); Zone 5

This elepidote rhododendron has firm, 4-in (10-cm) long leaves and 3-in (7-cm) wide delicate pink flowers with a dark pink blotch. It blooms in early May. The plant is a 1958 introduction of A. M. Shammarello, South Euclid, Ohio, and is rated 3/3.

***Rhododendron* 'Pink Pancake'** (*R.* 'Chinyeyi' × *R. nakaharae*) 6 in (15 cm); Zone 5

This prostrate evergreen azalea spreads to 2 ft (60 cm), hugging the ground as its thin branches creep along the contours of the soil. The 1.5-in (4-cm) wide wavy flowers are pink with a darker blotch and large for the size of the plant. They open in early to late July in my garden. This is the lowest growing but fastest spreading of Polly Hill's hybrids from her North Tisbury garden on Martha's Vineyard in Massachusetts. In winter I provide some protection for these attractive dwarfs in the form of a few branches from a Christmas tree or a hemlock. These branches shade the plant from the winter sun and, by catching the dry leaves that the wind blows into them, help moderate the freezing and thawing of the soil.

***Rhododendron* 'Pink Radiance'** 5 ft (1.5 m); Zone 6

This vigorous evergreen azalea has 2-in (5-cm) long leaves and 2.5-in (6.4-cm) wide radiant pink flowers. The narrow lighter stripes on the exterior sides of the petals capture and amplify the sunlight shining through them. This is another fine creation of the Long Island, New York, hybridizer, Louis A. Hindla. The plant was patented (#4535). It blooms in late April to early May.

***Rhododendron* 'Pink Twins'** (*R. catawbiense* × *R. haematodes*) 4 ft (1.2 m); Zone 5

This elepidote rhododendron with attractive 3.5-in (9-cm) long leaves of dark green color has pure pink hose-in-hose flowers, in trusses of 15 blossoms, which open in late May. The plant tends to grow low and wider than tall, which allows for a better display of the light pink flowers against the foliage. *Rhododendron* 'Pink Twins' is also known by its synonym, *R.* 'Cathaem No. 4'. It was hybridized in 1935 by Joseph B. Gable, Stewartstown, Pennsylvania, and described and registered in 1991 by Gable Study Group, Vienna, Virginia. It is rated 4/3. I planted two large specimens of this beautiful hybrid in my garden, but both succumbed to root rot, perhaps because they grew in low locations in very rich moist soil. I will grow the plant again but this time in a drier, more elevated site with less rich soil.

***Rhododendron* 'Pioneer'** (*R.* 'Conemaugh' × *R. mucronulatum*) 5 ft (1.5 m); Zone 4

This lepidote rhododendron with 2.5-in (6.4-cm) long semi-deciduous to deciduous leaves has abundant clear pink flowers, 1.5 in (4 cm) in diameter. It grows taller than wide, usually with several upright stems. This unregistered hybrid of Joseph B. Gable, Stewartstown, Pennsylvania, blooms in late March or early April. Also known as *Rhododendron* 'Gable's Pioneer', it is rated 4/3.

***Rhododendron* 'P.J.M.'** (*R. carolinianum* × *R. dauricum*) 4 ft (1.2 m); Zone 4

This lepidote rhododendron has 2-in (5-cm) long leaves that turn mahogany in the fall, a color they retain through the winter until early spring when they provide a complementary dark background for the brilliant lavender flowers (Plate 73). The hybrid is used extensively in North America and elsewhere. It is an unregistered hybrid of P. J. Mezitt, Weston Nurseries, Hopkinton, Massachusetts, raised before 1967. It is rated 4/4.

Rhododendron prinophyllum 5 ft (1.5 m); Zone 4

Roseshell Azalea; Rose Azalea; Early Azalea; Honeysuckle Azalea; Mountain Azalea

This North American deciduous azalea is native from New England to Indiana, and south to Missouri and Virginia. It will reach 5 ft (1.5 m) in 10 years, but its ultimate height may be well over 10 ft (3 m). The leaves are up to 2.5 in (6.4 cm) long, and the clove-scented, tubular, 1.5-in (4-cm) wide flowers are bright to deep pink or violet red. The blossoms appear in early May with the leaves. In the wild, the plant may have hybridized with other species; the least contaminated forms, mainly in the Virginia Blue Ridge Mountains, suggest that this is one of the more primitive species among North American deciduous azaleas. Prior to the 1970s, it was known as *Rhododendron roseum*. It is rated 3/2.

Rhododendron prunifolium 4 ft (1.2 m); Zone 5

Plumleaf Azalea; Red Azalea

This North American deciduous azalea is native to a narrow range of the coastal plain in southern Georgia and Alabama. Despite its southern origin, the plant is hardy in Connecticut, though the flower buds freeze in severe winters. The leaves are light green and up to 5 in (13 cm) long, and the 1.5-in (4-cm) wide tubular flowers are orange-red. The species is rated 4/3. The plant blooms late in the season, stretching the flowering time of the genus *Rhododendron* in my garden for a period of more than 4 months, from the first blooms of *R. mucronulatum* and *R. dauricum* in April to the last blossoms of *R. prunifolium* in late July to late August.

This species underscores the adaptability of the flora of eastern North America.

Many plants whose native range is 1000 miles (1600 km) south survive the New England climate despite prolonged periods of temperatures below 0°F (−18°C). Among them are not only some of our most beautiful azaleas, but also flowering trees such as *Franklinia alatamaha, Stewartia ovata* f. *grandiflora, Halesia monticola,* and *Chionanthus virginicus.* It could be reasoned that as the glaciers of the various ice ages advanced southward, they pushed the cold climate in front of them, and as they receded northward, they pulled the southern flora and silva behind them. Since such an event could have occurred more than once over the ages, the various genera adapted to the changing latitudes as they travelled up and down the Eastern seacoast. After the most recent glaciation 18,000 years ago, some species remained in the South and did not make yet another journey north. Nevertheless, their genes from past generations retained the hardiness, and the plants can survive and even flourish at our latitude.

Rhododendron pseudochrysanthum 1–3 ft (0.3–0.9 m); Zone 6

This elepidote rhododendron with 3-in (8-cm) long silver-indumented leaves produces 2-in (5-cm) wide bell-shaped blooms that begin as dark pink buds and in late April open into pale pink or white flowers with rose or crimson markings, in trusses of up to 20 blossoms. The plant is native to Taiwan at elevations of up to 13,000 ft (3900 m). It is a variable species occurring in several sizes. Its hardiness in our climate is questionable, despite the often quoted −10°F (−23°C) hardiness rating. I lost two plants of the species over the past several years. I hope that the third one will survive and flourish. The species is rated 3/5.

Rhododendron racemosum 2–5 ft (0.6–1.5 m); Zone 6

This lepidote rhododendron has small decorative leaves, 0.5–2 in (1.3–5 cm) long, that are dark green and smooth on top and silver beneath, with the scales clearly visible. The white to deep rose flowers are small, only about 1 in (2.5 cm) wide, but they almost completely cover the upper ends of the slender branches, creating the effect of flower racemes (from which the plant derives its name). The species is rated 4/3. My specimen did poorly the first 2 years in a location sometimes recommended for it, a moist spot with northern exposure. It has done considerably better in a drier, warmer woodsy position where it is protected from the north winds as well as from direct sun in winter.

***Rhododendron* 'Ramapo'** (*R. fastigiatum* × *R. carolinianum*) 2 ft (0.6 cm); Zone 5

This lepidote rhododendron has tiny 1-in (2.5-cm) long dusty blue leaves and small violet flowers. It was introduced in 1940 by Guy G. Nearing, Ramsey, New Jersey, and is rated 3/4.

Rhododendron recurvoides 2 ft (0.6 m); Zone 6

This elepidote rhododendron from the high mountains of Myanmar (formerly Burma) has 2.5-in (6.4-cm) long, thick, narrow leaves that are smooth and glossy above, with a white or tawny indumentum beneath. The 2.5-in (6.4-cm) wide whitish rose, bell-shaped flowers are in trusses of four to seven blossoms and open in late April to mid May. The species is a member of the Taliense series of rhododendrons, which includes plants with some of the most exceptional foliage in the genus; *Rhododendron recurvoides* is in the top rank and is rated 3/5. The plant in my garden has survived a winter which, though not particularly cold, was very injurious to many shrubs. Yet, the little specimen showed only minor signs of stress.

***Rhododendron* 'Red Head'** (*R.* 'Atrosanguineum' × *R. griersonianum*)
5 ft (1.5 m); Zone 6

This elepidote rhododendron with 4.5-in (11-cm) long dark green matte leaves bears 2-in (5-cm) wide flowers of strong red, opening in early May. The plant needs protection from the midday sun year round, as well as from the cold winds of winter, but even in an ideal location the leaves often winter-burn and the flower buds occasionally freeze. The plant, a relatively little known unregistered hybrid of Joseph B. Gable, Stewartstown, Pennsylvania, is probably better suited for more southerly climates. It is rated 3/3. There is another unregistered hybrid by the same name, produced by R. Henny. It, too, is generally unknown.

Rhododendron reticulatum 6 ft (1.8 m); Zone 6

This deciduous azalea comes from the mountains of the central islands of Japan. The reticulate leaves, which visibly display their raised veins, have a rhombic shape, a feature that was reflected in a name given to one of the plant's forms, once ranked as a separate species, *Rhododendron rhombicum.* The flowers, which open before the leaves in late April, are 1–2 in (2.5–5 cm) wide and purple with a few darker spots. The plant is rated 4/3.

***Rhododendron* 'Rocket'** (*R.* 'Cunningham's White' × red *R. catawbiense*)
5 ft (1.5 m); Zone 5

This elepidote rhododendron has 4-in (10-cm) long lush green leaves that appear to burst with vigor. The 2.5-in (6.4-cm) wide vivid pink flowers, with a scarlet blotch and ruffled edges, open in early May, creating a perfect background for the stamens that are almost white. The bush is aptly named as it seems eager to grow. A 1958 introduction of A. M. Shammarello, South Euclid, Ohio, it bears the rating of 3/5.

***Rhododendron* 'Rosebud'** (*R.* 'Louise Gable' × *R.* 'Caroline Gable')
3 ft (0.9 m); Zone 6

This evergreen azalea has 1.5-in (4-cm) long leaves and 1.5-in (4-cm) wide clear pink, double flowers in the shape of tiny roses. The shrub stays low for many years, blooming in mid June after most other azaleas have finished their blossoming period. It is a superior introduction of Joseph B. Gable, Stewartstown, Pennsylvania.

***Rhododendron* 'Roseum Elegans'** (*R. catawbiense* hybrid) 6 ft (1.8 m); Zone 4

This elepidote rhododendron has excellent 5-in (13-cm) long leaves and 2.5-in (6.4-cm) wide lavender-pink flowers in large trusses. Though most gardens contain at least one plant of this hybrid, it is not appreciated by rhododendron specialists because of its "ordinary" color. But, the plant is valued for its extraordinary vigor, beautiful growth habit, and pest and disease resistance. The quality rating of 2/3 does not do this hybrid justice; rather, it seems to reflect the fact that the plant has been around for a long time and has become very common. In my garden, this rhododendron is considered one of the unfailing ironclads; it has never disappointed me.

There are eight versions of *Rhododendron* 'Roseum Elegans' in the trade, all with the same parentage. I grow three forms: one with the classic rhododendron growth habit and foliage, and bluish lavender flowers; the second, of a somewhat lesser firmness and compactness, with pinker flowers; and the third, with flowers of rich purple, a lovely color by any standards. *Rhododendron* 'Roseum Elegans' was hybridized in the mid 1800s by Anthony Waterer, Woking, England.

***Rhododendron* 'Royalty'** 3 ft (0.9 m); Zone 6

This evergreen azalea with semi-deciduous dark green leaves has 1.5-in (4-cm) wide violet flowers with a red blotch. It blooms in late May. The bush has a low, spreading habit, and it appears to be hardier than the −5°F (−21°C) sometimes indicated. In severe winters it drops almost all its leaves, except for a few narrow leaflets at the tips of its branches. It was hybridized by Joseph B. Gable, Stewartstown, Pennsylvania, and introduced by a Mid-Atlantic nursery.

Rhododendron roxieanum* var. *oreonastes 3 ft (0.9 m); Zone 5

This elepidote rhododendron comes from the southeastern Himalayas. It has narrow, 3-in (8-cm) long heavy-textured leaves that are dark green and shiny above and with a thick rust-colored indumentum beneath. Rated 3/5, it is another Taliense series plant with excellent foliage. The flowers are campanulate, 1.5 in (4 cm) long and as wide, creamy white with a touch of rose. They open in late April. The species was discovered by the Scottish explorer George Forrest, who named it for the wife of a friend stationed in China, Mrs. Roxie Hanna. My little specimen of *Rhododendron roxieanum* var. *oreonastes* is the dwarf alpine form. Despite its indicated hardiness, it is severely damaged in difficult winters.

***Rhododendron* 'Scarlet Wonder'** (*R.* 'Essex Scarlet' × *R. forrestii* var. *repens*)
2 ft (0.6 m); Zone 5

This elepidote semi-dwarf rhododendron has oval 2-in (5-cm) long glossy leaves that display their prominent veins to advantage. The 2-in (5-cm) wide campanulate flowers, opening in early May, are brilliant scarlet red. The plant, a hybrid of Dietrich Hobbie of Germany, was introduced by LeFeber & Company in 1965 and is rated 4/5.

Rhododendron schlippenbachii 4 ft (1.2 m); Zone 4

This deciduous azalea comes from eastern Manchuria, eastern Siberia, and Korea, where it was discovered in 1854 by the Russian Navy officer Baron A. von Schlippenbach. The leaves are light green, broad, up to 5 in (13 cm) long, and in whorls of usually five at the ends of the branches. The fragrant flowers, which open between late March and late April, are single, up to 4 in (10 cm) in diameter, purplish white flushed with violet-red, with a brown-dotted throat, in trusses of three to six blossoms. Color varies from plant to plant; in the darker shades, the shrub is considered to be the most beautiful azalea of all. In my garden, the plants of this species are in woodsy locations where they have adequate light and are protected from the midday sun by tall trees. The species is rated 4/3.

***Rhododendron* 'Schneebukett'** (*R.* 'Mrs. J. G. Millais' × *R.* 'Bismarck')
5 ft (1.5 m); Zone 6

This elepidote rhododendron from Germany is still relatively new. It has large elliptic leaves and 3-in (8-cm) wide clear white flowers with a red blotch, in trusses of 18 to 26 blooms. Its name is German for 'Snow Bouquet'. The plant is a hybrid of H. Hachman and was registered by G. Stuck in 1983.

***Rhododendron* 'Scintillation'** (parentage unknown) 5 ft (1.5 m); Zone 5

This elepidote rhododendron has oval 6-in (15-cm) long shiny leaves that clothe the plant in the most attractive manner. The large, dense flower trusses, 6 in (15 cm) in diameter, contain up to 15 blossoms. Each flower is 2.5 in (6.4 cm) wide, pink with bronze markings in the throat, ruffled, and fragrant, opening in late May (Plate 17). The shrub is vigorous, healthy looking, bushy, and symmetrical. The plant as well as the flower buds are hardy to −15°F (−26°C). This is one of C. O. Dexter's masterpieces produced between 1925 and 1942 and registered by Paul Vossberg, Westbury, Long Island, New York, in 1973. It is rated 4/4.

***Rhododendron* 'Senegal'** (*R. keiskei* × *R. carolinianum* var. *album*)
3 ft (0.9 m); Zone 5

This lepidote rhododendron of semi-dwarf stature has small leaves and light-yellow flowers that open in late April. The growth is dense and rounded. It is a hybrid of David G. Leach, North Madison, Ohio.

Rhododendron serpyllifolium 2.5 ft (0.8 m); Zone 6

This deciduous to semi-deciduous azalea is native to the Japanese islands of Kyushu, Shikoku, and the southern half of Honshu. The leaves, which are narrow and less than 1 in (2.5 cm) long, are among the smallest in the genus *Rhododendron*. The 0.5-in (13-mm) wide flowers are rose-pink, funnel-shaped, and mostly solitary, opening in late April. The plant is suited for bonsai and for the tiny slope of my rock garden where it has prospered for years. It is rated 3/3.

Rhododendron serrulatum 5 ft (1.5 m); Zone 6
Southern Swamp Azalea; Hammocksweet Azalea

This North American deciduous azalea is native to the coastal plain from North Carolina to Florida and west to Alabama, Mississippi, and Louisiana. The leaves are 3 in (8 cm) long, and the white to pale violet flowers are 1 in (2.5 cm) wide and funnel-shaped, with a fragrance of cloves on most bushes, opening from late May to August. The species is, essentially, a southern counterpart of the northern *Rhododendron viscosum* (swamp azalea), which is very heavily represented in my garden. Despite the duplication that it would create, I obtained three small specimens of *R. serrulatum* to compare the two species and their respective performance in a cold climate. The plant is rated 2/3.

***Rhododendron* 'Sham's Pink'** (*R.* 'Boule de Neige' × *R. catawbiense* red seedling)
4 ft (1.2 m); Zone 5

This elepidote rhododendron with 4-in (10-cm) long leaves has 2.5-in (6.4-cm) wide very light pink flowers with slightly darker edges in ball-shaped trusses. It blooms in late May. The growth is irregular and somewhat unruly, so the plant should be shaped and trained severely when young. This cultivar was introduced and registered by A. M. Shammarello, South Euclid, Ohio, in 1972, and is rated 3/2.

***Rhododendron* 'Shanghai'** [(*R.* 'Mrs. Furnival' × *R. catawbiense album*) × unnamed seedling] 6 ft (1.8 m); Zone 6

This elepidote rhododendron has 4.5-in (11-cm) long leaves and 3.5-in (9-cm) wide clear pale pink flowers with darker margins and bold orange-yellow spotting. The flowers, which are arranged in ball-shaped trusses of up to 18 blossoms each, open in late May. David G. Leach, North Madison, Ohio, hybridized this cultivar and registered it in 1973. It carries the rating of 4/3.

***Rhododendron* 'Skyglow'** (parentage unknown) 3 ft (0.9 m); Zone 6

This is an elepidote rhododendron with 3.5-in (9-cm) long yellow-green leaves, and mildly scented, 3-in (8-cm) wide peach-colored flowers that open in early June. Neither the foliage nor the growth habit is particularly attractive. The plant, which has a tendency to spread, should be trained by pinching the lead bud and, with the help of supports and small stakes, should be forced to grow in a more compact fashion. Despite its shortcomings, the plant has its admirers, perhaps as a potential parent and source of the longed-for yellow flowers. Warren Baldsiefen, Rochelle Park, New Jersey, named and introduced it before 1966 but, before him, C. O. Dexter used it in his breeding program. It probably came from England to Farquhar's Nursery in Massachusetts, and from there to Dexter and Baldsiefen. The plant is bud hardy to about −5°F (−21°C) and in my climate needs a sheltered spot. It is rated 3/2.

***Rhododendron* 'Small Wonder'** [*R.* 'Fanfare' × (*R.* 'Prometheus' × *R. forestii* var. *repens*)] 5 ft (1.5 m); Zone 5

This elepidote rhododendron has 3-in (8-cm) long leaves and 2-in (5-cm) wide red flowers with light centers and wavy petals, up to seven per truss, opening in late April. The plant was hybridized and registered by David G. Leach, North Madison, Ohio, in 1973, and is rated 4/4.

Rhododendron smirnowii 3 ft (0.9 m); Zone 5

This elepidote rhododendron is native to the Caucasus Mountains where it was discovered in the 19th century. The leaves are dark green, 6 in (15 cm) long, leathery, shiny above and covered beneath with heavy indumentum that changes from white to brownish as the new leaves mature. The flowers are 3 in (8 cm) in diameter, pale rose to rose-purple, with wavy edges, and appear in late May. The 10-year height of this species is indicated as only 3 ft (90 cm), but recently I received a 20-year-old plant that towers well over 7 ft (2.1 m). The name is pronounced as if the *w* were a *v*. The species is rated 3/3.

***Rhododendron* 'Snow's Red'** (parentage unknown) 5 ft (1.5 m); Zone 5

This elepidote rhododendron has 3.5-in (9-cm) long leaves and 3-in (8-cm) wide blossoms of strong clear scarlet in trusses 5 in (13 cm) in diameter. The flowers open in early May, and the plant's growth is rounded and bushy.

***Rhododendron* 'Stewartsonian'** 3 ft (0.9 m); Zone 6

This evergreen azalea has 1-in (2.5-cm) long leaves that turn dark red in winter. The 1.5-in (4-cm) wide flowers are a clear, bright red, which is considered the richest red among hardy evergreen azaleas. The blossoms open in early May. The plant is a cross by Joseph B. Gable, Stewartstown, Pennsylvania.

***Rhododendron* 'Strawberry Ice'** 5 ft (1.5 m); Zone 5

This deciduous azalea has 3-in (8-cm) long leaves and large pink flowers with a yellow blotch, opening in early May. It is usually considered an Exbury hybrid, although at least one author, Christopher Fairweather in *Rhododendrons and Azaleas for Your Garden* (1979, 92) writes that it is a "plant from the Knap Hill stable."

***Rhododendron* 'Tiffany'** (*R.* 'Anna Baldsiefen' × *R. keiskei*) 1.5 ft (0.5 m); Zone 5

This semi-dwarf lepidote rhododendron with 1-in (2.5-cm) long leaves produces small star-shaped flowers with pink petals and an apricot spot in the throat, opening in early May. The subtle combination of hues and the profuse blossoms present a lovely sight when a well-grown plant is in full bloom. The cultivar was introduced by Warren Baldsiefen, Rochelle Park, New Jersey, in 1972, and is rated 3/3.

***Rhododendron* 'Tow Head'** (*R. carolinianum* var. *album* × *R. ludlowii*)
1 ft (0.3 m); Zone 5

This dwarf lepidote rhododendron bears 1.5-in (4-cm) long dark green leaves with scales on both surfaces. The flowers are 1.5 in (4 cm) wide, bright greenish yellow spotted with orange, in small trusses of five, opening in late April. This hybrid of David G. Leach, North Madison, Ohio, was registered in 1969, and is rated 3/5.

***Rhododendron* 'Tradition'** (unknown origin) 5 ft (1.5 m); Zone 6

This evergreen azalea with 1-in (2.5-cm) long leaves has clear pink, 1.5-in (4-cm) wide flowers that open in early May. The bush grows and blooms best in full sun, but flowers remarkably well even in medium shade where it provides a welcome touch of color for nearly 2 weeks. The interesting pattern of its foliage adds to its attractiveness for the remainder of the year.

***Rhododendron* 'Trilby'** (*R.* 'Queen Wilhelmina' × *R.* 'Standley Davies')
5 ft (1.5 m); Zone 5

This elepidote rhododendron has 4.5-in (11-cm) long matte green leaves. The 3-in (8-cm) wide flowers, opening in late May, are a beautiful deep red that, for the plant's hybridizer, must have evoked the image of George du Maurier's tragic heroine Trilby. It is a hybrid of C. B. Van Nes, Boskoop, Holland. My plant tends to bloom profusely in alternate years and, despite the favorable cold-rating for the bush as a whole, the flower buds are damaged in temperatures of −5°F (−21°C). Nevertheless, in good years, it is a very beautiful plant. It is rated 3/4.

***Rhododendron* 'Trude Webster'** (*R.* 'Countess of Derby' × *R.* 'Countess of Derby')
5 ft (1.5 m); Zone 6

This elepidote rhododendron has 7-in (18-cm) long leaves and, reputedly, 5-in (13-cm) wide pink flowers that open in early May. I have never seen the flowers, as on my plant they have frozen every one of the 5 years I have had the specimen. This highly rated West Coast hybrid fares poorly in my garden and climate. My impression is that its hardiness is overstated for our conditions. It is a 1951 introduction by Greer Gardens, Eugene, Oregon, and is rated 5/4.

***Rhododendron* 'Twilight Pink'** [(*R. fortunei* × *R.* 'Alice') selfed × *R.* 'Comstock']
4 ft (1.2 m); Zone 6

This elepidote rhododendron with light green leaves has very large flowers of transparent light pink. The plant, sold to me by a Long Island nursery, was incorrectly labeled as *Rhododendron* 'Dorothy Amateis'. It was not in bloom at the time, but when the large buds opened a few days later, it was a beautiful sight. Although the color was not exactly a strong pink, the size and form of the blossoms were outstanding. Nevertheless, the flower buds have made it through only one of the four subsequent winters. I think that even the quoted −5°F (−21°C) hardiness is optimistic for Connecticut's climate. The hybrid is a 1988 introduction of Greer Gardens, Eugene, Oregon, and is rated 4/4.

Rhododendron vaseyi 5 ft (1.5 m); Zone 4
Pinkshell Azalea

This North American deciduous azalea comes from a native range limited to a few counties in North Carolina; it has now escaped from cultivation and is spreading in parts of New England. It prefers but does not insist on wet situations and sites along streams and in high forests. The leaves are 2–5 in (5–13 cm) long, with wavy margins, and turn brilliant red in autumn. The 2-in (5-cm) wide flowers, opening in late April before the leaves unfold, are rose or occasionally pure white (forma *album*). They are two-lipped and differ from blossoms of other plants in the genus, except those of the related species, *Rhododendron canadense*. A well-grown *R. vaseyi* creates a uniquely delicate and airy image that has made it a popular subject among many gardeners overseas. The plant was discovered by George Vasey in 1878. I planted many specimens of this species in my garden, both white and rose. They look at home in the rather naturalistic environment, but I have seen them in more formal gardens where they looked very appropriate as well. The species is rated 4/4.

***Rhododendron* 'Veesprite'** (*R. impeditum* × *R. racemosum*) 1.5 ft (0.5 m); Zone 6

This dwarf lepidote rhododendron has leaves less than 1 in (2.5 cm) long and small 1-in (2.5-cm) wide rose flowers in terminal clusters of three to five blossoms. It blooms in late April. The plant is probably somewhat more tender than the often-quoted hardiness of −10°F (−23°C). Nevertheless, in a sheltered spot it has done relatively well in my garden. It is a 1968 introduction of R. Forster of the Horticultural Research Institute, Ontario, Canada.

Rhododendron vernicosum 5 ft (1.5 m); Zone 5

This elepidote rhododendron is native to very high elevations of southeastern China. It has 5-in (13-cm) long leaves which, when rubbed or heated, become shiny as if varnished (hence the Latin *vernicosum*). The 3-in (8-cm) wide flowers opening in late May vary from white to rose, sometimes with red markings, and occur in trusses of up to 12. My plant has lived through several severe winters but was damaged when for a year or two it grew in a location where the winter sun shone directly on it. It clearly needs filtered shade in winter as well as some mulch. It is rated 2/2.

***Rhododendron* 'Vernus'** (*R.* 'Cunningham's White' × *R. catawbiense* red hybrid) 5 ft (1.5 m); Zone 4

This elepidote rhododendron has 5-in (13-cm) long leaves and 2-in (5-cm) wide pale pink flowers. It blooms in late March or early April, soon after *Rhododendron mucronulatum*, and is a welcome touch of pink in the early spring landscape. It was hybridized by A. M. Shammarello, South Euclid, Ohio, and introduced by David G. Leach, North Madison, Ohio, in 1962. It is rated 3/3.

Rhododendron viscosum 5 ft (1.5 m); Zone 5

Swamp Azalea; White Swamp Azalea; Clammy Azalea; Swamp Honeysuckle

This North American deciduous azalea has a native range from Maine to Ohio and south to Tennessee and Georgia. The leaves are 2.5 in (6.4 cm) long, and the white narrowly tubular flowers are 1.3 in (3.5 cm) wide and of equal length, four to nine per cluster (Plate 46). The blossoms emit a delicious fragrance of cloves. The species blooms very late into the season, some blossoms opening in late June, while other bushes are still in full flower in late July. It is an impressive sight to see plants 10–12 ft (3–3.5 m) tall and 5–8 ft (1.5–2.4 m) wide covered with the pure white blooms, their fragrance penetrating every corner of the garden. There were dozens of *Rhododendron viscosum* specimens on the property when I moved in, and they all are still here, but now that so many have grown tall and wide, I will have to move several of them to other locations. The species is rated 3/3.

PLATE 46. The small white flowers of *Rhododendron viscosum* (swamp azalea) with no indication of the powerful spicy fragrance with which they permeate a garden from mid June till late July.

***Rhododendron* 'Vulcan'** (*R.* 'Mars' × *R. griersonianum*) 5 ft (1.5 m); Zone 5

This elepidote rhododendron has 4.5-in (11-cm) long dark green pointed leaves and 2.5-in (6.4-cm) wide bright red flowers that almost glow in the green landscape in early June (Plates 15, 71). The plant is quite hardy, but in an occasional winter the leaves suffer burn when positioned in direct sun. In some years, a significant number of the flower buds may freeze. Despite these shortcomings, the bush is well worth planting in Connecticut's climate. A 1938 hybrid of John Waterer, Bagshot, England, it is rated 4/4.

***Rhododendron* 'Waltham'** (*R.* 'Wilsonii' × *R. carolinianum*) 2 ft (0.6 m); Zone 4

This lepidote rhododendron has 1.5-in (4-cm) long dark green leathery leaves and 1.5-in (4-cm) wide light pink flowers in small trusses, opening in early May. The growth is low and spreading. The hybrid, which takes its name from a Massachusetts town of the same name, was raised by R. L. Ticknor and introduced by E. V. Mezitt, Weston Nurseries, Hopkinton, Massachusetts. It is rated 3/4.

Rhododendron weyrichii 5 ft (1.5 m); Zone 6

This deciduous azalea is native to the Japanese islands of Kyushu and Shikoku, and the Korean island of Cheju in the East China Sea, where it was discovered by Russian Navy surgeon Dr. Weyrich. The leaves are rhombic-ovate, 3.5 in (9 cm) long, and the 2.5-in (6.4-cm) wide funnel-shaped flowers are orange-red or dark red, appearing in late April before the leaves unfurl. The plant in my garden has survived several severe winters in good condition. It is rated 3/3.

***Rhododendron* 'White Rosebud'** (parentage unknown) 3 ft (0.9 m); Zone 6

This evergreen azalea with 2-in (5-cm) long leaves has pretty, 2-in (5-cm) wide pure white, double flowers that resemble miniature roses (reminiscent of, but larger than, Joseph B. Gable's pink *Rhododendron* 'Rosebud'). It blooms in late May. The plant is hardy in my garden, though some flower buds freeze in severe winters. It is a hybrid of August E. Kehr, Hendersonville, North Carolina.

***Rhododendron* 'Wilhelmina Vuyk'** (*R. kaempferi* hybrid × *R.* 'J. C. Van Tol') 3 ft (0.9 m); Zone 5

This evergreen azalea has 2-in (5-cm) long light green spring leaves that fall off in early winter, and smaller but darker green summer leaves that remain on the branches for a year. The gray-green foliage is covered with short brownish hairs. The flowers are single, 2.5 in (6.4 cm) in diameter, white with a chartreuse blotch, and lightly fragrant (Plate 47). Every second year the bush is completely covered with gorgeous flowers, but the years in between are only marginally less profuse. The blossoms begin to open by late May, and fresh buds continue to unfold gradually so that in some years the full effect lingers for weeks.

The plant has some enemies which, if not controlled, can spoil the show. It may become infested with *Pealius azaleae* (azalea white fly) and *Tetranychus bimaculatus* (red spider mite), especially if grown in the sun where, of course, it blossoms the best. In very damp years, it may be also affected by mildew that covers the leaves and causes

PLATE 47. A very old and beautiful evergreen azalea specimen of *Rhododendron* 'Wilhelmina Vuyk', in mid May.

them to drop prematurely. All three of these problems, and probably others as well, are solved by spraying in mid May and mid June with a mixture of sulfur-based fungicide and a miticide. As much as I dislike this chore, it is the only way to keep the plant beautiful.

When I brought the shrub 20 years ago from a property on Long Island, it was a grandmother plant even then; it is perhaps 50 years old by now, but continues to be full of vigor and beauty, and is worth the little time and effort I give it. It is a 1921 hybrid of Aart Vuyk of the Vuyk van Nes Nursery, Boskoop, Holland. Though its registered name is *Rhododendron* 'Wilhelmina Vuyk', the world knows it mostly by its synonym, *R.* 'Palestrina'.

***Rhododendron* 'Wilsonii'** (*R. ciliatum* × *R. glaucophyllum*) 3 ft (0.9 m); Zone 5

This lepidote rhododendron has beautiful dark green leaves resembling those of *Laurus nobilis* (laurel) and can provide an elegant touch to a limited space in a garden. The light rose-pink blossoms, opening in mid June, are small, tubular, and of lesser importance than the foliage. Most *Rhododendron* 'Wilsonii' specimens are not grown for their flowers, but rather for their leaves. The plant is quite hardy in Connecticut's climate, though the flower buds freeze once in two or three winters. It is sold also under the name *R.* 'Laetevirens'.

***Rhododendron* 'Windbeam'** (*R.* 'Conestoga' hybrid) 4 ft (1.2 m); Zone 4

This lepidote rhododendron has 3-in (8-cm) long dark green rounded, shiny, aromatic leaves that are heavily covered with scales beneath. The flowers are 1 in (2.5 cm) wide, apricot fading to light salmon, and very profuse; they open in late April. The plant is a cross by Guy G. Nearing, Ramsey, New Jersey, made in 1958 from *Rhododendron* 'Conestoga', which in turn is a 1955 grex by Joseph B. Gable, Stewartstown, Pennsylvania, made from *R. racemosum* and *R. carolinianum*. Though the plant in my garden is in shade for more than half a day, it flowers abundantly. It is rated 4/4. There is also a dwarf version of *R.* 'Windbeam' growing in my rock garden that is expected to reach about 1.5 ft (50 cm) in 10 years.

***Rhododendron* 'Windsor Buttercup'** (hybrid from Exbury material) 5 ft (1.5 m); Zone 5

This deciduous azalea has 3.5-in (9-cm) long light green leaves and 3-in (8-cm) wide clear yellow flowers that open in early May. The plant was developed at the Windsor Great Park from plants presented to King George of England by Lionel de Rothschild of the Exbury Estate.

***Rhododendron* 'Wissahickon'** (parentage unknown) 6 ft (1.8 m); Zone 5

This elepidote rhododendron has light green 4-in (10-cm) long leaves and bright red 2-in (5-cm) wide blossoms in loose trusses. It blooms in late May. It is an open, even leggy, plant that should be trained when young by removing the vegetative lead buds on all branches in late winter so as to encourage branching. The flower buds are hardy to −5°F (−21°C). This hybrid is a cross by C. O. Dexter, and is rated 3/3.

***Rhododendron* 'Wyanokie'** (*R.* 'Conestoga' hybrid) 3 ft (0.9 m); Zone 5

This lepidote rhododendron with 3-in (8-cm) long leaves has small white flowers in tiny 2-in (5-cm) wide ball-shaped trusses. It blooms in early May. It is another floriferous hybrid by Guy G. Nearing, Ramsey, New Jersey, made in 1958 from the *Rhododendron* 'Conestoga' grex of Joseph B. Gable, Stewartstown, Pennsylvania. It is rated 3/3.

***Rhododendron* 'Yaku Princess'** (*R.* 'King Tut' × *R. yakushimanum* 'Koichiro Wada')
3 ft (0.9 m); Zone 6

This elepidote rhododendron has 3.5-in (9-cm) long leaves that are shiny above and indumented beneath. The 2.5-in (6.4-cm) wide apple-blossom pink flowers fade to lighter pink. Up to 15 flowers occur in a ball-shaped truss, and they open in late May. This plant is a 1977 hybrid of A. M. Shammarello, South Euclid, Ohio, and is rated 4/4.

Rhododendron yakushimanum 4 ft (1.2 m); Zone 4

This elepidote rhododendron comes from the small Japanese island of Yaku (Yakushima) in the Tokara Strait of the East China Sea, where it is found on the steep peaks shrouded in mist and clouds for the greater part of the year. It is a variable species of uncommon charm, beauty, and hardiness. The leaves on most forms are about 4.5 in (11 cm) long, narrow, curved downward, shiny on top, and heavily indumented with a silver or brown felt beneath.

The unusually beautiful flowers begin in late April and early May as dark rose-colored buds, opening into clear-pink blossoms that mature pure white. At the beginning, all three colors are present on the bush at the same time, creating an apple-blossom effect of rare loveliness and purity. The shrub is beautiful all year long. New foliage, indumented on both sides, covers the plant with subtle silver or golden hues for several weeks in June and July. It is a dense and well-shaped bush that keeps its leaves for 5 years, one of the most evergreen of the evergreen rhododendrons.

There are many desirable forms of this species. In my garden, the loveliest is a plant 2.5 ft (80 cm) high and 4 ft (1.2 m) wide, which came from an Oregon nursery under the name *Rhododendron yakushimanum* 'Gossler Narrow Leaf'. It is the species at its best in all respects but one: it skips a year after one or two years of profuse blossoms. Another form, *R. yakushimanum* 'Apple Blossom', is a dwarf that will remain under 1 ft (30 cm) in height for many years. The third, *R. yakushimanum* 'Mist Maiden', a special selection by David G. Leach, North Madison, Ohio, as well as the fourth, *R. yakushimanum* 'Phetteplace', are among the tallest forms and are expected to reach 5–6 ft (1.5–1.8 m) in 10 years. In almost any form, *R. yakushimanum* is a first-class rhododendron. It is rated 5/5.

Rhododendron yedoense* var. *poukhanense 4 ft (1.2 m); Zone 5

This evergreen azalea has 3-in (8-cm) long leaves that remain on the branches until late fall when most of them drop off. In winter, only tiny tufts of small, narrow leaves remain at the branch tips. The foliage is sparsely covered with short hairs. The 2-in (5-cm) wide flowers are single, bright reddish violet with a darker blotch, and mildly fragrant. They appear in early April. This form was used extensively as one parent in the hybridizing program of Joseph B. Gable, Stewartstown, Pennsylvania, and by the U.S. Department of Agriculture, Glenn Dale, Maryland. The species is native to Korea (notably the Poukhan Mountain) and Japan. Before it became known to botanists, its double-flowered form, grown in Japanese gardens as Botan-Tsutsutsi (peony azalea), made its appearance first and was afforded the rank of a species called *Rhododendron yedoense* (from Yedo, now Tokyo). The rank was taken away when the real species appeared, but the name remained. Thus the wild species is called *R. yedoense* var. *poukhanense*, while the garden variety is called simply *R. yedoense* ('Yodogawa' azalea).

ROSA (ROSACEAE) Rose

There are 150 to 200 species in the genus *Rosa,* all native to the Northern Hemisphere. Only a handful are in cultivation in their pure form; the hundreds of millions of rose bushes grown all over the world (360 million estimated) are nearly all hybrids. A few are of an ancient origin with their pedigree long forgotten, and the remainder are crosses mostly less than 150 years old.

The scientific classification of roses is an ongoing process. As with other genera, there is no absolute agreement on what belongs where, neither is there any unanimity on the practical grouping of roses in the trade. Some divisions currently in use are based on the plants' physical characteristics, such as bush roses, miniature roses, climbing roses; other divisions reflect the time when the hybrids were raised, as is the case with the old roses; and, still other divisions describe the plants' flowering habits, as in polyanthas, floribundas, and hybrid perpetuals. In the largest group, the hybrid teas, it is the parentage that is the unifying factor.

The three or four dozen rose bushes growing in my garden (the exact number depends on the severity of the previous winter) may be placed in six groups:

1. Species. There is only one true species rose in my garden, *Rosa palustris,* an old resident that was here long before I came.

2. Old roses. These hybrids, created mostly in the past century or earlier, were raised from roses that were then in general cultivation and which comprised, among others, *Rosa* × *alba* (the albas), *R.* × *borbonica* (the bourbons), and *R. damascena* (the damasks). They are attractive shrubs with good foliage and full, old-fashioned rose blossoms. Hardy probably to zones 4 and 5, many are exceptionally fragrant, resistant to disease, and able to grow and bloom well even in poor soils and light shade. But, despite their undisputed assets, they are not entirely a rose lover's dream come true. Most of them bloom only once in a season. Some grow too tall and wide and must be supported against a wall or by wooden posts, and require a good pruning in early spring if they are to be kept within bounds. Still, they are such cultured denizens that no informal garden should be without them.

   The albas were probably developed before the Middle Ages, descending most likely from *Rosa damascena* or *R. gallica*. They are among the most beautiful of old roses. The bourbon roses are thought to have arisen on L'Isle de Bourbon (now called Reunion) in the West Indian Ocean, from a cross between the old China rose named *R.* 'Parson's Pink', and the damask rose called *R.* 'Quatre Saisons', both of which grew profusely on the island. The seeds of the cross were sent to France in the early 19th century and the resulting seedlings were used extensively for hybridizing with various types of roses that were then in cultivation in Europe.

3. Hybrid perpetuals. This is a somewhat newer group of hybrids that came into existence in the early 1800s. Later, toward the end of the century, they were replaced by the hybrid teas as the leading group. The hybrid perpetuals are mostly crosses of the ever-blooming but tender species, *Rosa chinensis,* with hardier stock, such as the damasks. They are vigorous and hardy, if not necessarily perpetually blooming, and their flowers are of substantial size with a fairly wide range of colors. Some are strongly scented.

4. Hybrid teas. This is the most favored class of roses today. Their blooms are usually large and well-shaped, and come in all colors except true blue, which does not yet exist in roses, although efforts are continuing to produce a blue rose. Some believe that a blue rose once existed but was lost centuries ago, perhaps having been bred out of existence in the quest for new colors.

   Some hybrid teas have a reasonably strong fragrance which, however, mostly pales against the powerful perfume of the old roses. Many bloom all summer long and rebloom in the fall. They derive their name from the fragrance of their tender ancestors, *Rosa chinensis* and its varieties, which were imported to Europe in the late 1700s. Peter Malins and M. M. Graff write in *Peter Malins' Rose Book* (1979, 3):

   > Their light fragrance resembled that of the chests in which tea was shipped from the Orient. It was so distinct from the heavy perfume of the familiar Damasks, Gallicas and Albas that it earned its bearers the name of Tea-Scented Chinas. Both the name and the scent are inherited by their progeny, the Tea Roses and our modern Hybrid Teas.

   The first hybrid tea is thought to be *R.* 'La France' produced in 1867 (probably from *R.* 'Madame Victor Verdier' crossed with tea rose *R.* 'Madame Bravy' or possibly a seedling of *R.* 'Madame Falcot').

   These gorgeous creations did not come without a price. Many are not reliably hardy and must be protected by the cumbersome procedure of hilling soil around them, or, as an alternative method practiced in my garden, they undergo the expensive and laborious trial-and-error process, an induced form of natural selection, by simply allowing the tender ones to perish. Those that live become the mainstay of the rose garden. There is almost no help forthcoming from the rose-growing community in determining in advance how hardy a given rosebush is. In the past two decades I have lost as many roses to severe winters as are currently growing in my garden.

   Another price gardeners pay for the hybrid teas' beautiful color shades, especially those in the yellow, orange, peach, amber, salmon, scarlet, and related tones, is mildew and blackspot. These pathogens entered the hybrid tea bloodlines through a cross with the brilliant yellow and copper *Rosa foetida,* which provided the desired hues, but which also carried a strong inclination toward the diseases.

5. Floribundas. This is a relatively recent class that resulted from crossing hybrid teas with polyanthas. The flowers are sometimes similar in quality to hybrid teas, usually appearing in clusters at the branch terminals. Another class, not unlike the floribundas, is still recognized in some quarters. It is a group called the grandifloras. It was invented in the 1950s to accommodate the then-new U.S. hybrid *Rosa* 'Queen Elizabeth'. It is a rather artificial class, now used only in the United States and possibly in France, but no longer recognized in the United Kingdom and most other countries. I have not used the grandiflora class in the descriptions, but instead have placed hybrids thus designated (in some books and catalogues) with the floribundas.

6. Polyanthas. This rather small class of mostly small roses includes hybrids with tiny blooms and low growth that are sometimes used as ground covers. The first commercially viable polyantha is thought to be *Rosa* 'Paquerette', an offspring of a low-growing form of the Japanese species, *R. multiflora,* and an

undefined hybrid of *R. chinensis*. It was raised, together with several other repeat-blooming seedlings of that parentage, by Jean Sisley of Lyon, France, and introduced by the nurseryman Mr. Guillot in 1875.

The rose descriptions that follow contain the parentage of hybrids (where available), plant height, and hardiness zone. As to the height, it should be borne in mind that most rosebushes are pruned every year to a few inches above the ground, and the subsequent year's height heavily depends on the intervening winter and the adequacy of spring rains. As to resistance to cold, this too is an uncertain element as dependable information is hard to come by or does not exist. I have included hardiness standings obtained from a few available sources, but mainly I have indicated estimated ratings based on a plant's performance in my garden. Commercial rose growers seldom, if ever, provide this essential information except to say, for example, that their "roses thrive all over the country." They do not mention, of course, the special protection the plants require. Since I do not transfer small mountains of soil to cover my bushes every autumn and then uncover them in spring, I lose a few roses almost every winter.

The descriptions also include the class to which the rose was assigned, together with the color and the presence of smell. The last two items are stated in somewhat general terms. A very precise characterization is difficult as both are rather subjective perceptions. In addition, they may vary, depending on the climate, the weather, and the time of the year; the subtle blossoms of autumn often render a different kind of color and fragrance than the lush and eager blooms of spring.

The following roses currently grow in my garden.

***Rosa* 'Allgold'** (*R*. 'Goldilocks' × *R*. 'Ellinor LeGrice') 2.5 ft (0.8 m); Zone 5

This yellow floribunda has no fragrance. In the 8 years it has grown in my garden, it has never exceeded its designated height. Its foliage is small, dark green, shiny, attractive, and quite resistant to diseases. The 3-in (8-cm) wide flowers are deep yellow and fade only slightly as they mature. The bush has survived Connecticut's winters well even though in some years its canes freeze to the ground. It was raised by E. B. LeGrice in the United Kingdom in 1956.

***Rosa* 'Amber Queen'** 3 ft (0.9 m); Zone 5

This amber-yellow floribunda is fragrant. A relative newcomer to my garden, the plant has shiny foliage and somewhat smaller apricot-yellow flowers with light fragrance. The blooms occur singly or in clusters of up to 10.

***Rosa* 'American Pride'** 5 ft (1.5 m); Zone 5

This red hybrid tea is lightly fragrant. A tall-growing bush, it has semi-glossy dark green foliage that unfolds red when young. The 5-in (13-cm) wide flowers begin bright red and mature deeper red, their light fragrance sometimes disappearing entirely. The flowers are occasionally too heavy for the slender stems and hang to the ground. The bush was raised in the United States in 1978.

***Rosa* 'Arizona'** 4 ft (1.2 m); Zone 6

This bronze-yellow floribunda is not reliably hardy. It has not been especially vigorous in my garden and seems to require a long time to recover from the winter before it begins its normal spring growth. The foliage appears to be resistant to diseases, and the 3.5-in (9-cm) wide blossoms have a light fragrance.

***Rosa* 'Broadway'** 5 ft (1.5 m); Zone 5

This bicolor (yellowish and red) hybrid tea is a fragrant, vigorous bush with attractive foliage. The 4-in (10-cm) wide flowers, borne in clusters, are creamy white to clear yellow in the center and dark pink toward the margins. The plant was raised in the United States in 1985.

***Rosa* 'Camelot'** (*R.* 'Circus' × *R.* 'Queen Elizabeth') 5 ft (1.5 m); Zone 6

This coral-red floribunda is fragrant. The shrub is upright and vigorous, with dark green, leathery, disease-resistant foliage. The 4-in (10-cm) wide flowers are very double, with up to 55 petals, and have a spicy fragrance. This rose blooms well throughout the season. It was raised by Swim and Weeks in the United States in 1964.

***Rosa* 'Carefree Beauty'** (unnamed seedling × *R.* 'Prairie Princess') 5 ft (1.5 m); Zone 4

This pink floribunda is lightly fragrant. It is a vigorous and tall-growing shrub with attractive foliage and somewhat thin but appealing growth habit. It fits best in an informal open landscape rather than in the company of hybrid teas in a formal rose garden (Plate 48). The handsome flowers, which are radiant pink and 5 in (13 cm) wide, appear throughout the season. If left to mature on the bush toward the end of summer, the blossoms turn into colorful fruits. Even after a severe winter, there are seldom any dead branches requiring removal. However, I do some spring pruning to maintain the desired size and shape. The plant is resistant to diseases but I still include it in my normal rose maintenance program. It was raised by Griffith Buck at Iowa State University, Ames, Iowa, in 1977.

PLATE 48. *Rosa* 'Carefree Beauty' in early June, with much more to recommend it than just low maintenance.

***Rosa* 'Dana'** 3.5 ft (1.1 m); Zone 6

This rose-pink hybrid tea is pleasantly fragrant. A bush of upright growth with medium-green foliage, it bears 3.5-in (9-cm) wide flowers. It is not a vigorous plant.

***Rosa* 'Diamond Jubilee'** (*R.* 'Marechal Niel' × *R.* 'Feu Pernet-Duchet') 4 ft (1.2 m); Zone 6

This creamy-white hybrid tea is fragrant but rather tender. An upright shrub with shiny foliage, it has 5-in (13-cm) wide pleasantly scented ivory flowers with shades of pink. It was raised in the United States in 1947 and introduced by Jackson & Perkins.

***Rosa* 'Double Delight'** (*R.* 'Granada' × *R.* 'Garden Party') 3.5 ft (1.1 m); Zone 5

This bicolor (ivory and red) hybrid tea is fragrant. A plant with a good growth habit and dark green glossy leaves, it has large, well-shaped flower buds. The 5-in (13-cm) wide flowers have creamy-white centers surrounded by bright cherry-red outer petals, some blooms having more red than others. The scent is very pleasant. The bush has survived several severe winters in good condition. It was raised in the United States in 1977.

***Rosa* 'Felicite Parmentier'** 4.5 ft (1.4 m); Zone 5

This plant, with an informal and attractive growth habit, belongs to the alba group of old roses. It is an attractive landscape shrub with clean grayish green leaves and very double, strongly fragrant 2.5-in (6.4-cm) wide light pink to white flowers in clusters of three to five. It was introduced by Mr. Jacques in France in 1827.

***Rosa* 'Forty-Niner'** 4 ft (1.2 m); Zone 5

This hybrid tea is a vigorous, upright bush with good foliage and 4-in (10-cm) wide bright red flowers, some petals having a touch of yellow on their outer sides. The blossoms are strongly and pleasantly fragrant.

***Rosa* 'Fragrant Cloud'** (unnamed seedling × *R.* 'Prima Ballerina') 5 ft (1.5 m); Zone 5

This orange-red hybrid tea has a strong and pleasant fragrance reminiscent of the damask roses. A sturdy, bushy plant with attractive dark-green glossy leaves, it bears 5-in (13-cm) wide flowers, which begin as well-shaped buds and open into attractively formed blooms but soon lose their good shape as they expand. The flowers occur in terminal clusters, and a partial disbudding allows fewer but larger and better shaped blossoms to develop. The plant is known in Europe by its synonyms *Rosa* 'Duftwolke' and *R.* 'Nuage Parfume'. It was raised by Mathias Tantau in Germany and introduced in 1963.

***Rosa* 'Fragrant Memory'** 5 ft (1.5 m); Zone 5

This rose-pink hybrid tea is fragrant. A slender bush with excellent foliage, it is a profuse bloomer bearing 4.5-in (11-cm) wide flowers of good form. It was previously known as *Rosa* 'Jadis'.

***Rosa* 'Frau Karl Druschki'** (*R.* 'Merveille de Lyon' × *R.* 'Madame Caroline Testout') 7 ft (2.1 m); Zone 5

This hybrid perpetual has one failing, and only one: it has no fragrance. In other respects it is a superior plant. The foliage is light green and leathery, and the plentiful, large globular flowers are of hybrid tea quality. Though scentless, they are uniquely pure, clean, almost an artificial white. The bush blooms in early summer, with a repeat flowering in autumn. It has been known in various times and places as *Rosa* 'Snow Queen', *R.* 'Reine de Neiges', and *R.* 'White American Beauty'. The plant in my garden is the climbing version of *R.* 'Frau Karl Druschki' developed by Mr. Lawrence in the United Kingdom in 1906. The original bush form was raised by P. Lambert in Germany in 1901.

***Rosa* 'Garden Party'** (*R.* 'Charlotte Armstrong' × *R.* 'Peace') 6 ft (1.8 m); Zone 5

This ivory white hybrid tea is hardy and has a strong and delicious fragrance. An upright plant, it has attractive, large glossy foliage and 5-in (13-cm) wide well-shaped blooms of heavy substance, with the typical high centers of hybrid teas. Some blossoms have up to 30 clear white petals with pink margins. Raised by H. D. Swim in the United States in 1959, it was introduced by Armstrong Nurseries.

***Rosa* 'Golden Wings'** [(*R.* 'Soeur Therese' × *R. pimpinellifolia altaica*) × *R.* 'Ormiston Roy'] 5 ft (1.5 m); Zone 4

This yellow fragrant hybrid is a tall bush, sometimes described as a member of the shrub roses. The plant is well suited for an informal landscape. The foliage is attractive, and the 5-in (13-cm) wide single flowers have an almost ethereal beauty (Plate 49). The petals are bright yellow in the center, fading to lighter yellow or almost white toward the margins. At the base of the broad petals is a tuft of large golden stamens. The fragrance is faint but distinct. The bush begins blossoming very early, blooms almost continuously, and remains in flower the longest of all my roses. The canes should be shortened by one-third in early winter, and in early spring the older branches should be pruned out. In this manner, the bush continues to rejuvenate, avoiding potential legginess. These pruning principles can well be applied to all taller landscape rosebushes including the old roses. *Rosa* 'Golden Wings' was raised by Roy Shepard in the United States and introduced in 1956.

PLATE 49. The unassuming beauty of *Rosa* 'Golden Wings' in late May.

***Rosa* 'Heirloom'** (unnamed seedling × unnamed seedling) 3 ft (0.9 m); Zone 5

This lavender, fragrant hybrid tea requires more than the normal amount of protection against diseases. The 3.5-in (9-cm) wide flowers are an attractive deep lilac when they first open, but as they mature the pretty hue fades into a dusty purple-gray. This phenomenon, which is rather common to the lavender-colored roses, is caused by the diminution of a red pigment, an essential ingredient of purple, as the blossoms lose their freshness. When new, the flowers are very full and, since they grow in terminal clusters, they tend to weigh down the weak stems. A regular removal of spent blossoms and diligent disbudding of excessive buds not only lightens the heavy load, but also encourages production of larger, better-formed roses. *Rosa* 'Heirloom' was raised in the United States, and introduced in 1972.

***Rosa* 'Intrigue'** 3 ft (0.9 m); Zone 7

This red-purple floribunda is strongly and pleasantly fragrant but not reliably hardy. If winters are mild, it is a vigorous shrub with large dark-green leaves that first unfold copper-red, creating an interesting two-tone pattern. The 3-in (8-cm) wide flowers with about 20 petals are a somewhat unusual red-purple color and grow in terminal clusters. Although the plant has not come through every Connecticut winter unscathed, thus far it has always grown back and bloomed well. It was raised in the United States in 1984. There is another red rose by the same name, sold mostly in Europe, which was raised in Germany in 1978.

***Rosa* 'John F. Kennedy'** 5 ft (1.5 m); Zone 6

This white hybrid tea is not reliably hardy. The foliage is rich green and attractive, and the 5-in (13-cm) wide ivory-white pleasantly fragrant flowers are well-formed and produced singly or in clusters. As with most other roses in my garden, the main attraction in choosing this hybrid was its fragrance and, as with many, the lack of hardiness was revealed only too late. Although in milder years it may grow to more than 6 ft (1.8 m) in height by midsummer, the bush freezes to the ground in most winters. Still, it has always recovered and bloomed. It was raised in the United States in 1965.

***Rosa* 'Joseph's Coat'** (*R.* 'Buccaneer' × *R.* 'Circus') 6 ft (1.8 m); Zone 6

This tricolor (orange-yellow-red) floribunda is lightly fragrant and not reliably hardy. The plant is often classified as a climber, but it looks best as a free-standing shrub or as a pillar rose. It also looks quite appropriate leaning on a 4-ft (1.2-m) high boundary wall. I planted my specimen on the cool north side of a wall, with the long canes and attractive foliage clambering over the stones into the sun. The leaves are disease resistant, and the 3.5-in (9-cm) wide flowers display several distinct shades of color at the same time. In a cluster, one blossom may be bright orange, another yellow, and a third bright red (Plate 50). Even on the same bloom, petals may show two or more colors. The shrub can be an outstanding addition if used as a landscape plant, away from other roses. It blooms profusely in late June to early July and does not let up very much until fall. It requires heavy winter mulching around its roots, a practice to be used with discretion on roses as the mulch may harbor spores of blackspot and mildew. The mulch should be removed in spring. Nevertheless, even with protection, the canes freeze to the ground in some winters. *Rosa* 'Joseph's Coat' was introduced in the United States in 1964.

PLATE 50. The colorful blossoms of the somewhat tender but beautiful *Rosa* 'Joseph's Coat' in early June.

***Rosa* 'Karl Herbst'** (*R.* 'Peace' × *R.* 'Independence') 3 ft (0.9 m); Zone 5

This deep red hybrid tea is lightly fragrant. It is a vigorous, free-flowering bush with glossy foliage that begins copper-red when it first unfolds. The blooms have a full form but only a light scent. The plant does best in sunny and dry weather. It was raised by W. Kordes in Germany in 1950.

***Rosa* 'King's Ransom'** (*R.* 'Golden Masterpiece' × *R.* 'Lydia') 4 ft (1.2 m); Zone 7

This yellow lightly fragrant hybrid tea is not reliably hardy. Nonetheless, in warm years it is a vigorous, upright shrub with light green foliage and 5.5-in (14-cm) wide deep yellow flowers of a somewhat looser form than is the rule for most hybrid teas. The blooms grow in terminal clusters and have only a fleeting fragrance. The bush flowers profusely in the summer and in the fall, with some blossoming in between. Some winters it dies to the ground but recovers and usually blooms well. It was raised in the United States in 1961.

***Rosa* 'Koenigin von Danemark'** 5 ft (1.5 m); Zone 5

This pink, very fragrant old rose, a member of the alba group, is of medium vigor and somewhat lax growth, with branches often weighed to the ground with blooms unless held up by supports. The flowers, which are 2.5 in (6.4 cm) in diameter and somewhat smaller than on other albas, open a darker carmine-pink and mature to a soft rose-pink. The blossoms, especially when young, occasionally display the quartering pattern typical for many old roses. The bush blossoms in June and there is no recurrent bloom. It was raised by J. Booth, Flottbeck Nurseries of northern Germany (then a part of Denmark), in 1816 and registered in 1826.

Rosa 'Lagerfeld' 5 ft (1.5 m); Zone 6

This light lavender floribunda is very fragrant. A moderately vigorous bush with healthy and attractive foliage, it is named for French dress designer Karl Lagerfeld. The 3.5-in (9-cm) wide blossoms are very light lavender fading into an unattractive noncolor. The catalogue gave no inkling of this unfortunate peculiarity, but the scent is quite strong and pleasantly perfumy.

Rosa 'Louise Odier' 5.5 ft (1.7 m); Zone 5

This old rose with soft pink, very fragrant flowers belongs to the bourbon clan. The growth is tall and vigorous, and the foliage is light green. The 3.5-in (9-cm) wide flowers are well-formed, sometimes with concentric circles of petals resembling camellia blossoms, and sometimes quartering in the classic old rose fashion. The fragrance is strong and pleasing. *Rosa* 'Louise Odier' was raised in France in 1851.

Rosa 'Madame Hardy' 5.5 ft (1.7 m); Zone 5

This old rose of the damask group has white, very fragrant blossoms and upright, vigorous growth. The branches are covered with abundant, attractive light green foliage, and the 3.5-in (9-cm) wide profusely borne flowers are creamy white or very pale pink maturing pure white. A blossom may have as many as 200 petals, all emitting a strong, delicious scent with a hint of lemon. The central petals are folded inward exposing a green eye in the middle. The shrub is the most popular rose of its type, and some gardeners consider it the most beautiful rose in existence. It is disease resistant and hardy in my climate, but blooms once in mid to late June and does not rebloom. It was raised in France in 1832 by Mr. Hardy and named for his wife.

Rosa 'Madame Isaac Pereire' 8 ft (2.1 m); Zone 5

This rose-pink, very fragrant old rose reaches 7–8 ft (2.1–2.4 m) tall in a year or two and requires a support such as a strong trellis, a fence, or a stone wall (Plate 51).

PLATE 51. The raspberry-scented old rose, *Rosa* 'Madame Isaac Pereire' in early June.

My specimen found such a spot which not only supports it, but also eliminates the need for weeding (at least on one side of the bush), an advantage considering the long and thorny canes. The foliage is light green and attractive but less disease resistant than other old roses. The large blossoms, sometimes up to 5 in (13 cm) in diameter, are very doubled and show quartering when mature. Their intense fragrance, reminiscent of raspberries, is considered by some to be the most powerful of all rose fragrances. The plant begins blooming in mid to late June; the early blossoms may be malformed, but as they continue to unfold well into September, they become more and more attractively shaped. It was raised by Mr. Garcon, in France, in 1881.

***Rosa* 'Marie Louise'** 4 ft (1.2 m); Zone 4

This rose-pink, very fragrant and beautiful damask grows lower than most old roses. It has a bushy growth and excellent foliage that is quite disease resistant. The glowing pink flowers are large and sometimes weigh down the slender branches (Plate 52). Their fragrance is strong and sweet. The bush blooms in late June to mid July and does not rebloom. It was raised in the gardens of Malmaison, the site of Empress Josephine's great collection of roses.

PLATE 52. An old rose from Empress Josephine's garden, *Rosa* 'Marie Louise' in mid June.

***Rosa* 'Mirandy'** (*R.* 'Night' × *R.* 'Charlotte Armstrong') 4 ft (1.2 m); Zone 5

This hybrid tea has dark velvety red, fragrant blossoms and a well-branched vigorous growth habit with attractive foliage. The new red leaves add an interesting two-color effect. The 4.5-in (11-cm) wide flowers are full, containing up to 50 petals, and display the classic high-centered hybrid tea form as they reach their fully open stage. Their color does not change as the blossoms age, and their fragrance resembles the damask scent. This rose was raised by Dr. W. E. Lammerts in the United States in 1945.

***Rosa* 'Mister Lincoln'** (*R.* 'Chrysler Imperial' × *R.* 'Charles Mallerin')
5 ft (1.5 m); Zone 5

This hybrid tea has dark red, fragrant blossoms. Peter Malins and M. M. Graff, in *Peter Malins' Rose Book* (1979, 22), write that this hybrid "is the full, heavily scented crimson rose traditionally favored by male gardeners." Mr. Malins probably knew that, as for years he observed and overheard the visitors to the Brooklyn Botanic

Garden, Brooklyn, New York, where he was the chief rosarian. The bush is upright and vigorous, and has good foliage. The dark red blossoms have high centers and are filled with many fragrant petals. Flower production tends to slow down in summer. This rose was raised by Swim & Weeks in the United States in 1964.

***Rosa* 'New Day'** (*R.* 'Arlene Francis' × *R.* 'Roselandia') 4 ft (1.2 m); Zone 5

This hybrid tea of vigorous growth produces canary yellow, fragrant blossoms on sturdy canes that bear attractive foliage with prominent veins. The clear and luminous flowers are delightfully scented (a rarity for yellow roses) with a spicy fragrance. Their high-centered hybrid tea form lasts for several days, even after the outer petals expand. The bush is hardy and disease resistant. It was raised in Germany in 1977 and introduced in the United States by Jackson & Perkins.

***Rosa* 'Oklahoma'** 5 ft (1.5 m); Zone 5

This hybrid tea is a well-branched and vigorous shrub with large, dark green foliage and 4.5-in (11-cm) wide velvety red, very fragrant flowers with high centers. The rich color does not diminish or change with age. This hardy and desirable bush was raised by Swim & Weeks in the United States in 1964.

***Rosa* 'Orange Ruffles'** 3.5 ft (1.1 m); Zone 5

This hybrid tea is a vigorous grower with dark green disease-resistant foliage. Its 3.5-in (9-cm) wide high-centered flowers have ruffled orange petals and a pleasing fragrance.

Rosa palustris 7 ft (2.1 m); Zone 4

Swamp Rose

This wild North American rose ranges from Newfoundland to Minnesota, south to Arkansas, and east to Florida. The 6-in (15-cm) long leaves have five to nine leaflets, each up to 2 in (5 cm) long, pointed at both ends and with finely toothed margins. The five-petaled bright rose-pink single flowers, 2 in (5 cm) in diameter, occur in small clusters or solitary, are mildly but pleasantly fragrant, and appear in modest numbers all over the bush from May to August. The rounded red hips are 0.5 in (13 mm) wide. This plant, which grew on my property before I came here, has increased by suckering to cover a wider but not excessively large area in a swampy location that is in shade but has full exposure to the light from the north. The bright little roses are welcome when they spring up periodically against the dark background of the wood behind them.

***Rosa* 'Peace'** {[(*R.* 'George Dickson' × *R.* 'Souvenir de Claudius Pernet') × (*R.* 'Joanna Hill' × *R.* 'Charles P. Kilham')] × *R.* 'Margaret McGredy'}
6 ft (1.8 m); Zone 5

This hybrid tea grows tall and upright, and its foliage is dense, healthy looking, glossy, and relatively disease resistant. The flowers are up to 6 in (15 cm) wide, high-centered, yellow edged with pink in summer, and almost pure yellow in autumn. The bush is vigorous, but if pruned too severely in late winter it may produce long shoots in spring that bear no flowers for the first several weeks. They break, however, later in the season.

The history of this king of roses is as unique as the plant itself. It was raised by the famous and prolific French hybridizer of roses, Francis Meilland, and named for his mother, Madame Antoine Meilland. It flowered for the first time in 1942, the year Germany invaded France. Meilland smuggled some cuttings of the bush to the U.S.

consul and for 3 years had no idea of what happened to them. After the German army withdrew from occupied France, Meilland finally learned that the rose had become popular in the United States. At a meeting on the United Nations charter, the delegates' conference tables were decorated with the blossoms of Mr. Meilland's rose, which, to honor the occasion, was renamed *Rosa* 'Peace'. Although it bears this name in most countries, in France it is still called *R.* 'Madame A. Meilland'; in Germany, it goes by the name *R.* 'Gloria Dei'; and in Italy, it is known as *R.* 'Gioia'.

***Rosa* 'Pink Peace'** [(*R.* 'Peace' × *R.* 'Monique') × (*R.* 'Peace' × *R.* 'Mrs. John Laing')] 4 ft (1.2 m); Zone 5

This hybrid tea is vigorous, upright, and disease resistant. The 6-in (15-cm) wide flowers are radiant pink and pleasantly scented. They bear no resemblance to *Rosa* 'Peace' in color or shape. The plant was raised by Francis Meilland in France in 1959.

***Rosa* 'Pristine'** (*R.* 'White Masterpiece' × *R.* 'First Prize') 4 ft (1.2 m); Zone 5

This hybrid tea is a bush of slender growth and restrained vigor, with large dark green glossy, disease-resistant foliage. The 5.5-in (14-cm) wide lightly fragrant, opalescent flowers begin as beautifully formed vase-shaped buds, which retain their good form well after they unfold into white blossoms with pink margins. The bush was raised in the United States in 1978.

***Rosa* 'Proud Land'** (*R.* 'Chrysler Imperial' × red unnamed seedling) 5 ft (1.5 m); Zone 5

This hybrid tea is a vigorous plant that must be restrained if it is not to grow too tall. This task can be accomplished even during the growing season by cutting the flowers with stems 3 ft (90 cm) long if necessary, regardless of how many five-leaflet leaves are removed. The foliage is large and healthy looking, and the 5.5-in (14-cm) wide flowers unfold from dark red buds to brilliant crimson blossoms visible from a distance. Their fragrance is delicious. A prolific bloomer, this rose was raised in the United States in 1969.

***Rosa* 'Queen Elizabeth'** (*R.* 'Charlotte Armstrong' × *R.* 'Floradora') 5 ft (1.5 m); Zone 5

This floribunda (sometimes still classified as a grandiflora) is an upright and vigorous plant with dark green leaves and bronze new foliage. The 4-in (10-cm) wide flowers are clear pink and lightly scented. Occurring singly or in clusters, the blooms are high-centered when young but become cupped with age. In the early part of the season, the plant may produce some vigorous blind shoots that will blossom later in summer. Disease resistant and hardy, this rose was raised by Dr. W. E. Lammerts in the United States in 1954.

***Rosa* 'Royal Highness'** (*R.* 'Virgo' × *R.* 'Peace') 4 ft (1.2 m); Zone 7

This hybrid tea is a tall, upright growing shrub with light green, leathery foliage, which regrettably is susceptible to black spot and should be protected regularly. The 5-in (13-cm) wide flowers with up to 45 petals are high-centered, light pink, and scented. They open abundantly throughout the season and are easily marred by rain. The plant is not hardy in my garden and usually freezes to the ground. It was raised in the United States by Swim & Weeks and introduced by Conard-Pyle in 1962.

***Rosa* 'Seashell'** 3.5 ft (1.1 m); Zone 7

This hybrid tea is a bush of modest vigor with dark green glossy foliage and 4-in (10-cm) wide apricot-colored flowers with high centers and pleasant scent. It is a slow starter and may require several years to become firmly established, provided it does not perish first in a cold winter. It seems to require more than the usual amount of protection against diseases. It was raised in Germany in 1976.

***Rosa* 'Sheer Bliss'** (*R.* 'White Masterpiece' × *R.* 'Grand Masterpiece') 4 ft (1.2 m); Zone 6

This hybrid tea is an upright but bushy plant with strong canes and light green matte foliage. The beautiful 5-in (13-cm) wide flowers are creamy white with blush pink centers and the classic hybrid tea form. The fragrance is not especially strong but it is very pleasant. The bush blooms well into fall with blossoms becoming more graceful with the advancing season. This rose was raised in the United States and introduced by Jackson & Perkins in 1987.

***Rosa* 'Shreveport'** (*R.* 'Zorina' × *R.* 'Ulve Seeler') 3.5 ft (1.1 m); Zone 6

This floribunda is vigorous and bushy; it has large matte leaves that unfold bronze when young. The 3.5-in (9-cm) wide, orange-red, lightly fragrant blooms with up to 30 petals, assume a cupped form when they fully open. It was introduced by Armstrong Nurseries in 1981.

***Rosa* 'Sweet Surrender'** (Unnamed seedling × *R.* 'Tiffany') 4 ft (1.2 m); Zone 7

This hybrid tea is an upright but bushy plant with large matte foliage that opens dark maroon when young. The 4-in (10-cm) wide flowers are light pink and strongly scented. The plant blooms well in summer and fall, but has not proven reliably hardy in my garden. It was raised in the United States in 1983.

***Rosa* 'The Fairy'** (*R.* 'Paul Crampel' × *R.* 'Lady Gay') 2 ft (0.6 m); Zone 5

This dwarf polyantha is bushy and sufficiently procumbent to be used sometimes as a groundcover. However, in my garden it has been trained upright and grows through a wire hoop that keeps it from sprawling on the ground and from being splashed with soil in rain. The tiny 1.5-in (4-cm) wide bright pink flowers have up to 30 petals. They begin to open in July and continue with some interruptions until frost. This rose was raised by J. & A. Bentall in the United Kingdom in 1932. It is sometimes erroneously listed as a sport of *R.* 'Lady Godiva'.

***Rosa* 'Tiffany'** (*R.* 'Charlotte Armstrong' × *R.* 'Girona') 4 ft (1.2 m); Zone 5

This hybrid tea is an upright but bushy plant with glossy dark green disease-resistant foliage. The 4-in (10-cm) wide flowers are bright salmon-pink to golden-yellow toward the base of the petals. The blooms open singly or in clusters throughout the season. Their fragrance is reminiscent of the old roses. The plant was raised by R. V. Lindquist in the United States and introduced in 1954.

***Rosa* 'Tip Toes'** 3 ft (0.9 m); Zone 6

This hybrid tea is a bush with large deep-green leaves and 3.5-in (9-cm) wide apricot-pink velvety flowers that have a classic high center and a pleasant fragrance.

***Rosa* 'Tropicana'** [(unnamed seedling × *R.* 'Peace') × (unnamed seedling × *R.* 'Alpine Glow')] 4 ft (1.2 m); Zone 5

This hybrid tea is a vigorous, upright bush with attractive matte leaves and 5-in (13-cm) wide radiant orange-red blossoms with up to 35 petals, high centers, and light but distinctive scent. In spring, the flowers grow singly, but by autumn they appear in clusters of up to five per stem. The plant requires regular protection from diseases. It is known in Europe as *Rosa* 'Superstar'. There is also a climbing version of the rose. *Rosa* 'Tropicana' was raised by Mathias Tantau in Germany and introduced by Jackson & Perkins in 1960.

***Rosa* 'V for Victory'** 5 ft (1.5 m); Zone 5

This hybrid tea is a sturdy bush with leathery foliage and attractive, light green new growth. The 5-in (13-cm) wide faintly fragrant flowers are ivory-white to light yellow toward the base of the petals. The blossoms grow in clusters of up to four.

***Rosa* 'White Lightnin'** 5 ft (1.5 m); Zone 6

This floribunda is a vigorous shrub with dark green glossy leaves and red new foliage. The 3.5-in (9-cm) wide flowers are white, occasionally touched with a faint blush of pink in the center, growing singly or in clusters. The fragrance of *Rosa* 'White Lightnin' has a trace of lemon blossoms. This good all-season bloomer was raised by Swim & Christensen in the United States in 1980.

Santolina chamaecyparissus (Compositae) 1.5 ft (0.5 m); Zone 7
Lavender Cotton

There are about eight species in the genus *Santolina,* all from the Mediterranean region. In my garden, *S. chamaecyparissus* barely makes it from one year to the next, but it is such an interesting little subshrub that I try to keep it alive against all odds. One of these springs, it just may not be there. The foliage is silver-gray all year long, except in early spring when the new growth is light green. The shrublet may be pruned to the base in April, which will discourage production of the small yellow blossoms that brighten the silvery cushion but which spoil the overall appearance of the interesting aromatic foliage. The best location for the little plant is in full sun, protected from north winds. It can grow in relatively poor but well-drained soil. In winter, evergreen branches from a Christmas tree or a hemlock may be placed over the shrub, but not too thickly as the plant could rot under a heavy mulch.

Sarcococca hookeriana* var. *humilis (Buxaceae) 1 ft (0.3 m); Zone 6
Sweet Box; Christmas Box

The genus *Sarcococca* has some 14 species, all native to the Himalayas and southeastern China. *Sarcococca hookeriana* var. *humilis* is a low, stoloniferous, evergreen shrub that grows well even in heavy shade where it forms a sparse but attractive ground cover. The leaves are evergreen and glossy, and the inconspicuous white flowers are fragrant. They are particularly welcome since they appear in late winter and very early spring. A sprig with a few blossoms brought into the warmth of a house will provide a pleasant scent for an entire room. In my garden, the plant grows in a small wood where it receives no direct sunlight once the trees above it leaf out in spring. It has been spreading very slowly. Though sometimes rated as hardy to only zone 7, it has not shown much stress in our winters.

SPIRAEA (ROSACEAE)

There are nearly 100 species of deciduous shrubs in the genus *Spiraea,* all native to the Northen Hemisphere. Among them is the pretty and popular *S. prunifolia* (bridalwreath) as well as weedy bushes of the northeastern woods. All prefer rich, moist soil in sun, but grow and bloom satisfactorily in light shade. They have masses of fibrous roots which make them easy to move.

***Spiraea japonica* 'Shibori'** 3 ft (0.9 m); Zone 5

Spiraea japonica 'Shibori' was introduced by Wayside Gardens Nurseries, Hodges, South Carolina, as *S. japonica* 'Shirobana', but the name was changed several years ago. The foliage is light green, and the flowers appear in terminal corymbs consisting of many tiny blossoms in colors from white and light pink to red, all at the same time. The plant blooms from midsummer to late fall. To produce as many of the flower-bearing shoots as possible, the bush should be pruned in March or early April, cutting all branches to about 3–4 in (8–10 cm) from the base.

Spiraea latifolia 3 ft (0.9 m); Zone 2

Broadleaf Meadowsweet

This North American species ranges from Newfoundland to Michigan, south to New York, and along the Appalachian mountains as far south as North Carolina. It grows in damp meadows and thickets, and along streams. The light green leaves are 1–2 in (2.5–5 cm) long and 1 in (2.5 cm) wide. The white or pale pink flowers, which are arranged in conical clusters 2–4 in (5–10 cm) long at the tips of slender branches, appear from June to September. The shrub is abundant but not objectionable in my garden. A second, very similar species called *Spiraea alba* (narrowleaf spiraea) differs from the former mainly in the narrower width of its leaves and in its flowers, which are always white.

Spiraea tomentosa 3 ft (0.9 m); Zone 4

Steeplebush; Hardhack

This North American species ranges from Nova Scotia to Manitoba and south as far as Tennessee and Arkansas. A denizen of sites similar to those suitable for *Spiracea latifolia,* this species differs from *S. latifolia* in having smaller, heavily veined leaves, green on top and densely covered with tawny or rust-colored indumentum below. The thin branches are also densely coated with the rusty wool. The pink flowers are arranged in a dense spirelike cluster and occur in June to September.

SYRINGA (OLEACEAE) Lilac

The genus *Syringa* comprises some 30 species of deciduous shrubs and small trees native to eastern Asia and the Himalayas, as well as to southeastern parts of Europe, the ancestral home of the most widely planted member of the genus, *S. vulgaris.*

Lilacs are easy to grow, but a few maintenance rules may well be observed to achieve good results. The plants grow best in full sun, though light or partial shade still allows an acceptable production of blooms. They can be moved with relative ease in late fall or early spring, and are indifferent to soil pH, although some gardeners believe that a neutral soil is best for them. Just in case this assumption is correct, and since our soils are acidic, I scatter wood ashes or small quantities of lime around my lilacs every other winter.

If not sprayed with sulfur or another fungicide, lilac leaves inevitably become covered with mildew at the end of summer. While this pathogen is said to cause no serious harm to the plants, I still protect the bushes with a mild fungicide two or three times a year to keep their leaves shiny green until frost.

Lilacs have a tendency to send up suckers from their roots. These suckers should be cut off at ground level, unless additional plants are needed. In that case, the suckers can be dug up in March and grown in the nursery for a year or two. A few suckers may be left in place if an old plant needs rejuvenating. For that purpose, only the strongest shoots are chosen; if they continue to grow well, the old stems are then removed one or two at a time. In this way, an old bush can be renewed in 2 or 3 years.

On rare occasions, a lilac may be attacked by borers whose presence is clearly evident by the sawdustlike material around the holes through which they entered the stem. The infected parts of the plant should be cut off below the damaged area and burned.

Syringa* × *chinensis (*S.* × *persica* × *S. vulgaris*) 15 ft (4.6 m); Zone 3

Chinese Lilac; Rouen Lilac

This is said to be the first lilac hybrid ever introduced, a chance seedling discovered in 1777 in a botanical garden in Rouen, France. The foliage is smaller than that of *Syringa vulgaris,* as are the panicles of purple flowers, whose fragrance is strong and pleasant. The bush in my garden was planted more than 10 years ago and, true to the lilac tradition, it took its time and finally began blossoming only 3 or 4 years ago. The appearance of the plant is rather informal and the bush is best suited for the natural environment on the edge of my wood where it may not have to be restrained in its growth. The plant used to be known in the trade as *S. rothomagensis,* but this name has no botanical standing.

***Syringa meyeri* 'Palibin'** 5 ft (1.5 m); Zone 5

Meyer's Lilac 'Palibin'

Syringa meyeri is native to the Far East. It was named for F. N. Meyer, an official of the U.S. Department of Agriculture who brought it from northern China in the early 1900s. The species is small compared to other lilacs, and the cultivar 'Palibin' is even smaller, taking many years to reach its maximum height of 5 ft (1.5 m). The leaves and the small 4-in (10-cm) high panicles of purple blossoms match the plant's restrained stature. The flowers are considered among the most fragrant of the lilacs.

Syringa vulgaris 20 ft (6 m); Zone 4

Common Lilac

Syringa vulgaris has hundreds of named cultivars which are sometimes called hybrids; nonetheless, many are just different versions of the species. Some were introduced in the 19th century by French nurseryman Pierre Louis Victor Lemoine, but new varieties are constantly being introduced from other sources. They come in single or opulently double flowers in a broad range of colors. Most of them are richly fragrant. Two cultivars of *S. vulgaris* grow in my garden. The first, *S. vulgaris* 'Ellen Willmott', is a pure white, double-flowered variety with a particularly strong fragrance. The second, *S. vulgaris* 'Sensation', has single, fragrant, deep red-purple flowers on which each little petal is edged with a narrow margin of white. The effect is quite attractive, but the bush has been known to occasionally lose this characteristic and revert to a single color.

Taxus (Taxaceae) 60 ft (18 m); Zones 2–6

Yew

The genus *Taxus* consists of eight species that differ from each other mainly in their growth habit, their linear 1-in (2.5-cm) long foliage, and their hardiness. Their native range covers the entire Northern Hemisphere. Only about half the species are widely cultivated, but hundreds of hybrids and cultivars are grown in the temperate zones of the world. Some are among the most popular and frequently used evergreens. On female plants, the dark foliage is brightened in late summer by scarlet arils, which are 0.5 in (13 mm) in diameter and contain a hard seed.

There are many *Taxus* plants in my garden; some were planted by the builder, but many more sprouted throughout the woods from seeds dropped by birds. The handsome dark green yew foliage used to be a welcome respite for the eye in winter in the all-brown deciduous forests—until the deer population explosion came. The animals eat every evergreen seedling whether of *Taxus* (yew), *Tsuga* (hemlock), *Pinus* (pine), or *Thuja* (arborvitae), and they are now devouring wild flowers from *Sanguinaria* (bloodroot) to *Trillium*. The *Taxus* plants must be protected with a repellent or plastic netting if they are to survive.

The *Taxus* species and hybrids in my garden are difficult to identify. Due to heavy interbreeding and the considerable number of forms and cultivars within each species, the taxonomy of the genus is very confusing. One of my upright-growing plants could be *T.* × *media* 'Hicksii' (Hicks yew), a cultivar introduced in the early 1900s by the Hicks Nurseries, Westbury, New York. It is a form of *T.* × *media* (Anglojap yew), which itself is a hybrid of *T. baccata* (English yew) and *T. cuspidata* (Japanese yew), but it could also be the fastigiate form of the English yew, called *T. baccata* 'Fastigiata', which was found on an Irish farm in 1870 and became known as the Irish yew. The other plants in my garden are hybrids and cultivars of untraceable origins.

Thymus vulgaris (Labiatae) 6 in (15.2 cm); Zone 4

Common Thyme

There are several hundred species in the genus *Thymus,* all native to the Eurasian continent and the southern coast of the Mediterranean Sea. They are mostly evergreen, creeping, sun-loving, and drought-tolerant aromatic subshrubs that have been cultivated in North America since the 1600s. Their exact identity is sometimes difficult to trace as they have hybridized freely. Some escaped from cultivation hundreds of years ago and populate wild areas far from civilization. For example, the plant in my garden was a gift from a friend who dug it up on the property around his ski cabin in the mountains of New York State. My identification of it as *T. vulgaris* is only tentative, as it could be a hybrid. Many types of thyme are available in nurseries under trade names that usually reflect the color of their leaves or leaf margins, or the kind of aroma the foliage emits. For example, the hybrid, *T.* × *citriodorus* (*T. pulegioides* × *T. vulgaris*), has the pleasant and refreshing smell of lemons when the leaves are crushed or stepped on, and varieties, *T.* 'Aureus' and *T.* 'Silver Queen' have light yellow and white leaf margins, respectively.

VACCINIUM (ERICACEAE) Blueberry; Huckleberry; Cranberry; Bilberry

There are some 150 species in the genus *Vaccinium*, all native to the Northern Hemisphere and heavily represented in eastern Asia and North America. This is a difficult group to comprehend: some botanists describe certain plants as cultivars while others treat them as separate species. Some believe there should be one *Vaccinium* genus while others believe several genera would be more appropriate.

Many *Vaccinium* species are deciduous, but some are evergreen. There are small trees among them as well as diminutive creepers. Most have in common the typical small urn-shaped blossoms, up to 0.5 in (13 mm) long and 0.25 in (6 mm) wide, varying in color from white to pink to purplish pink and even red. They may be arranged in pendant clusters or they may occur singly, and they never fail to attract honeybees and bumblebees.

Since *Vaccinium* species are ericaceous plants, they require acidic soils. Some prefer moist and even wet situations, and a few grow in poor dry soils. My garden contains several species and varieties of *Vaccinium*. Some plants are more than 50 years old; they were more than 10 ft (3 m) high with trunks 5 in (13 cm) in diameter when I came. New seedlings are still coming up, but I do not consider them weedy; these are wonderful plants to have. In early May, as they become covered with their interesting flowers, the garden begins to buzz with hundreds of bees. In late June and through July, thousands of berries begin to appear, at first shiny green and then dark blue and black, some dusted with white bloom. At that time, flocks of birds begin their daily visits and the state of agitation does not cease until most of the fruit is gone.

There is one more season when these species excel. In autumn their 2-in (5-cm) long elliptic to oval leaves are among the most colorful of all plants. They turn vivid red and remain on the branches for up to 3 weeks. About five varieties of *Vaccinium* grow in my garden.

Vaccinium corymbosum — 12 ft (3.7 m); Zone 3

Highbush Blueberry; Swamp Blueberry; Whortleberry

This handsome, deciduous North American shrub ranges from Nova Scotia to Wisconsin and south to Florida. It grows mostly in wet places and swamps, but in my garden it flourishes also in drier locations. The thick trunks of the very old bushes are covered with cinnamon-colored bark that peels in thin flakes closer to the ground. The species is the parent of many cultivated varieties that were selected for the size, flavor, and abundance of their fruit. I purchased two cultivars, which must be protected from birds by plastic netting. The first, *Vaccinium corymbosum* 'Herbert', bears later in the season and produces berries that from the first picking are up to 1 in (2.5 cm) in diameter. The second cultivar, *V. corymbosum* 'Blueray', has the advantage of keeping its fruit on the branches for weeks until most of the berries are ripe and can be picked at one time.

Vaccinium macrocarpon — Mat-forming vine; Zone 2

Cranberry; Large Cranberry; American Cranberry

This North American evergreen trailing shrub has thin branches up to 3 ft (90 cm) long. Its native range reaches from Newfoundland to Minnesota, and south to Arkansas and North Carolina. The flowers are pink with four recurved lobes, solitary or in groups of two to four. The fruit, a large red berry up to 0.75 in (19 mm) in diameter, has a sour taste. This is the Thanksgiving cranberry of the United States. The plant grows in wet, peaty locations.

Vaccinium vitis-idaea* var. *majus Creeper to 8 in (20 cm); Zone 2

Cowberry; Foxberry; Cranberry

This evergreen creeping shrub is native to Europe and northern Asia. In my garden it grows in a low dampish spot, creeping thinly over an area of several square feet but never covering the ground. There is also a smaller-leaved variety native to the northern regions of North America, called *Vaccinium vitis-idaea* var. *minus*, which I do not grow.

VIBURNUM (CAPRIFOLIACEAE)

Many of the 225 species that comprise the genus *Viburnum* are desirable garden plants. Some have attractive flowers, others have good deciduous or evergreen foliage, and the blossoms of many are deliciously scented. A significant number of the species have bright fruit that remains on the branches well into the winter, delighting the esthetic sense of humans and providing a rich supply of food for birds. Generally, viburnums are native to the Eurasian and North American continents. Eight *Viburnum* varieties grow in my garden.

Viburnum acerifolium 6 ft (1.8 m); Zone 3

Mapleleaf Viburnum; Dockmackie; Arrowwood; Possum Haw

This North American deciduous shrub ranges from Quebec to Minnesota and south to Alabama and Georgia. It is not a bush I would plant in a garden, but since it was here, I maintain a few specimens for their white flowers and the attractive 4-in (10-cm) wide mapleleaf-shaped foliage that turns purplish red in autumn. The abundant blue-black berries also add to the shrub's appeal. The plant spreads by underground runners and must be regularly restrained if large thickets are not desired.

Viburnum* × *burkwoodii (*V. carlesii* × *V. utile*) 6 ft (1.8 m); Zone 5

This mostly deciduous hybrid was raised in 1924 by Burkwood and Skipwirth in England. It has very fragrant pinkish flowers and 4-in (10-cm) long foliage that turns reddish in the early autumn before it falls. It is a vigorous grower and is easy to propagate, which tends to ensure that the plants in the trade are grown from cuttings on their own roots. This, in turn, precludes the occurrence of a disease that kills other viburnums that are difficult to root and must be grafted, thus providing a sensitive area for the disease's entry.

Viburnum carlesii 5 ft (1.5 m); Zone 5

Korean Spice Viburnum; Fragrant Viburnum

This deciduous species is native to Korea and was introduced to North America in 1902. It is less vigorous than *Viburnum* × *burkwoodii*, but it is one of the most sweetly scented shrubs in nature. The leaves are 4 in (10 cm) long, and the white flowers occur in 3-in (8-cm) wide cymes. Since the species does not root easily, it is usually grafted on a more reliable stock. The graft union is sometimes attacked by a graft blight for which there is no cure and which nearly always kills the shrub. I planted the bush to please my wife who particularly enjoys the fragrance of its blossoms as they perfume a wide area of the garden. The plant has survived for many years and I hope that it is now out of danger. Should it die, I will plant another specimen as we do not want to be without *V. carlesii*.

Viburnum dentatum 10 ft (3 m); Zone 3

Arrowwood

This North American deciduous species ranges from New Brunswick to Florida and Texas. It occurs in several forms, some of which have been proposed by botanists as separate species. The form growing in my garden has attractive roundish leaves 2–3 in (5–8 cm) in diameter, with sharply pointed deep teeth on the margins and prominent veins. The flowers are white and in 3-in (8-cm) wide cymes, and the fruit is blue-black, rounded, and 0.25 in (6 mm) long. The straight, upright branches add to the attractive appearance of this shrub which is handsome enough to maintain in a few specimens.

***Viburnum plicatum* 'Mariesii'** 10 ft (3 m); Zone 4

Maries' Doublefile Viburnum

This is a beautiful cultivar of *Viburnum plicatum* (Japanese snowball). It grows as a large shrub or a small tree with tiered horizontal branches that are covered with thick, dark green, pleated, deciduous, 3.5-in (9-cm) long leaves. From the upper side of each branch, almost along its entire length, rises a double row of white lacy flowers that give the bush a most unusual and elegant look. Each of the flat 3-in (8-cm) wide blossom cymes consists of a central cluster of inconspicuous fertile blooms and an outer ring of showy, white, sterile petals whose sole purpose is to attract insects to pollinate the fertile parts of the flower. The inner portion produces fruits that ripen red and, remaining at that stage for some time, eventually turn black later in the season. The plant is easy to propagate. Ten years ago, I layered a branch in a friend's garden. It rooted easily and a few months later I planted it in my garden. It grew into a tall shrub from which I took two cuttings that today are also blooming bushes. The plant flowers abundantly even in relatively heavy shade, but in full sun with plenty of moisture it is a very beautiful shrub.

Viburnum* × *pragense (*V. rhytidophyllum* × *V. utile*) 12 ft (3.7 m); Zone 5

This hybrid was raised in 1959 by Josef Vik in Prague. It is a vigorous, hardy, and beautiful plant with long narrow leaves that display prominent veins. The evergreen foliage is shiny green on top and covered with a silvery white indumentum beneath, which shows attractively when the leaves move in a stiff breeze. The clusters of pinkish white flowers are large, but they have no fragrance. Nevertheless, in winter, when the foliage of *Viburnum* × *burkwoodii* and *V. rhytidophyllum* looks mangy and winter-burned, *V.* × *pragense* looks as fresh as it did in early fall.

Viburnum prunifolium 15 ft (4.6 m); Zone 3

Black Haw; Sweet Haw; Sheepberry; Nannyberry; Stagbush

This deciduous North American species is native from Connecticut to Iowa, south to Texas, and east to Florida. It is an attractive shrub or a small tree with abundant white flowers in 4-in (10-cm) wide cymes in May. Its fruit, sometimes 0.5 in (13 mm) long, is the largest of all viburnums. It is used for preserves and is edible after frost, provided the birds leave it alone until then. The leaves turn red in autumn. The species was plentiful in my garden when I came and is seeding itself freely, though it is not weedy.

Viburnum rhytidophyllum 9 ft (2.7 m); Zone 5

Leatherleaf Viburnum

This rather massive Chinese bush has thick, leathery, ovate, 7-in (18-cm) long leaves that are evergreen in more southerly latitudes but do not fare too well in Connecticut winters. Nevertheless, in spring the plant recovers quickly, and by the time the yellowish white flowers in 8-in (20-cm) wide cymes appear in mid May, it looks very handsome again. The blooms have no agreeable fragrance.

Vinca minor (Apocynaceae) 6 in (15 cm); Zone 4

Common Periwinkle; Myrtle

Approximately 12 species comprise the genus *Vinca*. All are plants of Eurasian origin that are widely planted in many parts of the world. *Vinca minor* is among the better evergreen ground covers. Its dark green, lustrous leaves create a fine texture and pattern in shady spots unsuitable for many other plants. The lilac-blue flowers, 1 in (2.5 cm) in diameter, appear in spring and add further to the plant's attributes. Nevertheless, once well-established, and if grown in rich, organic soil, *V. minor* spreads relentlessly, sending its slender runners far outside its confines. In smaller areas it must be strictly controlled.

Of the several attractive cultivars, *Vinca minor* 'Aureo-variegata' with gold leaf margins and light blue flowers is one of the best. It is particularly welcome in a darker spot of the garden. Both the species and the cultivar in my garden are labor-intensive ground covers. First, weeds grow easily through a vinca cover and must be periodically removed. Second, the new long and persistent runners must be frequently headed back.

Yucca filamentosa 3 ft (0.9 m); Zone 4

Adam's Needle; Bear Grass

The genus *Yucca* has about 40 species, all native to North America. Only a few are hardy in northerly latitudes. They are stemless or with short woody trunks, with evergreen, tough, swordlike leaves that grow stiffly upright, crowding around the center. The leaves grow from a thick rhizome that on some species was used as food by Native Americans and is still so used in Central and South America. Until I installed a fence, the yucca plants in my garden used to be heavily damaged by deer that stripped the green substance off the long foliage down to the whitish fibrous structure of the leaves. The thick rhizomes are also eaten by deer and by rodents. Plants that are damaged severely do not produce the beautiful 5-ft (1.5-m) high spikes of white bell-shaped flowers that in July create the festive effect of a large candelabrum.

PLATE 53. *Actea pachypoda* (white baneberry) against the lichen-covered stone wall.

PLATE 54. The steel-blue blossoms of the North American wild flower, *Amsonia tabernaemontana* (bluestar), in late May.

Nonwoody Plants (Herbs)

Achillea millefolium (Compositae) 2 ft (0.6 m); Zone 3

Common Yarrow; Milfoil; Sanguinary; Thousand Seal; Nose-bleed

There are about 100 species in the genus *Achillea,* native mostly to Europe and Asia but naturalized as weeds in all temperate zones of the world. *Achillea millefolium* is a perennial herb with strongly aromatic leaves up to 10 in (25 cm) long, dissected into many fine segments. The small flowers, arranged in dense flat clusters at the top of the stems, are usually white, but in recent years the plant has been widely hybridized and is now available in colors ranging from pink to red and yellow. This species prefers a sunny dry location and grows even in poor soil.

Actea pachypoda (Ranunculaceae) 3 ft (0.9 m); Zone 3

White Baneberry; White Cohosh; Doll's Eyes

The genus *Actea* contains about eight species native to the temperate zones of North America and Eurasia. *Actea pachypoda* is a name applied to plants of North American origin, while the Eurasian plants are called *A. spicata*. All are perennial herbs with large compound leaves of five or more sharply toothed leaflets. The flowers are arranged in racemes consisting of many small blossoms with tiny, barely distinguishable petals. Each flower matures into a poisonous 0.25-in (6-mm) long white berry with a small black dot at its tip. As a garden subject, the plant is particularly effective in the fall when the spires of ivory berries provide a bright accent in the darkened landscape (Plate 53). *Actea pachypoda* is sometimes called *A. alba*.

Adiantum pedatum (Polypodiaceae) 1.5 ft (0.5 m); Zone 4

Maidenhair Fern; Five-finger Fern; American Maidenhair; Northern Maidenhair

The genus *Adiantum* includes more than 200 species of mostly tropical ferns, although a few are from the northern temperate regions. *Adiantum pedatum* is mainly a North American plant that ranges from Nova Scotia to Alaska and south to California and Louisiana, with some colonies found also in northeastern Asia. It is a deciduous and hardy yet refined fern with slender, brownish black stalks divided at the top into two recurving branches. Each branch bears thin branchlets with fanlike leaflets somewhat resembling the leaves of the maidenhair tree, *Gingko biloba*. The dark brown branched rootstock spreads extensively and sends up new clusters of fronds throughout the growing season. The plant is decorative and easy to grow, preferring shady locations. It does have one enemy, however: slugs. Unless controlled by slugbait from very early spring, these pests can eat all the new fronds the plant can produce. (See also "Ferns.")

***Ajuga pyramidalis* 'Metallica Crispa'** (Labiatae) 2 in (5 cm); Zone 6

Bugleweed; Spinach Ajuga

The genus *Ajuga* contains about 40 species, all native to Eurasia. Some are short-lived perennials while others are stoloniferous ground covers that spread aggressively and are not suited for restricted areas. *Ajuga pyramidalis* 'Metallica Crispa' is a well-mannered cultivar. Instead of stolons, it has rhizomes that slowly cover the allotted area with dark, evergreen, crinkled foliage. In early summer, 4-in (10-cm) tall spikes of dark blue flowers rise above the dense carpet. This cultivar is an ideal ground cover for partial shade and for protecting a steep bank from erosion. In my garden it is slightly damaged in most winters.

Amsonia tabernaemontana (Apocynaceae) 3 ft (0.9 m); Zone 4
Bluestar; Blue Dogbane; Willow Amsonia

The genus *Amsonia* contains about 20 species of perennial herbs native to North America and eastern Asia. *Amsonia tabernaemontana* is a North American species ranging from Virginia to Georgia, west to Missouri, and south to Texas. It is perfectly hardy in New England. The plant forms large clumps of slender stems with scattered, alternate, narrow leaves 2–4 in (5–10 cm) long. The stalks terminate in loose clusters of blue starry flowers 0.75 in (2 cm) in diameter. Opening in late May to early June, the blooms are pale steely blue, a hue not commonly encountered in nature (Plate 54). As with other blue blossoms, the true shade of this pretty North American wild flower is impossible to reproduce on film. The plant is not demanding as to growing conditions, but prospers best in light shade in rich moist soil. It seldom needs dividing, but if additional plants are needed, it is easy to cut a portion of the clump with a spade and move it elsewhere.

ANEMONE (RANUNCULACEAE) Wind Flower

The genus *Anemone* comprises up to 120 species of perennial herbs of varying sizes, native mostly to the temperate zones of the Northern Hemisphere. The compound leaves are divided into many segments, often feathered into long plumes. The flowers are mainly solitary, consisting of small bushy rings of yellow stamens, sometimes surrounding a small green ball in the center. The blossoms lack petals but are subtended by showy sepals in white, red, blue, rose, yellow, and other colors. Some anemones are among the earliest flowers of spring, while others bloom well into October or until frost. I grow six varieties in my garden, all hardy and easy to grow if their modest demands are met.

Anemone blanda 5 in (13 cm); Zone 5
Wind flower

A native of southeastern Europe, Asia Minor, and southwestern Siberia, this hardy anemone is among the first flowers to open in spring. The attractive blossoms are 2 in (5 cm) wide and come in colors ranging from clear blue to pink, pink-purple, and white. A well-established planting covers the ground completely with the pretty blooms. The leaves, which are divided into many segments, disappear by midsummer. The small irregular tubers are planted in the fall and should be soaked for several hours before they are put into the ground, generally not more than 3 in (8 cm) deep. Once established, the plants seed themselves generously if the ground is reasonably moist. They grow best in sun or light shade under deciduous trees.

PLATE 55. A bed of *Anemone* × *hybrida* (Japanese anemone) in mid September.

Anemone* × *hybrida (*A. hupehensis* var. *japonica* × *A. vitifolia*) 6 ft (1.8 m); Zone 6
Japanese Anemone

This large hybrid is sometimes sold as *Anemone japonica*. The compound, heavily divided leaves are up to 12 in (30 cm) long, and the tall, sturdy stems provide a support for many slender 12-in (30-cm) long stalks that terminate in single, smooth, and elegant 3-in (8-cm) wide blossoms with seven or more broad sepals. The flowers are usually ivory-white and have in the center a small wreath of bright golden stamens circling a tiny 0.25-in (6-mm) wide radiant light green globe (Plate 55). The abundant tall stems make sumptuous cut flowers for a tall floor vase, and by removing the spent blossoms as they fade, the great bouquet lasts a week or more in a cool room or an entry hall. *Anemone* × *hybrida* begins to bloom in early September and continues until frost.

If the first frost comes early one year, it is worth saving the beautiful flowers and the dozens of buds the plant will have produced by the end of August by covering plants with a sheet of plastic. With the autumn often warming up again into Indian summer, the buds will keep opening well into October or even November. By early winter, this great volume of lush vegetation turns brown and the plants go dormant until spring. At that time they can be divided or thinned out, a job required every few years since the original plants spread by thin rhizomes into masses of new plants.

This anemone does best in rich, moist soil in sun or partial shade, preferably along a fence or some other barrier to support it in wind and heavy rain. There are several cultivars available, some differing very little from each other. Cultivars 'Alba' and 'Honorine Jobert' have white single flowers of great purity and refinement; 'Prince Henry' has flowers of strong rose-pink; other cultivars have flowers of darker pink to light red.

Anemone nemorosa 9 in (23 cm); Zone 4

European Wood Anemone

This charming anemone is native to the colder zones of the Eurasian continent. It spreads willingly by rhizomous roots 0.1–0.25 in (3–6 mm) thick, but it never becomes weedy. It is difficult to reproduce from seed, which is reluctant to germinate unless fresh. On the other hand, if the seed is allowed to drop to the ground or collected and scattered immediately upon ripening, it produces a thick growth of new seedlings in a year or two. The leaves, 6–10 in (15–25 cm) long, are typical for the genus and are divided into many smaller segments. The flowers, up to 1.5 in (4 cm) in diameter, have six to eight sepals and are usually white, although color cultivars are available. I grow *Anemone nemorosa* 'Major' (with large white flowers); 'Allenii' (blue); 'Rosea' and 'Rubra' (both pink); 'Royal Blue' (purple); and a cultivar that has double flowers with numerous white and green sepals mixed in a dense tuft. All varieties are attractive, but mass plantings of the simple white version, especially 'Major', are the most beautiful. The plant does best in rich, moist soil under deciduous trees whose bare branches polarize and moderate the strong rays of the early spring sun which otherwise wilt the delicate blooms.

Anemone pulsatilla. See ***Pulsatilla vulgaris.***

Anemone quinquefolia 12 in (30 cm); Zone 4

Wood Anemone; Wind Flower

This plant is somewhat similar to *Anemone nemorosa*. It is native to North America ranging from Quebec to Iowa, and south to Tennessee and the Carolinas. The rhombic-shaped compound leaves consist of several leaflets. The flowers have five to seven white sepals, are about 1 in (2.5 cm) wide, and grow on stems up to 12 in (30 cm) tall. The flowers open in late spring. The plant tends to be a sparse bloomer and prefers woodsy, moist, moderately acidic soils.

Anemone sylvestris 18 in (46 cm); Zone 4

Snowdrop Anemone

Though reminiscent of both *Anemone nemorosa* and *A. quinquefolia*, this anemone is larger in all its aspects. The white fragrant flowers, up to 3 in (8 cm) in diameter, open from April through July. The species, which is native to eastern Europe and Siberia, is a beautiful plant for wild locations but should be kept out of smaller areas as it spreads aggressively by underground stolons. Light shade and a humus-rich acidic soil with good drainage suit this species best.

Anemone vitifolia 3 ft (0.9 m); Zone 4

Grape Leaf Anemone

This Himalayan native resembles *Anemone* × *hybrida* for which it served as one parent. The large divided leaves have a vague similarity to grape leaves, hence the botanical and the common names. The flowers are silvery pink and 2–3 in (5–8 cm) in diameter, and open from September through October if they are not cut down by early frost. The large flower cymes make this an excellent cut flower, but they also make the stems top heavy. A temporary support may be necessary. Like other anemones, this species prefers humus-rich, slightly acidic soil that is moist but well drained. The plants in my garden are of the cultivar *A. vitifolia* 'Robustissima', but I am not certain how they differ from the typical version of the species.

Anemonella thalictroides (Ranunculaceae) 9 in (23 cm); Zone 4

Rue Anemone

This North American plant ranges from Maine to Minnesota, and south to Oklahoma and Florida. It is the only species in the genus *Anemonella*. As the epithet indicates, the foliage strongly resembles that of *Thalictrum* (meadow rue). The plant is low growing and delicate looking. The white to pale pink or purple flowers have no petals but are subtended by five to ten sepals and are up to 0.75 in (2 cm) wide. It is a most endearing wild flower growing in rich, open woods and blooming in April and May. There are several cultivars in my garden, including a purple version and a very beautiful tiny double-flowered form.

AQUILEGIA (RANUNCULACEAE) Columbine

The genus *Aquilegia* contains about 70 species, mostly hardy perennial herbs native to the temperate zones of the Northern Hemisphere. Many have been hybridized and become popular garden subjects. Almost all are attractive and interesting plants that are suitable for the cultivated as well as the wild garden. They are said to prefer light sandy loam in light shade, but my plants grow, bloom, and multiply prolifically in almost any situation where I have scattered the seeds. Since they are not long-lived, plantings sometimes disappear after 4 or 5 years and may have to be reestablished in new areas.

The plants bloom even in heavier shade, a location that seems to have the advantage of keeping to a minimum the infestation by *Phytomyza aquilegiviora* (columbine leaf miner), which sometimes ravishes plants grown in full sun. This insect can be controlled by picking off infested leaves as soon as they appear, and by removing spent foliage in late fall and destroying it in a fire or incinerator.

Aquilegias are particularly welcome when planted in groups along shady paths where their refined foliage and colorful blossoms create an airy effect. I grow five varieties of *Aquilegia*.

Aquilegia caerulea 2.5 ft (0.8 m); Zone 4

Rocky Mountain Columbine

This western species, one of the prettiest aquilegias, is the state flower of Colorado. The long-spurred flowers are usually cerulean blue to darker blue. Since the home of this species is in the mostly calcareous Rockies, I scatter some wood ashes around the roots of my plants every winter to sweeten the acidic soil. The plants are prospering because or, maybe, in spite of the ashes.

Aquilegia canadensis 2.5 ft (0.8 m); Zone 4

Wild Columbine; American Columbine; Rock-Bells; Meeting-Houses; Honeysuckle

The range of this plant reaches from Quebec to Wisconsin, and south to Texas and Florida. Every gardener has an opinion on the beauty of flowers, and I think that this plant is nature's masterpiece when it comes to columbines. It is tall, vigorous, undemanding, and still very lovely (Plate 33). The flowers are reminiscent of 1.5-in (4-cm) long yellow chimes, shading to red and hanging from long slender stems. Each blossom has five petallike sepals and five real petals that are extended upward in the form of hollow spurs, terminating in tiny balls that secrete nectar. A well-grown stand of *Aquilegia canadensis* in bloom is a beautiful sight. The plant seeds itself readily, especially in dappled shade and in the margin of woods, in moist, rich well-drained loam. It blooms from April through July.

***Aquilegia flabellata* 'Nana Alba'** 6 in (15 cm); Zone 3

This is a white-flowered dwarf form of the blue-purple Japanese species *Aquilegia flabellata*. The foliage is lush light green, and the flowers are shorter and fatter than those of the North American columbines. This hardy plant is well-suited for a partly shaded spot in a rock garden. It blooms in April and May.

***Aquilegia* 'Nora Barlow'** 2.5 ft (0.9 m); Zone 4

This cultivar is a curiosity with excellent foliage and strange double flowers. The white, pink, and green petals are mixed together, and the flowers look more like tiny hedgehogs than the blossoms of a columbine. The plant seeds itself too readily.

Aquilegia vulgaris 1.5 ft (0.5 m); Zone 4

European Crowfoot

This European species has dark green foliage and rather heavy looking but interesting dark purple flowers with hooked spurs. It grows well in damp light shade where it seeds itself, though not too prolifically as it probably prefers soils that are somewhat less acidic than those in my garden.

ARABIS (CRUCIFERAE) Rock Cress

The genus *Arabis* includes some 100 species native to North America and Eurasia. Some are weedy annuals or biennials growing 4 ft (1.2 m) tall, while others are desirable creepers with white, pink, or rose-red flowers that are well suited for a sunny rock garden. I grow two species of *Arabis*.

Arabis alpina 12 in (30 cm); Zone 5

Mountain Rock Cress

Arabis alpina comes from the mountains of Europe. In rich soil, it grows to 12 in (30 cm) in height and survives even in poor soils where it remains a low, slowly spreading mat. The leaves are light green, slightly shiny, and about 1 in (2.5 cm) long with two or three teeth on either margin. The flowers, growing in short racemes, are usually white, as in the variety 'Snow Cap', but may be also rose-red, as in 'Rosea'. They appear in mid to late spring. My plants grow in a wall by the pond and have produced a few seedlings even in that vertical position. The species is similar to *A. caucasica*, so the two species are sometimes difficult to distinguish from one another.

Arabis caucasica 12 in (30 cm); Zone 5

Wall Rock Cress

This species is native to southeastern Europe, Asia Minor, and eastward to the mountains of Iran. It is more widely planted and available from nurseries than is *Arabis alpina*. The foliage is larger, often 2.5 in (6.4 cm) long, with several teeth on each margin, and is covered with thin whitish pubescence. The flowers are white, 0.75 in (2 cm) wide, and fragrant, growing in 2-in (5-cm) long racemes and, opening from early to late spring (Plate 20). The plant grows well in dry sunny locations, but in my garden has grown for many years also in nearly full shade in rich woodsy soil where it tends to become less compact but still attractive.

Aralia nudicaulis (Araliaceae) 1 ft (0.3 m); Zone 3
Wild Sarsaparilla

There are some 30 species in the genus *Aralia,* native to North America and parts of Asia, particularly the Malay Peninsula. Several are shrubs, and some are 45-ft (14-m) high trees. *Aralia nudicaulis* is a North American herb ranging from Newfoundland to Manitoba and south to Tennessee and Georgia. The plant has only one leaf on a naked 1-ft (30-cm) high stalk, which arises directly from a pencil-thick root creeping just below the forest litter. The leaf is divided into three parts each of which has five pointed and sharply toothed leaflets 4–5 in (10–13 cm) long. The thin flower stalk, shorter than the leaf, also rises directly from the rootstock and it, too, is divided toward the top into three clusters, each bearing naked greenish white blossoms that mature into small black berries. The aromatic root is sometimes used as a substitute for regular sarsaparilla. The plant spreads slowly in rich moist woods and margins and seldom needs to be weeded out.

Arisaema triphyllum (Araceae) 2.5 ft (0.8 m); Zone 5
Jack-in-the-pulpit; Indian Turnip

The genus *Arisaema* consists of some 190 species of tuberous herbs, some with flowers of unusual, even peculiar shapes, native mostly to the Eurasian landmass. *Arisaema triphyllum* is a North American species ranging from New Brunswick to Manitoba and south to Mississippi and Florida. It has one or two leaves on long bare stalks, divided into three leaflets, each of which may be up to 6 in (15 cm) long. The flower (Preacher Jack) is a 0.4-in (1-cm) thick club-shaped spadix 3 in (8 cm) long that rises from the bottom of the "pulpit," a wider tube formed by a modified leaf called a *spathe.* The leaf formation extends in the back above "Jack" to create a roof over the "pulpit."

This inflorescence, occurring from March to June, may be in colors varying from light green to dark reddish brown, often with dark vertical markings on the "pulpit." The colors, and some variations in the foliage, have caused several botanists to attempt to divide the species into varieties, subspecies, and even additional species. Names such as *Arisaema stewardsonii, A. atrorubens, A.* 'Zebrinum' and others have appeared in some publications. From year to year, specimens in my wet wood occur that fit some of these descriptions, but they live out their life cycle and in their place arise dozens of new plants with yet different characteristics. It would seem that the plant is variable by nature and that many of the versions in my garden are nothing more than forms of the same species.

By late summer the interesting flowers begin to mature into large clusters of brilliant red berrylike fruits that extend the appeal of this exotic-looking plant well into the autumn. Birds, squirrels, and mice eat the fruits and scatter the seeds, spreading the plant and assuring its continued presence in the damp, shady areas of the wood. The plants grow from rounded rhizomes 1–2 in (2.5–5 cm) in diameter that were once used by Native Americans as food and that are still used medicinally. It appears that *Arisaema triphyllum* is indifferent to soil acidity. Although it is sometimes recommended for neutral soils with pH 6.0 to 7.0, many of my plants grow satisfactorily even in pH below 5.0.

Asarum europaeum (Aristolochiaceae) 4 in (10 cm); Zone 5
Wild Ginger

The genus *Asarum* is comprised of about 75 species native mostly to Asia, particularly Japan, and represented also in Europe and North America. *Asarum europaeum* is an attractive evergreen ground cover with uniformly green, kidney-shaped leaves on thin 4-in (10-cm) long petioles. The small, dark brown, pitcher-shaped flowers are huddled at the base of the plant, which grows best in shaded locations in rich, moist soils of moderate acidity, although in my garden it seems to tolerate a pH as low as 5.0. There are several desirable North American species, including *A. shuttleworthii* from the Southeast and *A. caudatum* from the Northwest. *Asarum canadense,* which is native to the entire eastern half of North America, is deciduous; it is a vigorous plant that may become invasive. The roots of *Asarum* species are aromatic, but despite its common name, the genus bears no relation to real ginger.

Asclepias tuberosa (Asclepiadaceae) 2 ft (0.6 m); Zone 4

Butterfly Weed; Pleurisy Root; Tuberroot

Most of the 200 species of the genus *Asclepias* (milkweed) are native to North America and Africa. Though the majority have a milky sap that flows when a part of the plant is broken or damaged, *A. tuberosa* lacks this feature.

This species is a very attractive North American wild flower ranging from Vermont to Nebraska and from Colorado to Florida. The tall, erect stalks are covered with narrow 4-in (10-cm) long leaves, and both stalks and leaves bear thin silky hairs. The flowers appear at the top of the stems in 4-in (10-cm) wide cymes that are favored by butterflies. Their color is mostly vivid orange-red, but occasionally also yellow, rose-red, or white individuals occur.

The plant has a long thick root that has been used in medicine and that tends to be difficult to dig up and move. Nonetheless, with abundant pollination assured by the plant's popularity among insects, there are always more than adequate supplies of seeds, which germinate even if planted in the most rudimentary manner in slightly stirred soil, whether rich or poor, in a sunny dry location, and which bloom in a year or two. The long, pointed beanlike seedpod contains dozens of flat seeds, 0.24 in (6 mm) across, that are attached to 1-in (2.5-cm) wide fluffs of white down. All this is neatly and tightly folded into the narrow cylindrical seed container that splits open when ripe, releasing one of the parachutes at a time and allowing the autumn breeze to carry it to new sites. Unless the seed finds a patch of disturbed, dry, soft ground in the sun, it will not germinate. The plant seldom becomes weedy.

ASTER (COMPOSITAE)

A genus of 250 to 500 species, the asters are native to North and South America, Eurasia, and Africa, but are absent in Australia. Eastern North America alone is home to more than 75 species. Around the turn of the 20th century, English hybridizers combined several of the North American species and created plants with larger, fuller, and more colorful blossoms than the individual species. The new hybrids bloomed toward the end of September and, since September 29th is St. Michael's Day, they soon became known as Michaelmas-daisies.

Every year when the blossoms of wild asters first appear, they signal that summer is coming to an end. As if they were trying to hold back the inexorable march of the seasons, they burst onto the worn-out-green landscape with large patches of color varying from silvery white to rich purple. The plants finally give up after several hard frosts, when it is certain that the warm sun will not be returning until next spring.

Asters are present in my garden in considerable numbers but their precise recognition is difficult in some cases. Listed below are the few species that offered the least resistance to my efforts for correct identification.

Aster divaricatus 3 ft (0.9 m); Zone 4

White Wood Aster

This North American plant ranges from Maine to Ohio and south to Alabama. Among the identification marks are the broad 4-in (10-cm) long leaves with toothed margins that are heart-shaped near the lower part of the main stem, and more oval with a sharp tip toward the upper end. The dark reddish brown stalk is smooth, slender, and somewhat zig-zagged. The circle of flower rays is usually white, 1 in (2.5 cm) in diameter, and the small central disk of tiny tubular flowers is yellow turning brownish with maturity. The plant grows on the edges of woods and shrubbery borders and, though somewhat untidy and ragged looking, it is welcome here as a member of the original flora that has populated my backyard.

Aster dumosus 2 ft (0.6 m); Zone 4

Bushy Aster; Rice-button Aster

The range of this aster covers nearly the entire eastern half of North America. The leaves are small and narrow, and the slender upper branches bear 0.5-in (13-mm) wide flower heads with 15–20 white to pale lavender rays.

Aster linearifolius 2 ft (0.6 m); Zone 4

Stiff Aster; Savory-leaf Aster; Pine-starwort

This is one of the more compact North American asters. It ranges from Newfoundland to western Pennsylvania and south to Georgia and Tennessee. The stalks are rather densely covered with stiff, narrow leaves bearing minute bristly hairs. At the top, the stalk terminates in several short branches each of which ends in a solitary flower head with 10–15 narrow, bright blue or purplish blue rays.

Aster novae-angliae 6 ft (1.8 m); Zone 3

New England Aster

This is probably the most showy of the wild asters. It ranges from Quebec to Alberta and south to Colorado and Tennessee. The stems are clad with long, narrow leaves clasping the stalk. At the top of the stem are several small branches, each with a flower up to 2 in (5 cm) wide. In the center of the blossom is a bright yellow disk 0.5 in (13 mm) in diameter, surrounded by 40–50 narrow rays, usually a rich, deep purple. Sometimes the plant needs staking as it becomes top heavy in rains.

Aster novi-belgii 4.5 ft (1.4 m); Zone 3

New York Aster

The native habitat of this aster reaches from Newfoundland to Georgia, mostly along the Atlantic coast. The leaves near the base are up to 7 in (18 cm) long, narrow, with smooth, untoothed margins, partially clasping the stem. As the plant matures, the lower foliage browns and falls. The flower heads are 1 in (2.5 cm) in diameter, with 15–25 light blue or violet-blue rays.

Astilbe (Saxifragaceae) 5 ft (1.5 m); Zone 5

The genus *Astilbe* includes about a dozen species of perennial herbs native to the Himalayas, China, Korea, and Japan, and two species from North America. Most of the plants I grow are probably hybrids created by Oriental and European gardeners since 1800. I can identify only one, *Astilbe* × *arendsii* 'Deutschland', because I remember ordering it and because it is the only white astilbe of low growth in my garden. It is a cross of *A. chinensis* var. *davidii* with several species. The other astilbes in my garden vary from pink to red, but their identity remains unknown.

Except on a few dwarfs, the foliage of astilbes is large and heavily dissected into elegant plumes. The flowers, appearing from June through August, are in tall, feathery panicles in colors from pure white to many shades of pink and bright red. The plants prefer very rich organic soils with plenty of moisture. They do best in shady locations but will grow in the sun if water is available. All are long lived; some of my plants grew along the brook under total neglect for 20 years and, when moved to a more favored area, perked up and developed again into handsome specimens.

***Athyrium goeringianum* 'Pictum'** (Polypodiaceae) 1.5 ft (0.5 m); Zone 3
Japanese Painted Fern

The majority of the 25 species in the genus *Athyrium* are distributed over the Eurasian landmass and North America, but *A. goeringianum* is native only to Japan. The attractive cultivar 'Pictum' is a popular subject in the gardens all over the world. The arching deciduous leaves are generously touched with silver-gray on each leaflet and the stems are reddish brown. This cultivar grows best in a shady, moist position, in soil with adequate organic matter. Reproduction by division is easy in early spring. (See also "Ferns.")

Aurinia saxatilis (Cruciferae) 6 in (15 cm); Zone 3
Basket-of-gold; Goldentuft Madwort; Goldentuft Alyssum; Gold Dust

The genus *Aurinia* has seven species native to central and southern Europe and Asia Minor. Until recently, the plants were grouped with species of the genus *Alyssum*. They differ from them, however, in the structure and shape of their foliage.

Aurinia saxatilis grows into a large mat of brilliant yellow flowers opening in early spring. It spreads its woody roots near the surface of the soil into 6–12 in (15–30 cm) wide cushions and prefers full sun and a well-drained position. It grows even in soil of low fertility.

Caltha palustris (Ranunculaceae) 1 ft (0.3 m); Zone 4
Marsh Marigold; Meadow-bright; Kingcup; May-blob

The 15–20 species in the genus *Caltha* are native to the Northern and the Southern hemispheres. *Caltha palustris* ranges over the entire northern temperate zone of Eurasia and North America, reaching as far south as Tennessee. There appear to be no significant regional differences in the plant populations. As its epithet indicates (*palustris* means "of swamps"), this species grows in marshy ground in sun or under deciduous trees that do not leaf out until the plant is well into its growing and blooming cycle. The leaves are heart-shaped, 2–5 in (5–13 cm) wide, lustrous, and lush green; they are sometimes used in salads, especially when young. The flower heads are up to 2 in (5 cm) in diameter and consist of a bunch of orange stamens surrounded by five or six large, showy bright yellow sepals. Cultivars with larger or double flowers have been selected and are available under names such as 'Monstruosa' ('Monstrosa Plena'), 'Multiplex', and others.

CAMASSIA (LILIACEAE) Camass; Camas; Quamash; Camosh

This North American genus contains five species. All are western plants except one, *Camassia scilloides*, which comes from central portions of the United States. The bulbs from which camassias grow are edible. Native American tribes on the West Coast fought battles over the fields where they grew. Planted in the fall in holes 4–5 in (10–13 cm) deep and 10 in (24 cm) apart, the bulbs may be left undisturbed for many years. Moist, rich, nearly neutral soil in cool, partly shaded locations suits them best. The long, narrow grasslike foliage is folded along the middle and grows from the base of the plant. The flowers appear in late May to early June in terminal racemes on erect stalks that are taller than the leaves. Individual blossoms are up to 1.3 in (3.2 cm) in diameter, with five or six narrow petals somewhat loosely arranged in colors varying from light to dark blue or rarely white. I grow two *Camassia* species.

Camassia cusickii 2.5 ft (0.8 m); Zone 4

This is a tall, robust plant. The flowers are over 1 in (2.5 cm) wide and are a somewhat stronger blue color than the flowers of *Camassia quamash*. This species comes from a narrow range in northeastern Oregon.

Camassia quamash 2 ft (0.6 m); Zone 4

This species ranges from Alberta and British Columbia south to Oregon and Montana. Its botanical name is the original Native American name, and from it was derived the designation of the genus. Sometimes this species is known under the name *Camassia esculenta*. The color of the blossoms varies from plant to plant. My specimens have light steel-blue flowers.

CAMPANULA (CAMPANULACEAE) Bellflower

The genus *Campanula* comprises as many as 300 species native mostly to the Northern Hemisphere. Some come from North America, but the majority are from southern and eastern Europe and the Caucasus Mountains. Many are annual or perennial weeds, although a significant number are desirable garden plants. Over the years, I have grown many species of *Campanula* in my garden and some are no longer here; the seven species listed below endure and flourish.

Campanula carpatica 18 in (46 cm); Zone 3
Carpathian Harebell

This east European plant usually grows well over 1 ft (30 cm) in height, except in its dwarf forms which remain at about 6 in (15 cm). It spreads into compact clumps of rounded leaves from which rise thin, leafless pedicels topped with erect, blue bell-shaped flowers 1–2 in (2.5–5 cm) in diameter. The plant prefers well-drained organic soil in full sun. Cultivar 'Wedgewood Blue' is particularly attractive.

Campanula elatines 6 in (15 cm); Zone 5
Adriatic Bellflower

Since this *Campanula* species is native to the chalk mountains on both sides of the Adriatic Sea, the addition of lime to the acidic soil in my garden has been beneficial. This is a variable species and, in its best forms, an excellent subject for sunny, drier locations and rock gardens, where it spreads slowly into a low, broad mat of sharply toothed, rounded leaves through which rise racemes of blue campanulate flowers 0.5–1.0 in (1.3–2.5 cm) in diameter. One of my plants, *C. elatines* var. *garganica* 'Starry Blue', is positioned vertically in a retaining wall 3 ft (0.9 m) above the channel on the west side of the pond. It receives abundant light, but moisture is scarce; still, it grows and blooms well.

Campanula glomerata 2.5 ft (0.8 m); Zone 3
Clustered Bellflower

This is a Eurasian native that has become established as a wild flower in North American roadsides and empty lots. The tall stems, with lance-shaped leaves up to 5 in (13 cm) long, bear dense terminal clusters of dark purple, blue, or occasionally white bells 0.75–1 in (2–2.5 cm) long. The plants in my garden are situated in moist but well-drained organic soil in a mostly sunny location. All are *Campanula glomerata* 'Joan Elliot', a variety with somewhat larger, up-facing, dark blue flowers.

Campanula persicifolia 2 ft (0.6 m); Zone 3
Willow Bellflower; Peach-bells

This variable species is common throughout the Eurasian landmass. It spreads slowly by runners into colonies of nearly evergreen narrow leaves 6 in (15 cm) high, from which rise 2-ft (60-cm) high stems with campanulate flowers that are 1.5 in (4 cm) long and deep blue to white in color. I started a patch of blue-flowered *Campanula persicifolia* from seeds collected 20 years ago in a European garden. The patch now covers an 8 sq ft (0.7 sq m) area.

Campanula portenschlagiana 6 in (15 cm); Zone 4

This species from northern Croatia is similar to *Campanula elatines*. The difference lies mainly in the shape of its bells, which are more funnelform and not lobed beyond the middle. The bells are up to 0.75 in (2 cm) long. The rounded foliage remains green through most of the winter.

Campanula poscharskyana 6 in (15 cm); Zone 4

This is another plant from the southeastern Alps. It is also similar to *Campanula elatines* and is sometimes listed as a variety of that species. It is, however, more vigorous and can become rampant, a tendency it is displaying in my garden even under the severely restrained conditions of its current planting site, where it hangs out of a small pocket of arid soil in the wall above the pond (Plate 61).

Campanula rotundifolia 18 in (46 cm); Zone 3
Bluebell; Harebell; Common Harebell

This rather dainty species grows in clumps of 0.5-in (13-mm) wide rounded leaves and tall, slender stalks with thin racemes of nodding, usually blue, bells 0.5 in (13 mm) in diameter. Sometimes the species is called the bluebells of Scotland. The flowers are often white, and the plant is native from Alaska through northern Asia and the entire European continent.

Chimaphila maculata (Pyrolaceae) 10 in (25 cm); Zone 3
Spotted Wintergreen; Spotted Pipsissewa

There are seven or eight species in the genus *Chimaphila*. Four or five are Eurasian plants, and the other two are native to North America. *Chimaphila maculata* ranges from New Hampshire to Michigan and south to Tennessee and Alabama. It grows in dry open woods in very acidic soils of pH 4.0 to 5.0, where it spreads very slowly by thin underground stems, never becoming thick or abundant. The evergreen leaves are lance-shaped, deeply toothed, up to 2 in (5 cm) long, and dark green with distinctive white markings along their midrib. In early summer, 6-in (15-cm) tall slender stems arise from the leafstalks and terminate in a small umbell of three to five white or pinkish, waxy, lightly fragrant flowers 0.75 in (2 cm) across.

The plant grew naturally in my garden and the few specimens that were here are still with me. Occasionally, I add some iron sulfate or slices of an old lemon (pH 2.5–3.5) over the roots to ensure that the plants will not perish should the acidity of the soil diminish due to some unexpected cause, such as leaching from alkaline pockets below or near the plants.

The second North American species, *Chimaphila umbellata,* is similar to this one, but its leaves are uniformly light green. Currently it does not grow in my garden.

CHRYSANTHEMUM (COMPOSITAE)

The genus *Chrysanthemum* has 100–200 species of mostly perennial herbs and subshrubs native to Eurasia, with a few coming from southern Africa. The foliage of many chrysanthemums is strongly aromatic, and that of several species is used for the manufacture of the insecticide pyrethrum. The plants have been extensively hybridized to produce unusual flower forms such as the "football mums", showplants with "spider" or "spoon" petals, and many other large and beautiful or odd-looking versions. There are also modest little chrysanthemums that have nothing more to recommend them than the open, friendly face of an ordinary daisy. I grow three species of *Chrysanthemum.*

Chrysanthemum leucanthemum 3 ft (0.9 m); Zone 4
Oxeye Daisy; White Daisy; Field Daisy; Marguerite; Whiteweed

This is the ubiquitous Eurasian species that has become a favorite garden plant, and a pernicious weed, all over the world. Cultivars with lower growth habit, larger flowers, or other desirable characteristics have been selected and are available. While common, a well-grown plant of the typical version is an excellent addition to a perennial border where it provides an abundance of long-stemmed flowers without which no summer bouquet would be complete.

Chrysanthemum nipponicum 3.5 ft (1.1 m); Zone 5
Montauk Daisy; Nippon Daisy; Nippon Chrysanthemum

This species has soft woody stems and in time becomes rather shrubby. As its epithet indicates, it comes from Japan. The leaves are up to 3.5 in (9 cm) long and 1 in (2.5 cm) wide, toothed or with smooth margins, darker green above and lighter beneath, with a strong but agreeable chrysanthemum scent. The tall stalks are covered with leaves and terminate with large white daisies that begin opening in mid September. There is always an abundant supply of new buds the size of a marble that keep unfolding for many weeks until frost. In autumns with late or mild frosts, the last great daisies finally turn brown by early or mid November.

Chrysanthemum weyrichii 10 in (25 cm); Zone 4

This stoloniferous plant also comes from Japan where it was discovered by Dr. Weyrich, a surgeon in the Russian Navy. The leaves are fleshy and heavily dissected, and the stems are prostrate, sending up short stalks with daisylike flowers 1.75 in (4 cm) in diameter, in colors from white to pink. The modest specimen that I planted in the wall above the pond channel creeps vertically through every crack it can find between the stones, surviving the aridity of the location and producing a few rose-pink flowers throughout the season (Plate 56).

PLATE 56. Clinging to a wall, *Chrysanthemum weyrichii* with a few humble daisies in late June.

Cimifuga racemosa (Ranunculaceae) 8 ft (2.4 m); Zone 4

Black Cohosh; Black Snakeroot; Cohosh Bugbane; Fairy Candles

This North American plant is one of 15 species that comprise the genus *Cimifuga,* a group of tall herbs from temperate latitudes of the Northern Hemisphere. It grows in rich soils in woods and other shady locations, and ranges from Massachusetts to southern Ontario and south to Missouri and Georgia. The stem, which between June and September develops a long wand of small white flowers, reaches considerable height. The foliage is usually divided into three smaller sections and they, in turn, are divided into three leaves 1–3 in (2.5–8 cm) long. The large plumes of the dissected leaves are an impressive feature which, together with the tall flower stems, make the plant a desirable background subject in a wild or woodsy garden. The roots are used for medicine.

Colchicum speciosum (Liliaceae) 8 in (20 cm); Zone 4

The genus *Colchicum* contains 65 species of mostly autumn-flowering bulbs native to Europe, the Mediterranean, and central Asia. The name is derived from the land in the Caucasus by the name of Colchis, today's western Georgia, birthplace of Medea whom Jason met during his quest for the Golden Fleece. Medea helped Jason reach his goal and returned with him to his homeland, Iolcus, to become his queen, but she never gave up the magic potions and poisons brewed for generations by her fellow citizens in Colchis from toxic plants. The name of her country then became a synonym for natural poisonous substances. Centuries later, the Roman poet Quintus Horatius Flaccus wrote poems about the poisonous juices flowing from the Colchian chemists' vessels.

Both Medea and Horace knew of the deadly effects of the lovely autumn blooms of *Colchicum,* and so do the New England deer; they have never bothered the 1.5-ft (50-cm) tall, dark, lush green foliage of *C. speciosum* when it appears in spring. Nor do they ever touch the large chalices of naked blossoms that arise from the ground in early fall. The blooms are up to 4.5 in (11 cm) wide, light purple shading toward white in the center. The bright yellow stamens add an atttractive touch to the subtle hues of the flowers. Slugs are apparently immune to the colchicine in the flowers, which they can consume in a day unless slug bait has been generously applied in a wide circle around the blossoms.

Convalaria (Liliaceae) 6 in (15 cm); Zone 4

Lily-of-the-valley

Depending on the authority one is prepared to accept, there are either three or just one species in the genus *Convalaria*. The plant is native to East Asia, Europe, and the eastern mountains of the United States. To complicate matters further, specimens from each location have been introduced into each of the other two native ranges. Where pure native stands are reliably segregated, some variations in size and growth habit can be identified, but the differences are not sufficient to convince some botanists to assign them the ranks of two or three species.

In the trade, several cultivars have been selected. I have two or three plantings of *Convalaria*; none of them are particularly large or spreading, as is the case in some gardens. As to their identity, they could be either *C. keiskei* from Japan, *C. majalis* from Europe, or *C. montana* from the Blue Ridge Mountains. I also have a small planting of a pink cultivar, *C.* 'Rosea', whose off-color blossoms are hardly an improvement over the pure white flowers of the species. Aside from the lovely, fragrant bell flowers, *Convalaria* plants produce large orange berries that add color and interest to the planting in the fall. Since they, like the foliage, are poisonous, they remain on the stems unharmed well into winter.

Coptis groenlandica (Ranunculaceae) 3 in (7.6 cm); Zone 2

Common Goldthread; Cankerroot

The genus *Coptis* has about 10 species of rhizomous perennial plants native mostly to the northern zones of North America and a few to Eurasia. *Coptis groenlandica* grows in cool, shaded acidic soils from Labrador to Manitoba and south to New York, reaching as far as Tennessee along the mountain ranges. It covers small areas in moist woods, usually as a sparse ground cover, but it may grow into dense mats in favored spots. It requires strongly acidic soils with pH 4.0 to 5.0. The 1.5-in (4-cm) wide leaves are divided into three rounded lobes and rise from thin, golden-yellow rootlets that creep just below the ground litter. The tiny rhizomes have been used in the manufacture of a yellow dye and in medicines. The flowers are white, sometimes yellow, 1 in (2.5 cm) in diameter, with five to seven petallike sepals.

Crocus (Iridaceae) 4 in (10 cm); Zone 3

The genus *Crocus* is native to a wide area from the Atlantic Ocean, along both coasts of the Mediterranean Sea, to the Pamirs. There are about 80 species and hundreds of cultivars and hybrids of *Crocus*. Most are early spring flowering bulbs that give a winter-worn garden a colorful lift. Nevertheless, I gave up growing them in my garden a long time ago. As with tulips, what deer and rabbits did not consume, the mice and voles finished off in a season or two.

Yet, through the decades, two crocuses of unknown designation survived in my garden. One is a very early plant, probably a hybrid, that has grown into a large clump of radiant amethyst cups above the ground and a rich cache of small bulbs below. Occasionally, I uncover the little bulbs and plant a few in other locations with the hope that they, too, will remain undiscovered by predators.

The second little *Crocus* is clearly a species. The flower is small and slender, full of the innocence that only a wild flower can possess. I remember planting the tiny corms many years ago in a spot that has now become overgrown with shrubs. The fragile blooms still come up every spring and one of these years I will move some of them to a more open site. My most recent reluctant attempt to grow *Crocus* again is a small planting of a few bulbs of *C. vernus* 'Haarlem Gem'. It has handsome purple blossoms which, together with the foliage, must be sprayed diligently with a deer repellent.

CYCLAMEN (PRIMULACEAE)

Among the 15–17 species in the genus *Cyclamen,* I found 4 hardy enough in my garden. There are one or two other (*C. cilicium* var. *intaminatum* and *C. cilicium* var. *cilicium,* both from Turkey) that will probably survive here, but I have not grown them as yet. Cyclamens are native to a region from western Iran to parts of north Africa, various Mediterranean isles, and southern and central Europe. They prefer shady locations even at my latitude, but will survive in partial sun if the tubers are of a larger size when planted and if they are kept somewhat moist during their summer dormancy. Several of the tiny tubers my wife grew from seed perished the first summer, even though the sun reached them for only 2 or 3 hours in the afternoon. The others from the same seed packet, shaded by ferns, survived and flowered in 2 years from germination.

Cyclamens are perfect plants for shady nooks along a path or under a deciduous tree. All have fascinating flowers with inverted petals that give the illusion of a small butterfly with folded wings. They come in colors from light purple-pink to carmine red, and rarely white. Some are deliciously fragrant, and many have exquisitely marbled foliage that remains decorative and healthy-looking for a good part of the year. When established, they seed themselves readily.

In most species, once the blossom has matured, the thin, long pedicel winds into a tight ring with the seedpod in the center. When the coil has reached the soil level, it forms a lid over the pod as if to prevent easy access to it by ants and other potential predators. In spring, when the tiny round corms with small circular leaves appear among the large leaves, they can be gently pricked out and planted elsewhere. In some species, an old tuber may grow to the size of a dessert plate which, over the many weeks of its flowering season, may produce 100 blossoms or many more.

Cyclamen leaves and flowers are said to contain a toxic substance that makes them unpalatable to deer and rabbits. Thus far, my experience confirms this theory; I have not seen any damage on my plantings. As to the tubers themselves, they may be also safe from predators such as rodents. However, I have noticed that the plants are periodically investigated by squirrels, as evidenced by the narrow cavities dug in the soil just above the tubers, but the rodents cannot get to them because I enclosed the corms in a wire cage. At least one writer, whose name and book I no longer recall, commented on his or her experience when a large tuber was hollowed out, probably by squirrels. Taking a hint from this, I plant most of my cyclamens in an enclosure made of heavy-gauge galvanized wire mesh (see "Diseases and Pests"). The species that have proven hardy and successful in my garden are listed below.

Cyclamen coum 4 in (10 cm); Zone 5

This species is said to have acquired its name from the Dodecanese isle of Kos but, according to some reports, there is no sign of it on the island. It is native, however, to other locations in the Mediterranean region from Spain to Asia Minor and the Caucasus. The leaves are 2.5 in (6.4 cm) wide, shiny, mottled or uniformly green, usually red beneath. The flowers vary from carmine red to pink or white. They are usually fragrant and appear as early as March, except in warmer climates where they open throughout the winter. Though the species is sometimes considered somewhat tender in Connecticut's climate, it has survived several winters here. Many varieties, such as *Cyclamen coum* ssp. *caucasicum* 'Album' and *C. coum* 'Roseum', are available from nurseries and seed houses.

I have grown *Cyclamen coum* from seeds I gathered in June from blossoms that appeared in March. After the little round seedpods are opened, the seeds are spread on a sheet of paper to dry and then stored in a container that allows some air circulation. They are given a few weeks of post-harvest dormancy, then placed in a refrigerator for about 6 weeks before they are sown in a growing medium and covered with a thin layer of the same material or dry peat moss. It is recommended that seeds be germinated in the dark (the box is covered with cardboard) and in a cool temperature, such as that of a cool basement. I usually observe all these rules, and 70–90 percent of my seeds develop into tiny plants that are transplanted outdoors the following spring. I must admit, however, that on occasion I omitted some of the steps and the seeds still came up. If left outside, the seeds manage to grow into new plants without any help. I wonder whether they grow in my little boxes because of my complicated assistance or in spite of it.

Cyclamen fatrense 3 in (7.6 cm); Zone 4

This rare cyclamen comes from the Fatra hills of Czechoslovakia, its native range reaching to the foothills of the rocky Low and High Tatra Mountains 40 miles (60 km) to the northeast of the Fatra Hills. The plants in my garden have not yet experienced Connecticut's severest winters, but the nursery where I obtained the first tuber (Siskiyou Rare Plant Nursery, Medford, Oregon) rates them hardy to zone 4. The deep-pink flowers open in summer. The unmottled, uniformly green foliage is round, 1.5 in (4 cm) wide, and persists through most of the winter and spring. The fragrant blossoms are similar to those of *Cyclamen purpurascens* of which *C. fatrense* could be a variety or a subspecies. The plant is vigorous and seeded itself the second year. Seeds require one year to germinate.

Cyclamen hederifolium 4 in (10 cm); Zone 5

This species was called *Cyclamen neapolitanum* until a few decades ago. It is native to southern Europe and Asia Minor. The tubers grow slowly and live 50 and even 100 years, sometimes becoming 6–8 in (15–20 cm) wide. The bottom of the tuber is rounded, and the leaf and flower stalks, as well as some roots, grow from a broad depression on top of the tuber. The leaves vaguely resemble the foliage of some *Hedera* (ivy) species, whence the plant's epithet. The leaves are up to 5.5 in (14 cm) long and as wide, heavily marbled with attractive silver markings on top, and sometimes red beneath. The flowers are 1 in (2.5 cm) long, rose pink, occasionally white, and usually not fragrant (Plate 57). The plants bloom prolifically, normally beginning in early fall. Some of my plantings remain covered with blossoms until heavier frost, and in frost-free autumns, until mid November. The beautiful foliage persists through the winter and well into spring.

PLATE 57. A patch of *Cyclamen hederifolium* plants brightening a wooded path in mid October.

Cyclamen purpurascens 5 in (13 cm); Zone 5

This species comes from the mountainous regions of central and southern Europe. It used to be known as *Cyclamen europaeum*. The tubers grow to 1.5 in (4 cm) in diameter, sending up leaves 2 in (5 cm) wide, sometimes uniformly green but usually attractively mottled above and green or dark red beneath. The rather tall, slender pedicels bear 0.75-in (2-cm) long rose-pink or carmine-red flowers that are strongly scented. One of my plants is nearly 20 years old, and in years with adequate moisture it produces plenty of seedlings. It blooms in late summer to early fall.

CYPRIPEDIUM (ORCHIDACEAE) Ladyslipper; Lady's Slipper; Moccasin Flower; Whip-poor-will's Shoe

There are about 50 species in the genus *Cypripedium*, all terrestrial orchids native to North America and the Eurasian landmass. Their pleated leaves are usually broad, and the flowers are mostly solitary or in terminal racemes of a few blossoms each.

As with most orchids, their seeds are among the smallest seeds known. The orchid seeds are dustlike, even microscopic, and contain no endosperm, the condensed form of food usually available to seedlings in the early process of germination. Consequently, orchid seeds must rely on symbiosis, an intimate relationship with mycorrhizae fungi, some portions of which become submerged in the tissue of the seed's embryo and thus provide the seed with food from the soil until it can produce a leaf and manufacture its own nourishment by photosynthesis.

With a few exceptions, cypripediums are nearly impossible to grow in a normal garden. Unless they have grown in a given area naturally, there is little point in attempting to cultivate them. Even then success is not assured. One small native stand of *Cypripedium acaule* (pink ladyslipper) in my garden was suddenly attacked by a fungus that did not respond to any fungicides. All the plants in that location died within a year or two. There are other enemies that make culture of the ladyslippers a formidable challenge. These include mice and voles, and the devastating night-marauders, slugs. Nonetheless, under these trying conditions, I manage to grow two species in my garden.

Cypripedium acaule 18 in (46 cm); Zone 3

Pink Ladyslipper; Stemless Lady's Slipper; Pink Moccasin Flower

This North American plant is native from Newfoundland to Alberta, and south to Georgia, Alabama, and Missouri. It has two heavily veined, broad, pleated leaves 4–8 in (10–20 cm) long, growing directly from the root system. In May, a naked stalk rises between the leaves and terminates in a single pink flower in the form of a 2-in (5-cm) long pouch hanging forward from the base of side petals and sepals (Plate 58). This is one of the more distinctive blossoms in nature. Harold N. Moldenke, in *American Wildflowers* (1949, 382) described it in part as follows:

> The lip is somewhat obovoid, folded inward above, and has a fissure down its front. To this fissure lead scores of veins of deeper color which thus serve as the signposts (or "nectar guides") for the visiting insect. Insects' eyes are especially sensitive to changes in the intensity of color and these nectar guides . . . their color of continually increasing intensity . . . lead the visitor to the only spot where the slipper can be entered. Only large insects are strong enough to open the "door" and enter the flower.

After entering, the "door" closes behind the visitor and cannot be opened from the inside. Only by forcing its way past a sticky stigma, where the pollen on its back from

PLATE 58. A native stand of the orchid *Cypripedium acaule* (pink ladyslipper) in mid June.

another flower is safely removed, is the insect ready to leave, but not without first plastering its back again with new pollen which it takes to another ladyslipper. The complicated mechanism is a precaution against self-fertilization. Insects have been found eating their way through the flower's walls, and large dead bumblebees have been discovered inside, apparently unable to find a way out.

The plant grows only in soils of low pH, the optimal range being between 4.0 and 4.5. Though sometimes found on elevated swamp hammocks, the ladyslipper generally prefers locations that are somewhat dry, and where acidic mulch, such as pine or hemlock needles, is replenished annually. Some shade is desirable. However, if the essential mycorrhizal fungi are not present in the soil, the plant will eventually die out.

Cypripedium calceolus* var. *pubescens 2 ft (0.6 m); Zone 3

Large Yellow Ladyslipper; Golden-slipper; Large Moccasin Flower; Whippoorwill-shoe; Umbilroot; Nerveroot; Yellow Indian Shoe; Venus' Shoe; Noah's Ark

This robust North American variety (of the otherwise more slender Eurasian species *Cypripedium calceolus*) has a range similar to *C. acaule* except that it also grows farther west, as far as Washington State and Arizona. The stem is up to 2 ft (60 cm) high with several ovate veiny leaves up to 8 in (20 cm) long growing along its length. The flower is a pouch 0.75–2 in (2–5 cm) long, yellow, faintly fragrant, backed by three sepals and two narrow, spirally twisted, greenish yellow to purplish brown side petals. Each stem may have one or as many as three flowers.

The hairs of the plant may irritate the skin of some people. The orchid grows in a variety of habitats, but prefers swampy to wet woods. It has almost no restricted acidity range, doing well in soils of pH 5.0 to 7.0. It blooms in May and June, and an old clump may have many flowering stems. Where happy, the plant lives 50 years or much longer. It is the easiest of all slipper orchids to grow in a garden, but it must be vigorously protected against fungi, slugs, and snails. This task, though not necessarily pleasant, is not very difficult. An early application of fungicide, and a generous use of slug bait begun as early as March and continued through April, assures almost complete control. Thereafter, only an occasional follow-up is necessary.

Daffodil. See ***Narcissus.***

Delphinium (Ranunculaceae) 6 ft (1.8 m); Zone 4

The genus *Delphinium* has about 300 species native to many locations around the world. Some have been hybridized into tall, stately garden giants with long spires of single and double blooms each up to 1.5 in (4 cm) in diameter, in all shades of blue and violet as well as pink and clear white. The plants do best in rich sandy loam but grow in other soils as well. They prefer a nearly neutral reaction approaching pH 7.0. An open site with good air circulation is the most desirable location.

Among the plants in my garden are the 5-ft (1.5-m) tall *Delphinium grandiflorum* var. *chinense*, with dark blue flowers, and the bushy, compact, single-flowered *D.* 'Connecticut Yankees', a neat, trouble-free addition, welcome especially in a smaller space in the garden.

Several years ago I collected a few seeds of a plant that used to be included in the genus *Delphinium* but has now been reclassified under the genus *Consolida* (larkspur). The species, called *Consolida ambigua*, is an annual herb, native to the Mediterranean area and central Asia, with blue, white, or pink flowers. It seeds itself modestly on the edges of the wood and shrubbery borders without becoming weedy. It grows up to 1.5 ft (50 cm) in height.

DIANTHUS (CARYOPHYLLACEAE) Pink

The genus *Dianthus* encompasses several hundred species of annual, biennial, and perennial plants native mainly to Eurasia, with a few growing as far south as southern Africa. Though some species may grow 2–3 ft (60–90 cm) in height, most are low-growing or mat-forming plants. Many are suited for rock gardens and other dry places in full sun. The foliage is often dense and stiff, at times silvery gray, and usually decorative even without the flowers, which are generally very attractive, in colors that include all shades of pink and red as well as white and yellow. Eight varieties of *Dianthus* grow in my garden.

***Dianthus alpinus* 'Allwoodii'** 8 in (20 cm); Zone 3

This is a compact plant with silver-green foliage and many fragrant, fringed, sometimes double, flowers 1 in (2.5 cm) in diameter. The species, *Dianthus alpinus*, has white flowers and is native to the Carnic Alps and the limestone Kras Plateau of western Croatia and Slovenia. It has been frequently hybridized. The blossoms of 'Allwoodii' come in many colors, some with distinctive markings or a dark circle in the center. The cultivar is probably a cross rather than a natural selection. It originated at the Allwood Brothers Nursery, Hayward's Heath, England.

Dianthus armeria 16 in (40 cm); Zone 3
Deptford Pink

This is an annual or biennial herb from central and southern Europe and Asia Minor that has become naturalized throughout North America and other parts of the world. In July and August it produces heads of small red flowers. In my garden the flowers are a rich dark red, but I recall seeing the plant growing in the chalky soils of England where it was light rose-pink. It is more or less an attractive weed.

Dianthus barbatus 2 ft (30 cm); Zone 4
Sweet William

This European species may act as an annual, biennial, or a short-lived perennial. It is native from the Pyrenees to the Carpathians and escaped from cultivation and became naturalized in North America and China. The stems are about 12 in (30 cm) tall, though occasionally they may grow to 24 in (60 cm). The flowers, each 0.75 in (2 cm) wide, are velvety, in cymes of many blossoms, and occur in white, pink, and red, mostly with a darker ring in the center. Once established, *Dianthus barbatus* seeds itself unobjectionably.

Dianthus carryophyllus 2 ft (0.6 m); Zone 6
Carnation; Clove Pink; Divine Flower

This short-lived perennial grows about 10 in (25 cm) tall in the garden but may reach 2 ft (60 cm) or more under special cultivation by florists. The narrow, straplike foliage has a bluish cast. The flowers are more than 1 in (2.5 cm) in diameter and may be as much as 4 in (10 cm) wide if grown in a greenhouse. The blooms come in a wide range of colors, are often double with dozens of petals, and are usually strongly fragrant. The plant is grown in southern and southeastern Europe for production of perfumes, but is not particularly hardy in Connecticut. Its origin is somewhat unclear, although it is probably native to the Mediterranean region.

Dianthus deltoides — 8 in (20 cm); Zone 3

Maiden Pink

In nature, this European species grows in dry grasslands and other open spaces. In its compact forms, it is widely cultivated in rock gardens around the world. The foliage is grayish green with a slight white bloom, and the flowers are normally light pink. The blossom color is said to have given the plant its common name in England, where the plant is relatively rare, but where it apparently reminded someone of a maiden's blush. The species occurs in other colors as well, from white to scarlet.

Dianthus gratianopolitanus — 10 in (25 cm); Zone 3

Cheddar Pink

This species is native from France through central Europe, and as far east as Ukraine. It is rare in England where it is protected by law, but it was there that it was given its common English name after the chalk cliffs of Cheddar Gorge. The species provides an excellent evergreen edging, which is occasionally speckled with 0.75-in (2-cm) wide rose-pink flowers.

In addition to the normal version, I grow also the cultivar 'Karlik', which grows less than 6 in (15 cm) high and 18 in (46 cm) wide, with larger, very fragrant, pink flowers. This cultivar is probably of central European origin. Some of my plants of this cultivar are located in very dry pockets of a wall and will probably never grow more than 2 in (5 cm) high and a few inches wide.

Dianthus knappii — 16 in (40 cm); Zone 3

Yellow color is unusual in *Dianthus*. This species, which comes from the limestone mountains along the eastern Adriatic coast, does not spread into a mat as many other members of the genus. Rather, it forms a thin colony of individual plants whose only redeeming feature is the unspectacular heads of sulfur-yellow flowers each about 1 in (2.5 cm) in diameter.

Dianthus **'Zing Rose'** — 6 in (15 cm); Zone 4

This plant is probably a hybrid. It forms a broad, thick mat of dense foliage. The flowers are a strong, extremely bright rose color and enliven any dry, sunny spot, but which are best isolated from plants of gentler shades.

DICENTRA (FUMARIACEAE)

There are about 19 species in the genus *Dicentra,* native mostly to eastern Asia and North America. The leaves are compound, sometimes feathery, and the flowers are of unusual shapes arranged in one-sided racemes hanging on slender pedicels. Three species currently grow in my garden.

Dicentra cucullaria — 10 in (25 cm); Zone 3

Dutchman's Breeches

This North American wild flower grows in a range reaching from Nova Scotia to Minnesota and south to Missouri and Georgia. The divided leaves and the flower stalks rise directly from a small round tuber less than 0.5 in (13 mm) in diameter. The flowers are white, in the form of an inverted *v,* and definitely reminiscent of a pair of tiny upside-down pantaloons. The plant prefers rich moist soil in deciduous woods and other shady places where the sun can shine on it in early spring before the trees leaf out.

Dicentra eximia 12 in (30 cm); Zone 3
Wild Bleeding-heart; Plumy Bleeding Heart; Turkey Corn; Staggerweed
This North American plant is native to the mountains from New York to eastern Tennessee and Georgia. The bluish green foliage is heavily dissected. The one-sided racemes of pendant, light pink, rarely white, flowers are taller than the leaves and appear almost continuously through the growing season. This is an excellent wild flower, which is permanent and easy to grow in the woods and along shady paths.

Dicentra spectabilis 2 ft 90.6 m); Zone 3
Bleeding-heart
This Japanese species is a favorite garden plant around the globe. The large racemes of pendant flowers hover above the leaves, displaying dozens of heart-shaped light pink blossoms or, on 'Alba', pure white blossoms. The lush, light green divided foliage dies to the ground by midsummer or early fall. The plant is easy to grow in part shade, in rich, moist soil (Plate 20).

DIGITALIS (SCROPHULARIACEAE) Foxglove

The 20 species in the genus *Digitalis* are native from central Asia westward through Europe, and south to the Atlas Mountains of northwest Africa. They are mostly perennial or biennial, with tall wands of bell-shaped flowers in various colors. Two species of *Digitalis* grow in my garden.

Digitalis lutea 3 ft (0.9 m); Zone 5
This perennial plant from central and southwestern Europe and northwestern Africa bears yellow flowers along the tall, slender stems. It prefers deep, rich soil in partial shade along the edge of woods. It grows from a mass of fibrous roots and thus is easy to transplant, preferably in very early spring or in autumn.

Digitalis purpurea 4 ft (1.2 m); Zone 4
Common Foxglove
This is a biennial species that occasionally persists for 3 or more years. It is a variable plant occurring in several varieties and cultivars. Though its original home is assumed to be the western Mediterranean, there are wild stands of it throughout Europe and as far north as central Scandinavia. While it seeds itself readily, the plant is easy to control. The root system is shallow and the foliage large. A slight pull with a hand or a rake will uproot the plant, and the whole little mass of organic matter can become part of the surrounding mulch or be relegated to the compost pile. *Digitalis purpurea* is a plant for the wild or semi-wild environment. The tall spires with one-sided racemes of 1-in (2.5-cm) long bells brighten the shady nooks and woods at a time when the spring profusion of color has just faded (Plate 59). The colors vary from white to dark rose-pink. The plant is toxic and neither deer nor any other wildlife ever bother it. The foliage is used for the production of a very useful cardiac medicine digitalis.

PLATE 59. The thin spires of *Digitalis purpurea* (common foxglove) with the foliage of *Osmunda cinnamomea* (cinnamon fern) on the left and *O. regalis* (royal fern) on the right, in mid June.

DODECATHEON (PRIMULACEAE) Shooting Star; American Cowslip

The genus *Dodecatheon* includes 13 species from North America, mostly from the western slopes of the Rockies and Alaska, and one species from the northeast corner of Siberia. The foliage is smooth, growing in a rosette at the base of the plant, and the flowers are arranged in an umbel on top of a naked stem, 8–12 in (20–30 cm) high, nodding from slender pedicels. The flowers are about 1 in (2.5 cm) long, with five reflexed petals and a narrow cone of forward-jutting stamens. The entire blossom has an unmistakable resemblance to a dart or a shooting star. The plants grow best in well-drained soil in partial shade, in thin woods or open slopes, in soil pH that can vary from 4.5 to 6.0. I grow two species of *Dodecatheon*.

Dodecatheon meadia 18 in (46 cm); Zone 4

This plant is native to the eastern and central parts of North America, ranging from Pennsylvania to Alberta, and south to Texas and Alabama. The basal leaves grow to 12 in (30 cm) in length, and the tall flower stalks usually carry several of the interesting blossoms in colors from pinkish white to lavender. A well-grown plant is supposed to produce umbels with as many as 100 or more blossoms. I have not seen such profusion in my garden, but one day I will try to coax some of my plants to this kind of magnificent overproduction.

Dodecatheon pulchellum 10 in (25 cm); Zone 4

The range of this species reaches from southern Alaska and Vancouver Island to Oregon, and east to Montana and Wyoming. It is similar to *Dodecatheon meadia* but its blossoms are dark purple to lavender and its umbels tend to produce somewhat fewer flowers.

Doronicum cordatum (Compositae) 1.5 ft (0.5 m); Zone 4

Leopard's Bane

Doronicum is a Eurasian genus with some 30 species of perennial herbs with yellow daisylike flower heads up to 2.5 in (6.4 cm) in diameter. *Doronicum cordatum,* sometimes known as *D. caucasicum,* comes from southeastern Europe and western Asia. The heart-shaped, partly evergreen foliage is light green, rising to 8 in (20 cm) from spreading, underground stolons that in a few years form a colony several square feet (0.5 sq m) wide. The yellow ray flowers grow on 18-in (46-cm) high stems and open in June. The plant is attractive, particularly in an informal part of the garden where its space does not have to be restricted.

Dryopteris austriaca* var. *intermedia (Polypodiaceae) 1.5 ft (0.5 m); Zone 4

Evergreen Woodfern

The genus *Dryopteris* contains about 150 species of ferns native to North America, Europe, and Asia. They grow in the woods and are often moved to gardens or greenhouses where they are used as florists' greens. Native to North America and Eurasia, *D. austriaca* occurs in several distinct varieties of which variety *intermedia* has finely cut, feathery evergreen leaves. It grows abundantly in my wood.

Although the plant loses its erect stance in winter, the fronds remain green until they are replaced by new growth in spring. The leaves emerge into a vaselike shape from a thick central rootstock which the deer sometimes scoop out like the heart of an artichoke. Plants thus damaged usually do not recover. This fern grows best in moist, shady locations. (See also "Ferns.")

Echinacea purpurea (Compositae) 5 ft (1.2 m); Zone 4

Purple Coneflower

The North American genus *Echinacea* has three species ranging throughout the prairie states and south to Texas and Louisiana. *Echinacea purpurea* is a tall, stout plant with rough, sharply toothed leaves, and strong stems terminating in up to 24 large, sunflowerlike blossom heads each 3–5 in (8–13 cm) in diameter. The large, central brownish cones, the size of a small egg, are surrounded by long pink-purple rays (Plate 60). The plant grows in open areas and thin woods, preferring rich neutral soil. It may be divided in spring, but not too frequently as it takes a few years to reestablish itself. There are several cultivars available, including some with double and white flowers. The specimen in my garden, *E. purpurea* 'Bright Star', a typical pink-purple version, is a profuse bloomer.

***Empetrum eamesii* ssp. *hermaphroditum*.** See under **"Shrubs."**

***Epigaea repens*.** See under **"Shrubs."**

PLATE 60. The butterflies' favorite, *Echinacea purpurea* (purple coneflower) in early July.

Epimedium grandiflorum (Berberidaceae) 1 ft (0.3 m); Zone 6

The taxonomy of the genus *Epimedium* is somewhat unclear. There are about 20 species, but several have been crossed with each other and a clear distinction is not always possible. All are native to Europe and Asia. They make an excellent ground cover for partial shade, creeping by underground rhizomes and forming thin, attractive colonies which in spring are covered with equally airy flowers. Their foliage is similar to that of the North American plant, *Vancouveria hexandra,* except that it is lighter green and somewhat larger. The thin, wiry stems are usually bright red, and the flowers may be white, yellow, or red, occurring in loose panicles. The plants prefer woodsy soil and a sheltered location. Some winters the foliage may stay green, while at other times only dead leaves remain until the next spring. In a severe winter or a very dry summer, a planting may disappear.

Equisetum pratense (Equisetaceae) 1 ft (0.3 m); Zone 2

Shade Horsetail; Scouring Rush

The equisetums are close relatives, and the sole survivors, of the family of treelike plants that 300 million years ago covered vast areas of the Earth. They were so prevalent that their carbonized trunks and branches created inexhaustible deposits of black coal; their accumulated spores alone have turned into large beds of the bright-burning cannel or jet coal. There are 25 to 35 species in the genus *Equisetum* occurring all over the globe with the possible exception of Australia. About 10 species grow in northeastern North America. A precise differentiation is difficult because some species have many distinct forms.

In the process of identification, one of the principal characteristics of this genus is the pattern of the cross section of the stem. Each stem has three kinds of minute channels, and their size, shape, and relative position determine the species or the form. The plant growing in my wood matches reasonably closely the description of *Equisetum pratense.* It creeps thinly along the wet forest bottom but is said to reach down into the subsoil sometimes as much as 8 ft (2.4 m). Every 2–3 ft (60–90 cm), along its creeping rootstock, it sends up an articulated 8-in (20-cm) tall stalk with a few slender branches growing in symmetrical, tiered whorls. The stem and the branches are covered with minute particles of silica, and the plant is sometimes used for polishing, hence one of its common names.

Eranthis hyemalis (Ranunculaceae) 2 in (5 cm); Zone 4
Winter Aconite

This south European plant is a member of a genus of about seven species, all native to the Eurasian landmass. *Eranthis hyemalis* is one of the earliest flowering plants, with low, palmately dissected leaves and 1.5-in (4-cm) wide bright yellow or, rarely, white flowers. It blooms 2 weeks before most crocuses and seeds itself generously in locations with good soil and adequate moisture. The little tuberous rhizomes should be planted in very early fall, about 2 in (5 cm) deep, in sun or deciduous shade.

Erythronium americanum (Liliaceae) 10 in (25 cm); Zone 4
Yellow Adder's-tongue; Fawn Lily; Trout Lily; Dog-tooth Violet

Nearly all 25 species in the genus *Erythronium* are native to North America; only one species grows wild in Europe and east Asia. A majority of the species range along the western slopes of the Rocky Mountains, but the native habitat of *E. americanum* is the eastern half of the continent, reaching from Ontario to Minnesota, and south to Texas and Georgia. The bulbs, the shape and size of a dog's tooth, grow deep in the ground and send up a pair of gray-green leaves, 4–6 in (10–15 cm) long, heavily mottled with brown and white markings, a feature that gave the plant some of its common names. Between the two leaves rises a smooth stalk, 6–10 in (15–25 cm) high, bearing one nodding, bell-shaped, golden-yellow blossom 1–2 in (2–5 cm) long, and 1.5 in (4 cm) wide. Frequently, large patches of these plants grow in apparently ideal locations, but produce only single leaves and no flowers. Only plants with two leaves can yield a blossom, and it often takes many years for the corms to become large enough to flower. Some of the western species are not only larger and more beautiful, but apparently more floriferous. The plants grow best in shade in organic soils with plenty of moisture.

FERNS

There are some 10,000 species of ferns on this planet grouped into a great many genera. Some are distributed over five continents, while others are limited to specific narrow ranges. Every season these plants produce billions of spores so minute that they become an integral part of the normal atmospheric pollution. High-altitude winds carry the spores from place to place and around the globe several times before rain and snow wash them down. Some spores may germinate in several weeks while others take months to come alive.

The ferns' unique method of reproduction is cumbersome and complicated, but it must have served them well over the ages as they are among the oldest plants on earth. As an example, if a spore of *Dryopteris austriaca* (woodfern) lands in an appropriately moist and shady spot, and the temperature is favorable, it first develops into a tiny substance called *prothallus*. This minute, one-celled body quickly anchors itself to the soil with an extremely thin rootlike hair and begins dividing into more cells until it becomes a flat thin surface about 0.25 in (6 mm) wide. On its underside, it develops sexual organs; the male and female organs are at the opposite ends of this leaflike body. Each of the several female organs produces one egg, and each of the males produces several sperms. At the correct stage of maturity, and when at least a minute amount of moisture is present between the two ends, the male organs release their sperms into the moisture. The sperms propel themselves toward the female organs, which simultaneously begin turning the access openings to their eggs in the direction of the males. Once an egg is fertilized, it sends a tiny root into the soil and a small stem upwards. The stem then develops into the first small true leaf of a new fern.

With this perilous reproductive process, it is difficult to imagine how some ferns can become invasive. Nevertheless, there are species that can become a great nuisance in a restricted area of the garden. These are plants that, in addition to reproduction by spores, also have the ability to spread by underground rhizomes. Yet, many of our most attractive ferns remain for many decades, perhaps a century, where they began as a tiny spore.

For detailed information on the ferns in my garden listed below, see the individual descriptions entered in their respective alphabetical position.

Adiantum pedatum
Athyrium goeringianum 'Pictum'
Dryopteris austriaca var. *intermedia*
Onoclea sensibilis
Osmunda cinnamomea
Osmunda claytoniana
Osmunda regalis
Polypodium virginianum and *P. vulgare*
Polystichum acrostichoides
Pteridium aquilinum
Thelypteris noveboracensis

FRAGARIA (ROSACEAE) Strawberry

The genus *Fragaria* contains 12 species widely scattered throughout Eurasia and North as well as South America. They are low-growing plants with three-part leaves and small racemes of white flowers with five rounded petals. The "fruits" are fleshy, edible, and delicious, ripening usually bright red and studded with dark red "seeds" (achenes), or white with beige achenes. The fruit, not a true berry, is a soft, fleshy, egg-shaped mass. The seeds (achenes) are actually the fruits. There are several *Fragaria* species and cultivars in my garden.

Fragaria vesca 8 in (20 cm); Zone 3
Wild Strawberry; Woodland Strawberry; Sow-teat Strawberry

This species has long, arching runners that root readily when they touch open ground. The leaves have sharply toothed leaflets, and the white flowers, about 0.75 in (2 cm) in diameter, have five rounded petals subtending a tuft of yellow stamens and anthers. The "fruit" is red and distinctly egg-shaped (plate 61). The plant comes from Eurasia, but one version, *Fragaria vesca* var. *americana*, is native to North America. The European plants have also been introduced to, and become naturalized in, North

PLATE 61. In late May, the ripening fruit of *Fragaria vesca* (wild strawberry), and the red-streaked white blossoms of *Rhododendron* 'Lady Robin', as a backdrop for *Campanula poscharskyana* (bellflower) hanging from the top of a wall.

America, joining the extant native population and probably hybridizing with it. Several cultivars and forms have been separated and are available in trade.

I have introduced cultivars said to have been derived from this species. Known as "alpine strawberries," they have no runners and grow in one spot for many years before they disappear. They seed themselves freely and come true from seed, making attractive edging plants, or just a handsome, almost evergreen, groundcover. I grow three red cultivars: 'Alpina', 'Baron Solemacher', and 'Improved Rugen'. I also grow the white *Fragaria vesca* f. *alba* which seems sweeter, probably because the "fruit" has a chance to ripen a little longer; the birds are less attracted to it because of its lack of red color.

Fragaria virginiana 8 in (20 cm); Zone 3
Virginia Strawberry

This species is so similar to the natural version of *Fragaria vesca* that I have some difficulty separating the two. Among the identifiable differences are the leaflets of *F. virginiana,* which have shorter petioles and sharper and larger teeth on their margins, and the "seeds", that are pressed into deep pits on the "fruit" mass rather than just sitting on its surface as on *F. vesca.*

FRITILLARIA (LILIACEAE)

Fritillaria is a genus consisting of some 100 species of bulbous herbs native to Eurasia, northwestern Africa, and northwestern North America. Most species are hardy and interesting plants, and at least some have the distinction of having a skunklike odor that makes them unattractive to deer and other animals. It was this aspect, in addition to their beauty, that encouraged me to grow fritillarias. Several species currently grow in my garden.

Fritillaria imperialis 4 ft (1.2 m); Zone 6

Crown-imperial

This is a tall, stately species from northern India, Pakistan, and Afghanistan, which is sometimes thought to be too formal for a wild garden. I do not agree with this viewpoint; after all, in its native lands this species grows wild in much more informal environments than even my garden. Furthermore, if nature created these plants, and they survive in this climate, they are welcome in my garden.

The lush green foliage begins emerging from the still chilly soil in very early spring, soon lengthening into tall leafy stems. At the top is a large head of narrow leaves below which hang six or more bell-shaped flowers 2–3 in (5–8 cm) in diameter (Plate 62).

On *Fritillaria imperialis* 'Rubra', the blooms are bright red, while 'Lutea Maxima' has yellow blossoms. Both cultivars open so early in the year that they are occasionally nipped by frost. Even if some slight damage occurs during a frigid night and the plants hang dejectedly in the morning, they usually perk up quickly in the warmth of

PLATE 62. The green leafy stems and the bright blossoms of *Fritillaria imperialis* (crown imperial) defying cold temperatures in the bare landscape of early April.

the day. Nevertheless, in very cold springs it may be necessary to place a few tall stakes around the plants and wrap them with a sheet of plastic or cover them with a tall garbage can. The blooms of these plants are so impressive, so early and so long lasting that they are well worth the effort.

The bulbs are large, up to 6 in (15 cm) in diameter, and should be planted in early fall at least 6 in (15 cm) deep. A very sunny, well-drained but moist location, with rich organic soil is the most appropriate site. If possible, the site should be in the lee of tall trees or shrubs to protect the plants from the strong cold winds of the early season.

Fritillaria meleagris 12 in (30 cm); Zone 5

Checkered Lily; Snake's Head

This is a plant of modest proportions but considerable charm. It has pendant, 1.75-in (4.5-cm) long tulip-shaped blossoms whose colors vary from reddish and light brown to white. The petals are checkered with a small geometric pattern that is sometimes partly evident even in the all-white flowers. The plant is native from western Scandinavia through central Europe and east to the Caucasus. It prefers a sunny or semi-shaded position in well-drained soil. My plants have been seeding themselves acceptably in such a location.

Fritillaria michailovskyi 9 in (23 cm); Zone 4

This species comes from cold elevations in the high mountains around Mt. Ararat in eastern Turkey and western Georgia. It came to the attention of bulb growers only recently and is now becoming readily available. Between the long, narrow straplike leaves rise slender flower stems bearing one or two bell-shaped flowers, about 1 in (2.5 cm) long, and purple-maroon edged with golden-yellow. The bulbs should be planted in sun or part shade in well-drained soil. The plants produce abundant flat seeds 0.25 in (5 mm) in diameter that germinate in the following spring.

Galanthus nivalis (Amaryllidaceae) 8 in (20 cm); Zone 3

Snowdrop

Of the 12 species in the genus *Galanthus, G. nivalis* is the most popular and most widely planted. It comes from Europe and is now becoming naturalized in many parts of the world. Most springs, the first blossoms of *G. nivalis* manage to push through the snow and frozen earth by mid or late February. In mild winters they make their first appearance just after New Year. If the weather is not too frigid or too warm, they remain attractive for many weeks. Several cultivars are available including 'Flore Pleno', which has double flowers. A similar but larger species, *G. elwesii,* is also frequently planted, but I have not grown it as yet.

Galax urceolata (Diapensiaceae) 2.5 ft (0.8 m); Zone 5

Wandflower; Wand Plant; Beetleweed; Galaxy; Coltsfoot

This is the only species in the North American genus *Galax*. Although names such as *G. aphylla* and *G. rotundifolia* are freqently encountered, they have no valid botanical standing. *Galax urceolata* is native to a narrow range from Virginia to Georgia and Alabama, but is hardy in Connecticut and even farther north. It has attractive, evergreen, cordate leaves up to 5 in (13 cm) long that grow from a scaly rhizome which creeps just below the forest floor. The foliage is bright shiny green in summer, turning rich bronze in cold weather. The small white flowers appear from May to July on a 15-in (38-cm) high leafless stalk that rises directly from the rhizome. The plant requires rich, strongly acidic soil in shade where it will spread into an excellent, fully evergreen and permanent ground cover.

Gaultheria procumbens. See under **"Shrubs."**

Genista sagitalis (Leguminosae) 15 in (38 cm); Zone 5

There are some 90 species in the genus *Genista,* mostly woody plants and shrubs native to Europe and adjacent parts of Asia as well as certain sections of northern Africa. Some are equipped with sharp thorns while others resemble *Cytisus* (broom) species.

Genista sagitalis is a nonwoody plant with soft, flat, articulated, gray-green stems that are covered with thin hairs. The flowers in terminal inflorescences appear in June when the plant creates a tiny fall of golden-yellow color. The plant requires a dry, sunny location, preferably on a small slope where it can best display its interesting pendant growth.

GENTIANA (GENTIANACEAE) Gentian

In the past, the genus *Gentiana* was so large and contained such widely varied species that botanists deemed it necessary to divide it into three separate genera. Thus, in addition to *Gentiana,* there is now also *Gentianella,* and *Gentianopsis,* which, incidentally, includes the beautiful North American wild flower, *Gentianopsis crinita* (fringed gentian), a gem I have tried to grow without success. Most other plants we tend to associate with the name "gentian" remain in the genus *Gentiana,* which still counts some 200 to 350 species among it members. Many of them have blossoms whose blue color is seldom seen in the plant world and from which has arisen the color designation "gentian blue," a clear, cool, steely hue. When we see the blooms of certain gentians, we become convinced that they are the bluest color we are likely to see in nature, until we encounter the next, even bluer species that makes the previous one appear almost purple.

Some gentians are easy to grow, but many can be difficult unless their exacting requirements are fully met. Most require rich, moist acidic soil, but others prefer alpine scree with perfect drainage and light but constant moisture. I have grown several of the exquisite Himalayan and Japanese species, which have lived and bloomed for a few years, but, since they are short-lived plants even in their natural habitats and, because they did not reseed themselves readily, they eventually died out. I will try to grow them again in the future. Currently, there are four species in my garden, of which three bloom and reproduce without my help.

Gentiana andrewsii 1.5 ft (0.5 m); Zone 4

Closed Gentian; Bottled Gentian; Blind Gentian

This species is native to the eastern half of North America, ranging from Quebec to Manitoba and south to Arkansas and Georgia. In my garden, the plant often becomes top-heavy and sprawls over the ground, keeping only its flowering heads erect. The blossoms are up to 2 in (5 cm) long and narrowly ovoid. They appear to be tightly closed until I happen to observe a large bumblebee force its way inside and disappear entirely. After a few seconds, the bee reemerges and the blossom closes once again. The plants produce large quantities of tiny seeds that germinate easily in the partly shaded, moist site where they are located. A mature planting of *Gentiana andrewsii* presents a lovely sight, especially since the blue flowers do not appear until October.

A second, unidentified species of closed gentian grows on the same site as *Gentiana andrewsii*. It blooms in summer and completes its blossoming period 4 weeks before *G. andrewsii* begins to bud, thus totally precluding hybridization of the two. Except for larger leaves and earlier flowering on the unidentified species, the two plants are almost identical. I obtained the seed of the unnamed gentian in Tokyo many years ago at the large plant-store of Dai-ichi Engei, a prestigious name in that part of the world. The designation on the packet was *Gentiana scabra* Bunge var. *buergeri* Maxim. Nevertheless, after the first blossoming, it became evident that I did not receive the *G. scabra* I was seeking; clearly, it was mislabeled. Yet, since this plant and *G. andrewsii* are so similar and grow in the same location, I was able, unwittingly, to achieve the unusual effect of having an area covered with closed gentian blossoms from July to November with only a 4-week interval without color.

Gentiana cachemirica 12 in (30 cm); Zone 4

As its name indicates, this is a Himalayan gentian from Kashmir, a plant of great beauty but not of excessively long life (though I hope it will be with me for at least a few years). This species requires screelike conditions and an unfailing supply of moisture in summer. The flowers are large, elegant, up to 1.25 in (3.2 cm) long, gentian-blue striped on the outside of the chalice with yellowish white and darker blue. I placed my plant in the most favorable position I could find: a steep, semi-shaded slope in the rock garden, facing north, adding a mixture of sand and leafmold into the planting pocket. Now I mulch the plant heavily in winter with pine needles and keep it moist throughout the summer. Perhaps some of the many seeds it produces will germinate and thus continue the species' presence in my garden.

Gentiana scabra* var. *buergeri 12 in (30 cm); Zone 4

This is the splendid species I sought, but did not find, in Japan. I had to wait several years until a friend made me a present of this desirable plant. It is positioned under a large shrub of many canes, where *Vaccinium corymbosum* (highbush blueberry) and *Rhododendron viscosum* (swamp azalea) grow together next to a picket fence. The somewhat thin shade created by the mixed bush and the fence, the rich organic soil, and the elevated site must suit the gentian well because it has been eagerly spreading its wiry stems over the mulch of dry leaves fallen from the two acid-loving shrubs above. It seeds itself modestly. From September until early November, each of the plant's sprawling, slender stems produces a terminal cluster of up-facing blue bells. As with many late-flowering plants, the blossoms of this gentian open only on sunny days when the few insects active so late in the season are likely to come by. When the day is dark or rainy, the blooms remain closed.

GERANIUM (GERANIACEAE) Cranesbill

The genus *Geranium* includes about 300 species of herbs native mostly to Eurasia. Some are weeds that have become naturalized all over the world, but many are desirable plants for woodland gardens, as well as for hot sunny spots and rock gardens. The tender house plant that we incorrectly call "Geranium," hardy to zone 9, is a hybrid of several species belonging to the southern African genus *Pelargonium*. To complicate the issue further, both *Geranium* and *Pelargonium*, together with three other genera, belong to a larger group, the geranium family (Geraniaceae). I grow several varieties of *Geranium* in my garden.

Geranium maculatum 2 ft (0.6 m); Zone 3

This is one of the few geraniums native to North America. It ranges from Maine to Manitoba and south to Tennessee and Georgia. The leaves are divided into five parts, each sharply toothed. The 1-in (2.5-cm) wide lavender-purple flowers open between April and June. This geranium is one of the most common wild flowers, growing in open areas and thin woods where it seeds itself freely.

Where space permits, individual plants may be grouped into colonies to create an attractive deciduous ground cover with interesting patterns of the dissected foliage and a mass of color that remains modestly effective for several months in spring and early summer. The plant is easy to grow, is pest- and disease-free, and is largely indifferent to soil acidity, flourishing in pH 4.5 to 7.0. Several forms broaden the color range, including *Geranium maculatum* f. *albiflorum* with white blossoms. Also growing in my garden are the vivid blue *G.* 'Johnson's Blue' and the clear purple-pink *G.* 'Claridge Druce'.

Geranium sanguineum* var. *prostratum 6 in (15 cm); Zone 4

This European creeper hugs the ground or the rock it comes upon. With its rather thick rhizomous stems, it spreads in a slow, orderly manner never becoming rampant or objectionable. The leaves are small and numerous, forming a well-defined cushion that in spring becomes speckled with light rose-pink flowers 0.75 in (2 cm) in diameter. I planted one specimen in a vertical position in a wall where it forms an attractive but restrained cascade of grayish foliage and small pinkish blossoms in spring (Plate 63). The plant was obtained as *Geranium lancastrense* but that designation apparently has no botanical standing and is sometimes used incorrectly for *G. sanguineum* var. *prostratum*.

PLATE 63. The restrained creeper, *Geranium sanguineum* var. *prostratum*, in its moment of modest glory in early June.

Geum quellyon 'Mrs. Bradshaw' (Rosaceae) 2 ft. (0.6 m); Zone 5

Avens

There are about 50 species of perennial herbs in the genus *Geum,* native to Eurasia, North Africa, and North as well as South America. They have been frequently hybridized to produce garden specimens with brightly colored flowers opening in late spring and throughout the summer. *Geum quellyon* is a colorful species from Chile, and 'Mrs. Bradshaw' is an improved variety with 3-in (4-cm) wide very bright orange-red double flowers that appear from May to August. The plant is hardy and vigorous. It requires good garden soil in full sun and adequate moisture in summer.

Goodyera pubescens (Orchidaceae) 1 ft (0.3 m); Zone 3

Downy Rattlesnake Plantain; Latticeleaf; Scrofula Weed

The genus *Goodyera* has about 40 species of terrestrial orchids native mainly to Asia and North America. *Goodyera pubescens* is a North American species native from Maine and Ontario to Missouri and Florida. The leaves, which form a rosette at the base of the plant, are up to 2.5 in (6.4 cm) long, oval, and dark green with a unique and attractive network of white veins, which gave the plant its common name, latticeleaf. In July and August, a tall erect stem rises from the center of the leaves. The upper half of the stem is densely covered with small whitish flowers. This raceme matures into brownish spikes of dry capsules that could remind a casual observer of the tail of a rattlesnake. The plant prefers woodsy locations with dry or damp acidic soil of pH 4.0 to 5.0.

Haberlea rhodopensis (Gesneriaceae) 3 in (8 cm); Zone 6

There are only two species in the genus *Haberlea.* They resemble each other and both are native to a small range in Bulgaria. The foliage of *Haberlea rhodopensis* is covered on both sides with sparse soft hairs, and is somewhat larger than the foliage of, *H. ferdinandi-coburgii,* which is daintier and has leaves with smooth upper surfaces. My *H. rhodopensis* has grown for many years in a somewhat elevated spot in the shelter of a large stone in the rock garden. In most summers, it produces 4-in (10-cm) tall naked stems with nodding, pale-purple flowers that look very much like elongated versions of blossoms of the better-known but tender gesneriad, *Saintpaulia ionantha* (common African violet).

Hedera helix (Araliaceae) Vine to 20 ft (6 m); Zone 5

English Ivy

The Eurasian genus *Hedera* has only about five species, but some of them have hundreds of cultivars. *Hedera helix* occurs in the following versions: 'Baltica' from Latvia, 'Bulgaria', 'Hibernica' from Ireland, 'Poetica' from Italy, 'Scotica', 'Taurica' from Turkey, and innumerable others. If an evergreen cover for a brick wall or a large bare area in heavy shade is desired, then *H. helix* is the plant to do the job. But, in an average garden there is scarcely any place where its advantages can be fully realized. Having introduced it once or twice, I am now in the process of eliminating it.

Helianthus divaricatus (Compositae) 6 ft (1.8 m); Zone 4

Woodland Sunflower; Rough Sunflower

All 150 species in the genus *Helianthus* are American. Some are large invasive plants. *Helianthus divaricatus* earned its name by a distinguishing trait (*divaricatus* is Latin for spreading). This species is native to the eastern two-thirds of North America, growing mostly in dry wood margins and thickets. The plant is too vigorous for a

PLATE 64. The verdant foliage and the yellow blooms of *Helianthus divaricatus* (woodland sunflower) in the summer doldrums of late August.

garden, but a middle-sized clump at the edge of a wood becomes very decorative when dozens of 2-in (5-cm) wide yellow flowers appear in late summer and contrast brightly against the dark background (Plate 64). Once in several years it may be necessary to dig up the roots and discard most of them. As an alternative, the plants may be completely mowed down in several successive years while in full growth. Only a few will survive such an ordeal, but some will endure and flower again on a diminished scale.

HELLEBORUS (RANUNCULACEAE) Hellebore; Christmas Rose

The Eurasian genus *Helleborus* consists of about 20 species, some blooming during the coldest months of the year. All parts of the plants have been thought to be poisonous—at least since the days of Dioscorides, the follower of Socrates and Plato, who made a study of the medicinal properties of plants. No records are available on the identity of the poison, and one may even wonder whether it exists. Until I constructed a fence, every autumn and winter the deer systematically consumed substantial amounts of the handsome evergreen foliage of my *Helleborus* planting, yet I have never seen any of the animals ailing or dead. Currently, I grow two species, though I have tried, and failed thus far, to grow two or three others.

Helleborus abchasicus 1 ft (0.3 m); Zone 4

This species comes from the Caucasus. The foliage is evergreen and divided, and the flowers are carmine-red, drooping, and 2.5–3 in (6–8 cm) in diameter. If the weather is not too extreme, the flowers, which open as early as February, persist for many weeks.

Helleborus niger 1 ft (0.3 m); Zone 4

This is the classic Christmas rose of European woods. A handsome evergreen plant even out of bloom, it is particularly beautiful when the large blossoms of pure ivory open in the first warm days of late winter. The blooms are durable and cold-resistant, lasting for weeks before they begin turning darker beige-pink. Individual blooms may be 3 in (8 cm) or more in diameter. My planting is in a moist, rich soil near the border of the wood where it receives sun all winter but is completely shaded in summer. To the north is a 4-ft (1.2-m) high boundary wall that reflects a small amount of warmth from the winter sun, but deflects the cold north winds. Nonetheless, such protection is probably not necessary at this latitude as the plant is fully hardy in Connecticut. This species seeds itself freely so that I am able to start new plantings elsewhere in the garden.

Hemerocallis fulva (Liliaceae) 5 ft (1.5 m); Zone 4

Daylily

The genus *Hemerocallis* contains some 15 species, all native to Eurasia, especially the Far East. *Hemerocallis fulva* has spread widely and become ubiquitous in most parts of North America. I grow three varieties. 'Bonanza' is a 15-in (38-cm) high semidwarf plant with narrow, arching foliage and plentiful erect stems with colorful blossoms. The flowers have a dark red, well-defined, starlike center bordered by broad, bright yellow margins. This cultivar begins blooming in late July and continues well into September. Despite the fact that each blossom lasts only one day, there are always plenty of blooms on the small plant.

The second variety I grow is 'Hyperion', which is of normal stature though the flowers tend to be larger than the norm. The 3-ft (1-m) tall and slender stems are good for cutting since the buds unfold well in a vase. The very fragrant lemon-yellow blooms open in July and August.

The third variety, 'Stella D'Oro', has bell-shaped, 2.5-in (6.4-cm) wide golden-yellow flowers that begin to open in June and continue until early fall. The plant is less than 2 ft (60 cm) high. Many new varieties of daylilies appear on the market every year to the delight of dedicated fanciers of *Hemerocallis*.

HEPATICA (RANUNCULACEAE) Liverleaf

The 10 species that constitute the genus *Hepatica* are native to the northern areas of Eurasia and North America. They are mostly early blooming plants with blossom stems pushing through the cold soil as early as March. The leaves remain on the plants through the winter, eventually deteriorating into thin, leathery patches that disappear when new foliage unfolds in late spring. The flowers have no petals, but the sepals that subtend the numerous stamens are up to 1.5-in (4-cm) in diameter. There are usually five to nine sepals in colors from white to pink, purple, and blue. I grow three species of *Hepatica*.

Hepatica acutiloba 6 in (15 cm); Zone 4

Sharp-lobed Hepatica

As its name implies, the leaves of this hepatica are acute (i.e., sharply lobed), and the sepals of its flowers are bluish or white. This is a North American plant that ranges from Maine to Minnesota and south to Missouri and Georgia. It grows in partial shade in well-drained soil, that is rich in organic matter and has a nearly neutral reaction of pH 6.0 to 7.0.

Hepatica americana 6 in (15 cm); Zone 4

Round-lobed Hepatica

This North American species is native from Nova Scotia to Manitoba and south to Florida and Alabama. It is similar to *Hepatica acutiloba* but, as its common name indicates, the lobes of its three-part leaves are rounded. The sepals are white, pink, or light purple, approximately 0.5–1 in (1.3–2.5 cm) in diameter. *Hepatica americana* grows best in dry, rocky woods and hillsides, in soil that is decidedly acidic, with pH 4.5 to 6.0. It is sometimes called *H. triloba*.

Hepatica nobilis 6 in (15 cm); Zone 4

This European species has three-lobed leaves that are rounded and broader, more reminiscent (than those of the two North American species) of a liver. In ancient times it was believed that the outline of a plant's leaves, blossoms, or root had a significance in the life and health of humans. Thus the genus name is derived from the Latin *hepaticus,* meaning liver.

The blossoms of *Hepatica nobilis* are not substantially different from those of the other two species, though they tend to have stronger colors, usually pink or blue, against which the white stamens stand out very attractively. Like *H. americana,* This species is occasionally called *H. triloba*.

Hesperis matronalis (Cruciferae) 3 ft (0.9 m); Zone 4

Dame's Rocket; Sweet Rocket; Dame's Violet

The genus *Hesperis* contains about 24 species of mostly tall biennial and perennial herbs native to Europe and central Asia. *Hesperis matronalis* comes from central and southern Europe. In various parts of the world it escaped from cultivation and became a colorful, if somewhat weedy, addition to the roadside flora. In North America it associates freely with native *Phlox paniculata* (summer phlox). It usually blooms before *Phlox,* thus widening the period of color in locations where the two plants coexist.

PLATE 65. The late-June explosion of color in a planting of *Hesperis matronalis* (dame's rocket).

To a casual observer, the two species look so much alike they are often considered to be one and the same. Nevertheless, *Phlox paniculata* belongs to Polemoniaceae (the phlox family), while *Hesperis* is a member of Cruciferae (the mustard family). The flowers of *Phlox* have five petals united in a long tube, whereas those of *Hesperis matronalis* have only four petals and are usually pleasantly scented. The fruit of *Phlox* is a rounded dry capsule about 0.25 in (6 mm) in diameter, while that of *Hesperis matronalis* is a thin pod (silique) 0.1 in (3 mm) wide and up to 2 in (5 cm) long.

Hesperis matronalis is usually perennial but may occasionally act as a biennial. I have collected two or three plants along the road and planted them at the edge of my wood where they seed themselves more than generously (Plate 65). The planting becomes attractive as early as May and continues well into July when the companion *Phlox paniculata* (summer or fall phlox) joins the show. Thus the small area has some color from spring until frost.

Heuchera americana (Saxifragaceae) 2.5 ft (0.8 m); Zone 4

American Alumroot; Rock Geranium; Coralbells

Heuchera is a North American genus of some 35 to 50 species growing mostly on the western slopes of the Rocky Mountains, although a few species are native east of the Mississippi River. *Heuchera americana* is the most common of the eastern species, ranging from Connecticut to Michigan and south to Oklahoma and Georgia. The nearly evergreen leaves grow from the base of the plant on long, slender stalks. They are 3–4 in (8–10 cm) wide, with margins of seven to nine blunted lobes. The small but plentiful reddish flowers are arranged in loose, airy panicles. The plant favors well-drained open locations in humus-rich soil of pH 5.0 to 6.0. Hybrids with other species, particularly *H. sanguinea,* have been produced and provide a wider range of colors.

Impatiens pallida (Balsaminaceae) 5 ft (1.5 m); Zone 3

Jewelweed; Pale Touch-me-not; Balsam; Snap-weed

There are about 500 species in the genus *Impatiens* widely distributed in the tropical as well as the temperate regions of Eurasia, Africa, and North America. Some are tender plants grown by nurseries in flats for summer planting in city and country gardens.

Impatiens pallida is a North American annual ranging from Newfoundland to Saskatchewan and south to Kansas and northern Florida. The stems are thick and succulent, and the 1-in (2.5-cm) long canary-yellow or orange flowers mature into long green siliques that burst, when they are ripe or are touched, into five twisted bands, propelling their seeds several feet in all directions. This prolific weedy plant can take over the rich, moist bottom of my wood completely in two or three seasons unless restrained by the removal of all specimens of the species.

Despite my diligent effort to weed out *Impatiens pallida,* a few plants somehow manage to come up every spring. I tolerate a handful of specimens so that I can use their foliage to rub the sap of *Rhus radicans* (poison ivy) off my hands should I accidentally touch its leaves; I have eliminated poison ivy from my garden almost entirely, but birds keep introducing it and young seedlings occasionally appear where I expected them the least. The liquid from *Impatiens pallida* is said to neutralize the burning effects of the toxic and dangerous skin irritant in poison ivy, provided the cure is applied without delay. Though I have no scientific proof of its effectiveness, I still use the remedy and it does seem to work.

***Ipomoea tricolor* 'Heavenly Blue'** (Convolvulaceae) Vine to 12 ft (3.7 m); Zone 4
Giant-flowered Morning Glory

The 500 species that comprise the genus *Ipomoea* are a diverse collection of annual and perennial herbs and shrubs growing mainly in the temperate and tropical zones of the world. *Ipomoea tricolor* 'Heavenly Blue' is an annual vine that produces great quantities of flat, funnel-shaped, 4-in (10-cm) wide blossoms. The blooms open at sunrise and die by midday, unless the weather is cloudy and dark, in which case they may remain open until early or mid afternoon.

The color of the blossoms is an incredibly radiant sky-blue. In an attempt to capture it on a photograph, I have taken pictures of the blossoms on different types of film and under different light conditions: in early morning before the sun's rays reached them; during the bright noonday hours; and on dark cloudy days when it was necessay to activate the camera's flash. The prints and transparencies are never true blue, but instead, always come out purplish. It is evident that today's film emulsions are totally incapable of faithfully reproducing nature's blue colors.

The seeds of all *Ipomoea* species are planted in spring after the soil has warmed up. A wire or wooden fence displays the fleeting but abundant and beautiful blossoms most effectively.

IRIS (IRIDACEAE) Fleur-de-lis; Flag

The genus *Iris* counts over 200 varied species among its members widely distributed over the temperate and cold regions of the Northern Hemisphere. Some irises grow from bulbs, while others have rhizomes that sometimes may be only a slightly enlarged root. These rhizomatous types have been divided into three groups according to the kind of flowers they produce: pogon irises have bearded blossoms, apogon irises have beardless blossoms, and evansia irises have crested blossoms.

The pogon or bearded irises form an enormous group of hybrids and cultivars. They are the first irises that come to mind when we hear the word *iris,* the "flags" our mothers and grandmothers cultivated in their cottage and city gardens. These irises used to be called by the aggregate term German iris or *Iris Germanica* but, according to *Hortus Third* (Liberty Hyde Bailey Hortorium 1976, 599), that "designation is inexact and is now largely abandoned." These plants have a complex and mysterious lineage. They come in nearly all colors of the spectrum except true reds which will be difficult to attain given the pigments present in their genes (unless new genes are introduced from other genera). The collective common name (bearded iris) comes from the beard, usually in a contrasting color, located on top of the fall near the flower's center.

Although the bearded iris blossoms last only about a day, they are abundant and colorful. Every sunny garden should have at least a few of these plants. They require well-drained soil in full sun and should be divided every 3 years. Though they are easy to grow, they have one serious enemy—a borer that can destroy a planting in a year or two. The presence of this insect can be detected by the telltale, darker green, waterlogged streaks in the foliage. To avoid infestation, plants should be drenched with the appropriate control liquid as early as March and again later in the growing season. Once infested, a plant should be lifted just after flowering, the affected part of the rhizome cut off and reliably destroyed, and the remaining portion replanted after it is first dusted with sulfur to prevent rotting.

Six species of irises grow in my garden.

Iris cristata 6 in (15 cm); Zone 3

Crested Iris; Dwarf Crested Iris

This North American wild flower is one of six or seven species in the evansia (crested) group of irises. It ranges from Maryland to Missouri and south to Mississippi and Georgia, but is hardy in Connecticut and much farther north. The small straplike leaves, 3–6 in (8–15 cm) long, are typical for the genus. The 6–7 in (15–18 cm) high flower stems bear one or more pale blue to lavender blooms. On the upper side of each of the three sepals is a white elongated area in the center of which runs an orange fringed crest. In addition to the more common lavender version, there are cultivars with white flowers (e.g., *Iris cristata* 'Alba') and blue flowers (e.g., *I. cristata* 'Caerulea'). The plant grows best in rich acidic soil in partial shade. If it finds the location agreeable, it spreads into a low mat.

***Iris ensata*—Higo Strain** 2 ft (0.6 m); Zone 5

The species, *Iris ensata,* used to be called *I. kaempferi,* but that name is no longer accurate. *Iris ensata* belongs to the apogon (beardless) group of irises, and was used by Japanese gardeners in the past 300 years to develop splendid varieties such as the Higo strain. The Higo irises are tall and vigorous, with long narrow leaves, and have flowers in colors ranging from white to maroon-red, purple-blue, pink, and others. The blossoms of some named varieties are as broad as a small plate, often 8 in (20 cm) in diameter; others let their great falls arch downward, displaying veined markings of white, and still others have large, ruffled double flowers in pure pink and related subtle shades.

These plants prefer a moist location with good drainage, especially in winter, and acidic soil rich in organic matter, in sun or partial shade. Of the many beautiful varieties available, I limit myself to only three: 'Benibotan' with large pendant copper-red petals; 'Kumasumi-No-Uta' with double rose-colored blooms; and 'Murakumo' with large dark purple horizontal petals marbled with distinctive white veins. These cultivars are hardy at my latitude, but require 2 or 3 years to become fully established.

Iris japonica 2 ft (0.6 m); Zone 4

This species, native to China and Japan, is also a member of the evansia (crested) group of irises. The foliage is narrow, up to 2 ft (60 cm) long, and the flower stems of equal height culminate in two or three blossoms in colors from a subtle lavender-blue to white. The plant prefers a moist, partly sunny location with an acidic soil containing some organic matter.

***Iris pallida* 'Variegata'** 2 ft (0.6 m); Zone 4

Iris pallida is a pogon (bearded) species native to the southern slopes and valleys of the European Alps. *Iris pallida* 'Variegata' has leaves edged in ivory, which provide a harmonizing background for the sky-blue or light bluish purple fragrant blossoms that appear in June. The plant requires good, well-drained soil in full sun.

Iris tectorum 1 ft (0.3 m); Zone 4

Roof Iris; Wall Iris

This Chinese species belongs to the evansia (crested) group of irises. It has been cultivated in Japan as a living binder of thatched roofs, as its botanical and one of its common names indicate. The flowers are rather uniform lavender or azure-blue, though the cultivar 'Alba' has white blossoms. The plant can be somewhat temperamental. However, where satisfied it spreads and even seeds itself. Divisions may be made every 3 years, but if left undisturbed, *Iris tectorum* will form large attractive drifts. The species is fully hardy at my latitude, and with some winter protection it can be grown much farther north. Rich, well-drained soil in full sun or partial shade suits it best.

Iris versicolor 3 ft (0.9 m); Zone 4
Wild Iris; Blue Flag

This North American apogon (beardless) species is native from Labrador to Manitoba and south to Ohio and Virginia. The long leaves are only 1 in (2.5 cm) wide, and the tall flower stems bear slender flowers in blue-violet, lavender, or, rarely, white. The species likes rich, moist soil and favors wet meadows, stream banks, and marshes in sun or semishade. It is a very adaptable species and will cling to life for many years even under the most unfavorable conditions.

Jeffersonia diphylla (Berberidaceae) 1 ft (0.3 m); Zone 4
Twinleaf

There are two species in the genus *Jeffersonia;* one is from northeastern Asia, and the other, *J. diphylla,* is from eastern North America where it ranges from New York and southern Ontario to Wisconsin, and south to Alabama. The genus was named in honor of Thomas Jefferson, the science-oriented third president of the United States, who was particularly interested in botany. Both the plant's scientific epithet and its common name are derived from the form of the leaves which are divided into two more or less identical parts.

Together the kidney-shaped leaves measure about 5 in (13 cm) across. The leaf stalks grow from the base of the plant and are about 6 in (15 cm) high. The solitary white blossoms are 1 in (2.5 cm) in diameter, have eight petals and eight stamens, and appear in April and May on naked stalks taller than the leaves. The fruit is a dry capsule closed by a hinged lid that pops open when the seeds are ripe. The stem and the capsule resemble the tube and the bowl of a small tobacco pipe. The plant favors rich, moist open woods with acidic or neutral soil of pH 4.5 to 7.0.

Kniphofia uvaria (Liliaceae) 2.5 ft (0.8 m); Zone 6
Red-hot-poker; Tritoma; Torch Flower

There are 60 to 70 species in the genus *Kniphofia,* all native to southern and tropical Africa and the island of Madagascar. *Kniphofia uvaria,* from the southern parts of Africa, is probably hardy in Connecticut but, to be certain, I planted my specimen on the south side of a warm boundary wall, and I mulch it every winter with oak leaves and pine needles. The foliage is linear, up to 2 ft (60 cm) long and 0.75 in (2 cm) wide. It grows in profusion from the plant's base. The flowers, usually red, orange, or yellowish, appear in great numbers in 8–10 in (20–25 cm) long dense racemes at the top of a stout stem. The plant gives an exotic look to the spot in a garden where it grows.

LEUCOJUM (AMARYLLIDACEAE) Snowflake

The genus *Leucojum* consists of nine species of bulbous plants native mostly to central Europe and the western shores of the Mediterranean Sea. The long narrow leaves grow directly from the bulb as does the tall hollow flower stem bearing one or more nodding, graceful, bell-shaped flowers 0.75 in (2 cm) long. Each bell has six sharp tips on its margin, and each tip is decorated with a green or light brown dot. The name of the genus comes from the Greek *leukos* (white) and *ion* (violet), suggesting the violetlike fragrance of the flowers. The plants are hardy, easy to grow, and perform best if left undisturbed over the years. I grow three species, all attractive and, thus far, living up to their reputation as being deer-proof.

Leucojum aestivum 12 in (30 cm); Zone 5
Summer Snowflake

This species from central and southern Europe blooms in midspring, despite its Latin and common names suggesting summer blossoms. It is long-lived and with age gradually increases into a sizable clump of long narrow leaves and numerous flower stems, each with two to five white chimes. All growth aboveground disappears by midsummer. The bulbs are planted in September about 4 in (10 cm) deep. *Leucojum aestivum* 'Gravetye' (or 'Gravetye Giant') is more robust than the species, and its flowers are larger.

Leucojum autumnale 9 in (23 cm); Zone 6
Autumn Snowflake

This Mediterranean species lives up to its botanical and common names, blooming in autumn unless earlier watering or heavy rains bring on a premature blossoming in late summer. It is a dainty species with thin, grasslike foliage and slender flower stems that bear only one or two bells 0.5 in (13 mm) long. It comes from Spain and Portugal and should be mulched in northerly latitudes after winter sets in.

Leucojum vernum 12 in (30 cm); Zone 5
Spring Snowflake

This species blooms in very early spring, in full accordance with its names. In warmer climates it begins to open in March, but in Connecticut it waits until mid April. It likes full sun or partial shade and good, well-drained soil. The 1-in (2.5-cm) long solitary bells are tipped with green dots and have a pleasing fragrance. The species is native to central Europe. Variety 'Carpathicum' usually has two blossoms on each stem with yellowish brown dots.

LEWISIA (PORTULACACEAE)

All 15 to 20 species of this unique and attractive North American genus are native from the northern Rockies to southern California and Arizona. They are fleshy plants with thick roots and succulent foliage that is evergreen on some species, but disappears totally on others which become dormant shortly after blossoming. The plants insist on a dry, mostly sunny position with deep, loose, gravelly soil with perfect drainage and moderately acidic reaction of pH 5.0 to 6.0. On sites that do not dry out occasionally, the roots and foliage of these plants eventually rot. In my generally dampish bottomland with its abundance of shade, I had some difficulty in finding the proper locations. Nevertheless, there are one or two such spots, and my plants have been blooming and seeding themselves for many seasons. They do wear out after several years, so the small seedlings that occur in wetter years come in handy in perpetuating the plantings. Over time, I have attempted to grow four or five species and varieties, but now only two species grow in my garden, of which thus far only the first has become fully acclimated and feels at home.

PLATE 66. In late May, the candy-striped *Lewisia cotyledon* coexisting successfully with *Maianthemum canadense* (beadruby).

Lewisia cotyledon 10 in (25 cm); Zone 6

This species has a flat rosette of fleshy leaves that remain green throughout the year. The plant grows from a relatively long, thick root. From the rosette rise 10-in (25-cm) long sprays of open blossoms. Each flower is 1 in (2.5 m) in diameter with up to 10 petals in pink, orange, salmon, or white, often "candy-striped" in a stronger, complementary or contrasting color (Plate 66). The plant can take some shade, preferably from the afternoon sun. *Lewisia cotyledon* has been the most successful *Lewisia* species in my garden. Occasionally, I order a few new plants, but my own seedlings are usually sufficient to fill most of the gaps caused by attrition.

Lewisia rediviva 2 in (5 cm); Zone 3
Bitter Root

This *Lewisia* is the state flower of Montana. Its common designation gave its name to the Bitterroot River and the Bitterroot Range in the northern Rocky Mountains. This species grows from a substantial root which, true to its name, has a bitter taste when raw but is edible when cooked, and which was used as food by Native Americans and early colonists.

The botanical epithet means "reborn," a reference to the plant's ability to regenerate even after it has been dried out for a year. The plant requires excellent drainage, even drought conditions, if it can be arranged. Keeping my specimen dry during some of the rainy months is not easy. After it goes dormant following its flowering period in spring, I place a flat stone or a piece of slate over the spot where its fleshy quill-shaped foliage grew; the stone is supported on one side by a large pebble to shed the rain. I keep this little shelter in place until early spring.

This species produces its large ivory-white flowers with many petals just as the leaves begin to fade. It is relatively easy to start from seed.

***Ligularia przewalskii* 'The Rocket'** (Compositae) 6 ft (1.8 m); Zone 4

The genus *Ligularia* has an undetermined number of species, sometimes given as between 50 and 150, all native to Eurasia. These species are frequently but erroneously included in the enormous genus *Senecio* (2000–3000 species), but they are separate.

Ligularia przewalskii is a Chinese species with large deeply lobed and toothed leaves growing directly from the base. The flower stems tower above the foliage. The upper part of the stalk is a narrow raceme of many small, bright yellow flowers that contrast attractively with the dark reddish brown stem. The plant grows best in partial shade in rich, moist soil.

Lilium (Liliaceae) 3 ft (0.9 m); Zone 4
Lily

Lilium is a genus of about 90 species, all native to the Northern Hemisphere. These species grow from bulbs, rhizomes, or stolons, and many have grown in gardens for millennia. They are relatively easy to grow, although their foliage must be protected from deer and rabbits, and their bulbs from mice. They do best in deeply dug soil that is rich in organic matter, in sun or partial shade. If protected from predators, the plants are long lived and provide a nearly permanent addition to a garden. Many make excellent garden subjects in their natural forms, and great numbers of hybrids and varieties are also readily available.

Over the years, I have planted several native species of this genus, of which the spectacular *Lilium superbum* (turk's-cap lily) was the most desired. Nevertheless, the deer ate it to the ground every year until, finally, it did not come up. I still grow several lilies that somehow survive the hostile environment: *Lilium* 'Destiny' is a tall plant with large, six-petaled lemon-yellow flowers spotted chocolate-brown near the center. I also grow a few colorful 18-in (45-cm) high plants of unknown names. A bright orange plant of unknown origin, which has been with me for years, grows only to about 16 in (40 cm) in height. Last but not least, I have a roadside denizen, *L. lancifolium* (tiger lily), from the Far East that owes its continuing presence to the dozens of bulbils growing in the leaf axils along the thin, 6-ft (1.8-m) high stalk. These bulbils germinate readily and reach flowering size in a few years.

***Lithodora diffusa* 'Heavenly Blue'** (Boraginaceae) 12 in (30 cm); Zone 6

There are seven species in the genus *Lithodora,* most of them subshrubs native to western and southern Europe, north Africa, and Asia Minor. The old name for the genus, *Lithospermum,* is still occasionally encountered.

Lithodora diffusa 'Heavenly Blue' grows only about 3 in (8 cm) high but spreads over an area of nearly 2 sq ft (0.2 sq m), covering its hairy branchlets with bright sky-blue flowers in spring and, occasionally, in midsummer. This species comes from the very warm parts of Europe and Morocco and is not truly hardy in zone 6 nor is it known particularly for its longevity even in ideal circumstances. I placed my little specimen against a south-facing boundary wall, where it is kept warm by the winter sun but is shaded from the baking summer sun by a 4-ft (1.2-m) high *Vaccinium corymbosum* (highbush blueberry). The soil in which the lithodora grows is a loose, well-drained mixture of decomposed leaf mold of acidic reaction.

Lobelia cardinalis (Lobeliaceae) 3 ft (0.9 m); Zone 4
Cardinal Flower; Indian Pink

The genus *Lobelia* comprises some 375 species of mostly tropical herbs, shrubs, and trees. Some are weedy plants that populate stream banks and open areas of disturbed soil. *Lobelia cardinalis* is a North American species ranging from New Brunswick to Minnesota and south to Texas and Florida. The tall single flower stem is covered toward the top with many bright scarlet blossoms 1.5 in (4 cm) wide. Opening in late summer, this is one of the brightest wild flowers of its range. The plant does not persist too long in one place, but the seeds germinate readily and new plants can be produced with relatively little effort.

Lupinus polyphyllus (Leguminosae) 2.5 ft (0.8 m); Zone 5
Lupin

The genus *Lupinus* has about 200 species native to many parts of the world, but especially numerous in North America. The leaves are palmately compound, and the pealike flowers occur on tall, erect stems. Many of the species from the western states are grown as ornamentals in their natural version, but *L. polyphyllus,* native from Washington to California, has been widely hybridized to produce great spikes of flowers in a broad range of colors. The Russell hybrids are particularly attractive.

The plants need a well-drained location with soil of somewhat lower fertility, and are at home in partial shade or full sun. In the latter position plants should be mulched to keep their roots cool. Watering during dry periods is essential for normal growth. Removing spent flower spikes preserves a plant's energy and sometimes induces second blossoming.

LYCHNIS (CARYOPHYLLACEAE) Campion, Catchfly

The genus *Lychnis* consists of 35 species distributed throughout the temperate zones and the arctic regions of the globe. Some are suited for a cultivated flower border, but others are better used in the wild flower garden. I grow several varieties of *Lychnis.*

Lychnis alpina 1 ft (0.3 m); Zone 3

Lychnis alpina, sometimes listed as *Viscaria alpina* (catchfly), is a perennial plant native to Europe but occasionally occurring in the wild also in eastern North America. It has a small rosette of narrow leaves from which rises a 10-in (25-cm) high naked stem with a 1.5-in (4-cm) high inflorescence of 6–20 small rose-pink flowers. The plant grows and flowers even in a dry location where it seeds itself modestly. It is indifferent to soil pH level. It looks best in a semiwild garden. The larger, more vigorous version, *Lychnis alpina* 'Flore Pleno', is better suited for a cultivated garden.

Lychnis chalcedonica 2 ft (0.6 m); Zone 3
Maltese Cross; Jerusalem Cross; Scarlet Lightning; London Pride

This species, native to northern Russia, is a tall, stout plant with stems covered by 2–4 in (5–10 cm) long leaves. When grown in quantity, the plants create a verdant bank topped with many flaming scarlet inflorescences, each 2–3 in (5–10 cm) in diameter. Individual flowers are 0.75 in (2 cm) wide and are in the form of a star or cross formée, the emblem of the Knights of Malta. The plant grows best in full sun in good garden soil.

Lychnis flos-cuculi 1 ft (0.3 m); Zone 4
Ragged Robin; Cuckoo Flower

This European wild flower has become naturalized in North America from eastern Canada to Pennsylvania. In ideal locations, such as a sunny damp meadow, it grows 2 ft (60 cm) high, but in drier conditions it remains at 1 ft (30 cm) or less. The 2-in (5-cm) long oval leaves form flat, nearly evergreen rosettes on the ground, and from them grow slender stems with several pairs of narrow, clasping leaves. At the top of each stem are small but very visible panicles of rose-pink flowers, 1 in (2.5 cm) in diameter, with narrow, twisted, ribbonlike petals that give the flower cluster an untidy but definitely endearing appearance. I allow the plant to seed itself in a 2-ft (60 cm) wide strip along a sunny path and, after the flowers have matured and scattered their seeds, I mow the area down to the green basal rosettes.

LYCOPODIUM (LYCOPODIACEAE)

Clubmoss; Ground Pine; Running Pine; Princess Pine; Ground Cedar

The genus *Lycopodium* includes about 450 species of creeping evergreen plants widely distributed around the world. They are primitive creations of ancient origin, a tiny remainder of the clubmoss trees that, together with ferns and equisetums, formed the Earth's jungles more than 300 million years ago. The giant trunks and clouds of pollen of the Paleozoic Era became today's vast deposits of coal. Similar to their other venerable companions, lycopodiums reproduce from minute spores that are widely dispersed by wind or even a breeze. The spores are produced in large quantities and have been used extensively in industrial and commercial applications. They are so uniform in size that they were once used for microscopic measurements. Furthermore, since they ignite easily, they were part of early fireworks and photographic flashes, and, because they are water repellent, they were used as powder for dressing wounds, for coating pills, and as a fixative in wool dyes.

The spores of lycopodiums are neither male nor female. Before being capable of reproduction, the spores must first develop into an intermediate form, called a *gametophyte,* which in turn develops male and female organs. Only after their eggs have been fertilized do actual plants begin to grow. In some *Lycopodium* species the spores burrow deeply below the surface of the soil to perform this function, while in others it is accomplished on the surface. The study of the gametophytes is extremely difficult. Because of their minute size, it is almost impossible to locate them in the ground and follow their progress. It is believed, however, that it takes 7 years or more for a spore to develop into a gametophyte, and an additional 10 or more years to develop into a new plant.

Until recently, lycopodiums were ripped out by the ton for Christmas decorations. Now they are supposedly grown from cuttings for that purpose. More are destroyed today by builders, highway contractors, and even by unknowing gardeners. Although lycopodiums are difficult to transplant, if a stand is threatened plants can be carefully moved after verifying that an undamaged plant has a length of underground or surface runner with at least two or three whitish roots in good condition. The soil in the new location must be acidic (pH 4.0 to 5.0), well shaded, and kept constantly moist (though not wet) until the transplant is established. Several species of *Lycopodium* grow in my garden.

Lycopodium clavatum 6 in (15 cm); Zone 3

Running Clubmoss; Coral Evergreen; Staghorn Evergreen; Buckhorn; Wolf's Claw

This Eurasian and North American species has long, light green furry runners that travel on the surface of the soil, sending an occasional white root into the ground and producing erect branches up to 6 in (15 cm) high. In late summer or early fall some of the branches develop a thin stalk that terminates in one or more spore-bearing strobiles reminiscent of a tiny club (called *clava* in Latin). The strobiles mature in early winter and produce clouds of golden-yellow spores.

Lycopodium complanatum* var. *flabelliforme 5 in (13 cm); Zone 3

Running Pine; Christmas Green

This variety is native to the northeastern part of North America. It grows in tangled mats that send up a few upright stems terminating in two or three thin strobiles. The plant's little branchlets are bright green and many-forked, usually sprawling and less erect than branchlets on similar species.

Lycopodium lucidulum 8 in (20 cm); Zone 3
Shining Clubmoss

This rare species, native to North America, remains in one place for many years, creeping only very little. The roots are just below the surface of the soil, and the stems are heavily clad with evergreen, shiny, bristlelike leaves 0.4 in (1 cm) long. The spores are produced on the stems themselves, on narrow growths that look like smaller leaves. In addition, this species also reproduces by tiny bulblets occurring in the upper parts of some branches.

Lycopodium obscurum 10 in (25 cm); Zone 3
Tree Clubmoss

This species from North America and Asia looks like a tiny conifer tree. The thin, horizontal stems travel below the ground, and, about every 6 in (15 cm), send up erect shoots that branch into treelike forms. Each branchlet is densely covered with short, narrow, sharp-pointed, shiny evergreen leaves. The spore-bearing strobiles grow directly out of the tops of the branches without any stems.

Maianthemum canadense (Liliaceae) 5 in (13 cm); Zone 3
Beadruby; False Lily-of-the-Valley

There are only three species in the genus *Maianthemum,* all native to the northern regions of Eurasia and North America. *Maianthemum canadense* ranges from Labrador to British Columbia, and south to Tennessee and Delaware. The plant has up to three shiny green leaves on 5-in (13-cm) high stems, and clusters of small fragrant flowers above the leaves. It spreads by white, threadlike rhizomes that creep just below the ground and reach quickly into new areas, provided the soil is rich, moist, shaded, and strongly acidic, with pH 4.0 to 5.0. The leaves appear in early spring and within 2 weeks completely carpet the forest floor. The flowers occur in May and mature into pale, greenish beadlike fruits that become spotted brown and eventually ripen into red berries. By the end of summer, this lush ground cover disappears.

Mertensia virginica (Boraginaceae) 1.5 ft (0.5 m); Zone 4
Virginia Bluebells; Virginia Cowslip; Roanoke Bells

The genus *Mertensia* has about 45 species of perennial herbs native to Eurasia and North America. *Mertensia virginica* is a purely North American species with a native range from Ontario to Minnesota and south to Kansas, Alabama, and Georgia. The leaves are gray-green, oval, and to 5 in (13 cm) long. The flowers are nodding, 1-in (2.5-cm) long trumpets clustered at the ends of the tall stems. They open in April and May, at first as rose-pink buds, later changing to lavender-blue and eventually sky-blue bells (Plate 33). The foliage disappears after the flowers fade.

The plant prefers a moist, shady, location in the woods or along streams where it seeds itself generously. Upon germination, the tiny thick root with one little oval leaf can be moved to a new location before the leaflet shrivels and the seedling disappears for the season. The new plant will bloom in a year or two after transplanting. The species supposedly prefers neutral soil but it has grown, blossomed, and seeded itself prolifically in my garden's strongly acidic soils.

Mitchella repens (Rubiaceae) 1 in (2.5 cm); Zone 3
Partridgeberry; Squawberry; Two-eye Berry; Twinberry; Running Box

One of the two species in the genus *Mitchella* is from the Far East, and the second, *M. repens,* is a North American plant ranging from Newfoundland to Minnesota and south to Texas and Florida. Named for the early U.S. botanist Dr. John Mitchell, this genus contains plants that are among the most ideal ground covers for smaller areas. *Mitchella repens* is a very low, hardy evergreen, with small attractive leaves. If satisfied in its location, it produces small white flowers that mature into bright red berries that spark up the finely textured surface. The tubular blossoms are united into pairs. They are fragrant, and the red berries have a mild peppermint taste.

The plant does not survive in full sun. It requires at least partial shade and does well even in completely shaded locations. It grows best in moist, rich acidic soil with pH 4.0 to 5.0. In very dry summers it benefits from occasional watering. The foliage can be eaten by rabbits, slugs, and rodents and deer can rip out the slender stems mercilessly destroying many square feet of *Mitchella repens* in one visit. A cover of plastic netting usually prevents total destruction even though the deer's nimble tongues and lips are able to pull many of the thin runners through the openings.

Monarda didyma **'Adam'** (Labiatae) 3 ft (0.9 m); Zone 3

Oswego Tea; Oswego Beebalm; Scarlet Bergamot

There are about 12 species in the purely North American genus *Monarda. Monarda didyma* is native from Quebec to Michigan and south to Tennessee and Georgia. The tall stems, as well as the 4-in (10-cm) long leaves, are usually covered with thin hairs. The flowers, in showy terminal heads 1.5–2 in (4–5 cm) in diameter, are normally flaming red, a color which strongly attracts hummingbirds. Cultivar 'Adam' is bright scarlet, but many other versions range in color from white to salmon, violet, rose-pink, and other shades. The plant prefers moist situations along streams or low areas, but grows also in dry woods and other partly shady locations. It is rather indifferent to soil acidity, though the optimal rate is pH 5.5 to 6.5. If it is happy in a given spot, the plant will spread vigorously and must be restrained either by a natural boundary such as a stream, by an artificial barrier such as deeply imbedded rocks or boards, or by periodic intervention with a spade.

Myosotis scorpioides (Boraginaceae) 1 ft (0.3 m); Zone 4

Forget-me-not

The 50 species that comprise the genus *Myosotis* are distributed over five continents. *Myosotis scorpioides* is native to Eurasia and has naturalized through most of North America. It prefers moist or wet situations, but will grow in drier positions if sufficiently shaded. The 1-ft (30-cm) long stems often sprawl over the ground or float at water's edge. The flowers grow in loose cymes and are about 0.25 in (6 mm) wide, usually sky-blue with a yellow, pink, or white eye. The plant seeds itself freely and blooms in the fall of the second year from sowing.

Narcissus (Amaryllidaceae) 1.5 ft (0.5 m); Zone 3

Daffodil

Only a few of the 25 species in the genus *Narcissus* are in wide cultivation in their pure form. The plants most widely grown are either natural crosses or hybrids of garden and commercial origins. The genus is native to Europe and North Africa and has been subjected to many generations of hybridization and selection. This process is continuing and new, ever-more-spectacular plants are reaching the market.

Narcissi are valued for their early blossoms and their ease of cultivation as well as their beauty, but they have become popular also for their complete immunity to rabbits, deer, mice, and other predators who avoid the toxic leaves, blooms, and bulbs. I grow a number of varieties, and my desire to grow more is curbed only by lack of space. Of the hundreds of named varieties that are readily available, I selected and grow the following: 'Ambergate', 'February Gold', 'King Alfred', 'Mount Hood',

'Paola Veronese', 'Royal Victory', 'Suzie', 'Tahiti', 'World's Favorite' and others.

When planting a large number of bulbs, it may be advantageous to outline the design and the size of the new bed by first placing all the bulbs, about 8 in (20 cm) apart, over the ground in which they will be planted. I have found that the process can be further improved by digging up the entire outlined area to a depth of about 10 in (25 cm) rather than digging dozens or hundreds of individual holes. The excavated soil is mixed with leafmold, and a portion of this blend is spread over the bottom of the excavation to form a base 2–3 in (5–8 cm) thick. The bulbs are then gently pressed into the soft bed, some bonemeal scattered around each bulb, and the remaining soil placed over them until the top layer of the new planting is slightly higher than the surrounding soil to allow for settling.

Onoclea sensibilis (Polypodiaceae) 3 ft (0.9 m); Zone 4
Sensitive Fern; Bead Fern

This is the only species in the genus *Onoclea*. It is native to Eurasia and North America where it is found as far south as the Gulf of Mexico. Its regular (sterile) leaves have the general outline of normal fern leaves but are segmented only once compared with other ferns that usually have twice-pinnate leaves divided into much smaller surfaces. The second type of leaves on *O. sensibilis* are the fertile fronds appearing in late summer. Twice-pinnate, their smaller segments are rolled tightly into hard beads that contain and protect cases of spores. The effect is one of a stiff stalk studded with hard greenish brown balls, each 0.1 in (3 mm) in diameter.

The plant spreads vigorously by thick rootstock and must be rigidly contained or entirely excluded from all but the most extensive gardens. Native to my garden, I have hesitated to totally eliminate this unique fern as long as I am able to launch periodic eradication raids, always saving a few inches of the hazardous rootstock. The species acquired its botanical name, and one of its common names from its sensitivity to low temperatures: with the first light frost, the sterile fronds perish, leaving only the dark spikes of fertile fronds covered with the black pellets which, at some time during the winter, open and scatter their spores. (See also "Ferns.")

Orchis spectabilis (Orchidaceae) 8 in (20 cm); Zone 4
Showy Orchid; Woodland Orchid; Purple-hooded Orchid; Kirtle Pink

An estimated 600 to 800 genera comprise the orchid family, Orchidaceae, containing up to 30,000 species. Most orchids are epiphytic plants living on the surface of other plants, such as trees, and using them for support rather than as a source of nourishment, as do parasitic plants. About 50 species are terrestrial plants. *Orchis spectabilis* is a member of this group.

One of the most desirable North American wild flowers, *Orchis spectabilis* is native from New Brunswick to North Dakota, to southern New England and, along the Appalachians, to Georgia and Kentucky. From the base of the plant rises an upright stalk with two 5-in (13-cm) long smooth, oblong leaves, and a loose 4-in (10-cm) long raceme with 2 to 10 attractive, fragrant flowers. Each blossom, about 1 in (2.5 cm) long, has a white or purplish lip and a lilac or magenta hood. The blossoms appear in late April or early May and last through June.

The plant prefers shaded, low lying moist soil rich in organic matter and a pH of 5.5 to 6.5. If such conditions can be created, it will grow and multiply, doubling the number of flowering stems every year. However, the plant frequently falls victim to small and large predators. It should be protected from early spring until dormancy against slugs, snails, rodents, and insects. To keep it moist, I use a 2-in (5-cm) thick layer of pine needles as mulch.

Osmunda cinnamomea (Osmundaceae) 5 ft (1.5 m); Zone 4

Cinnamon Fern; Fiddleheads; Buckhorn

The genus *Osmunda* has 10 species that are scattered throughout the temperate and tropical regions of Asia and North as well as South America. *Osmunda cinnamomea* ranges from South America and the West Indies to northern North America and eastern Asia. The plant is very attractive at every stage of its growth. It begins in early spring with the coiled fronds (croziers) appearing in great numbers where the plant is plentiful, and adding bold and exotic forms to a landscape that for months had been scrubbed of all tender living matter by the winds and frosts of winter (Plate 20).

Over several days, these "fiddleheads" unfold into majestic, arching fronds. Soon from their middle emerge the tall, erect, fertile, "flowering" fronds that are actually stems with short branchlike leaves smothered with spore-bearing fruit dots (sori). Initially bright green, the flowering fronds change to golden brown, cinnamon-red, and then chocolate-brown before they wither away (Plate 67). The massive sterile foliage remains, creating constantly changing patterns as it bends and sways gently in the slightest breeze (Plates 3, 59). When autumn comes, the foliage turns reddish beige and yellow, then brown, before it disappears with the first frosts.

The plant has a massive system of black wiry roots that is very difficult to dig up, but does not spread. Most of the plants in my garden were here when I came and they still occupy their original locations, having grown only slightly larger. They must be 50 years old or more. Occasionally, with considerable effort, I dig up a few to make room for other plants, but I give these ferns away always somewhat reluctantly and with a slight sense of guilt.

Osmunda cinnamomea grows best in shady locations with rich moist soil of pH 4.0 to 6.5. Once established, it can stand a considerable amount of sun but, if adequate moisture is unavailable, the fronds shrivel and usually do not reappear until the next spring. (See also "Ferns.")

Osmunda claytoniana (Osmundaceae) 5 ft (1.5 m); Zone 4

Interrupted Fern

This fern is similar to *Osmunda cinnamomea* except that it lacks the colorful cinnamon-fruiting stems. Instead, fertile leaves appear as normal fronds, but about half way up their length two or three regular leaflets (pinnae) are missing. In their place are two to five pairs of short twice-pinnate leaflets that serve only to bear spores. The native range of this fern is identical to that of *O. cinnamomea,* and its growing conditions are similar also, though it will grow in somewhat less acidic soils. (See also "Ferns.")

Osmunda regalis (Osmundaceae) 4 ft (1.2 m); Zone 5

Royal Fern

This third *Osmunda* species in my garden differs considerably from the other two, mainly in the pattern and the general aspect of its foliage. The fronds are less segmented and more slender and wiry. The leaflets are oblong with smooth rather than serrated margins as in the other species (Plate 59). The spore-bearing fronds are similar to the sterile fronds except for their tips which become dense clusters of small leaves covered with spores. These tips are at first light green but turn brown as they mature. This elegant species grows in South America, Africa, Europe, Asia, and North America. In Europe, where it used to be plentiful, the wild population has declined significantly because of excessive collecting. The plant prefers rich, moist soils and tolerates a wider range of acidity, from pH 4.0 to 7.5. (See also "Ferns.")

PACHYSANDRA (BUXACEAE) Spurge

The genus *Pachysandra* is comprised of five species: four are native to eastern Asia, and one is North American. Much has been written about the excessive use of the alien, spreading *Pachysandra terminalis* in gardens and landscapes. Some critics recommend that its use be restrained in favor of native ground cover. At least one writer recommended the "native" *Vinca minor* (periwinkle) as a substitute.

It is true that the species can be planted in excess, but one could make a similar observation about many plants including, say, *Poa pratensis* (Kentucky bluegrass). Twenty years ago, my own garden had a number of areas covered with *Pachysandra terminalis*, and today the extent of these large patches is about the same. The plant is easily kept in bounds by a mower along the lawn margins or by pulling out the few runners that occasionally wander off into beds where they are not desired. On the other hand, where it is allowed to grow, *P. terminalis* performs a useful service by reducing weeding chores, by keeping the soil cool and moist for large ericaceous plants that grow through it, and by providing an esthetically appealing green carpet for nearly 52 weeks of the year. As to the "native" periwinkle and Kentucky bluegrass, they are both natives of the Old World. I grow two species of *Pachysandra*.

Pachysandra procumbens 1 ft (30 cm); Zone 5

Allegheny Spurge; Allegheny Pachysandra

This is the North American member of the genus native from Kentucky to Louisiana and east to Florida. It is similar to the familiar *Pachysandra terminalis* but its leaves are somewhat less shiny and lightly mottled with whitish markings. One out of two or three winters the foliage freezes and disappears. Albeit of southerly origins, the plant itself is hardy and has survived at least 10 years in Connecticut's climate.

Pachysandra terminalis 1 ft (30 cm); Zone 4

Japanese Spurge; Japanese Pachysandra

This is the widely used ground cover that is the subject of sometimes less-than-rational controversy. It is reliably evergreen, vigorous, attractive, and permanent (Plate 3). Though usually free of pests and diseases, it can become affected by both, especially if planted in very hot dry locations. I have such an area near the house where, in some years, hordes of caterpillars of an unidentified moth have nearly destroyed my planting. In very wet summers, a fungus seems to affect the leaves, turning their tips black and diminishing new growth. The solution obviously lies in replacing the pachysandra with a plant more appropriate for the location.

PAEONIA (PAEONIACEAE) Peony

There are about 35 species in the genus *Paeonia*. The large majority are herbaceous perennials, and the remainder are thinly branched shrubs with a few stiff, woody stems, called by the somewhat overstated common name, "tree peonies." Both groups include some of the most beautiful garden plants. All are native to Eurasia, with the exception of two species with somewhat less-than-spectacular blossoms that come from the western coast of North America and are not in general cultivation (*P. brownii* and *P. californica*). Most peonies have large, compound, and dissected leaves. Their great blooms are either double or single and, in either form, there are not many blossoms in my garden that match them in beauty.

At first grown as medicinal plants, peonies have been hybridized in the Orient and Europe for centuries, and the process goes on also in North America and Australia. They are easy to grow, especially if they are planted correctly from the begining. It is definitely worth the effort to dig a hole or a trench 1.5–2 ft (50–60 cm) deep and equally wide. The soil, before it is placed back in the excavation, should be mixed with rich organic matter, bonemeal, and a fungicide such as dust of sulfur. Peonies should be planted in October. I grow several herbaceous and tree peonies in my garden.

***Paeonia* 'Doris Cooper'** 3 ft (0.9 m); Zone 3

This herbaceous peony with deliciously fragrant, double, light pink flowers of medium size blooms late in the season. It was developed by Dr. H. C. Cooper, Portland, Oregon, and named for his daughter.

***Paeonia* 'Mrs. Franklin D. Roosevelt'** 3.5 ft (1.1 m); Zone 3

This is a herbaceous plant with large, light pink, fragrant, long-lasting blossoms. It grows tall and produces a significant number of blooms every season. It is a 1932 hybrid of Alonzo Barry Franklin, Minneapolis, Minnesota.

***Paeonia* 'Red Charm'** 3 ft (0.9 m); Zone 3

This herbaceous peony, a hybrid of *Paeonia officinalis* var. *rubra* and *P. albiflora,* became a sensation after its 1944 introduction by Lyman D. Glassock, Elwood, Illinois. The flowers are not fragrant, but they are enormous, double, bomb-type spheres of narrow petals in the center surrounded by a collar of broader petals, all in rich, radiant red. In some growers' opinion, if only one red peony can be grown, it should be this one. The plant blooms early and goes dormant before other peonies.

***Paeonia* sp.** 3 ft (0.9 m); Zone 3

The label on this pink-flowered herbaceous plant has long been lost. When I planted it in its present site about 20 years ago, I dug a hole just big enough to accommodate the 10-in (25-cm) wide root system rather than digging a more generous hole such as those I excavated for the other peonies. As a result, the specimen grows and blooms only modestly. It is living proof that when planting peonies, it is desirable to follow the principle of digging "broad and deep," and enriching the soil with plenty of organic matter.

Paeonia suffruticosa 7 ft (2.1 m); Zone 3

Tree Peony

The botanical epithet of this Himalayan species is considerably more appropriate than its common name. In Latin, *suffruticosa* means "shrubby," which describes the plant's semiwoody stems and branches much more accurately than does the adjective "tree." In the words of John C. Wister and Harold E. Wolfe (Wister 1962, 146), tree peonies are among "the most magnificent, most beautiful, and most interesting of all plants."

It is difficult to disagree with this assessment while observing the enormous blossoms of a plant such as *Paeonia suffruticosa* 'Nissho' (Japanese for 'Sunbeam'). The blooms are single, 8 in (20 cm) in diameter, with large flat petals of an iridescent orange-red, and a large tuft of contrasting yellow stamens in the center (Plate 67). It took my specimen 4 or 5 years from planting to begin flowering. Now it is 3 ft (0.9 m) tall and, by the time it matures at 6–7 ft (1.8–2.1 m), it could be producing hundreds of blossoms every season.

I grow two other tree peonies: *Paeonia suffruticosa* 'Kinshi' ('Golden Bird'), a hybrid of *P. lutea* with rich, double, many-petalled golden yellow blooms that have a satin sheen; and *P. suffruticosa* 'Sahohime', which has large semidouble flowers with white petals, purple markings toward the center, and ivory stamens (Plate 67).

PLATE 67. A mid-May display of the silky orange blooms of *Paeonia suffruticosa* 'Nissho', and the great white disks of *Paeonia suffruticosa* 'Sahohime' (tree peonies), with the fruiting fronds of *Osmunda cinnamomea* (cinnamon fern) in the center.

PAPAVER (PAPAVERACEAE) Poppy

Most of the 50 species in the genus *Papaver* come from Eurasia and a few are native to the western part of North America. They are easy to grow in most soils and seed themselves freely. Two species currently grow in my garden.

Papaver orientale 3 ft (0.9 m); Zone 3

Oriental Poppy

This is a perennial plant native to southwestern Asia but widely planted and hybridized around the world. It grows easily in many types of soil and has become naturalized in some parts of North America. The robust, dissected hairy leaves grow in large rosettes, and in May and June sturdy stems arise from the rosettes with large blossoms, sometimes 6 in (15 cm) in diameter. The petals are usually bright orange-red, but many hybrids and cultivars are available in colors from white to salmon, pink, or purple. These are among the longest-lived poppies.

Papaver rhoeas 1.5 ft (0.5 m); Zone 3

Field Poppy; Corn Poppy; Flanders Poppy

This is the annual orange-red poppy of Eurasia which, together with *Centaurea cyanus* (cornflower) and *Chrysanthemum leucanthemum* (ox-eye daisy), is a major ingredient in the colorful, early summer meadows of the Old World. *Papaver rhoeas* has become naturalized in some parts of North America, but in the acidic soils of my garden it dies out after a few years and has to be replanted with fresh seeds.

About 100 years ago, an English clergyman, Rev. W. Wilks, of the Shirley vicarage, developed a special strain of poppies with a broad range of pastel colors. They have become known as the Shirley poppies and are now widely planted in all parts of the world. In my garden, their colors remain true for 2 or 3 years, but by the fourth generation, they revert to the original red-orange, with some plants retaining their double-flower character for several years. In any color, *Papaver rhoeas* and its derivatives are among the most attractive annuals.

PHLOX (POLEMONIACEAE)

Approximately 60 species comprise the genus *Phlox,* all North American natives except one, *P. sibirica,* which comes from northern Asia. Many of the species are desirable garden plants in their natural forms, while others have undergone an extensive hybridization and selection process that has produced a range of cultivated plants with larger and more numerous blossoms. There is a tall, stately phlox, as well as a phlox in the form of dense mats of procumbent creepers only a few inches high. The larger plants, particularly, must be protected from deer. Phloxes have been heavily hybridized in North America as well as Europe, Australia, and Asia and are now appearing as refined selections and crosses with blossoms of clear, unmuddied colors. I grow several varieties in my garden.

Phlox carolina 3.5 ft (1.1 m); Zone 3

Thick-leaf Phlox; Carolina Phlox

This species ranges from Maryland to Indiana and south to Florida. The sturdy stems, which have 5 to 12 pairs of thick, smooth lance-shaped leaves up to 5 in (13 cm) long, in May to July produce panicles of attractive five-parted flowers about 0.75 in (2 cm) in diameter. The prevalent color is purple, but cultivars in other shades are common. *Phlox carolina* 'Miss Lingard' (white) and 'Rosalind' (pink) are particularly attractive. *Phlox carolina* is sometimes called *P. suffruticosa.*

Phlox divaricata 1 ft (0.3 m); Zone 3

Wild Sweet William; Wild Blue Phlox

This *Phlox* species is native from Vermont to Minnesota and Nebraska, and south to Texas and Florida. It is a slender, somewhat hairy plant, with several pairs of narrow 1–2 in (2.5–5 cm) long leaves along a thin stalk that terminates in a small cyme of pale-blue to lilac flowers. The corolla has five petallike lobes, each notched on the margin. The plant prefers light shade and humus-rich soil of nearly neutral reaction. The optimal pH level is 6.0 to 7.0, although the species grows and flowers well even in more acidic soils (Plate 70). If its requirements are met, the plant spreads slowly into nearly evergreen plantings which at flowering time become airy patches of bluish mist.

Phlox paniculata 6 ft (1.8 m); Zone 3

Perennial Phlox; Summer Phlox; Fall Phlox

This species is the most reminiscent of the normal garden phlox. It is native to the southerly two-thirds of North America and has been cultivated for many generations in its natural form as well as in numerous hybridized versions. In good soil and partial shade, it may grow to 6 ft (1.8 m), but 4 ft (1.2 m) is more normal. The stems are strong and upright, uniformly green along their entire length, clad with a dozen or more pairs of large lance-shaped, strongly veined leaves up to 6 in (15 cm) long. A similar species, *Phlox maculata,* differs from *P. paniculata* mainly in having smaller leaves and having stems that are visibly spotted with purplish blotches. The range of the two species is similar, although *P. maculata* grows in more southerly latitudes.

The flowers of both species, arranged in panicles several inches long, are usually pink-purple, but also white and many shades in between. The plants, especially those of *Phlox paniculata,* are abundant along country roads and in margins of woods. The rich reddish purple plants in my garden have seeded themselves abundantly over the years; by culling unwanted colors at blossom time, I have been able to create a sizable bed of the interesting shade. Planted near or mixed with *Hesperis matronalis* (dame's rocket), *Phlox paniculata* can extend the combined flowering season of these two unrelated plants from late April until frost. *Phlox paniculata* has been known also as *P. decussata* but that name is used mainly for the European hybrids. And, to compound the confusion, the term is sometimes misapplied also to *P. maculata* and *P. carolina*.

Phlox stolonifera 10 in (25 cm); Zone 3

Creeping Phlox

This species is native from Pennsylvania to Georgia and Tennessee, but is hardy much farther north. The foliage is evergreen, fairly dense, spatulate, growing on creeping stolons, and reaching only a few inches in height. From April to June, the broad mats of small leaves send up flowering stems up to 10 in (25 cm) high, with cymes of purple-blue flowers 0.5 in (13 mm) in diameter. The species prefers moist, shady locations and, while an assiduous spreader, it is not extremely difficult to keep within bounds. A patch of creeping phlox along a shady path or under a tree is pretty at any time of the year, and particularly at blooming time. There are several desirable cultivars of which *Phlox stolonifera* 'Blue Ridge' is among the best.

Phlox subulata 6 in (15 cm); Zone 2

Moss-pink; Moss Phlox; Mountain Phlox

This is a cushion-forming, sun-loving, colorful phlox native from New York to Michigan and south to Tennessee and South Carolina. From the creeping stems rise numerous thin branches that become smothered with needlelike leaves up to 1 in (2.5 cm) long. In April and May the entire plant is covered with 0.5-in (13-mm) wide blossoms in rose pink, white, blue, and many other colors. This species is perfectly suited for a sunny stone bank or a warm rock garden where it provides a neat and tidy evergreen patch throughout the year, coming alive with color at blossom time. Among the many cultivars, 'Klima's Beauty' is one of the best.

Platycodon grandiflorus (Campanulaceae) 2.5 ft (0.8 m); Zone 3

Balloon Flower; Chinese Bellflower

There is only one species in the genus *Platycodon,* a native of the Far East. The plant has firm, erect stems branched toward the top, which are sparsely covered with smooth, sharply toothed leaves up to 3 in (8 cm) long. In summer, the top branchlets bear terminal flowers, 2–3 in (5–8 cm) in diameter, in the form of open, sharp-tipped bells mostly in shades of blue, but sometimes white, and pinkish ivory. Some cultivars have double flowers. Before the buds open, they expand into sizable, five-sided, hollow spheres that give the plant its common name, balloon flower. The plant prefers sunny, open positions, and should be left undisturbed for many years.

Podophyllum peltatum (Berberidaceae) 1.5 ft (0.5 m); Zone 4

Mayapple; Wild Lemon; Raccoon Berry; Wild Jalap

The genus *Podophyllum* has two, possibly a few more, species native to North America and Asia. *Podophyllum peltatum* is a North American plant ranging from Quebec to Minnesota and south to Texas and Florida. The single erect stalk is usually 1 ft (30 cm) or more in height, and at the top has one or two deeply divided peltate leaves that look like small umbrellas. In the fork, where the petioles of the two leaves meet, appears a solitary white blossom 1 in (2.5 cm) or more in diameter. The bloom has six sepals, which drop off when the bud opens into a flower with six or nine petals. The number of stamens equals the number of petals or is exactly double.

The blossoms occur only on plants that have two leaves. The fruit is a large berry, 1–2 in (2.5–5 cm) in diameter, in the shape of a small lemon. It is the "apple" that gave the plant the name, mayapple, and although it is edible, it may give discomfort to some people. Native Americans and early settlers used the fruit to cure various ailments. The plant's fleshy underground rhizome yields a toxic substance, podophyllum, from which a compound has been recently refined that appears to have the capability of selectively destroying undesirable types of cells in humans.

Polygala pauciflora (Polygalaceae) 4 in (10 cm); Zone 3

Fringed Polygala; Fringed Milkwort; Flowering Wintergreen; Gay-wings; Bird-on-the-wing

There are 500 to 600 species of woody plants and herbs in the genus *Polygala* (milkwort), native to Eurasia, Africa, and the Americas. Their habitat reaches from the subarctic regions to the tropics. *Polygala pauciflora* is a North American wild flower, a tiny, evergreen creeper ranging from New Brunswick to Minnesota and south to Virginia. It is seldom more than a few inches high, and it spreads very slowly, eventually thinly covering an area of 1 sq ft (0.1 sq m). The dark green leaves are about 1.5 in (4 cm) long, and the unique, dainty blossoms are 0.75 in (2 cm) long.

The plant is not very floriferous; in fact, the flowers occur with some paucity (hence the epithet *pauciflora*), usually two or three blooms per smallish plant. They are, however, very bright rose-purple, rarely white, and their form is most unusual. The small petals are rolled into one tube about 0.25 in (6 mm) wide and 0.75 in (2 cm) long. At the tip of the petal, which forms the lower part of the tube, is a bushy, fringed, bright yellow crest. In the back, the little tube is subtended by two winglike sepals, each 0.5 in (13 mm) long, of equally bright purple-pink hue. The plant grows best in part shade in humus-rich soil of pH 4.5 to 5.0. It can be grown in the garden if its demands are met, but it must be diligently protected against fungus and slugs.

POLYGONATUM (LILIACEAE) Solomon's Seal

The genus *Polygonatum* includes about 30 species of perennial herbs native to North America and Eurasia. Its common name is derived from the intaglio-shaped scars that remain on the thick, horizontal rhizome after the leafy stems break off at the end of each season. The stalks are usually 1.5–2 ft (50–60 cm) high and may grow to 6 ft (1.8

m) on certain species. They are clad with numerous alternate leaves up to 5 in (13 cm) long, which are smooth, shiny, and with parallel veins. From the leaf axils, singly, in pairs, or in clusters, hang greenish white flowers in the form of narrow, 0.75-in (2-cm) long bells. The blossoms mature into blue-black berries each containing several seeds. The plant prefers moist, woodsy soil and can take a considerable amount of shade. Three species grow in my garden.

Polygonatum biflorum 3 ft (0.9 m); Zone 4
Small Solomon's Seal

This North American species is native from Connecticut to western Ontario and Nebraska, and south to Texas and Florida. The arching stems bear whitish flowers that occur singly or in groups of two or three. The plant spreads by stolons or by seed and grows best in some shade.

Polygonatum commutatum 6 ft (1.8 m); Zone 4
Great Solomon's Seal

This larger polygonatum grows over a wide range from New Hampshire to Manitoba and south to Mexico. The leafy plumes grow much taller than those of *Polygonatum biflorum* and the flowers occur in pairs or up to 10 per cluster.

***Polygonatum odoratum* var. *thunbergii* 'Variegatum'** 3 ft (0.9 m); Zone 4

Polygonatum odoratum is native throughout Eurasia, but the attractive variety *P. odoratum* var. *thunbergii* 'Variegatum' comes from Japan. Its foliage is rich green with margins of bright yellow, and the 1-in (2.5-cm) long slender white bells, occurring in two-flowered peduncles, are pleasantly fragrant. As with all polygonatums, the leafy stalks turn light yellow in the fall and remain standing for 2 weeks or more adding a touch of bright color to the brown forest floor.

Polypodium virginianum (Polypodiaceae) 3 ft (0.9 m); Zone 5
Rock Polypody; American Wall Fern

A vast number of *Polypodium* species grow in greatly varied locations and latitudes of the world. In recent years, some botanists divided this large genus into more than 20 genera. *Polypodium virginianum*, and *P. vulgare* (European version of the former) retain their membership in the genus *Polypodium*, which keeps its old name unchanged. They are small, attractive, fully evergreen ferns. In my garden, both grow in moist, shady locations with a northern exposure. The two species look identical to me but, according to *Hortus Third* (Liberty Hyde Bailey Hortorium 1976, 898), *P. vulgare* may produce much longer fronds, up to 36 in (91 cm) long, and the rhizome is sweet to the taste, whereas *P. virginianum* has fronds only 8–10 in (20–25 cm) long and the rhizome is not sweet to the taste. Since I know which is which in my garden, I have no need to sample the flavors. (See also "Ferns.")

Polystichum acrostichoides (Polypodiaceae) 2.5 ft (0.8 m); Zone 4
Christmas Fern; Dagger Fern; Canker Brake

The genus *Polystichum* has about 120 species growing on five continents. *Polystichum acrostichoides* is native to northeastern United States where it populates woods, open slopes, and rocky outcroppings. It is fully evergreen and remains very attractive throughout the year. In the past it was used for Christmas decorations but this practice, fortunately, has now been generally abandoned. Large clumps of this fern can be easily divided into many smaller plants. I have used such divisions to line the small banks along some paths; the fronds cover the open soil quickly and prevent erosion by rains, while adding their interesting evergreen pattern to the path all year long. The plant prefers shady, moist locations in good soil. It grows in pH 4.5 to 7.0. (See also "Ferns.")

PRIMULA (PRIMULACEAE) Primrose

The genus *Primula* is comprised of some 400 species of perennial plants native mostly to the Old World, with a few coming from the tropical and temperate zones of North America. Many of the more attractive species are from the Himalayas. These species thrive in cool, shady locations with adequate moisture during the growing season. Some flourish in full sun if their feet are in wet ground. The majority of primulas are suited to a small garden, but they can also be at home in open woods, a cool bed on the shady side of a house, or in a low, damp spot along a wooded path. I grow several varieties of *Primula*.

Primula denticulata 10 in (25 cm); Zone 4

This Himalayan species has large crinkled leaves with toothed margins and flowers that are arranged in ball-shaped inflorescences. The individual blossoms begin to open as soon as the little ball is barely out of the ground, usually with the earliest flowers of spring. As the weather grows warmer, the naked stalk supporting the flower-ball begins to lengthen until it stands 8–10 in (20–25 cm) high, the dense floral cluster expanding to 2 in (5 cm) or more in diameter. The typical color is lilac, but there are plants also with white, pink, and red flowers ('Alba', 'Rosea', and 'Rubra'). *Primula denticulata* var. *cashmeriana* has flowers of pure lavender and tends to grow lower, usually 4–6 in (10–15 cm) high.

The species strongly prefers semishaded locations as direct hot sun wilts its foliage and allows the flower stems to become soft and bend to the ground under the weight of the heavy cluster. The plants can be left alone for several years, although the best blossoms occur on specimens that have been in place for 2 or 3 years, deriving considerable benefit from a division after 5 or 6 years. If the soil is sufficiently moist, the primulas seed themselves and provide an abundant supply of new plants to replace those that have completed their life cycle.

Primula japonica 3 ft (0.9 m); Zone 4
Candelabra Primula

This is one of the most spectacular primulas. It is called the candelabra primula because the flowers are arranged in horizontal tiers. From a base rosette of large leaves rises a strong leafless stalk that eventually grows to 2.5–3 ft (80–90 cm). About 8 in (20 cm) above the ground, a small circle of flower buds surrounds the stem; it widens as the individual blossoms begin to open, the first of several tiers that will eventually unfold. The central stalk continues to lengthen, growing a few inches above the first tier, and repeating the earlier process (Plate 68). In a week or two, the sturdy stalk will have five or six whorls, the lower already changing into a circle of seed capsules, and the uppermost just opening its buds into the attractive 1-in (2.5-cm) wide blossoms.

Primula japonica requires a very rich soil and plenty of moisture. It tolerates even boggy conditions during the growing season. The plants are not long lived, but they seed themselves freely so that there is never any dearth of new seedlings. The large

PLATE 68. A shady bed of *Primula japonica* (candelabra primula) in late May.

foliage disappears by late fall or early winter, but by midspring the tight buds begin to peek through the soil, and in a few weeks the area is filled again with the imposing flower heads.

Primula* × *polyantha 8 in (20 cm); Zone 5

Polyanthus

This is a class of hybrids produced many generations ago, most likely from three European species, *Primula veris, P. elatior,* and *P. vulgaris.* Polyanthus primroses come in many colors, including yellow, white, pink, red, coffee, cocoa, sky-blue, purple blue, as well as dark bicolors with golden margins and yellow eyes in the center. In addition, there are various forms, including miniatures and robust plants 6–8 in (20 cm) high. The foliage is lush green and healthy looking, and remains so through the winter. Like all primulas, these hybrids like rich, shady, moist situations (Plate 69). If allowed to dry out, their leaves will almost certainly be infested with various juice-sucking insects that turn the foliage into whitish, pale-yellow fiber.

Primula sieboldii 5 in (13 cm); Zone 5

This species is native to northeast Asia. The leaves are scalloped around the edges, and appear crinkled because of their pronounced veins. The foliage fades away toward the end of summer, so the growing site should be well marked to avoid damage to the dormant plants. A practical solution is to place *Primula sieboldii* in a separate bed or in a planting of azaleas and rhododendrons which is never cultivated and is generally kept moist. The mulch should then be rather thin, perhaps 0.75 in (2 cm) of pine needles or 1 in (2.5 cm) of shredded leaves.

The flowers of *Primula sieboldii* are 0.75–1 in (2–2.5 cm) in diameter, in umbels of up to 10 blossoms on stalks growing above the foliage. Each of the long petals is deeply notched, giving the blooms a rather delicate look. The usual color is a very

PLATE 69. *Primula* × *polyantha* (polyanthus) along a narrow path in early May.

light purple, and most new seedlings have this somewhat washed-out hue. Nevertheless, there are dozens of cultivars available in a great variety of colors including white, dark purple, red, pink, and many other pure shades. Typically, most of the blossoms will have a unique two-tone effect, the upper sides of the petals a lighter shade and the lower sides a darker, stronger version of the same color.

This aspect, and the snowflake pattern of the blossoms, lend *Primula sieboldii* a singularly lacy appearance. In addition to the home-grown seedlings, my garden contains *P. sieboldii* 'Fimbriated Red', with deeply serrated edges on the bright red petals, and 'Musashino', with large-petalled blossoms, rose-pink on top and darker pink on the reverse side.

Primula veris 8 in (20 cm); Zone 4

Cowslip

This species is among the most beloved of European spring wild flowers, native to most of the continent and the British Isles. It prefers streamsides and damp meadows but grows in any location that is not too dry and too hot. The fresh green foliage is evergreen, and the flowers, while not spectacular, are bright, interesting, and always welcome. They grow in one-sided umbels of 7 to 10 pendant bells, each 0.5 in (13 mm) wide, in various shades of yellow. In my garden, probably as a result of open pollination from other primulas, seedlings with dark orange-red blossoms have appeared (Plate 70).

The blooms of *Primula veris* are scented with the kind of fragrance that is sometimes called the "scent of wild primroses," and which is often found also in other spring flowering plants and shrubs. The species is easy to grow and multiply. A gardener may almost wish that it would become weedy.

PLATE 70. The yellow flowers of *Primula veris* (cowslip) with its orange open-pollinated hybrids, and a volunteer seedling of the blue *Phlox divaricata* (wild sweet William) in mid May.

Primula vulgaris 5 in (13 cm); Zone 4

Primrose

This is another popular wild flower of the Old World. It is sometimes called the English primrose, although it is native throughout a major part of Europe, and east to the Caucasus and northern Persia. A low, ground-hugging plant with crinkled leaves, it has yellow up-facing flowers, 0.75 in (2 cm) wide, growing from the base on thin 2–5 in (5–13 cm) long stems, one flower per stem. There are cultivars in a wide range of colors, including white, purplish red, red, sky-blue, purple-blue, pastel pink, and others. The plant is easy to grow and multiply by division or seed.

Pteridium aquilinum (Polypodiaceae) 3 ft (0.9 m); Zone 3

Bracken; Brake; Pasture Brake; Hogpasture Brake

This large deciduous fern grows the world over, and its widely distributed populations have been divided into 12 varieties. A tall plant, this species spreads vigorously by a thick rootstock that travels long distances in great depth, sometimes as deep as 10 ft (3 m) below the ground level. The single fronds rise along the horizontal rhizomes and, if left uncontrolled, take over large areas, shading the soil with their broad leaves and precluding smaller plants from taking hold. It is not a plant for a small- or even a middle-sized garden. The bracken croziers and rhizomes were once used for human consumption but now have been determined to be carcinogenic. The foliage is poisonous to cattle. I have been trying to eliminate *Pteridium aquilinum* from my garden for many years but, as of now, the battle is a standoff. (See also "Ferns.")

PULMONARIA (BORAGINACEAE) Lungwort

The genus *Pulmonaria* contains about 12 species native to Eurasia. Their foliage is large, usually uniformly green but on some species heavily spotted with whitish blotches. The 0.5-in (13-mm) wide flowers appearing in early spring are arranged in branched terminal cymes on stalks up to 1.5 ft (50 cm) high. The blossoms are usually blue but may be white or pink. The plant grows best in light or heavier shade in woodsy soil of no particular pH and spreads slowly by rhizomes or seeds into large clumps, seldom becoming weedy.

Because the genus belongs to the borage family (Boraginaceae), this species is sometimes identified by that name. The designations *Pulmonaria* and lungwort refer to the plant's use in past centuries in the treatment of lung diseases. Several varieties of *Pulmonaria* grow in my garden.

Pulmonaria angustifolia 1 ft (0.3 m); Zone 5

This European species has leaves with darker markings along the veins and flowers that appear in terminal cymes. The blossoms are usually blue but come also in rose and white.

***Pulmonaria arenaria* 'Rubra'** 1 ft (0.3 m); Zone 5

Pulmonaria arenaria is very similar to, and perhaps a variety of, *P. montana*. The foliage is light green, and the flowers are an unusual orange color that contrasts well with the bright green leaves. The plant is vigorous but not weedy, and grows well in shaded spots.

Pulmonaria montana 1.5 ft (0.5 m); Zone 5

This is a central European native with long narrow leaves covered with soft hairs, and violet flowers 0.75 in (2 cm) long. It is sometimes called *Pulmonaria rubra*.

Pulsatilla vulgaris (Ranunuculaceae) 1 ft (0.3 m); Zone 4
Pasque Flower

This European species is still occasionally called by its synonym, *Anemone pulsatilla*. Its common name, pasque flower, is sometimes used also for a somewhat-similar North American plant, *Anemone patens*. The foliage of *Pulsatilla vulgaris* is heavily dissected and forms large, lacy plumes. The flower stems terminate in blossoms in the shape of goblets up to 2 in (5 cm) wide, usually deep velvety purple. There are several cultivars available, including *P. vulgaris* 'Alba' (white) and 'Rubra' (red). *Pulsatilla vulgaris* ssp. *grandis*, native from central Europe to Ukraine, has dark purple blossoms that are larger than the blossoms of the species. All these variations grow successfully in my garden in rich, well-drained soil in full or nearly full sun. They begin blooming in April and continue through May into early June.

Pyrola rotundifolia* var. *americana (Pyrolaceae) 1 ft (0.3 m); Zone 4
Round-leaf American Wintergreen

The 12 species that comprise the genus *Pyrola* are native to the temperate zones of North America and Eurasia. *Pyrola rotundifolia* is a North American wild flower ranging from Newfoundland to South Dakota, and south to New Mexico and West Virginia. It is a creeper that spreads by long, thin stolons from which rise oval, shiny, leathery, evergreen leaves on long petioles. The flower stalks may reach 12 in (30 cm) or more. In June and July, the stalks develop narrow racemes of nodding, waxy-white flowers, each up to 0.5 in (13 mm) wide. The plant occurs in dry, sandy, very acidic soils of pH 4.5 to 5.5, and is not easy to transplant as the white, slender roots travel considerable distances under the forest litter. To move a plant from one site in a garden to another, these rhizomes must be taken in their entirety, together with the few leaves that grow along their length.

Ranunculus acris (Ranunculaceae) 1 ft (0.3 m); Zone 4
Tall Buttercup

Of the 250 species in the genus *Ranunculus,* two or three have been hybridized or selected for garden cultivation, and a few others are of garden quality in their natural form. The remainder are, to a large extent, weedy plants that infest cultivated areas and lawns. *Ranunculus acris,* native to Eurasia, may be counted among the latter, even though it is an attractive weed. The foliage is divided into three leaflets each of which is further dissected. The leaves rise on long petioles from a relatively thick, noncreeping cluster of roots. The flowers, about 1 in (2.5 cm) in diameter, have five bright yellow petals and a tuft of orange stamens in the center. In early spring the flower stalks and the rather attractive foliage are only a few inches tall, but by May they reach 1 ft (30 cm) or even more. The stems produce many flowers which mature into small ball-shaped clusters of achenes that scatter easily and root freely.

I have kept one plant in a dampish spot by a partly shady path where it enhances the rich green moss from which it is growing (Plate 71). To keep it from reseeding itself excessively, I snap off the spent flowers and little clusters of seeds every time I walk by, disposing of them where they cannot germinate. With its colorful blossoms and nearly evergreen foliage, the plant is too attractive to discard, but it must be strictly controlled.

PLATE 71. A late May view toward the pond with the small yellow flowers of *Ranunculus acris* (tall buttercup) by a narrow path, *Rhododendron* 'Vulcan' on the left, and *R.* 'Nova Zembla' (red) and *R.* 'Catawbiense Alba' (white) on the right.

Sanguinaria canadensis (Papaveraceae) 8 in (20 cm); Zone 3

Bloodroot; Red Puccoon

This early blossoming and attractive North American wild flower is the only species in the genus *Sanguinaria*. It yields orange-red sap when its rhizome is broken, and from this come its scientific as well as its common names. The word puccoon is of Algonquian origin. Native American tribes from Virginia and elsewhere used the plant juice as a pigment.

The species is native from Quebec to Manitoba and south to Texas and Florida. The thick horizontal rootstock pushes slowly through the earth or forest litter an inch or two (2.5–5 cm) below the surface, and sends up individual leaves and flower stalks. The leaf is palmately lobed, grayish green, and at first enfolds the single flower bud. With the warmer days of early spring, the flower stem lengthens and pushes out of the leaf's shelter. At its tip opens a single white blossom, 2 in (5 cm) in diameter, with 8 to 12 elongated oval petals. The bloom lasts only a day or so, but with enough plants, a bed of *Sanguinaria canadensis* produces many attractive flowers daily.

The plant is easy to grow from seed. It prefers rich, moist, well-drained soil with pH 6.0 to 7.0, though it blooms also in more acidic conditions. Deciduous trees allow the warming rays of the early sun to reach the plants, but protect them from the burning rays of late spring and summer so that the foliage can mature slowly over a longer period.

In 1916, in the countryside in Dayton, Ohio, a plant was found that had double flowers. It came to be known as *Sanguinaria canadensis* 'Multiplex', sometimes erroneously listed as 'Flore Pleno'. No other double bloodroot has been found since. Its blossoms are of uncommon refinement and beauty. Some measure 3 in (8 cm) in diameter or more and contain a great number of pure white petals that form gardenialike flowers. These blooms remain on the plant for many days, compared with the more fleeting beauty of the species' single blossoms. Though now more readily available, this treasure comes at a high price. Thus, it can be disheartening to see the plant eaten by rodents, or the leaves and blossoms devoured by deer. The loss of foliage weakens the rootstock and eventually kills the plant. To protect the rhizomes from mice, I make a large, flat cage of hardware cloth similar to one used for cyclamens and other vulnerable tubers, rhizomes, and bulbs (see "Diseases and Pests" for more detail).

Saponaria officinalis (Caryophyllaceae) 2 ft (0.6 m); Zone 5

Soapwort; Bouncing Bet

All 30 species in the genus *Saponaria* are native to Eurasia, but *S. officinalis* has made itself completely at home in North America and elsewhere in the world, becoming a common roadside weed. Weedy though it may be, it is still attractive. The upright or sprawling stems are covered with lance-shaped leaves, and the flowers are in terminal inflorescences with up to 12 blooms, each with five white or pinkish petals, opening from July to September. I have allowed two or three plants to become established at the edge of a *Pachysandra terminalis* bed along the street, and they have not gotten out of bounds. The roots of the species have been used in medicine. The leaves and stems form a soapy lather when wet and rubbed in one's hands, a feature that gave the plant its botanical name and one of its common names.

***Saxifraga* 'Whitehill'** (Saxifragaceae) 3 in (8 cm); Zone 4

Rockfoil

The genus *Saxifraga* encompasses some 300 species, which some botanists have grouped into several genera. These plants are native mostly to subarctic and alpine regions of Eurasia, North Africa, and North America, populating mountains and rocky outcroppings. Their leaves are usually clustered close to the ground, and their flowers are arranged mostly in thin racemes, panicles, and cymes on long, often drooping, stalks. Flowers may be white, yellow, purple, or pink. Sometimes the classification of the plants has been organized according to growth characteristics, such as encrusted leaves, mossy appearance, and others.

Saxifraga 'Whitehill' is of the encrusted group known as Euaizoonia. The leaves are small, fleshy, and blue-green, with slightly raised edges which are actually minute scallops. Each scallop is encrusted with a tiny deposit of lime. The plant prefers a well-drained but moist site in partial shade, a spot easily found in my rock garden, but one that regrettably is also a perfect breeding ground for slugs. Over the years these pests have consumed a small fortune in rare saxifrages, but apparently they are not attracted to the encrusted type which has prospered in its place for a long time. *Saxifraga* 'Whitehill' has a small cluster of white blossoms on a 6-in (15-cm) high stem.

Scilla siberica (Liliaceae) 6 in (15 cm); Zone 3
Siberian Squill

There are 80 to 90 species of small early flowering bulbs in the genus *Scilla*. All are native to Eurasia and North Africa. *Scilla siberica* from Russia has two to five straplike leaves up to 6 in (15 cm) high and 0.5 in (13 mm) in diameter, and a short scape of 1-in (2.5-cm) wide pendant flowers, usually in various shades of blue, although the white 'Alba' is particularly appealing. It likes a sunny position where, if left undisturbed, it forms sizable patches over the years. It does not require frequent thinning or transplanting.

***Sedum spectabile* 'Autumn Joy'** (Crassulaceae) 1.5 ft (0.5 m); Zone 3
Stonecrop

The genus *Sedum* contains about 600 species. In an effort to simplify its classification, botanists have divided the genus into eight informal groups. Their effort was not entirely successful as the nomenclature of sedums remains highly confusing. The plants are native to northern temperate zones as well as to tropical regions of the globe. Many are rock dwellers; some are indiscriminate spreaders that multiply by rooting each of their tiny succulent leaves as they drop off and touch bare ground.

Sedum spectabile 'Autumn Joy' is a restrained plant, and it is also one of the most attractive sedums. In good soil, it forms large clumps of gray fleshy leaves on tall stems terminating in broad flat heads of small flowers that begin in September as light pastel pink, change to darker pink in October, and dry into brownish shades for the remainder of the cold season. One of my plants is tucked into a pocket of poor, dry soil in the wall above the pond where it never grows more than a few inches tall, but retains all its other attributes.

Shortia galacifolia (Diapensiaceae) 8 in (20 cm); Zone 4
Oconee-bells

There are about eight species in the genus *Shortia*, all but one native to east Asia. *Shortia galacifolia* is a North American plant, one of the most beautiful native wild flowers. It ranges only in a small area of the Carolinas, southwestern Virginia, and northern Georgia. It was discovered for the first time about 200 years ago by a French plant explorer, but its existence was doubted by scientists and the species was soon forgotten. It took the faith and perseverance of a respected botanist of the mid 1800s, Dr. Asa Gray, to rediscover it. The plant then became known as the Lost Flower of South Carolina.

PLATE 72. *Shortia galacifolia* (Oconee-bells) in a pocket of rich, brown acidic soil in late April.

The foliage is shiny and evergreen, turning bronze in cold temperatures. The rounded leaves, with sharp teeth on the margins, are up to 3 in (8 cm) wide, rising from the plant's base on petioles 5 in (13 cm) long. The flowers are nodding translucent white or pinkish bells with fringed edges, about 1 in (2.5 cm) in diameter, hanging from 4-in (10-cm) high stems (Plate 72).

Though of southern origin, the plant is hardy far north and, according to Donald Wyman's *Ground Cover Plants* (1961, 158), it can withstand winter temperatures of −40°F (−40°C) with only a slight protection of oak leaves. It requires full shade and rich, moist, strongly acidic soil of pH 4.0 to 5.0. It can be divided successfully in very early spring or immediately after flowering, but seeds do not germinate readily.

SILENE (CARYOPHYLLACEAE) Campion, Catchfly

The genus *Silene* contains about 500 species of herbs native to the Northern Hemisphere. They are related to the genus *Lychnis,* and both genera are members of the pink family (Caryophyllaceae). The same common names are often used for plants of either genus, and it is sometimes difficult to determine to which genus a given species belongs. Two species of *Silene* grow in my garden, both in dry and sunny locations.

Silene caroliniana* ssp. *pensylvanica 1 ft (0.3 m); Zone 4
Pink Catchfly; Wild Pink

This North American subspecies ranges from New Hampshire to Ohio and south to Tennessee and South Carolina. The narrow grayish green leaves growing from the base are 2–3 in (5–8 cm) long, wider at the tips, and arranged in dense mats. In May and June tall stems arise from these mats, each with a small head of two or more bright pink, five-petalled flowers about 1 in (2.5 cm) in diameter. The sepals form a tube which is covered with sticky hairs that capture small insects, hence the common name catchfly.

Silene quadridentata 12 in (30 cm); Zone 5

This species comes from the mountains of southern and central Europe. It has light green leaves up to 3 in (8 cm) long and only 0.1–0.3 in (2–5 mm) wide. The cymes have small flowers with white, rarely pink or light purple, petals. The species is known also by its less frequently used synonym, *Silene pusilla*.

Sisyrinchium atlanticum (Iridaceae) 1 ft (0.3 m); Zone 3
Blue-eyed-grass

All 75 species in the genus *Sisyrinchium* are from North and South America. They are small, grasslike members of the iris family (Iridaceae) with thin, narrow, light green leaves. Each wiry stem produces one or several small flowers up to 0.5 in (13 mm) wide.

The blossoms of *Sisyrinchium atlanticum* have a corolla with six small sky-blue petallike segments that usually have small bristlelike points in the middle of their margins. In the center is a yellow eye that contrasts with the light blue flower. The roots are tiny but, if examined closely, resemble a miniature rhizome typical for irises. The plant seeds itself willingly and its few seedlings are seldom unwanted.

Smilacina racemosa (Liliaceae) 2.5 ft (0.8 m); Zone 3
False Solomon's Seal; Solomon's Feather; Solomon's Plume; False Spikenard

The 25 or more species in the genus *Smilacina* are native to Asia and North America. *Smilacina racemosa* is an attractive North American plant ranging throughout the United States and Canada. It spreads vigorously by thick rootstock, creating large areas of arching foliage in the woods and other shady spots with rich, moist soil, preferably of pH 5.0 to 6.0. The leaved stalks are up to 2.5 ft (80 cm) high, and from May to July produce 6-in (15-cm) long panicles of small whitish flowers at their tips. These inflorescences mature into bunches of 0.25-in (6-mm) wide round berries which at first are bright green but later become spotted with reddish brown markings, eventually ripening shiny red. The plant seeds itself generously in my wood and must be periodically weeded out, not an easy task considering the thick rhizome.

Soldanella carpatica (Primulaceae) 5 in (13 cm); Zone 5

The genus *Soldanella* includes eight species of European mountain plants. *Soldanella carpatica* (syn. *S. hungarica*) is native to the Carpathian mountains from Czechoslovakia as far east as western Ukraine, and south to the high elevations of the Balkans. It is a small, evergreen, alpine plant with dark green, round leaves 0.5 in (13 mm) in diameter. From the base rise taller stems with umbels of one to three fringed, blue-purple, nodding bells 0.75 in (2 cm) in diameter. The plant requires a moist, well-drained spot in shade.

Solidago (Compositae) 7 ft (2.1 m); Zone 3

Goldenrod

The genus *Solidago* has 130 species native mostly to North America but occurring in limited numbers also in South America, Eurasia, and the Azores. Most of them are tall plants that seed themselves prolifically and can easily become weedy. Still, they provide great golden-yellow sweeps of color in late summer and early autumn, a time when nature begins to tire from the profusion of summer. The plants are sometimes mistakenly blamed for hay fever. Some are rather similar to each other and are difficult to distinguish, even for a botanist. There are many specimens, and probably several species in my garden. I have been able to identify, with a small measure of confidence, only *Soldago bicolor* (white goldenrod). A second one, I believe, could be *S. uliginosa* (bog goldenrod). The names of the others remain an enigma.

Sternbergia lutea (Amaryllidaceae) 1 ft (0.3 m); Zone 6

Winter Daffodil; Lily-of-the-field

All five species that constitute the genus *Sternbergia* are native to Eurasia. They are bulbous plants, which in early fall send up narrow straplike leaves together with yellow funnel-shaped up-facing flowers about 1.5 in (4 cm) in diameter. They grow best in a sunny, dry location and rather heavy soil. The bulbs are planted in early September about 6 in (15 cm) deep.

Stylophorum diphyllum (Papaveraceae) 1.5 ft (0.5 m); Zone 5

Celandine Poppy; Gold Poppy; Yellow Wood-poppy

There are up to six species in the genus *Stylophorum,* all native to east Asia except one, *S. diphyllum,* which is North American and ranges from Pennsylvania to Wisconsin and south to Tennessee and Virginia. It is fully hardy in Connecticut and even

PLATE 73. The thick trunks of *Liriodendron tulipifera* (tulip trees) rising from a bed of yellow blossoms of *Stylophorum diphyllum* (celandine poppy) in late April. On the right, the lavender pink blooms of *Rhododendron* 'P.J.M.'.

farther north. As the epithet *diphyllum* suggests, the plant is two-leaved, and each leaf is heavily dissected. At the top of the stem are two to four flowers, each with two hairy sepals that drop off as soon as the 2-in (5-cm) wide blossoms open. The blooms, which unfold from March to May, have four broad, bright yellow petals that stand out in the woods where the species prefers to grow (Plate 73).

The plant spreads by seeds, forming large, colorful colonies that must be occasionally restrained by pulling out unwanted seedlings. It is a perfect plant for damp forest bottom with rich, neutral soil of pH 6 to 7, though it flourishes also in more acidic soil. If there is room and the plants are left undisturbed for a few years, they completely cover the ground with their attractive foliage that is speckled generously with the golden blossoms in early spring.

There is another celandine poppy (*Chelidonium majus*), which is only vaguely similar, and which has been introduced to North America from Eurasia. It has become a noxious weed with no redeeming value and should be eradicated whenever possible.

Symplocarpus foetidus (Araceae) 1.5 ft (0.5 m); Zone 3

Skunk Cabbage; Polecat Weed

This is the only species in the genus *Symplocarpus*. It is native to northeast Asia and North America where it ranges from Quebec to Manitoba and south to Northern Georgia and Tennessee. As implied by its names, when slightly bruised the plant emits an odor which approximates that of a skunk mixed with garlic. Evidently, the smell has protected this ancient species successfully through the ages. It is a very permanent plant growing from a long, stout deep-rooted rhizome that remains in the spot where it germinated almost forever.

The *Symplocarpus* flower is the earliest blossom of the year. It first appears as a spathe (a fleshy, modified leaf) in the shape and almost the size of a cupped hand, mottled on its outer surface with purplish brown markings. As the winter nears its end, this odd-looking bloom inexorably pushes upward from the root, its cellular respiration creating enough heat to melt the frozen earth, the snow, and the ice around it. At first it is tightly closed, but, as spring marches on, it half-opens into a hoodlike shield revealing at its bottom a spadix almost the size of a golf ball, speckled with tiny bisexual flowers (containing stamens as well as pistils).

Later, several leaves unfold, some of which may grow to the size of an elephant ear (Plates 1, 33). In shady, mucky woods with many skunk cabbage plants, the leaves cover the ground entirely. Despite its smell, *Symplocarpus foetidus* is a magnificent plant. Once established in a suitable location, the plant will stay for generations, giving the site a lush-green look during a major part of the growing season.

Tellima grandiflora (Saxifragaceae) 2 ft (0.6 m); Zone 5

Fringecups

The North American genus *Tellima* has only one species, *T. grandiflora*, which is native to western parts of Canada and the United States and is fully hardy in Connecticut. The leaves, which grow from the base on long petioles, have a rounded outline with scalloped margins and sometimes a slight point at the tip; they are somewhat reminiscent of the foliage of *Heuchera*. The flowers, too, have a casual resemblance to *Heuchera* blossoms, but rather than growing on branched scapes, they occur on slender unbranched stalks rising from the base. The individual small blossoms, up to 0.25 in (6 mm) long, are greenish but become reddish as they mature.

Thalictrum polygamum (Ranunculaceae) 8 ft (2.4 m)); Zone 4

Tall Meadow Rue; Muskrat Weed; King-of-the-meadow

The genus *Thalictrum* contains about 100 species of perennial herbs native mostly to the northern temperate zones of Eurasia and America. Some are low growing plants, and a few are tall, graceful denizens of northern meadows and open woods. The North American species, *T. polygamum,* ranges from Newfoundland to Ontario and south to Tennessee and Georgia. It has a stout stem with airy compound foliage, and its leaflets strongly resemble those of *Aquilegia* species. The flowers occur in large but sparse terminal clusters. Some flowers have only stamens while others have both pistils and a few stamens. The blooms appear between June and August.

Although growing to a considerable height, this polygamous plant can be an attractive addition even in a limited space where its elegant bearing and airy texture provide a point of interest. It grew in my garden when I came, and it continues to seed itself modestly in damp, shady locations as well as sunnier spots where it blooms more generously.

Thelypteris noveboracensis (Polypodiaceae) 2 ft (0.6 m); Zone 3

New York Fern; Tapering Fern

This is one of only a few northern species in the extensive genus *Thelypteris;* most of its other 500 members are tropical plants. The species is native to northeastern North America, ranging from Newfoundland to Minnesota and south to Arkansas and Georgia. The fronds are yellowish green, sharply pointed at the top and tapering to a few short greenish scales at the bottom. It is one of the most common ferns in its range, growing in sunny or partly shaded areas, occurring in thin woods and drier edges of marshes. Once established, the pest spreads relentlessly by dark brown rootstock, creeping just below the forest floor. It is very difficult to control. I have been pulling out the roots to keep the fern from taking over a stand of *Lycopodium obscurum,* but the progress is slow. (See also "Ferns.")

Tiarella cordifolia (Saxifragaceae) 10 in (25 cm); Zone 4

Foamflower

Of the six species that comprise the genus *Tiarella,* five are from Asia and one, *T. cordifolia,* is from North America. The latter ranges from New Brunswick to Michigan, south to New England and, along the mountain ranges, as far as eastern Tennessee. The leaves are cordate (i.e., heart-shaped at the base) and have up to seven toothed lobes. The margins are slightly more pointed but otherwise similar to the leaves of *Heuchera* species. The slender flower stalks are thinly covered with small white flowers along their upper part. One stalk by itself creates no dramatic effect, but in large colonies the flowers create the impression of a thin haze floating above the foliage. The plant does best in shady, cool, moist, and fertile locations, blooming from April to June. It is mostly indifferent to soil acidity and succeeds in pH 5.0 to 7.0.

***Tradescantia × andersoniana* 'Purple Dome'** (Commelinaceae)

Spiderwort; Widow's Tears 1.5 ft (0.5 m); Zone 4

The genus *Tradescantia* has over 20 species, all native to the Western Hemisphere. The straplike leaves of *T. × andersoniana* 'Purple Dome' are 12 in (30 cm) long and 0.75 in (2 cm) wide. The flowers are violet-purple on this cultivar but may be blue, white, and other shades. They open from June throughout the summer, sometimes reblooming in autumn until frost. The blossoms consist of three green sepals, three broad petals, six stamens, and a three-parted pistil. There are many buds in each terminal cluster but only one or two a day open into blossoms which unfold in the morning. By noon, the petals almost disappear, becoming drops of viscid liquid. The plant prefers semi-shaded positions in good soil of pH 6.0 to 7.0. Once established, it spreads rapidly and may require vigilant control. The cultivar is sometimes offered as *T. virginiana* 'Purple Dome'.

Trientalis borealis (Primulaceae) 9 in (23 cm); Zone 2
Starflower

The genus *Trientalis* contains four similar species, all native to the temperate and boreal regions of Eurasia and America. *Trientalis borealis* is a North American species that grows from Labrador to Saskatchewan and south to Ohio and Virginia. It is a fragile-looking plant that inhabits shady, humus-rich woods with strongly acidic soil of pH 4.0 to 5.0, and spreads by slender underground runners into unobtrusive but attractive colonies (Plate 74). At the top of each thin stalk is a flat whorl of 5 to 10 narrow, sharply pointed leaves, up to 4 in (10 cm) long. From their center, on 1.5-in (4-cm) long threadlike pedicels, rise two star-shaped flowers 0.75 in (2 cm) in diameter, with six or seven pointed white petals and golden stamens. The species is not easy to move. But, if threatened by a bulldozer, with patience during transplanting and care in providing a moist, acidic soil, it can be moved and grown successfully.

TRILLIUM (LILIACEAE) Wake-robin

There are about 30 species in the genus *Trillium,* all native to North America, the Himalayas, and eastern Asia. All parts of the plant above the stalk occur in threes or multiples of three. At the top of a tall, strong stem is a whorl of three broad leaves, and from their center arises a flower with three narrow green sepals and three petals in colors typical for each species or variety. The plant has six stamens, a three-celled ovary, and a three-celled fruit. Occasionally, atypical forms occur in nature, such as the beautiful double-flowered *T. grandiflorum* f. *petalossum* with blossoms of many petals and sepals, and leaves in fours, fives, and sixes. I have not yet grown this unusual gem. The mutations differ genetically from the types, and most of them have lost the ability to produce seeds and can be reproduced only vegetatively. Three *Trillium* species grow in my garden.

Trillium erectum 15 in (38 cm); Zone 4
Red Trillium; Purple Trillium; Wet-dog Trillium; Stinking Beth; Stinking Benjamin

The most common of the trilliums, this species is native from Nova Scotia to Minnesota and south to Georgia and Alabama. The leaves are diamond-shaped, and the flowers are usually dark red but may be deep purplish, greenish yellow or creamy white (var. *album*). Some plants are ill-scented and, judging by the proliferation of common names with that connotation, the malodorous specimens must be rather common. Nevertheless, I have not encountered any with that characteristic, and I wish that all my plants were in that category so that they might possibly escape the periodic plunder by deer.

Trillium erectum is easy to grow in moist, deep organic soil in nearly full shade. The preferred pH is 4.5 to 6.0, with optimal level of about 5.0 (Plate 75).

PLATE 74. A drift of *Trientalis borealis* (starflower) in mid May.

PLATE 75. *Trillium erectum* (red trillium) in early May.

Trillium grandiflorum 18 in (45 cm); Zone 4

White Trillium; Large-flowered Wake Robin

This *Trillium* species ranges over the same area as *T. erectum*. The white flowers are very attractive in their common form, but are exquisite in the rare double form (f. *petalossum*). The cultural requirements of this species are similar to the requirements of *T. erectum* except that the preferred pH levels are between 6.0 to 7.0.

Trillium undulatum 15 in (38 cm); Zone 4

Painted Trillium

This plant is similar to the above two species in its range as well as cultural requirements. One exception is the soil acidity. *Trillium undulatum* strictly insists on a very sour reaction, the optimal pH being 4.0 to 5.0. The flowers are white with purple markings at the base of somewhat wavy petals. It is not easy to meet the narrow range of conditions under which *T. undulatum* will prosper; however, if deep, humus-rich, cool, moist, and sandy woodland can be found, the required acidity can be achieved and maintained with the application of iron sulfate.

Tulipa linifolia (Liliaceae) 5 in (13 cm); Zone 4

After planting thousands of tulip bulbs over the decades which I lost to deer, and having promised myself that no tulip would ever again grow in my garden, *Tulipa linifolia* is my first, and perhaps, last concession.

The genus *Tulipa*, with 50 to 150 species, is native to Eurasia. These species have gone through centuries of horticultural breeding and selection after being introduced to Europe from cultivation in the gardens of medieval Turkey. *Hortus Third* (Liberty Hyde Bailey Hortorium 1976, 1132) suggests that these species may have "their ultimate origin in *Tulipa Gesnerana* or, in some cases, in the dwarf *Tulipa suaveolens* of southern Russia."

Tulipa linifolia comes from Uzbekistan. The foliage is thin and narrow, and the fire-engine-red flowers have six broad petals that seem large compared with the other parts of the plant. Growing naturally in large numbers, the plant must create spectacular sweeps in its native range.

Tussilago farfara (Compositae) 6 in (15 cm); Zone 3

Coltsfoot

There is only one species in the genus *Tussilago*. It is native to Eurasia and has become naturalized all over the world. The leaves are rounded, 8 in (20 cm) wide, green on top and heavily indumented with white felt beneath. The thick rootstock spreads below the ground at a speed of 12 in (30 cm) or more a year. Thus, the plant is obviously not suited to a small garden. Nevertheless, I have not eradicated it completely because of its very early flowers that appear long before the leaves. The blossoms are 1.25 in (3 cm) in diameter, a thick tuft of bright yellow rays that brighten the drab landscape of early spring.

Uvularia sessilifolia (Liliaceae) 1 ft (30 cm); Zone 4

Bellwort; Wild Oats; Little Merrybells

The genus *Uvularia* contains five species, all native to eastern North America. *Uvularia sessilifolia* ranges from New Brunswick to North Dakota and south to Alabama and northern Florida. It is a slender plant with a thin forking stem and 3-in (8-cm) wide smooth, sessile leaves. The creamy white flowers are pendant elongated bells about 1.25 in (3 cm) long, usually one or two on each of the two thin branches. The plant grows in humus-rich, moderately acidic soil with pH 5.0 to 6.0, in shady shrub borders or thickets. It is sometimes difficult to transplant because of its long roots but once established *U. sessilifolia* grows without much care except some watering in dry periods.

Vancouveria hexandra (Berberidaceae) 10 in (25 cm); Zone 5

Vancouveria is a genus of three species, all native to western North America. The genus was named for the English traveler Captain George Vancouver, who spent 4 years exploring North America's Pacific coast at the end of the 18th century. Species of this genus are rather similar to species of the Eurasian genus *Epimedium,* and both genera are members of the barberry family (Berberidaceae).

Vancouveria hexandra is a fine, deciduous, slowly spreading ground cover. Its thin, wiry stalks bear slender branchlets with 1.5-in (4-cm) long leaves in a shape that could be interpreted, with some license, as having six sides, and thus giving the species its botanical epithet. The margins of the leaves are somewhat harder than the rest of the surface. The 0.5-in (13-mm) long white flowers, appearing in May and June, are in panicles of up to 45 blossoms.

Veratrum viride (Liliaceae) 5 ft (1.5 m); Zone 4

White Hellebore; American Hellebore; Itchweed; Indian Poke

The genus *Veratrum* has about 45 species native to Eurasia and North America. *Veratrum viride* is native from New Brunswick to Minnesota and south to Georgia and Tennessee. The large, attractive leaves, up to 1 ft (30 cm) long at the lower part of the stem, are broadly elliptic with sharp tips at both ends, heavily veined and pleated. They grow along the entire stout stalk almost to the top, except for the uppermost 1–2 ft (30–60 cm) segment, which becomes an attractive panicle of yellowish green 1-in (2.5-cm) wide flowers. This is a handsome, nonspreading plant of sizable proportions which, nevertheless, would fit remarkably even into a small garden if a shady, wet or moist, informal corner could be found. The parts of the plant below the ground level yield a poisonous substance, which possesses medicinal properties and which is also used as an insecticide.

Viola (Violaceae) 8 in (20 cm); Zone 3

Violet

The genus *Viola* contains some 500 species of mostly perennial plants native to many parts of the world. In North America, they are among the most desirable garden subjects, as well as among the most bothersome weeds, whether in the garden or the lawn where they are particularly difficult to eradicate. Certain species are not easily distinguished from others, and this is further aggravated by their promiscuous nature which leads sometimes to new unidentified crosses.

There are probably several more species in my garden than those I have listed and identified with at least some confidence. *Viola canadensis* (Canada violet) has white flowers tinted purple in the back and grows 8 in (20 cm) tall. *Viola cucullata* (marsh blue violet) has violet flowers with darker throat and grows 6 in (15 cm) tall. *Viola lanceolata* (lance-leaf violet) has white flowers and long narrow leaves, and grows 6 in (15 cm) tall. *Viola odorata* (sweet violet) has heart-shaped leaves that are folded when young and purple fragrant flowers 0.75 in (2 cm) in diameter. *Viola odorata* 'White Czar' is a white version of *V. odorata,* a species of Old World origin. *Viola palustris* (marsh violet) has pale lilac blossoms with darker veins, and grows only 4 in (10 cm) tall. *Viola sagittata* (arrow-leafed violet) has violet purple flowers and grows 4 in (10 cm) tall. I often wonder what we would do without violets and, since we have them, what we should do with them.

Viscaria alpina. See ***Lychnis alpina.***

Waldsteinia ternata (Rosaceae) 3 in (7 cm); Zone 4

There are perhaps four species in the genus *Waldsteinia,* some native to North America and others native to Eurasia. *Waldsteinia ternata* is from the Old World, ranging from central Europe to Siberia and Japan. It is an excellent evergreen carpeter with leaves and flowers very similar to those of strawberries except that its blossoms are yellow. The fruit, an achene, is unlike that of strawberries and is generally not noticeable. The plant makes an attractive ground cover in shade, or in sun if moisture can be provided in very dry periods. Its spreading is slow and its coverage of the ground is effective. It is sometimes listed as *W. trifolia.* The North American species *W. fragarioides* (barren strawberry) is similar, but I have not grown it as yet.

Glossary

Achene. A small one-seeded fruit (e.g., strawberry).
Acidic soil. Soil with pH below 7.0.
Acute. Sharp.
Alkaline soil. Soil with pH above 7.0.
Alternate. Having leaves, branches, or buds arranged first on one side and then on the other at different levels. Compare Opposite.
Annual. Completing the life cycle, from germination to maturity and death, in one growing season.
Anther. The pollen producing and bearing part on top of a filament; together, the anther and filament form a stamen.
Aril. The fleshy covering of a seed, as on *Taxus* (yew).
Axil. The angle between a leaf petiole or a branch and the axis from which it arises.
Axillary. Occurring in an axil.
Axis (pl. **axes**). A stem or a branch from which arise lateral parts, such as branches or leaf petioles.
Biennial. Usually germinating and developing vegetative growth the first year, then flowering, fruiting, and dying the second.
Bract. A modified leaf borne at the base of a flower or subtending a cluster of flowers, as on *Davidia* or some *Cornus* flower configurations.
Bulbil, Bulblet. A small or secondary bulb usually borne in leaf axils, as on *Lilium lancifolium* (tiger lily), but also in place of flowers, borne in unusual places as on *Lycopodium lucidulum* (shining clubmoss).
Calcareous. Consisting of or containing limestone.
Calyx (pl. **calyces**). The external, usually green or leafy, outer whorl of sepals that encloses the flower petals before they open.
Campanulate. Bell-shaped.
Capsule. A dry seedpod consisting of two or more cells containing seeds.
Catkin. An elongated cluster of unisexual flowers, as in *Salix* (willow), *Betula* (birch), or *Quercus* (oak).
Chlorophyll. The green-coloring matter of plants.
Clone. The progeny produced asexually by cuttings, layers, micropropagation, or other vegetative means, and not by seed. See also **Cultivar** and **Variety.**
Compound. Divided into several more or less similar parts, usually used of a leaf.
Conifer. Cone-bearing (from Latin *conus* = cone, and *ferre* = to bear).

Cordate. Heart-shaped, usually used of a leaf with two rounded lobes at the base and an angle between them.

Corolla. A floral envelope. Its parts are usually separate, in which case they are petals, or they may be united and thus evident only as teeth, lobes, or slightly undulating tips, as in *Kalmia,* or they may not be evident at all.

Corymb. A flower cluster with a flat-topped or domed head in which the outermost flowers bloom first.

Cultivar (abbreviated to **cv.**). A horticultural variety originating and persisting under cultivation, or occurring in the wild and maintained in gardens. Names of cultivars are now formed from three words or less and are usually enclosed in single quotation marks.

Cyme. A flower cluster, often with a flat-topped appearance, in which the central or terminal flower opens first.

Deciduous. Leaf losing (from Latin *deciduus, decidere* = fall).

Dioecious. Having male (staminate) and female (pistillate) flowers on separate plants. Compare **Monoecious.**

Diploid. Having the basic two sets of chromosomes, a condition usual in most organisms. Compare **Triploid.**

Disc (disk) flower. One of the tubular flowers in the middle of the flower head, as in *Aster,* surrounded by ray flowers that usually look like narrow petals.

Double. Used of flowers having more than the usual or normal number of petals or other floral envelopes.

Drupe. A stone fruit in which the seed is enclosed in a stony inner portion, which in turn is surrounded by a fleshy or pulpy outer layer, as in peach or plum.

Elepidote. Without scales; large-leaved.

Elliptic, Elliptical. Oblong with rounded ends, widest near the middle.

Entire. Without lobes, teeth, or divisions; with a continuous unbroken margin.

Epiphytic. Growing on another plant but not taking nourishment from it.

Epithet. The word that follows the name of a genus and identifies the species.

Ericaceous. Belonging to the heath family (Ericaceae), and thus normally requiring acidic soils.

Even-pinnate. Used of a compound leaf without a terminal leaflet. Compare **Odd-pinnate.**

Fastigiate. Erect, narrow, with branches upright and clustered together.

Filament. A thin flexible object; for example, the threadlike stem that bears the anther in a flower stamen.

Genus. A group of plants marked by common characteristics and consisting of one or more species.

Glabrous. Hairless, smooth.

Glaucous. With blue or blue-gray powdery or waxy substance (bloom).

Grex. A group of different cultivars of the same parentage.

Herb. A nonwoody plant; a plant without a persistent stem above ground. Also, a plant valued for its medicinal, aromatic, or savory qualities.

Hose-in-hose. A flower growing out of another.

Immutable. Not capable of or susceptible to change.

Indumentum. A dense coating, especially of hairs or felt.

Inflorescence. A group, cluster, or arrangement of flowers.

Leaflet. One of the ultimate parts of a compound leaf.

Lepidote. Covered with scales; small-leaved.

Linear. Resembling a line; usually used of a leaf; elongated, with nearly parallel sides, as the foliage of many conifers.

Lobe. A protruding segment of a leaf, representing a division halfway to the middle or less. Also applicable to flowers.
Midrib. The central rib of a leaf or leaflet.
Monoecious. With male and female flowers separate but borne on the same plant. Compare **Dioecious.**
Oblong. Longer than broad, of fairly uniform width.
Obovate. Egg-shaped, having the broadest part above the middle.
Obovoid. Inversely ovoid; same as obovate but often referring to a solid body.
Odd-pinnate. Used of a compound leaf with one terminal leaflet. Compare **Even-pinnate.**
Opposite. Having leaves, branches, or buds arranged in pairs on opposite sides of an axis. Compare **Alternate.**
Oval. Egg-shaped.
Ovate. Egg-shaped, having the broadest part below the middle.
Ovoid. Same as ovate but often referring to a solid body.
Palmate. With lobes radiating like fingers from the palm of a hand.
Panicle. A branching inflorescence, with each branch branching again into a raceme or a corymb.
Pedicel. A stalk that supports an individual flower.
Peduncle. A stalk bearing a flower cluster, or a solitary flower when the inflorescence consists of only one flower.
Peltate. Shaped like a shield, with the stem attached to the lower surface rather than to the margin.
Perennial. Persisting for 3 or more years.
Petal. A modified leaf; a part of the corolla, usually showy.
Petiole. A slender stalk that supports a leaf.
Pinna (pl. **pinnae**). The smallest part of a pinnately compound leaf, as on ferns.
Pinnate. Constructed like a feather; used of a leaf with leaflets on both sides of the axis. Compare **Even-pinnate** and **Odd-pinnate.**
Pistil. The female sexual organ of a flower consisting of stigma, style (supporting the stigma), and ovary (where the seed forms).
Polygamous. Having unisexual and bisexual flowers either on the same plant or on separate plants of the same species.
Pome. A fleshy fruit, such as an apple.
Procumbent. Trailing or lying flat but not rooting.
Pubescent. Hairy; bearing short, fine hairs.
Raceme. An elongated inflorescence on which each flower has a short stalk.
Ray flower. One of the marginal flower parts that surround the disc flower, as in *Aster.*
Reticulate. Netlike.
Rhizome. An elongated horizontal stem that produces shoots above ground and roots below ground, and differs from a true root in having buds, nodes, and usually scalelike leaves.
Rhombic. Like a parallelogram in which the angles are oblique; diamond-shaped.
Samara. A dry one-seeded winged fruit, as in *Acer, Fraxinus,* or *Ulmus.*
Scape. A flower stalk; a peduncle arising at or beneath the ground, as in *Tulipa.*
Selfed. Self-pollinated.
Sepal. One of the modified leaves comprising a calyx, often green.
Serrate. Saw-toothed, with the teeth pointing forward.
Sessile. Attached directly by the base, without a stalk.
Silique. A narrow elongated two-sided capsule containing several seeds in each side and opening by sutures at either margin.

Simple. Used usually of leaves; not compound or divided into secondary units; having a blade in one piece.

Sorus (pl. **sori**). A cluster of spores on a fern. One of the dots on the underside of a fertile frond.

Spadix. A thick floral spike enclosed or subtended by a spathe.

Spathe. A sheathing bract or leaf surrounding a spadix, as in *Arisaema triphyllum*.

Spatulate. Spatula- or spoon-shaped.

Species abbr. **sp.** (pl. species abbr. **spp.**). A group of individuals with common characteristics. A part of a genus.

Stamen. The male organ of a flower, consisting of an anther and a filament.

Stigma. The sticky tip of the pistil that receives the male pollen.

Stolon. A horizontal shoot from the base of a plant that produces new plants at its tip.

Stratification. A method of storing seeds in layers alternating with moisture-holding materials, usually in a cool environment.

Strobile. A spike consisting of spore-bearing organs, similar to or synonymous with cone, as in *Lycopodium* and conifers.

Style. The portion of the pistil that connects the stigma with the ovary.

Subspecies abbr. **ssp.** A named subdivision of a species.

Taxonomy. The principles and study of the scientific classification of plants and other living organisms.

Triploid. Having three, rather than the usual two, basic chromosome sets. Compare **Diploid.**

Umbel. A flat-topped or rounded flower cluster in which the pedicels of the individual flowers rise from approximately the same point, usually at the top of a taller stem.

Understory. Undergrowth of a forest.

Unisexual. Having only male or only female flowers.

Variegated. Having markings of different colors.

Variety. Officially, varietas. A subdivision of a species.

Verticil. A whorl; a circle of flowers, leaves, or branches around a stem.

Bibliography

American Rhododendron Society. 1980. *American Rhododendron Hybrids.* Tigard, OR: n.p.

Beales, Peter. 1987. *Classic Roses.* New York: Holt, Rinehart and Winston.

Birdseye, Clarence, and Eleanor G. Birdseye. 1951. *Growing Woodland Plants.* New York: Oxford University Press.

Bruce, Hal. 1976. *How to Grow Wildflowers and Wild Shrubs and Trees in Your Own Garden.* New York: Alfred A. Knopf.

Cobb, Boughton. 1963. *A Field Guide to the Ferns and Their Related Families.* Boston: Houghton Mifflin.

Courtenay, Booth, and James Hall Zimmerman. 1972. *Wildflowers and Weeds.* New York: Van Nostrand Reinhold.

Dana, W. S. 1903. *How to Know the Wild Flowers.* New York: Charles Scribner's Sons.

Everett, T. H. 1981. *The N.Y. Botanical Garden Illustrated Encyclopedia of Horticulture.* New York: Garland.

Fairweather, Christoper. 1979. *Rhododendrons and Azaleas for Your Garden.* Nottingham, England: Floraprint.

Fisk, J. 1963. *Success with Clematis.* London: Thomas Nelson and Sons.

Gartrell, Robert D. 1977. *Notes to the New Hybridizer—My Experiences in Developing the Robin Hill Azaleas.* Unpublished.

Greer, Harold E. 1988. *Greer's Guidebook to Available Rhododendrons, Species and Hybrids.* Eugene, OR: Offshoot Publications.

Grimm, William Carey. 1962. *How to Recognize Trees.* New York: Castle Books.

———. 1966. *How to Recognize Shrubs.* New York: Castle Books.

———. 1968. *How to Recognize Flowering Wild Plants.* New York: Castle Books.

Harkness, Jack. 1978. *Roses.* London: J. M. Dent and Sons.

Harkness, J. L. 1979. *The World's Favorite Roses and How to Grow Them.* Maidenhead, England: McGraw-Hill Book Co.

Jaynes, Richard A. 1988. *Kalmia: The Laurel Book II.* Portland, OR: Timber Press.

Kingsbury, John M. 1965. *Deadly Harvest: A Guide to Common Poisonous Plants.* New York: Holt, Rinehart and Winston.

Klaber, Doretta. 1959. *Rock Garden Plants: New Ways to Use Them Around Your Home.* New York: Bramhall House.

———. 1964. *Gentians For Your Garden.* New York: M. Barrows.

———. 1966. *Primroses and Spring.* New York: M. Barrows.

Leach, David G. 1961. *Rhododendrons of the World.* New York: Charles Scribner's Sons.

Lee, Frederic P. 1958. *The Azalea Book.* New York: D. Van Nostrand.

Liberty Hyde Bailey Hortorium. 1976. *Hortus Third: A Concise Dictionary of Plants Cultivated in the United States and Canada.* 3rd ed. New York: Macmillan.

Lucas Phillips, C. E., and Peter N. Barber. 1981. *Ornamental Shrubs Hardy in Temperate Climates.* New York: Van Nostrand Reinhold.

Malins, Peter, and M. M. Graff. 1979. *Peter Malins' Rose Book.* New York: Dodd, Mead and Co.

Millar Gault, S., and Patrick M. Synge. 1985. *The Dictionary of Roses in Colour.* London: Michael Joseph.

Moldenke, Harold N. 1949. *American Wildflowers.* New York: D. Van Nostrand.

Nehrling, Arno, and Irene Nehrling. 1960. *Peonies, Outdoors and In.* New York: Hearthside Press.

Petersen, Roger Tory, and Margaret McKenny. 1968. *A Field Guide to Wildflowers of Northeastern and North-central North America.* Boston: Houghton Mifflin.

Phillips, Roger. 1978. *Wild Flowers of Britain.* London: Pan Books.

Pokorny, Jaromir. 1973. *A Color Guide to Familiar Trees, Leaves, Bark and Fruit.* Prague: Artia; London: Octopus Books.

______. 1974. *A Color Guide to Familiar Flowering Shrubs.* Prague: Artia; London: Octopus Books.

Sanecki, Kay. 1975. *The Pictorial Guide to Garden Flowers.* London: Marshall Cavendish Publications.

Slavik, Bohumil. 1973. *A Color Guide to Familiar Wild Flowers, Ferns and Grasses.* Prague: Artia; London: Octopus Books.

Spongberg, Stephen A. 1974. "A Review of Deciduous-Leaved Species of *Stewartia* (Theaceae)." *Journal of the Arnold Arboretum* (Cambridge, MA). Volume 55, Number 2.

Stevens, T. H. G. 1938. *Trees and Shrubs in My Garden.* Altrincham, England: John Sherratt and Son.

Taylor, Norman. 1953. *Color in the Garden. Fragrance in the Garden.* New York: D. Van Nostrand.

Wherry, Edgar T. 1948. *Wild Flower Guide.* New York: Doubleday.

Wister, John C., ed. 1962. *The Peonies.* Washington, DC: American Horticultural Society.

Wyman, Donald. 1961. *Ground Cover Plants.* New York: Macmillan.

______. 1969. *Shrubs and Vines for American Gardens.* Rev. ed. New York: Macmillan.

______. 1977. *Trees for American Gardens.* New York: Macmillan.

Index of Plant Names

Boldface numbers indicate pages of primary discussions.